Introduction to Political Sociology

The Social Anatomy of the Body Politic

second edition

ANTHONY M. ORUM

University of Texas at Austin

PRENTICE-HALL, INC., Englewood Cliffs, New Jersey 07632

Library of Congress Cataloging in Publication Data

Orum, Anthony M.
    Introduction to political sociology.

    (Prentice-Hall sociology series)
    Bibliography:
    Includes index.
    1. Political sociology.   I. Title.   II. Series.
JA76.078 1983   306'.2   82-16628
ISBN   0-13-491399-X

Editorial production and supervision by F. Hubert
Cover design by Barbara Shelley
Manufacturing buyer: John Hall

Prentice-Hall Sociology Series
Neil J. Smelser, editor

To my family—for all the moments they have given me

10   9   8   7   6   5   4   3   2   1

Printed in the United States of America

ISBN   0-13-491399-X

Prentice-Hall International, Inc., *London*
Prentice-Hall of Australia Pty. Limited, *Sydney*
Editora Prentice-Hall do Brasil, Ltda., *Rio de Janeiro*
Prentice-Hall Canada Inc., *Toronto*
Prentice-Hall of India Private Limited, *New Delhi*
Prentice-Hall of Japan, Inc., *Tokyo*
Prentice-Hall of Southeast Asia Pte. Ltd., *Singapore*
Whitehall Books Limited, *Wellington, New Zealand*

Credits

    Quotation on page 1 reprinted by permission of Hawthorn Books, Inc. from *Utopia* by
Thomas More. Copyright © 1949 Appleton-Century-Crofts, Inc. All rights reserved.

Quotations on page 1 and page 209 reprinted from William L. Riordon, *Plunkitt of Tammany Hall: A Series of Very Plain Talks on Very Practical Politics,* with an introduction by Arthur Mann. Copyright 1963 E. P. Dutton & Co., Inc.

Quotation on page 54 reprinted from Max Weber, *The Protestant Ethic and the Spirit of Capitalism,* translated by Talcott Parsons with a foreword by R. H. Tawney. Copyright © 1958 Charles Scribner's Sons. By permission of Charles Scribner's Sons and of George Allen & Unwin, Ltd., England.

Quotation on page 72 reprinted from Talcott Parsons, *The System of Modern Societies.* Copyright 1971 Prentice-Hall, Inc. By permission of the publisher.

Quotations on pages 96-97 reprinted from Talcott Parsons, "An Outline of the Social System" in Talcott Parsons et al., eds., *Theories of Society: Foundations of Modern Sociological Theory,* vol. 1. Copyright © 1961 by The Free Press, a division of Macmillan Publishing Co., Inc.

Quotation on page 106 reprinted from Jean Jacques Rousseau, "The Social Contract," in *The Essential Rousseau,* trans. Lowell Bair. Copyright 1974 New American Library. By permission of the publisher.

Quotation on page 106 reprinted from Niccolo Machiavelli, *The Prince,* translated and edited by Thomas G. Bergin. Copyright 1947 AHM Publishing Corp., Arlington Heights, Ill. By permission of the publisher.

Quotation on page 125 from page 171 of Volume II, Chapter XX from *Democracy in America,* by Alexis de Tocqueville, translated by Henry Reeve, revised by Francis Bowen, and edited by Phillips Bradley. Copyright 1945 Alfred A. Knopf, Inc. By permission of the publisher.

Table 6-1 from Thomas R. Dye, Eugene R. DeClercq, and John W. Pickering, "Concentration, Specialization, and Interlocking Among Institutional Elites," *Social Science Quarterly,* vol. 54, no. 1 (June 1973), table 1 and pp. 17-19. Copyright 1973 University of Texas Press. By permission of University of Texas Press.

Table 6-2 adapted by permission from "The Polls: The Question of Confidence," by Everett Carll Ladd, Jr., *Public Opinion Quarterly,* vol. 40, no. 4 (Winter 1976-77), p. 545. Copyright 1977 by The Trustees of Columbia University.

Quotations on pages 170, 172, 173, and figure 7-2 adapted from Floyd Hunter, *Community Power Structure: A Study of Decision Makers.* Copyright 1953 The University of North Carolina Press. By permission of the publisher.

Table 7-1 from Amos Hawley, "Community Power and Urban Renewal Success," *American Journal of Sociology,* 68 (January 1963). Copyright 1963 University of Chicago Press. By permission of University of Chicago Press.

Quotation on page 198 from James Madison, "Federalist Paper Number 10," in Alexander Hamilton, James Madison, and John Jay, *The Federalist Papers,* with an introduction by Clinton Rossiter. Copyright 1961 New American Library. By permission of the publisher.

Table 8-1 adapted from Angus Campbell, Philip E. Converse, Warren E. Miller, and Donald E. Stokes, *The American Voter.* Copyright 1960 John Wiley & Sons, Inc. By permission of the publisher.

Figure 8-1 adapted from Norman H. Nie with Kristi Andersen, "Mass Belief Systems Revisted: Political Change and Attitude Structure," *Journal of Politics,* vol. 36, no. 3 (August 1974), figure 4, p. 558. Copyright 1974 Southern Political Science Association. By permission of the publisher and of the author.

Table 8-1 adapted from Angus Campbell and Donald E. Stokes, "Partisan Attitudes and the Presidential Vote," in *American Voting Behavior,* ed. Eugene Burdick and Arthur J. Brodbeck. Copyright © 1959 The Free Press of Glencoe, a Corporation. By permission of Macmillan Publishing Co., Inc.

Contents

PART THREE   POLITICAL PARTIES, PARTICIPATION, AND THOUGHT

8 POLITICAL PARTIES AND POLITICAL PARTISANSHIP   198

9 CITIZEN PARTICIPATION IN POLITICS   235

10 THE FORMS AND ORIGINS OF POLITICAL THOUGHT   254

PART FOUR   POLITICAL DEVELOPMENT AND CHANGE

11 NATION BUILDING IN THE MODERN WORLD   281

12 SOCIAL AND POLITICAL MOVEMENTS   311

Preface

In the several years since the first edition of this book appeared I have learned from colleagues both the advantages and disadvantages, the strengths and weaknesses, of what I said. As a result of these comments, and some of my own qualms with portions of the first edition, I have made three major changes in this, the second edition. I have added an extension to the chapter on Karl Marx. In this section I discuss some of the twentieth century figures who elaborated and added to the Marxist heritage; I also provide a brief discussion of the contributions of Friedrich Engels. I also have thoroughly changed two chapters from the first edition—the chapter on power and influence in America, and the chapter on socialization. In the case of the former I have tried to create a more comprehensive, yet necessarily looser, survey of key trends in American society in the twentieth century. I hope to have succeeded in this effort, in particular to have promoted deeper thought on the nature of power and influence under contemporary conditions. With the chapter on socialization I have essentially discarded the chapter from the first edition. I—and I have learned other teachers—always found this chapter too painfully tedious and dense. In its place I have introduced an entirely new chapter, on political thought. This is the most speculative chapter of the entire work, drawing its inspiration from the logic of dialectical analysis. I try in this chapter to illuminate the various forms of political thought that exist in the world of politics, and to combine them into a single analytical framework. I think this new frame of reference, while speculative, works to a certain degree; and I know that I am considerably happier with it than I was with my earlier chapter. Elsewhere in the book I have made a number of minor alterations, but the basic themes, ideas, and analyses of the first edition remain otherwise intact.

As in the case of the first edition, I again owe my initial thanks of appreciation to my wife, Amy, and to my son, Nicholas. This time around we all took a vacation in Colorado, thanks to the generosity of my mother-in-law, Grace Wexler, and it made the completion of the changes all the easier. I also want to thank the reviewers who offered such helpful detailed criticisms on my revision of the first edition, in particular, Dick Braungart, Patricia Lengermann, Irving Tallman, Neil Smelser, and, most especially, Thomas Guterbock. Tom Guterbock provided the most detailed and thoughtful review of any book I have ever seen; he acted, in effect, as my alter ego. I am very grateful he took the time and care he did for he helped me to save myself from needless errors, and to add important references and citations to various chapters. Finally, Susan Taylor and Barbara DeVries have helped me to expedite the completion of this revision, and to get on with my other pressing obligations. They were very gracious and kind, maintaining the standards of cordiality and good sense which, since the days of Ed Stanford and Irene Fraga, I have come to associate with Prentice-Hall.

My typewriter has not changed since the first edition; it remains an ever loyal, if a bit wiser, friend.

ACKNOWLEDGMENTS FROM THE FIRST EDITION

In writing any book, I suppose, one accumulates quite a few debts to friends, colleagues, and family; having taken almost four years to write this one, I seem to have created quite a long list. Not the least of my debts are to my wife, Amy, and my son, Nicholas, who genuinely did forego some pleasures they wished for, including, among others, a couple of nice vacations and too many weekends to count. In allowing me to persist in the writing and thinking required by this book, they have helped me enormously. Moreover, by being around when I needed them, to cheerfully absorb my grumpy moods and graciously reflect on my tentative new ideas, they proved to be absolutely irreplaceable. I am grateful that they have put up with me.

I also owe much to several people directly connected with Prentice-Hall. Several years ago Ed Stanford suggested that I undertake to write this book, or, at least, something like it; neither he nor I expected that it would take quite so long. He has been extremely kind in the interim, between conception and birth, never especially nasty, never forcing me to come up prematurely with the finished product, and always encouraging about the worth of the final manuscript. Irene Fraga, his trusted assistant and clever manipulator of impatient authors, has been equally helpful, even though at times I may have carelessly tossed too anxious a word in her direction. She has helped me out with the small things, as well as helped with the larger questions, like whether the book was any good or not. Neil Smelser, who serves as the editor of the Prentice-Hall Sociology Series, has my lifelong thanks and respect for his assistance. He was sufficiently gracious and kind to take chapters of mine, more or less as they first came off my typewriter, and promptly to provide me with his reactions—comments that always were incisive, intelligent, and generally closed with a kind word on how well things were going. Scholarship is, as most writers know, an awfully lonely undertaking; Neil helped to make it much less lonely, and much more exciting. I thank them all.

Among my old friends there are several who helped in important ways and to whom I will always remain grateful. Everett Wilson, my very first teacher of sociology, assisted by reading the original manuscript and, with his usual eye for detail, identified weak spots in grammar and in sociology. Mayer Zald, a friend from my frist days in graduate school at Chicago, also read the manuscript and gave me important suggestions on places where my argument was unclear, my reference and knowledge too sparse. I am glad that they were, and remain, my teachers and friends. At the University of Texas, Louis Schneider, Norval Glenn, and Kenneth Wilson were all extremely helpful to me: Lou gave freely of his rich and penetrating knowledge of social theory, among other things; Norval kindly permitted me to give him a couple of chapters to read, for which he gave me his customary intelligent (and gentle) criticism; Ken was a very good friend, reading materials as well as helping to buoy my spirit in the early phases of this work. In addition, Marilyn Prentice, a dear family friend, gave up several of her summer afternoons over the past couple of years to cheer me up, to arouse me to take on that next chapter that lay ahead of me.

Several other people who have helped me on occasion and to whom I shall always be available for whatever help I might provide them are Antonio Ugalde, James Bill, John Higley, Herbert Hirsch, Bernard Farber, Mark Fossett, Dennis Roncek, Joe Feagin, and several reviewers from Prentice-Hall. Sharon Moon and Lindsey Woodruff were particularly helpful in the preparation of the typed manuscript, itself. All of these people are to be thanked for the many improvements they made on the manuscript; I, alone, take responsibility for its weaknesses.

I want to end my acknowledgments by recognizing a helper who has been invaluable but often goes unmentioned by other authors—my dear friend and most constant companion, my IBM Selectric II. I only wished that all my friends were so responsive and attention to my every word.

CHAPTER ONE
Introduction

In other places where they speak of the common good, every man is looking out for his own good. But in Utopia where there is no private property and where they zealously pursue the public business, there the name common- wealth is doubly deserved.

THOMAS MORE, *Utopia*

Show me a boy that hustles for the organization on election day, and I'll show you a comin' statesman.

WILLIAM L. RIORDON, *Plunkitt of Tammany Hall*

This is a book about politics but with a special twist. It is an effort to introduce you to the social circumstances of politics, that is, to how politics both is shaped by and shapes other events in societies. Instead of seeing the political arena and its actors as independent from other happenings in a society, this book treats that arena as intimately related to all social institutions—for example, to the family, as well as to the economy. The field of study encompassed by this particular view has become known as political sociology. Although the roots of this field reach far back into intellectual history, it only recently became a special area of inquiry because of the pioneering work of several social scientists. The major figures in the creation of this field have been Reinhard Bendix and Seymour Martin Lipset. This book repre- sents an attempt to carry on the tradition of scholarship that these two men helped to shape and that numerous other scholars now carry on with considerable ingenuity and passion.

VISIONS OF SOCIETY AND POLITICS

Unlike some other disciplines, political sociology is crosscut by several different visions of what society and politics are all about. Still, there is a basic agreement on the imagery employed to make sense out of the world—an imagery that construes this as a world in which there exists both a social and a political order and in which one seeks to discover how these two orders are related. This imagery can be traced to the currents of thought that prevailed during the nineteenth century; all social thinkers tended to think of the world as somehow divided between society and state. This conception was the intellectual product of fundamental transformations occurring in Western Europe; it helped observers to organize their thoughts about what was happening and assisted them in making out the connections between the actions of government and the actions of various social groups, including classes and specific occupational organizations. The imagery continues to dominate the thinking of political sociologists today, though now we are a bit more self-conscious and sophisticated about the nature of the connections between social and political orders. In particular and in contrast to many nineteenth century thinkers, we now realize that the institutions of the state, or the political arena, may often exercise as profound an influence over social development as the institutions of society exercise over politics. Thus, it is perhaps too simple to conclude, as Marx did, that those who occupy the offices of government are merely the henchmen for the wealthy groups in a society; it is however, equally simple-minded to believe that those who act as the governors can operate independently of the various class and ethnic groups that dominate so many of today's nations.

What political sociology has done is to provide both the basic imagery as well as certain specific visions that lead scholars to inquire into the social nature of politics. Three such visions dealt with in this book are those of Karl Marx, Max Weber, and Talcott Parsons. Each of these represents a powerful and tantalizing way for thinking about politics; each dominates the thinking of a fairly large body of scholars who practice the art of political sociology.

NATURE AND DISTRIBUTION OF POWER

We would all agree, I think, that the essence of politics is power. Thus, any pursuit that seeks to unravel some of the mystery about politics must address itself, in the course of that inquiry, to the nature and distribution of power in a society. Conventional thinking would have us believe that those who wield power in a society must be those who occupy the principal offices of the political arena—the heads of government and the leaders of political parties, among others. Political sociology, however, does not adopt this conventional view either of politics or of power; it makes both the source and the exercise of power into a problem rather than a definition. Marx perhaps first noted that power may not necessarily be held by those whom we think hold it in modern societies, that is, the politicians. Other scholars continue the study of power inspired by the same sort of critical stance toward society as that assumed by Marx.

Much of the work of political sociologists has been addressed to the matter of power and influence and of who holds these rather important commodities in both new and old societies. There has, however, been considerably more headway in the effort to lay out a compelling theoretical portrait than there has been in the hard research required by this subject. For example, C. Wright Mills furnishes a broad panorama of power in the United States as does Robert Dahl, even though their portraits differ in quite fundamental respects. The differences between their views, echoing some of the differences between Marx and other major visionaries of political sociology, remain for the most part unresolved by the evidence on power in America or in other Western nations. This is an intellectual impasse that the reader ought to come to appreciate and to use to further an understanding of how one constructs a theory of politics of how one assembles evidence for that theory.

PARTIES AND PARTISANSHIP

One of the topics that tended to elude the visions of the great nineteenth century theorists such as Marx and Weber but has attracted the attention of many contemporary students of politics is that of political parties. Parties represent a relatively modern institution. They achieved their first major successes at about the turn of the nineteenth century in the United States, and elsewhere they really did not represent a live and active institution until at least the second half of the nineteenth century. Today, however, they seem to be permanent and present in virtually every advanced and developing nation of the world. For many modern students of society and politics, parties have become the critical focus of politics; they are the very organizations through which power is sought and won or lost.

There is a fair amount of attention to political parties in this book because of the prominent position they occupy in the world. They are examined both as institutions, or as agencies capable of affecting the tides of opinion in the political arena, and as links between the mass of citizens and the government. One of the interesting things that students of modern politics have discovered is that parties represent a very significant force in the political lives of citizens; they are either embraced as a kind of guide to electoral behavior or, as is happening with increasing frequency, rejected in favor of an independent position on political issues. Moreover, concern with the fundamental imagery of political sociology—with the links between the social and political orders—also leads to inquiries into the ways in which differences in partisan affiliation are associated with differences in group membership in society, for example, between socioeconomic groups or ethnic groups.

There are opportunities other than parties that exist for the involvement of citizens in the political arena. There are many voluntary associations that dot the political landscape in advanced societies—the sort that captured the attention of Alexis de Tocqueville on his visit to the United States in the nineteenth century. Americans seem to specialize both in the production and in the enjoyment of such activities and to use them as another means for the expression of influence and power. Nonetheless, not all citizens are able to take advantage of them. The very poor, for example, tend to participate at much lower rates than the very rich; this has prompted not only theoretical interest but also considerable concern among those who wish for political activity on the part of all citizens. Recent scholarship on citizen involvement in the various outlets in the political arena has also raised serious questions about the rationality of the underlying motivation for such activity; if individuals wish to advance their own self-interests, then involvement in political associations and other such groups is hardly a satisfactory means.

One of the issues that has preoccupied students of politics, at least since the days of Marx, has been that of the nature of beliefs in political and social orders. Marx, as we shall learn, was much concerned with the character of belief and, in his early works especially, devoted considerable attention to its analysis. Eventually beliefs for Marx came to be identified with those beliefs that serve to sustain the reigning powers, and to be called, in particular, ideology. Weber, too, expressed a concern with this issue, though his concern focused more directly on the legitimacy, or legitimations, that sustained the system of ideas in any given society. And Parsons as well took up the matter, in the form of an interest in the nature of values and norms. We devote a part of our analysis in this book to the nature of political belief and thought. We do so in a rather speculative manner, in a fashion that, as you will discover, comes to incorporate principles of dialectical analysis as a means of uncovering the several dimensions of political thought. This analysis is undertaken in conjunction with our section on the nature of parties and participation, though the implications and consequences of belief range far beyond these phenomena themselves. In fact, Antonio Gramsci, the great Italian radical theorist, believed that political thought and the institutions that produced it were absolutely central to maintaining the rule of the dominant classes.

POLITICAL CHANGE

Any reputable field of political inquiry cannot fail to examine the nature of power, and it can hardly overlook the issue of political change. In a sense, the visions of society and politics that represent the heart of political sociology—those of Marx, Weber, and Parsons—represent an effort to understand modern societies. Marx sought to explain the development of capitalism in the nineteenth century; Weber, the distinctive emergence of rationalization in the West; and Parsons, the evolution of the most advanced of modern societies. Included in this sort of intellectual ambition is the attempt to discover what it is that promotes political change, both the unique features of the modern polity, its existence as a nation-state, and the common vehicles of much of that change, reform and revolutionary movements.

Nation building has become a useful phrase to describe the effort by political scientists and sociologists, among other social scientists, to comprehend the sequence of steps that leads to the modern nation-state. Clearly, some present societies have been more successful in achieving the accouterments of nationhood—for example, a centralized governmental administration—than others; this observation has promoted some of the most imaginative and exhaustive research in recent studies of politics. While there are some common features among nation-states, there are also some very critical differences, particularly between those with democratic and those with totalitarian institutions. These differences have also prompted some of the most imaginative and detailed of historical investigations; these pursuits are likely to continue for as long as important differences remain in the political structures and values of present societies.

Reform and revolutionary movements—agents of political and social change—have perhaps drawn as much careful observation from contemporary political sociologists as any other subject. In large measure this springs from the desire of many scholars to help to change the world as well as to understand it; this is the sort of passion to be an activist-intellectual that moved Marx, Weber, and many other nineteenth century intellectuals. Presently there are a number of competing interpretations both of the nature of such movements and of their origins. Some observers emphasize the broad economic undercurrents that give rise to such activities, while others stress the minute social-psychological mechanisms that convert an angry citizen into an active dissident. In this area of study, as in that of power, there is something of an intellectual impasse over equally sound interpretations, and the student would be well-advised to examine and reflect critically on the merits of the competing views. Though it is true that different aspects of movements, for example, their leadership as compared to their initial origins, necessarily call for separate interpretations, it is also true that some of the theories about movements are deficient from their fundamental premises to their implications for politics. These are issues that are dealt with in detail later in this book.

DIVERSITY AND RICHNESS

The basic dilemma that faces anyone who tries to make some sense of the field of political sociology lies in the choice between emphasizing a few common threads and perspectives and attending to the rather expansive and often overwhelming number of ideas and topics invented by political sociologists. I have solved this dilemma by attempting to identify both the common threads and the vast coverage of materials, attending perhaps more to the latter than to the former. The few common themes, I think, are evident in the magnificent visions of society and politics provided by the principal intellectual voices in political sociology, those of Marx, Weber, and Parsons. They have set out an agenda that today's students of politics seek to follow to a certain degree. Where this agenda has not fully fit the facts of modern politics and where there are questions to be asked that were not clearly addressed by the great visionaries, then scholars have embarked on their own tentative sorts of research, and thus, political sociology has grown a bit unevenly. I look at the somewhat rambling character of the topics and themes in political sociology more as a challenge than as an obstacle; it is an area of diversity that, like the real world, can often be considerably more stimulating than frustrating.

Another aspect of the diversity of political sociology is that it permits the student to integrate ideas from a wide variety of disciplines. Although the images of society and polity set the stage for our study, they by no means restrict the sort of actors or floodlights that play upon it. Thus, the study of psychology, history, or economics as well as political science are most useful in examining politics in the way that political sociologists choose to do. Indeed, political sociologists are perhaps at the forefront of those scholars who believe that the various distinctions among disciplines are rather artificial, if not handicaps; they seek to break down such barriers by drawing upon a wide variety of bodies of knowledge to examine, probe, and illuminate the nature of politics.

SPECIAL CONTENTS AND VIEWS
OF THIS BOOK

In the effort to present a broad and accurate portrait of political sociology, I have done a couple of things in this book that are a bit different from those that might have been done by my friends and colleagues in this field. First, I have tried to illuminate the often abstract character of concepts by referring mainly to materials from the United States—its present as well as its past. Where possible, I have also tried to point out differences between the character of politics in the United States and elsewhere, particularly in Western Europe. Still, this attempt to draw in the comparative materials has not gone quite as far as I would have wished, and I hope that both students and instructors might introduce as many materials from other nations as possible to highlight the special features of the American setting and to flesh out the contents of the concepts used by political sociologists. Second, I have presented the theories on a particular subject and then evaluated them in terms of available evidence and, occasionally, in terms of the requirements of a good theory. Where it has been impossible to resolve the differences between theories on the basis of known facts or to dismiss a particular theory because it does not fit what we know about the world, then I have said as much. Thus, in addition to the general diversity of ideas in this book, the reader also confronts an effort to present differences among theories and unresolved issues. The world about us is not a neat and tidy place in which all our ideas are confirmed by our observations; there is no reason to sugarcoat a book about this world and, especially, its politics—that would demean a reader's intelligence. The ideas in this book, just like those present in the world, demand that we think and reflect.

If there is a single lesson that I have tried to get across in this book, apart from the many substantive ones, it is this: One must approach the world in a state of curiosity and openness, be willing to arrive at conclusions about the world, be sufficiently resilient to formulate tough statements of opinion, and be persistent enough to discover whether or not those judgments are accurate. This is what politics often proves to be about; it is what the enterprise of learning must be about.

CHAPTER TWO
The Vision of Karl Marx

Within the capitalist system all methods for raising the social productiveness of labour are brought about at the cost of the individual labourer; all means for the development of production transform themselves into means of domination over, and exploitation of, the producers; they mutilate the labourer into a fragment of a man, degrade him to the level of an appendage of a machine, destroy every remnant of charm in his work and turn it into a hated toil; they estrange from him the intellectual potentialities of the labour-process in the same proportion as science is incorporated in it as an independent power; they distort the conditions under which he works, subject him during the labour-process to a despotism the more hateful for its meanness; they transform his lifetime into working-time, and drag his wife and child beneath the wheels of the Juggernaut of capital. . . . But all methods for the production of surplus-value are at the same time methods of accumulation. . . . It follows therefore that in proportion as capital accumulates, the lot of the labourer, be his payment high or low, must grow worse. Accumulation of wealth at one pole is, therefore, at the same time accumulation of misery, agony of toil, slavery, ignorance, brutality, mental degradation, at the opposite pole.

KARL MARX, *Capital*

All fields of knowledge have been influenced by a few persons of singular thought and insight. Philosophy was shaped by Plato and Aristotle; astronomy by Copernicus and Galileo; physics by Newton and Einstein; medicine by Harvey; biology by

Darwin; and psychoanalysis by Freud. Political sociology is no exception. This and the following two chapters review the work of three scholars who have furnished many of its most fundamental ideas.

The first person discussed is Karl Marx. He is in many ways the most prominent, a figure of enormous complexity and learning. Marx might be claimed as the father of political sociology, much as Auguste Comte is claimed to be the father of sociology. No doubt Marx would disdain the title for a number of reasons; nevertheless, it is abundantly clear that he gave birth to more provocative and fruitful ideas than any sociologist—living or dead—interested in the study of politics. Ideas such as class conflict and themes such as the economic roots of political ideology certainly owe, if not their origins, their intellectual prominence to him.

The other two figures considered are Max Weber and Talcott Parsons. Weber was a German scholar of unparalleled learning who helped to originate a number of significant themes that have clarified and supplemented those of Marx—among them bureaucracy and status categories. Parsons is perhaps the most prominent of contemporary social theorists. His ideas about society as a social system and about the subsystems within it, for instance, have been adapted by a number of current scholars who are interested in the comparative study of politics. His theories have had substantially less impact on political sociology than those of Marx and Weber for one major reason—they understate the considerable differences of power, wealth, and beliefs that are evident among people and groups in modern societies.

The conventional way to discuss the ideas of different scholars is to select the most original and salient ones of each figure and then to contrast them with those of other figures. Useful as that approach might be, it has two principal drawbacks. First, one often draws distinctions between ideas that are not strictly comparable. Second, ideas taken out of the context of thought in which they were developed often become distorted and misshapen; generations of students, as a consequence, may possess clear conceptions of incorrect ideas. To offset both difficulties, the discussion in this and the next two chapters relies on addressing the same important questions of each scholar. These queries highlight how each scholar views the nature of society, the nature of the polity, and the types of links between them—in short, the major issues of political sociology.

KARL MARX (1818-1883)

In writing of the influence of Karl Marx, Isaiah Berlin remarks:

> If to have turned into truisms what had previously been paradoxes is a mark of genius, Marx was richly endowed with it. His achievements in this sphere are necessarily ignored in proportion as their effects have become part of the permanent background of civilized thought.[1]

[1] Tom Bottomore, ed., *Karl Marx* (Englewood Cliffs, N.J.: Prentice-Hall, Inc., 1973), p. 68.

Many of us, for instance, subscribe to the view that there exist some groups of which we are aware and with which we identify based on common levels of wealth and property—more succinctly, social classes. Marx helps us to appreciate the significance of this idea. Many of us believe, further, that people's ideas about politics or about religion are in some manner influenced by their wealth or property. Marx (and others) have had a major influence over our thought on this matter. Finally, there are many of us who adopt the position that there are marked inequalities of wealth and power in modern societies and that these inequalities may become the source of major ideological struggles. Again, Marx helps us to recognize this aspect of many societies.

Ironically, many people whose own intellectual heritage owes the most to the theories of Marx are also among his most vociferous detractors, mainly because some of his theories have been employed as programs for political parties and whole nations; Marx has even become the omnipresent symbolic figurehead for many of these nations. His ideas have become Marxism, and thus people are either for or against them, regardless of their truth or insight. This holds true for no other figure whom we consider. Consequently, his ideas are carefully presented and quoted when it seems warranted.

Marx occupied various roles during his lifetime. He was, on occasion, a philosopher of history, an economist, a revolutionary, a sociologist, and a historian.[2] Rarely did he bother to reveal the role he occupied at any time, producing innumerable and interminable controversies over the content of his writings. At the outset of the discussion, therefore, it is important to understand the exact nature of these different roles and the manner in which Marx attempted to join them creatively.

For Marx, as all scholars, there is an inherent tension between the role of a practical human being and the role of a student of society and ideas. The former calls for practical action, involves one in the immediacies of everyday life, and, above all else, requires moral commitments. The latter calls for a theoretical and dispassionate stance—for an unbiased observation of things as they are, have been, and will be. Scholars such as Max Weber who recognize the tensions springing from the dilemma of occupying two seemingly contradictory roles choose to divorce one from the other explicitly; the man of action, with his opinions, should make those opinions known *only outside* of the academy and scientific discourse, and the man of thought, with his ideas, is obliged to render those ideas known *only within* the confines of the academy.

In his typical fashion, Marx chose to resolve the tension created by the seeming contradiction by wedding the roles into one. To illustrate, as a historian and sociologist, Marx believed that through the careful study of history one could discover the main principles that bring about historical change and development. Furthermore, he claimed that he and Engels had hit upon these basic principles

[2] He wrote a number of volumes by himself, such as *Capital*. For much of his adult life he also worked in close collaboration with his friend and fellow revolutionary Friedrich Engels, writing such manuscripts as *The Communist Manifesto*. Throughout, however, Engels remained the junior partner in their intellectual ventures, as he admitted at Marx's graveside.

with the theory of dialectical materialism. Certain aspects of this theory are discussed in detail later; for now it suffices to say that the theory asserts that the proletariat, or working classes, would emerge victorious from a revolutionary confrontation with the capitalists, or owners of industrial enterprises, during the modern capitalist era.

As a social philosopher, Marx believed that his theory of change was itself the product of historical development, that is, the development of society under capitalism in the nineteenth century had enabled some men, like himself and Engels, to grasp the principles of historical change. When change in society was imminent, he thought, some men would become armed with a theoretical understanding of it much as other men might become armed with weaponry.[3]

(It should be remarked that Marx believed that all the ideas of men were the product of social and historical circumstances. Most men—proletarians *and* capitalists—were so constrained by their social class interests even during eras of imminent change that they were incapable of comprehending the principles and the coming of change by themselves. A few men were capable of achieving the necessary transcendence of their own times and their own class biases, for example, he and Engels.)

For Marx, it was only a small step to achieving the synthesis between his knowledge of change acquired as a theorist and his desire for change growing out of revolutionary convictions. Equipped with an understanding of change, he believed it incumbent on himself, as an advocate of revolution, to spread such understanding among the principal beneficiaries of change, the working classes, in order to enlighten them as well as to hasten change. Theory of change and action to change were married; theory and action were combined. He wrote in *Contribution to the Critique of Hegel's Philosophy of Right*: "Just as philosophy finds its *material* weapons in the proletariat, so the proletariat finds its *intellectual* weapons in philosophy."[4]

If we understand that Marx achieved this remarkable synthesis between the demands and constraints operating on him, then many seemingly paradoxical elements of his thought and action are clarified. There are some scholars, for instance, who believe that Marx's emphasis on determinism, that is, the inevitability of historical change, and his advocacy of revolution on behalf of the working classes are contradictory; they argue that if change is inevitable in history and if the working classes are destined to come to power, then free will, in the form of man as a voluntary revolutionary, is impossible, nay futile. Yet Marx effected a marriage of the two; Lewis Feuer writes of Marx's doctrine:

> It called upon human beings for a supreme deed of free will, that of intervening in their history with a revolutionary act and creating their own society.

---

[3] Georg Lukács, *History and Class Consciousness,* trans. R. Livingstone (London: The Merlin Press, Ltd., 1971).

[4] Robert C. Tucker, ed., *The Marx-Engels Reader* (New York: W.W. Norton Co., Inc., 1972), p. 23.

But it did so with a necessitarian vocabulary, so that the working class in its highest moment of freedom was fulfilling historical necessity. Freedom and determinism were joined in a dialectical unity. The language of liberty always had its deterministic semantic commentary, and the mystic revolutionist became one with the scientist.[5]

Like many marriages, this was not always a happy one, and on occasion one role, such as that of the scientist, took priority over the other, such as that of the revolutionary. Yet on the whole, Marx managed to unify them as few scholars, before or since, have done.

Another key to understanding Marx is that certain themes preoccupied him throughout his life, despite their being cloaked in somewhat different guises. The most important was that of alienation; it drew upon the humanist and rationalist traditions of the eighteenth century and was heavily discussed in his early manuscripts as well as implicit in many of his later economic manuscripts. Men, as social beings, are alienated—that is, estranged from their own unique creative capacities and from their capacity to empathize with one another. The principal causes of alienation are the institutions of society, in particular social classes and the division of labor; while the principal manifestation of alienation is man's belief that social institutions are immutable—that such institutions possess a life of their own. Other sociologists have adopted somewhat similar ideas, albeit with a different slant. For example, the French sociologist Emile Durkheim maintains that the division of labor, as all social facts, represents a phenomenon of a genre or kind unto itself.

Marx's position has its own peculiar twist. In truth, he maintained, social institutions are *not* immutable but are rather continually being created by men, in the past, during the present, and into the future. Further, Marx assumed, all history, in particular the continuous unfolding and changing of social institutions, is moving toward a single goal of eliminating alienation among men and, thus, revealing to them that they are the masters and creators of their own social world. Each major stage in historical development brings with it greater progress toward this goal—an increasing capacity for societies to permit men to be freed from the constraints of alienation, to be freed from social institutions. The final attainment of this goal would come about with the collapse of capitalism and the advent of communist society. Communist society for Marx *had* to be a society without social classes, since it was classes that gave birth to man's alienation.

Marx's ideas about alienation and especially about the inevitable movement of history toward its elimination provide another instance of the synthesis that he attempted to achieve between his science and ethics, between his role as a theorist and his role as a man of political action. This feat, however, entails a potentially serious hazard, at least insofar as the interpretation of Marx's scientific observations is concerned. If the social scientific claims and the ethical ones are so interwoven in Marx, the man, can we distinguish them from one another in Marx, the writer? The distinctions can be drawn.

[5] Lewis Feuer, ed., *Marx and Engels: Basic Writings on Politics and Philosophy* (Garden City, N.Y.: Doubleday and Co., 1959), p. xi.

MARX'S IMAGE OF THE SOCIAL ORDER

There are various ways that sociologists choose to talk about the nature of society, or the social order. Here we have selected three concepts that sociologists use, and we shall employ them as a means of eliciting the major features of Marx's vision of the world, and of the visions later of Max Weber and Talcott Parsons. Having done so, we shall then be in a position to draw pointed comparisons among the views of the three scholars. The concepts we shall refer to are *social stratification, social organization,* and *social system. Social stratification* is rather straightforward—it refers to the nature and composition of the social hierarchies in a society, and in the case of Marx, in particular, to his conceptions of social class. *Social organization* is a somewhat more general term, but sociologists currently use it to refer to specific types of groups, or collectivities, that exist in the social world. For Marx, as we shall soon discover, organization seemed to play a minor role, but in the case of both Weber and Parsons it played a very important role in shaping their visions of the world. Finally, there is the conception of *social system.* Generally this refers to the form in which the theorist casts the broad details of his or her view, the logical and substantive structure of the picture of the social world. Marx clearly possessed a vision of a social system, though one of his own special making; so, too, did Parsons, but as we shall learn, Max Weber did not. There are implications that follow not only from the existence of differing conceptions of the social system held by each theorist, but also from the absence of such a conception as with Weber. These issues, too, we shall discuss at the conclusion of this section on theory.

There is one further point that we need to make clear, about our discussion of Marx, in particular. Here we shall concentrate only on what he had to say about the nature of capitalist societies, that is, nations like England and France as they existed in his lifetime. Although he devoted some attention to other societies in earlier epochs, most of his intellectual effort was spent on the analysis of capitalism. Our discussion here, therefore, will not do him and his work a serious injustice. Let us turn, then, to discuss the details of Marx's vision of the social world.

Social Stratification

Man's primary role in life, Marx argued, is that of a producer; this is a result of the fact that survival requires him to meet the needs of food and shelter. The tools and technical instruments that he employs in production as well as the social forms in which he works, for example, factory system or plantation, generate the system of stratification in every society.[6] The groups or strata that comprise the stratification system are referred to as social classes. In mature capitalist society there are two principal classes: the capitalists, a small minority of the population, and the proletariat, the large majority. Both groups derive from the production

[6]Karl Marx, "The German Ideology: Part I," in *The Marx-Engels Reader,* Tucker, pp. 110-64.

process but differ about an essential fact—the capitalists own the means of production, that is, the technological and scientific apparatus, and the proletariat own nothing but their labor power. Ownership of property, moreover, entitles the owners to be the sole beneficiaries of the fruits of that process, profit or, technically, surplus value.

The subsequent discussion of Marx relies almost exclusively on this portrait of two principal social classes. However, it is important to consider briefly some ambiguities in Marx's conception of social class. In *The Communist Manifesto*, a political manuscript written with Friedrich Engels and published in 1848, in addition to the capitalists, or industrial bourgeoisie, and the proletarians, or working classes, Marx spoke of the "lower-middle class, the small manufacturer, the shopkeeper, the artisan, the peasant . . . [the] 'dangerous class,' the social scum."[7] In *The Class Struggles in France*, a historical analysis of the regimes of Louis Phillipe and Louis Bonaparte, he wrote of the "finance aristocracy . . . [the] industrial bourgeoisie . . . [the] petty bourgeoisie . . . and the peasantry."[8] There are other instances when Marx wrote of these additional classes as well, and this inevitably raises questions about what he had in mind when he wrote of social class.

Since Marx died before he was able to clear up this issue, a great deal of controversy as well as scholarship developed around it. For didactic purposes, the social class division between capitalists and proletarians is relied on but not without good reason. This is the conception employed throughout Marx's abstract analysis of the economic development of capitalism.[9] In addition, this conception figures more prominently in his political analyses of capitalism. In *The Communist Manifesto*, for instance, Marx and Engels portrayed the two final political camps of capitalism as the industrial bourgeoisie, or capitalists, and the proletariat. All additional classes, they claimed, would be incorporated into either one of these groups. Finally, this conception is the most compatible with Marx's overall definition of capitalism, namely, private ownership of the means of production. Defining social class and the foundations of capitalism in the very same terms was a deliberate ploy that allowed Marx to predict the collapse of capitalism and the capitalist class at one and the same historical instant.[10]

[7]Feuer, *Marx and Engels,* pp. 17-18.

[8]Ibid., p. 282.

[9]Since Marx, like every other sociologist, could not conduct such experiments in the real world, he conducted them in the abstract. The results, no less significant for being obtained in such a manner, indicated among other things the manner in which capitalist enterprises would grow. Defects in the actual economic principles employed by Marx, owing largely to the source of them, David Ricardo, rendered many of his predictions wrong or indeterminate. For example, see Fred M. Gottheil, *Marx's Economic Predictions* (Evanston, Ill.: Northwestern University Press, 1977). Such is the fate of many of our scientific predictions, however good they might appear for a time.

[10]Even when Marx wrote of the capitalist and the proletariat classes, he seemed confused about what they represented. On occasion he wrote of them as though they were real groups. However, he usually viewed them as abstract entities that were useful for conducting analyses and making predictions [Stanislaw Ossowski, *Class Structure in the Social Consciousness* (New York: Free Press, 1963)]. More important, if Marx meant to define the capitalist and

Social Organization

Social organization, Marx believed, is an important element of the social order. One of the two results of the process of production is the social form in which men work; the other result is stratification. In *Capital*, for instance, the three stages in the development of the mode of production are handicraft guilds, manufacturing, and factories characteristic of capitalist nations in the nineteenth century. Further, Marx observed:

> As co-operation [among workers] extends its scale, this despotism [by the capitalist] takes forms peculiar to itself ... now, he [the capitalist] hands over the work of direct and constant supervision of the individual workmen, and groups of workmen, to a special kind of wage-labourer. An industrial army of workmen, under the command of a capitalist, requires, like a real army, officers [managers], and sergeants [foremen, overlookers], who, while the work is being done, command in the name of the capitalist. The work of supervision becomes their established and exclusive function.[11]

The fine details of the structure of industrial organization, and social organization generally, were of little consequence to Marx, however. The administrative hierarchy of industrial organizations constitutes, for all intents and purposes, the identical social groups as the stratification hierarchy of society, the capitalists and the proletarians. This blending of the principles of social stratification with social organization leads to unavoidable analytical pitfalls, among them a frequent confusion between the *abstract* entities of social class generated by private ownership of the means of production and the *concrete* forms represented by the owners and workers in industrial enterprises. Max Weber later more clearly distinguished and examined the separate and independent dynamics of social organization.

Social System

Marx held two related images of the social system: one abstract, the other concrete. The abstract conception has come to be known as his theory of economic determinism and depicts the social system as consisting of two principal parts, a substructure and a superstructure. The substructure comprises the primary and

proletarian classes by their relationship to property, there must be one additional social class under capitalism, the landed aristocracy—a remnant of feudalism whose property consists, not of the technical and scientific apparatus, but of land. There then appear to be three main social classes under capitalism, not two: the capitalists, owners of the technical and scientific apparatus of production; the landed aristocracy, owners of land; the proletariat, owners of no property, simply their labor power. These, incidentally, were the three principal classes that Marx defined in the third volume of *Capital*. Nevertheless, if Marx had remained alive long enough he would probably have argued that as capitalist societies matured—and no capitalist society in the late nineteenth century could be considered mature, not even England—land would diminish in importance as a source of profit, thereby leaving only the two great classes, the capitalist and the proletariat.

[11] Karl Marx, *Capital* (Moscow: Foreign Languages Publishing House, 1961), I, 332.

most essential characteristics of the social system: the process of production, the social form of production, and the stratification system built upon production—in other words, the network of economic institutions and relationships. The superstructure, a derivative and secondary component of the system, comprises religion, politics, philosophy, and law. The two major parts are interdependent—the activities of the substructure exert substantial, if not exclusive, influence on the superstructure. For instance, in *Capital* Marx wrote:

> The religious world is but the reflex of the real [substructural] world. And for a society based upon the production of commodities, in which the producers enter into social relations with one another by treating their products as commodities and values, whereby they reduce their individual private labour to be the standard of homogenous human labour—for such a society, Christianity with its *cultus* of abstract man, more especially in its bourgeois developments, Protestantism, Deism, &c., is the most fitting from of religion.[12]

Consistent with this overall portrait is Marx's assertion that any changes in the economic sphere of society temporally precede and ultimately shape changes in the other spheres.

The second image that Marx held of the social system asserts that the two principal social classes growing out of the economic process in society, the capitalist and the proletariat, are continuously in conflict. The tension between them derives from the division of labor, in particular private ownership of the means of production, and pervades the entire social system. Given this high level of tension, a major problem is posed: How is social order maintained? According to Marx, the two classes do not possess equal resources—the owners of the means of production possess all the resources of society, while those persons employed in the use of the means of production possess none of them. The resources, in turn, are used by the owners of industry to suppress the antagonism of those employed in the factories. Further details of this second image are discussed in the section, "Marx's Image of Why Men Obey."

Both images have come under attack. Inasmuch as they are related and the second is discussed in greater detail shortly, the more abstract conception is focused on. The first and most trivial criticism was enunciated most clearly by the German Social Democrat Eduard Bernstein, who claimed that the wide variety of men's motives cannot be reduced simply to economic ones. Marx never claimed they could or meant to imply as much with his images of the social system.

A second issue begins with the assertion that the first image of the social system makes Marx a technological determinist. Certainly, he encouraged this particular interpretation; in one of his more widely quoted passages he observed:

> The organization and division of labour varies according to the instruments of labour available. The hand mill implies a different division of labour from that of the steam mill. To begin with the division of labour in general, in

[12] Ibid., p. 79.

order to arrive at a specific instrument of production—machinery—is therefore to fly in the face of history.[13]

Writing later in *Capital*, he noted the profound effects of the introduction of machinery. Handicraft guilds and manufacture were eliminated by the large-scale machinery of the factory system of production; machinery in one sphere of industry, spinning, created the apparent necessity for it in another sphere, weaving; machinery, in general, revolutionized the entire production process, from agriculture to transportation; and, finally, machinery was the instrument of production that was primarily responsible for the worker's sense of alienation.[14] Although one cannot, therefore, deny that Marx believed technology was a major component in the development of society, to him the more fundamental issue was the control of the productive forces, not the productive forces themselves.

The most general issue of all is a criticism leveled at Marx for unduly emphasizing economic forces in the ebb and flow of social change. There are those scholars, such as Alfred G. Meyer, who assert that if the social system is a "going concern," then its various constituent parts are in some form of interdependence; changes in one part of the system, so this argument goes, bring about changes in another part of the system, and in turn, the latter may subsequently affect the former.[15] For instance, changes in the network of economic institutions may result in changes in the political institutions, and at some later point in time, the political institutions may bring about changes in the economic ones.

In the final analysis, Marx might concede some ground to those who criticize him in this regard, but it is doubtful that he would go quite so far as Engels who, in a letter to Franz Mehring in 1893, wrote that "once a historical element has been brought into the world by other, ultimately economic causes, it reacts, can react on its environment, and even on the causes that have given rise to it."[16] Economic conditions for Marx provided the solution to many mysteries of his day, intellectual and practical. Today, many of men's actions and beliefs are not puzzles because of Marx's profound insight and conviction.

MARX'S IMAGE OF THE POLITICAL ORDER

Contemporary political sociology relies on a distinction between the social order, which consists primarily of the economic, religious, and kinship systems, and the political order, which consists exclusively of the state and related institutions. This section examines Marx's view of the political order, employing again a general

[13]T. B. Bottomore and Maximilien Rubel, *Karl Marx: Selected Writings in Sociology and Social Philosophy* (London: C.A. Watts Co., Ltd., 1963), p. 93.

[14]Marx, *Capital,* I, 383-86.

[15]Alfred G. Meyer, *Marxism: The Unity of Theory and Practice* (Ann Arbor, Mich.: The University of Michigan Press, 1963).

[16]Tucker, *The Marx-Engels Reader,* p. 409.

scheme that permits a comparison and contrasting of the ideas of Marx with those of the other theorists. Four elements figure in this scheme that alone or in combination are used to discuss the substance and mechanics of the political order: political rulers; state machinery, including the bureaucracy and legislature; ancillary organizations such as parties; and the political system.

Political Rulers

For Marx, the political rulers of a society are an important element of the political order. His primary concern with them centered on a single issue. To what extent do the political rulers govern in favor of the interests of a particular social class? At the most abstract level, the rulers under capitalism govern in favor of the capitalists. In concrete historical cases, the picture is not so simple, however. Sometimes the political rulers seem to rule less on the behalf of a particular class than in their own special interests. The best example is found in Marx's discussions of Louis Bonaparte:

> The proper form of [the bourgeois Republicans'] joint-stock government was the *Parliamentary Republic,* with Louis Bonaparte for its President. . . . In their uninterrupted crusade against the producing masses they were, however, bound not only to invest the executive with continually increased powers of repression, but at the same time to divest their own parliamentary stronghold—the National Assembly—one by one, of all its own means of defense against the Executive. The Executive, in the person of Louis Bonaparte, turned them out. The natural offspring of the "Party-of-Order" Republic was the second Empire.
>
> The empire, with the *coup d'etat* for its certificate of birth, universal suffrage for its sanction, and the sword for its sceptre, professed to rest upon the peasantry, the large mass of producers not directly involved in the struggle of capital and labour. It professed to save the working class by breaking down Parliamentarism, and with it, the undisguised subserviency of Government to the propertied classes. It professed to save the propertied classes by upholding their economic supremacy over the working class; and, finally, it professed to unite all classes by reviving for all the chimera of national glory.[17]

Bonaparte, in other words, successfully captured the machinery of government in France and used it for his immediate ends rather than for advancing the interests of a special class; his own benefits gained in ascendancy in the degree to which he effectively played one social class off against another.

Even when the political ruler appears to have severed his connection with particular classes completely, his leadership still has the ultimate effect of furthering the interests of the propertied classes, that is, the capitalists, the financial aristocracy and the landed aristocracy:

> Under [the regime of Louis Bonaparte] . . . bourgeois society, freed from political cares, attained a development unexpected even by itself. Its industry

[17]Marx, "The Civil War in France," in *The Marx-Engels Reader,* Tucker, p. 553.

and commerce expanded to colossal dimensions; financial swindling cele-
brated cosmopolitan orgies; the misery of the masses was set off by a shame-
less display of gorgeous, meretricious and debased luxury.[18]

Hence, the fit between theory and empirical reality is clearly more comfortable in
Marx's analyses of political rulers than in the case of his analysis of social class; con-
sciously or unconsciously the leadership of political rulers favors the interests of
those social classes who privately control property.

State Machinery

The state machinery of capitalist societies is comprised of "organs of standing
army, police, bureaucracy, clergy and judicature," plus the parliament.[19] This
machinery develops policies that serve to the advantage of the capitalists; this is
consistent with Marx's abstract view of the political order. In *Capital*, for instance,
he claimed that the British Parliament passed many laws that were principally
designed to extend the workday of the laborers and, thus, to increase the profits,
or surplus value, of the capitalists.[20]

There are exceptions even to this rule. Specifically, Marx observed in France
several different political factions and parties within the National Assembly that
contended with one another for control of the government and manifested little
unity among themselves. The absence of harmony among the political groups,
Marx believed, simply reflected underlying social class differences, and the opposing political programs sprang from *different forms* of property:

> Legitimists and Orleanists, as we have said, formed the two great sections of
> the Party of Order. Was that which held these sections fast to their pre-
> tenders and kept them apart from one another nothing but lily and tricolour,
> house of Bourbon and house of Orleans, different shades of royalty, was it
> the confession of faith in royalty at all? . . . What kept the two sections
> apart . . . was not any so-called principles, it was their material conditions of
> existence, two different kinds of property, it was the old contrast of town
> and country, the rivalry between capital and landed property.[21]

Continuing in the same vein, he provided one of the clearest expositions of his
theory about the connections between material conditions and political views:

> Upon different forms of property, upon the social conditions of existence
> rises an entire superstructure of distinct and characteristically formed senti-
> ments, illusions, modes of thought and views of life. The entire class creates
> and forms them out of its material foundations and out of the corresponding
> social relations. . . . If Orleanists and Legitimists, if each section sought to
> make itself and the other believe that loyalty to their two royal houses

[18] Ibid.

[19] Ibid., p. 552.

[20] Marx, *Capital*, I, chapter 10.

[21] Marx, "The Eighteenth Brumaire of Louis Bonaparte," in *The Marx-Engels Reader*,
Tucker, p. 459.

separated them, it later proved to be the case that it was rather their divided interests which forbade the uniting of the two royal houses. And as in private life one distinguishes between what a man thinks and says of himself and what he really is and does, still more in historical struggles must one distinguish the phrases and fancies of the parties from their real organism and their real interests, their conception of themselves with their reality. Orleanists and Legitimists found themselves side by side in the republic with equal claims. If each side wished to effect the *restoration* of its *own* royal house against the other, that merely signifies that the *two great interests* into which the bourgeoisie is split—landed property and capital—sought each to restore its own supremacy and the subordination of the other.[22]

If the state machinery does not clearly govern in favor of the capitalists, there is not yet a single dominant social class, but there are contending ones whose power derives from different forms of property and wealth.

Ancillary Organizations

Marx devoted little attention to the characteristics of ancillary organizations associated with the state, including political party organizations or the interest groups and voluntary associations that Alexis de Tocqueville found so prominent in American social and political life.[23] Perhaps the only such organization that occupied his scholarship at all was the Paris Commune, but his analysis of it, at least its organizational characteristics, was extremely sketchy.

Political System

According to Marx, the political system consists of two elements: political rulers and their staffs, and the state machinery. His distinction between these two elements, the state and civil society, parallels his use of the substructure-superstructure scheme. The state is men in the political order; civil society is men in the

---

[22] Ibid., pp. 459-60.

[23] Although Marx paid little attention to such groups, Engels seems to have considered them important, particularly in the United States. In the introduction to Marx's *The Civil War in France,* he wrote:

> Nowhere do "politicians" form a more separate and powerful section of the nation than precisely in North America. There, each of the two major parties which alternately succeed each other in power is itself in turn controlled by people who make a business of politics, who speculate on seats in the legislative assemblies of the Union as well as of the separate states, or who make a living by carrying on agitation for their party and on its victory are rewarded with positions. It is well known how the Americans have been trying for thirty years to shake off this yoke, which has become intolerable, and how in spite of it all they continue to sink ever deeper in this swamp of corruption. It is precisely in America that we see best how there takes place this process of the state power making itself independent in relation to society, whose mere instrument it was originally intended to be ... [We] find here two great gangs of political speculators, who alternately take possession of the state power and exploit it by the most corrupt means for the most corrupt ends—and the nation is powerless against these two great cartels of politicians, who are ostensibly its servants, but in reality dominate and plunder it. (Tucker, *The Marx-Engels Reader,* pp. 535-36.)

production process and social classes. Civil society is also the more fundamental dimension; man's citizenship in the state, for instance, simply is one more illustration of his alienation from his true destiny and powers.[24]

Marx had considerably less to write about the political order of capitalism during his lifetime than about its economic institutions because of the determinative role he assigned the latter. His shortcomings in this regard were made all the more evident by Weber's detailed and expert discussion of political institutions.

MARX'S IMAGE OF WHY MEN OBEY

One of the main issues for political sociology concerns the nature and foundations of men's obedience in society. Solutions to the problem vary, of course, depending on the theorists; generally, the solutions portray the manner in which a theorist deals with power and authority. Marx's solutions furnish one of the principal images in modern political sociology.

Why do members of the working class in capitalist society obey the capitalists? Marx's assumption is that the division between the capitalists and the proletarians is antagonistic—each class is in conflict with the other. Furthermore, the capitalist class wishes to advance its own goals, notably to continue the accumulation of capital. In order to accomplish this, it obviously must convince the proletariat to continue to work in its factories and industries; it must, in short, convince the proletariat to obey its commands to work.

The obedience of the working class to the capitalists, insofar as industrial work is concerned, is *not the product of blatant coercion*; divorced as they are from the ownership of any of the technical means of production, the proletarians have no choice but to work for the capitalists.[25] Their daily livelihood depends on the use of these instruments, and thus, they obey the commands of the capitalists out of sheer necessity. From the perspective of the capitalist class, the first of the principal devices that account for the obedience of the proletariat is *the capitalists' ownership of the means of production.*

Not content simply to demonstrate the power of the capitalists in economic institutions, Marx proceeds to make one of his renowned theoretical leaps, albeit one consistent with his general view of the world: Dominance in the economic institutions of society produces, ipso facto, dominance in every other main sphere

"free labor" [margin annotation]

[24] Marx, "On the Jewish Question," in *The Marx-Engels Reader,* Tucker, pp. 24-51.

[25] In recent years, some sociologists have become attached to a polarity between conflict theories and consensual theories. The theories of Marx are frequently referred to as conflict theories. Those who adopt this point of view also stretch it too far by asserting that Marx believed societies were held together by virtue of the coercive powers of the dominant social classes, the capitalists. Nothing could be further from the truth. For information on those who appear to adopt this point of view about conflict see, for example, Ralf Dahrendorf, *Class and Class Conflict in Industrial Society* (Stanford, Calif.: Stanford University Press, 1959); and Seymour Martin Lipset, *Political Man* (Garden City, N.Y.: Doubleday and Co., 1960). Also see our discussion later in this chapter of the writings of Antonio Gramsci on coercion and, in particular, his concept of hegemony.

of society. In other words, by virtue of their control of the working classes in the economic institutions of society, the capitalists also control the working classes in all other enterprises and institutions. The reasons for this assumption, of course, are less than obvious. Why should power in economic institutions be generalized to power in all other institutions?

There are any number of answers. One of the most plausible is that capitalists are, by definition, men of wealth, and wealth permits them to "purchase" people in positions of state power. Furthermore, control over those individuals who occupy positions of state power means control over the physical means of force. Hence, the capitalists are able to secure the obedience of the working classes outside of economic institutions through their indirect control over the means of physical force.

To this argument Marx would respond that, though it is partly correct, it obscures the real basis for noneconomic power of the capitalists. Concealed in the claim that economic wealth guarantees the capitalists political or other forms of power is the real basis for the power of the capitalists outside of the economic realm, namely, *the hegemony of their system of values.* Their control in this respect is akin to that of any other dominant class in any other age:

> The ideas of the ruling class are in every epoch the ruling ideas: i.e. the class which is the ruling *material* force of society, is at the same time its ruling *intellectual* force. The class which has the means of material production at its disposal, has control at the same time over the means of mental production, so that thereby, generally speaking, the ideas of those who lack the means of mental production are subject to it.[26]

"One man, one vote" and "equal rights for all," for instance, represent elements of the belief system of the capitalists that effectively act to secure the obedience of the proletariat in the political order of society; with adages such as "time is money," they persuade the working-class members that they are fulfilling their own best interests by remaining obedient to the institutions of capitalism. Thus, the second principal device that the capitalists use to generate obedience from the working classes is *their control of the means of communication.*[27]

Marx's insightful analysis of these matters glosses over a number of important issues, however. For one thing, it fails to specify *how* the hegemony of the beliefs of the capitalists is attained. Are there particular agencies, for example, the family

---

[26] Marx, "The German Ideology," in *The Marx-Engels Reader,* Tucker, p. 136.

[27] Comparatively few scholars actually recognize the prominent role that the system of values and their dissemination play in securing the power of the capitalist class over the proletariat. One who does, however, makes it an integral part of his interpretation of Marx's ruling class:

> The basis on which the power of the ruling classes rests in Marxian view, is *the control which it wields over the essential means of production and communication.* It is this control which enables a class to exploit all those classes which do not have such control to maintain economic, social and political inequalities. It is this control which makes a class into the *ruling class.* (Meyer, *Marxism,* p. 20.)

or school, that spread the beliefs? Perhaps the most fundamental question of his analysis is raised by Joseph Schumpeter: How is it that some people come to own the means of production *in the first place*? Marx deals with this problem by introducing the notion of primitive accumulation. "The so-called primitive accumulation . . . is nothing else than the historical process of divorcing the producer from the means of production."[28] Piracy, usury, and the dispossession of journeymen and apprentices by guildmasters are among the several ways in which owners of industry initiate and foster the growth of their own capital resources. Yet the notion of primitive accumulation, and the particular routes whereby it is achieved, beg the question of how certain people become capitalists. "Force-robbery-subjugation of the masses facilitating their spoliation and the results of the pillage in turn facilitating subjugation," as Schumpeter observes, "this was all right of course and admirably tallied with ideas common among intellectuals of all types. . . . *But . . . it does not solve the problem, which is to explain how some people acquired the power to subjugate and rob* [my italics] ."[29] Marx really solved this issue by fiat; other scholars consider it substantially more problematic.

In sum, the obedience of the proletariat derives from the control of the capitalists over the means of production and communication. Obversely, the power of the capitalists comes essentially from their ownership of these resources.

MARX'S IMAGE OF CHANGE

Often scholars claim that the entire thrust of Marx's analysis of capitalism, as well as of other societies, is concerned with change. Broadly speaking, this is a justified, if nevertheless oversimplified, portrayal of his ideas. For Marx, the basic principles of capitalism contain elements that promote both stability and change, order and disorder; over time, change takes priority over stability, and the very mechanisms that once served to advance the growth of capitalism act to transform it. Among such principles are surplus value, or the mechanism that leads to the profit of the capitalists; the divorce of the majority of the population, the working class, from the ownership of the means of production; and, at the most general level, the alienation of man in capitalist society.

The Breadth and Depth of Change

Marx was interested in the most fundamental sort of change best characterized as *qualitative* rather than *quantitative*. The tensions that stem from the basic contradictions in capitalism are spread out over a long period of time. Eventually they accumulate, producing a stark contrast between the capitalists and the proletariat; they end with the victory of the proletariat and the establishment of an

[28] Marx, *Capital*, I, 715. Our discussion here is indebted to the great insights of Antonio Gramsci and Georg Lukács, two Marxists whose writings we discuss at length below.

[29] Joseph Schumpeter, *Capitalism, Socialism, and Democracy*, 3rd ed. (New York: Harper & Row, Publishers, 1962), p. 17.

entirely new society grounded in new economic and social principles as, for example, public ownership of property. In this regard, Marx's concern with change fundamentally differs from that of many other social theorists.

Worldwide rather than simply national change was of primary interest to Marx, even though he—as well as loyal followers—was often absorbed by the potential for revolutionary changes in individual countries. Capitalism, he felt, was destined to become a worldwide phenomenon because of its own internal dynamics, the growth and incessant search for profits, and consequently, the proletarian revolution would become a universal phenomenon. There is evidence of this realization, for example, in *The Class Struggles in France*:

> The development of the industrial proletariat is, in general, conditioned by the development of the industrial bourgeoisie. Only under its rule does the proletariat gain that extensive national existence which can raise its revolution to a national one, and does itself create the modern means of production, which become just so many means of its revolutionary emancipation. Only its rule tears up the material roots of feudal society and levels the ground on which alone a proletarian revolution is possible.... The industrial bourgeoisie can rule only where modern industry shapes all property relations to suit itself, and industry can win this power only when it has conquered the world market, for national bounds are not wide enough for its development.[30]

Marx went on to argue that the revolution of February 1848 in France was aborted precisely because the conditions of economic growth had not yet permitted the rise of a nationwide, much less worldwide, industrial bourgeoisie (capitalist class) and proletariat.

A third facet of this dimension of change involves the contrast between political change and social change. The distinction was a crucial one for Marx and stemmed from his parallel contrast between the state and civil society. Consistent with his general perspective, he believed the change that took place only in the realm of state power, that is, change of officeholders or even of the entire regime, represented just the first stage toward effecting a complete change of society. State power certainly had to be acquired by the proletarian forces, and so the revolution was initially a distinctly "political" one. Once state power had been secured, then the whole economic and social edifice on which capitalist society rested, namely, private property and social classes, would have to be eliminated and, with it, state power itself. Evidence of Marx's view of this matter is found in his discussion of the Paris Commune of 1871:

> Its true secret was this. It was essentially a working-class government, the product of the struggle of the producing against the appropriating class, the political form at last discovered under which to work out the economic emancipation of labour.

---

[30] Feuer, *Marx and Engels*, p. 291.

Except on this last condition, the Communal Constitution would have been an impossibility and a delusion. The political rule of the producer can not coexist with the perpetuation of his social slavery. The Commune was therefore to serve as a lever for uprooting the economical [*sic*] foundations upon which rests the existence of classes, and therefore of class-rule. With labour emancipated, every man becomes a working man, and productive labour ceases to be a class attribute.[31]

Finally, the one aspect of Marx's view of change that leaps first into people's minds is the violence associated with change. Marx's praise for the Paris Commune of 1871, his and Engels's rhetoric in *The Communist Manifesto*, his disdain, as an older man, for the slow programs of other socialists, and his very image of change as qualitative create a vision of an abrupt rending of capitalist society. As a general portrayal that image is correct and compatible with Marx's view of himself as a dedicated, militant revolutionary. As a scholar, however, Marx recognized exceptions; the classic one was that of England:

We now come to the Chartists, the politically active portion of the British working class. The six points of the Charter which they contend for contain nothing but the demand of Universal Suffrage, and of the conditions without which Universal Suffrage would be illusory for the working class; such as the ballot, payment of members, annual general elections. But Universal Suffrage is the equivalent of political power for the working class of England, where the proletariat forms the large majority of the population, where, in a long, though underground civil war, it has gained a clear consciousness of its position as a class, and where even the rural districts know no longer any peasants, but only landlords, industrial capitalists [farmers] and hired labourers. The carrying of Universal Suffrage in England would, therefore, be a far more socialistic measure than anything which has been honoured with that name on the Continent.
Its inevitable result, here, is the *political supremacy of the working class* [italics left out and selective for emphasis].[32]

Even so, political supremacy of the working class is only a prerequisite for fundamental, social change; it is unclear whether Marx intended also to assert that fundamental change in England could occur nonviolently. All things considered, he probably did not.

The Logic of Change

The theory of dialectics and of dialectical change is one of the most important doctrines outlined by Marx. It is a theory he took over from G.W.F. Hegel, the great German philosopher. How much Marx retained of Hegel's own dialectical vision, apart from the fact that he inverted Hegel's idealism into materialism,

---

[31] Marx, "The Civil War in France," in *The Marx-Engels Reader,* Tucker, p. 557.

[32] Bottomore and Rubel, *Karl Marx,* p. 200.

remains a matter of considerable debate among Marxist and non-Marxist scholars, alike.[33]

Initially the dialectic may be thought of as comprised of three basic elements: a thesis, an antithesis to the thesis, and a synthesis. Such a scheme is correct, but it fails to convey the dynamic qualities of the dialectic. Defining the terms, a synthesis is the capitalist society; the thesis is the capitalist class; and the antithesis is the proletariat class. By definition the relationship between the capitalist and proletarian classes is antagonistic. Both classes, furthermore, only exist in relationship to each other—there can be no capitalist class without a proletarian class, and vice versa. The theory of change embedded in this logic is that capitalist society creates sources that serve *to sustain and to undo* it as a form of society: the one the capitalist class, the other the proletarian class.

Specifically, under capitalism the capitalist class owns the technical and scientific apparatus of production. To further their own interests, the growth of capital, they employ workers. It is in the very nature of the relationship between the capitalist and workers that the former benefit and the latter suffer; for instance, the capitalists are those who reap profits, or surplus value, while the workers are those who receive nothing but subsistence wages. Both groups require the continued services of one another—the capitalists as a means of accumulating capital, and the laborers as a means of sheer survival; neither group can remain independent of the other:

> Capitalist production . . . of itself reproduces the separation between labour-power and the means of labour. It thereby reproduces and perpetuates the condition for exploiting the labourer. It incessantly forces him to sell his labour-power in order to live, and enables the capitalist to purchase labour-power in order that he may enrich himself. . . . It is the process itself that incessantly hurls back the labourer on to the market as a vendor of his labour-power, and that incessantly converts his own product into a means by which another man can purchase him. . . . Capitalist production, under its aspect of a continuous connected process, of a process of reproduction, produces not only commodities, not only surplus-value, but it also produces and reproduces the capitalist relationship; on the one side the capitalist, on the other the wage-labourer.[34]

From the capitalist's point of view, of course, the situation is fine so long as he can maintain the worker in his service. Two things keep the worker from leaving: the economic fact of capitalism, that the worker is a free labourer who possesses no means of production of his own, and the ideological fact of capitalism, that the

---

[33] For two very different readings of the Hegelian influence on Marx, see, on the one hand, George Lukács, *History and Class Consciousness: Studies in Marxist Dialectics* (Cambridge, Mass.: The MIT Press, 1971), and, on the other, Louis Althusser and Etienne Balibar, *Reading Capital,* 2nd ed., trans. Ben Brewster (London: NLB, 1977, Part I).

[34] Marx, *Capital,* I, 577-78.

worker believes that his work for the capitalist is done for his—the worker's—own best interests.

Those conditions that benefit the capitalist and burden the labourer ultimately become inverted so that it is the capitalist who suffers and the laborer who profits, in the figurative sense. Thus, from the capitalist's point of view, the mechanism that produces his profit will turn to his disadvantage and lead to the rebellion of the laborer. This inversion is evident throughout many passages of *Capital*, but one passage will suffice:

> The law by which a constantly increasing quantity of means of production, thanks to the advance in the productiveness of social labour, may be set in movement by a progressively diminishing expenditure of human power, this law in a capitalist society—where the labourer does not employ the means of production, but the means of production employ the laborer—undergoes a complete inversion and is expressed thus: the higher the productiveness of labour, the greater is the pressure of the labourers on the means of employment, the more precarious, therefore, becomes the condition of their existence, viz., the sale of their own labour-power for the increasing of another's wealth, or for the self-expansion of capital.[35]

In brief, the laws that once served to expand capitalism and to accumulate wealth for the capitalist class are the very conditions that will destroy capitalism and with it the capitalist class.

The tension between the capitalist and the proletarian classes is resolved through the formation of a new form of society under the sponsorship of the proletariat; its principal policy calls for the abolition of all social classes. This new society, communist society, represents to Marx the *final* synthesis, since the driving motor, class struggle, of all previous development has been eliminated. Some of its more salient features are discussed shortly.

As Hegel had done with his own scheme, Marx, too, claimed that dialectics came virtually to an end, in his case with the demise of capitalism. Yet, as a system of logic, dialectical principles imply a recurrence of the thesis-antithesis-synthesis sequence. Hence, why should the shift to communism represent the *final* synthesis? In fact, *there is no reason implicit in the logic of dialectics to support the idea that communist society is the final synthesis.* To arrive at this conclusion, Marx seems to have felt compelled to superimpose his ethical standards onto the dialectic itself and, in particular, to represent the proletariat as a "universal class" embodying all the sins and all the promise of mankind. The proletariat is different from all previous social classes, and therefore, the class whose ascendancy would radically alter all previous history by dispelling it.[36]

---

[35] Ibid., pp. 644-45.

[36] Schlomo Avinieri, *The Social and Political Thought of Karl Marx* (Cambridge: Cambridge University Press, 1968).

The Antecedents
of Revolutionary Change

Over the years, scholars have become interested in pinpointing the special circumstances that Marx believed would lead to the formation of a revolutionary movement among the working classes. Several have been identified. They represent the consequences of the economic motor of capitalism—the continuous drive for and accumulation of profits—and can be decomposed into two categories, economic and social (see figure 2-1). Although most of these conditions are generally discussed in terms of their consequences for the formation of a revolutionary movement among the working classes, their principal effect is to create a distinctive division between the capitalist and the proletarian classes. Once such lines are drawn, Marx believed, the illusions of capitalism would be revealed to the working classes, thereby producing a revolutionary movement. For their part, the capitalists would control state power, but inasmuch as they represent the old class structure of capitalism, their power would be doomed to be overthrown by the proletariat.

Economic Antecedents. Marx expected that the lust of the capitalists for profits would eventually produce an overabundance of commodities—a surplus that exceeded the capacity of the world market to absorb it. Most of the economic antecedents of revolution stem from this central premise. The first of these are the periodic crises and falling profits of capitalists. As Marx and Engels observed in *The Communist Manifesto*:

> It is enough to mention the commercial crises that by their periodic return put on its trial, each time more threateningly, the existence of the entire bourgeois society. In these crises a great part not only of the existing products but also the previously created productive forces are periodically destroyed. In these crises there [appears] an epidemic that in all earlier epochs would have seemed an absurdity—the epidemic of over-production.[37]

Marx's second economic antecedent of revolution is the centralization of capital; a diminishing proportion of the owners of industries come to possess an increasingly greater proportion of the wealth—an exaggeration of capitalism's tendency for wealth to be controlled by a minority. "That which is now to be expropriated is no longer the labourer working for himself, but the capitalist exploiting many labourers. This expropriation is accomplished by the action of the immanent laws of capitalist production itself by the centralization of capital. One capitalist always kills many."[38] One of the effects of centralization is presumably to make the source of oppression and the fact of oppression more visible to the working classes.

Another effect of centralization is proletarization, a critical antecedent of revolution. Expropriated from the means of production formerly controlled by

[37]Feuer, *Marx and Engels,* p. 12.
[38]Marx, *Capital,* I, 750.

28

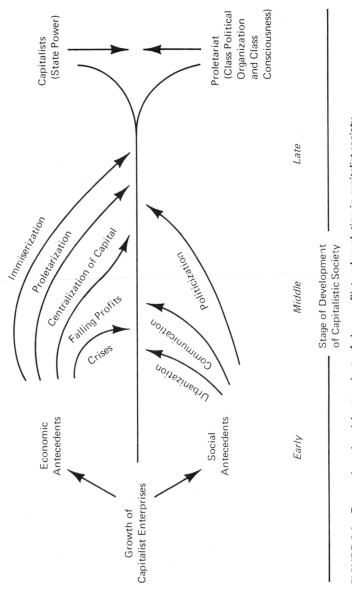

FIGURE 2-1 Economic and social antecedents of class conflict and revolution in capitalist society

them, many capitalists are compelled to join the ranks of the working class in order to survive; in effect, they are downwardly mobile. "Entire sections of the ruling classes are, by advance of industry, precipitated into the proletariat, or are at least threatened in their conditions of existence. These also support the proletariat with fresh elements of enlightenment and progress."[39]

The last of the major economic antecedents of revolution is also the one open to the most diverse readings. According to Marx, the financial conditions of the average worker would worsen as a result of the growing numbers of economic crises and the steady displacement of workers by the introduction of technology. In particular, a large surplus population of laborers, an industrial reserve army, would be created, leading to a reduction in workers' wages and to a general burden on the working class.

The industrial reserve army, however, represents only one part of a much broader process, *Verelendung*, or increasing misery. "Accumulation of wealth at one pole is, therefore, at the same time accumulation of misery, agony of toil, slavery, ignorance, brutality, mental degradation, at the opposite pole, i.e. on the side of the class that produces its own product in the form of capital."[40] Disputes arise among scholars about whether Marx intended to argue that the *absolute* wages of the working class would diminish, that is, that there would be a decline in the general wage level of the working class; or whether he meant to claim that there would be an absolute rise in the general wage levels throughout society but a decline in the *relative* wage level of the proletariat, that is, their share in the national income. The former has become known as the "vulgar" reading of Marx, the latter as the "relative deprivation" reading; these are two interpretations we again encounter in chapter 12. The dispute is more than academic; if Marx meant to imply that the lot of the working class would become progressively worse in absolute terms, then he was clearly mistaken, and this might account for the absence of the revolution he predicted.

While the controversy is likely to rage for a long time, with reputable scholars giving arguments for one or the other interpretation, the most sensible statement is that of Ronald L. Meek:

> There does indeed exist, we may plausibly argue, at any rate in a kind of "pure" capitalist system, an "innate tendency" towards "increasing misery" in Marx's sense, but for various reasons this "innate tendency" has been "off-set" or "counteracted" in our own times by various factors which Marx abstracted from his model. . . . If we adopt a Leninist line, we may put the blame on imperialism; or we may point, alternatively or in addition, to the great wages of technical innovation and consequent increases in productivity which have occurred since Marx's time, to the immense growth in the extent and power of trade unionism which has increased the power of the workers to press for a higher share of the growing national product, to the change in the aims of the trade union movement which has made it more interested

[39] Feuer, *Marx and Engels*, p. 19.
[40] Marx, *Capital*, I, 644-45.

in getting what it can out of the capitalist system than in putting an end to it, and to the growth of the socialist sector of the world which has made the capitalists more willing to grant the workers the wage increases they demand.[41]

These and similar reasons, including other defects in Marxian economic principles, are often asserted by observers of contemporary politics who wish to explain why Marx's expectations for revolution failed to materialize. Of course, the extent of trade unions in the United States and Great Britain, among other countries, are important differences from Marx's day and perhaps undercut the pivotal element in the Marxian scheme of things. Yet these arguments, after all, only consider *one* of several antecedents that Marx believed would produce revolution and, thus, provide only partial accounts for the absence of revolution.

Social Antecedents. A *leitmotif* characteristic of Marx's thought is an alleged opposition between town and countryside. The theme is evident in Marx's emphasis on urbanization in promoting revolution. The congregations of workers drawn into urban areas possess a far greater potential for revolution than the peasants and farmers in the country. There are two reasons for this: the workers in the urban centers are generally employed in factories, thus encountering the most degrading and dehumanizing forms of work, and sheer density of numbers present a potential for the organization of revolutionary movements, a fact peculiarly characteristic of urban centers.

A second social antecedent of revolution stems from urbanization, namely communication. Communication among the workers is essential to the formation of a revolutionary movement, mainly because it enables them to recognize the similarity of their experiences and to develop common beliefs:

> Now and then the workers are victorious, but only for a time. The real fruit of their battles lies not in the immediate result, but in the ever expanding union of the workers. This union is helped on by the improved means of communication that are created by modern industry and that place the workers of different localities in contact with one another.[42]

The importance of communication among the working class is that it serves to counteract the control of the capitalists over the means of communication in society as well as the general hegemony of the capitalist system of values.

The last of the major social antecedents required for the development of revolutionary movement on the part of the working classes is their politicization. There are two sources of this politicization: one that occurs almost naturally as a result of the encounters between the workers and the capitalists is trade-unionism, and the other that is brought into the working classes from without is the effort by

---

[41] Ronald L. Meek, "Marx's Doctrine of Increasing Misery," *Science and Society,* 26 (Fall 1962), 436-37.

[42] Feuer, *Marx and Engels,* p. 16.

revolutionaries like Marx and his compatriots to direct the politics of the working class. Marx and Engels noted this latter process in *The Communist Manifesto*:

> Finally, in times when the class struggle nears the decisive hour, the process of dissolution going on within the ruling class, in fact within the whole range of old society, assumes such a violent, glaring character that a small section of the ruling class cuts itself adrift and joins the revolutionary class, the class that holds the future in its hands. [So] now a portion of the bourgeoisie goes over to the proletariat, and in particular a portion of the bourgeois ideologists, who have raised themselves to the level of comprehending theoretically the historical movement as a whole.[43]

The two sources, of course, are not necessarily compatible. Indeed, it is on matters of the precise form of this politicization that loyal followers of Marx's doctrines have become divided.

Class Consciousness.   Perhaps the most significant component in the Marxian scheme of revolution and, more broadly, of change is class consciousness. It is also the component least understood. In order for the working-class members to overthrow the capitalists, they have to become aware of themselves as a class. Adapting terminology from Feuerbach, who himself took over terms ultimately traceable to Kant, Marx asserted that the proletariat had to transform itself from a *Klasse an sich*, a class simply by virtue of similar economic and social conditions, to a *Klasse für sich*, a class whose members were aware of those conditions.

What precisely constitutes this phenomenon of class consciousness? Marx came closest to giving his most concise and clear conceptual exposition of it in *German Ideology*: "The separate individuals form a class only insofar as they have to carry on a common battle against another class; otherwise they are on hostile terms with each other as competitors."[44] Class consciousness consists of two elements: the shared awareness among a group of people that they are on hostile terms with another group of people, and a shared desire for united action against this group of people.[45] Class consciousness among the members of the proletariat, in particular, means that as a group they are aware that the capitalists are oppressing them and, further, that they are convinced of the need for collective action to be taken against the capitalists.

Political organization probably plays a major part in the formation of class consciousness. What precise form does such political organization assume, especially among the proletariat? Many scholars and revolutionaries believe that the trade-union movement that emerged among working-class groups worldwide represents the "false consciousness" of the workers, not a genuine class consciousness. They

---

[43] Ibid., p. 17.

[44] Tucker, *The Marx-Engels Reader*, p. 143.

[45] There is one additional element that figures into class consciousness on a philosophical plane—the class of people must be aware of their coming ascendancy to power in society (Lukács, *History and Class Consciousness*).

maintain that trade unions generally accept the standards and ethics of capitalism and thus are unprepared to overthrow the capitalists and establish a new society to benefit the majority of the citizens. In recognition of this, more militant followers of Marx, Lenin the chief one among them, argue that trade unions must be combatted:

> There is a lot of talk about spontaneity, but the *spontaneous* development of the labour movement leads to its becoming subordinated to bourgeois ideology ... for the spontaneous labour movement is pure and simple trade unionism ... and trade unionism means the ideological subordination of the workers to the bourgeoisie. ... [The task of the Social Democrats in Russia would be] to combat spontaneity, to divert the labour movement, with its spontaneous trade-unionist striving, from under the wing of the bourgeoisie and to bring it under the wing of revolutionary Social-Democracy.[46]

Since Marx, the best political form that would allow the working class to meet their own needs and goals has been an issue on which differences in persuasion and tactics emerge, even among the most devoted loyalists to Marx. There are those, such as the German Social Democrat Edward Bernstein, who adopted a reformist position and argued that the chief goal should be to improve the working conditions of the working classes; if these are improved under the regime of capitalism, then there is no need for revolution. Others, including Lenin, adopted a more militant position and argued that the main goal should be to liberate the proletariat; this is an action that requires an overthrow of the entire structure of capitalist society. No doubt such struggles and differences will long persist.

THE UTOPIAN VISION:
COMMUNIST SOCIETY

During his lifetime, most of Marx's attention was occupied with understanding and explicating the evils of capitalist society rather than with drawing up plans for the new, communist society. As a result, his ideas regarding communism were not developed in fine detail, even though they helped to furnish the basis for the establishment of the Bolshevik regime in Russia. Thus, in order to capture his vision, a picture of it must be constructed from diverse elements written at different times and in different stages of his maturity.

The principal change to be instituted under communism is the abolition of ownership of the means of production, including land, by the few, and the public ownership of them. All previous privileges built on the foundations of capitalism and providing wealth to single individuals or families are also eradicated. Thus, Marx and Engels wrote in *The Communist Manifesto* that there would be "heavy progressive or graduated income tax ... [and] ... [abolition] of all right of

[46] Lenin, *What Is to Be Done?* (New York: International Publishers, 1943), p. 41.

inheritance."[47] Everyone, under communism, is liable to labor and has to contribute to the process of production. Furthermore, the labor of children in factories is outlawed, and free education is provided to them.

These and other changes are centralized in the apparatus of the state. The state machinery is captured by the proletariat as a result of their revolution; in order to achieve the transition to communism, those individual members who occupy positions within the state machinery left over from capitalism are expected to lay down specific policies. There had to be, Marx believed, a "revolutionary dictatorship of the proletariat."[48]

What did Marx have in mind when he spoke of the dictatorship of the proletariat? Detractors of Marx claim that he envisioned a society and state just like capitalism but with representatives of the working classes occupying positions of power. Proponents argue that Marx believed the state would only operate as an administrative agency. To be sure, on both philosophical and moral grounds Marx wished for state power to vanish after the establishment of communism, but he was ambivalent about how soon or how readily such power might be eliminated.

In this dispute, the final answer is to be found in Marx's historical analyses, in particular his examination of the Paris Commune of 1871. Judging from his description and portrayal of the commune, Marx apparently felt that it represented, for all intents and purposes, a living example of the new, worldwide communist society:

> The direct antithesis to the empire was the Commune. . . . The first decree of the Commune . . . was the suppression of the standing army, and the substitution for it of the armed people. The Commune was formed of the municipal councillors, chosen by universal suffrage in the various wards of the town, responsible and revocable at short terms. The majority of its members were naturally working men, or acknowledged representatives of the working class. The Commune was to be a working, not a parliamentary, body, executive and legislative at the same time. . . . [The] police was at once stripped of its political attributes, and turned into the responsible and at all times revocable agent of the Commune. So were the officials of all other branches of the Administration. From the members of the Commune downwards, the public service had to be done at *workingmen's wages*. The vested interests and the representation allowances of the high dignitaries of State disappeared along with the high dignitaries themselves. Public functions ceased to be the private property of the tools of the Central Government. . . . [The] Commune was anxious to break the spiritual force of repression, the "parson-power," by the disestablishment and disendowment of all churches as proprietary bodies. . . . The whole of the educational institutions were opened to the people gratuitously, and at the same time cleared of all interference of Church and State. . . . The judicial functionaries were to be divested of that sham independence. . . . Like the rest of public servants, magistrates and judges were to be elective, responsible and revocable.
>   The Paris Commune was, of course, to serve as a model to all the great industrial centres of France.[49]

[47] Feuer, *Marx and Engels*, p. 28.
[48] Marx, "Critique of the Gotha Program," in *Marx and Engels*, Feuer, p. 127.
[49] Tucker, *The Marx-Engels Reader*, pp. 554-55.

It is more than evident from these pages that, if Marx did view the Paris Commune as the example for future communist societies, then the state was merely to serve administrative purposes. To insure that those who occupied positions in the state did not become a new class unto themselves, their wages were to be the equal of other wages in the commune, and as officials, they were to be "elective, responsible, and revocable." Such a position underscores the fact that Marx's view of the new communist state was clearly an antiauthoritarian and antibureaucratic one.[50]

However much one might appreciate Marx's position with regard to the role of the state, it is quite clear from developments since his death in 1883 that those placed in control of the state machinery as a result of revolution are not so easily displaced from office or from power. Indeed, Marx seems to have seriously underestimated the problems involved in dismantling or, at any rate diminishing, the powers of the bureaucratic machinery of the state. Likewise, he overestimated the tendency for those who occupy the positions of power, in the state machinery or in other large-scale organizations, to freely relinquish those positions to other members of the public. Both forms of oversight, in fact, became central concerns for other sociologists interested in politics—the former for Max Weber, the latter for Roberto Michels.

Like all great thinkers, Marx managed to fashion a vision of the world that has inspired many future generations of scholars, political activists, and laypeople, alike. He captured dominant tendencies in the development of modern society and succeeded in showing how they would unfold in the decades following his own death. Later thinkers and activists, drawn into the camp of the Marxists by the magnificence of this vision, have sought to amend, to refine, and to make relevant to contemporary society the claims Marx advanced a century ago. We shall turn now to consider some of the most important of these contributions.

EXTENSIONS OF THE MARXIST VISION:
THE MARXISTS

What did Marx really mean by the nature of social classes and class consciousness? What did he truly intend to be the connection between the nature of theory and of praxis? What is the relationship between the writings of the young Marx, who wrote in the manner of a philosopher, and the mature Marx, who conceived the work of *Capital* as a scientific treatment of capitalist society? How do the writings of Marx, which deal with the development of capitalism through the mid-nineteenth century, actually bear upon the workings of capitalist and noncapitalist societies in the twentieth century? These are among the many questions that both sympathetic and unsympathetic students and scholars have raised in conjunction with the effort to better understand the writings of Marx since his death in 1883. Here in this section we shall very briefly consider some of the major contributions that have come to constitute the corpus of Marxist writings over the past century. In particular, we

---

[50] Ralph Miliband, "Marx and the State," in *Karl Marx,* Bottomore, pp. 128-50.

shall discuss contributions to this literature made by Friedrich Engels, V. I. Lenin, Antonio Gramsci, Georg Lukács, Herbert Marcuse, Jürgen Habermas, and Louis Althusser.[51] While some of these ideas do not directly touch upon our concerns with the political sociology of Marx, they will still help us to gain firmer overall appreciation of his outlook and its vast influence on notable thinkers.

Friedrich Engels

Let us begin with the work of Friedrich Engels. As we have learned, Engels, son of a wealthy German businessman, befriended Marx in Paris in 1844, and soon thereafter they began their lifetime of intellectual partnership, surely one of the most fruitful the world has ever known. Engels, as we noted earlier, always remained the junior partner in this work. Still he did produce his own distinctive contributions, especially after Marx's death. In 1845 Engels published his first major work, *Condition of the Working Class in England*, a vivid and sympathetic account of the conditions of the working class in the industrial heart of England.[52] Among the ranks of those who have made a careful assessment of Marxist writings, Engels seems to have attracted the greatest admiration—and also stirred the greatest controversy—for his effort to interpret and to extend the theories which he developed alongside Marx.

It is in three works, *Anti-Dühring, Socialism: Utopian and Scientific*, and *The Origin of the Family, Private Property, and the State*, in which Engels's most distinctive contributions are to be found.[53] In *Anti-Dühring*, Engels embarks on a polemical attack against Dr. Eugen Dühring, a *Privatdozent* at Berlin University who in 1875 had proposed a new theory of socialism. *Anti-Dühring*, written without the aid of Marx but published supposedly with his tacit approval of its contents, is an effort to demonstrate the distinctive features of Marx's theory for capitalism, and to demonstrate how this theory is superior to that of the other socialist views of the day, particularly to that of Dühring, himself. The heart of the argument lies within the chapters subsequently revised and published separately as *Socialism: Utopain and Scientific*, for herein Engels depicts what he regards to be the intellectual roots of the philosophy which underlay Marx's approach, that which he calls *dialectical materialism*, as well as the scientific system to which it gave birth, that which he names *historical materialism*.[54] Moreover, he seeks at the

---

[51] For an excellent discussion of a number of the Marxist scholars and thinkers of the twentieth century, see Perry Anderson, *Considerations on Western Marxism* (London: Verso, 1979). Also, see David McLellan, *Karl Marx* (New York: Penguin Books, 1975).

[52] Friedrich Engels, *The Condition of the Working Class in England* (Moscow: Foreign Languages Publishing House, 1962).

[53] Friedrich Engels, *Anti-Dühring* (Moscow: Foreign Languages Publishing House, 1954); Friedrich Engels, "The Origin of the Family, Private Property, and the State," in *Selected Works in Two Volumes,* Volume II, Karl Marx and Friedrich Engels (Moscow: Foreign Languages Publishing House, 1951), pp. 155-296; Friedrich Engels, "Socialism: Utopian and Scientific," in *Selected Works in Two Volumes,* Volume II, Marx and Engels, pp. 86-142.

[54] These two names for the philosophy and science developed by Marx and Engels apparently were used for the first time here in Engels's work.

same time to show the differences among the various schools of socialist thought, devoting some attention to the ideas of Saint-Simon, a Frenchman whose writings influenced Marx's ideas on the working class and industry, Fourier, who adopted the dialectical method in the analysis of society, and Robert Owen, an Englishman who founded several utopian communities in the United States in the nineteenth century.

Engels argues that the philosophy of dialectical materialism is founded on the belief that all nature is involved in constant motion and change, establishing forms which, by virtue of natural processes of opposition, are ultimately surpassed, only to once again undergo the process of opposition and transformation. Tracing dialectics to the Greek philosopher Heraclitus, as well as to Fourier, he insists that it achieved its most perfect articulation in the writings of G.W.F. Hegel, the German philosopher who lived from 1770 to 1831.[55] But Hegel made a fundamental error, believing that dialectics was essentially based upon the movement and change of ideas. In natural and inevitable opposition to such a misconception arose the Marxian system, that of dialectical materialsm, which insists that nature, itself, is real, and that it encompasses the whole variety of animals, plants, heavenly bodies, and human beings known to humankind. Thus, Engels insists, modern science has shown that in these material objects and beings are to be found the inherent mechanisms of dialectics, the constant motion and change which Hegel had assumed somehow existed only in the unfolding of the Idea, or the Concept. In a most revealing passage Engels finds proof of the validity of dialectical materialism in the most recent scientific discovery of the day, that of Darwin's evolutionary laws: "[Darwin] dealt the metaphysical conception of Nature the heaviest blow by his proof that all organic beings, plants, animals, and man, himself, are the products of a process of evolution going on through millions of years."[56]

At the same time as he provides a clear statement of the origins and nature of the philosophy of Marx, Engels also provides a clear and incisive statement of the science which he and Marx invented, historical materialism. Historical materialism, he argues, is the true socialist science. It takes as the object of its concerns the working class and their liberation, but it construes this liberation as part of the inevitable evolution of mankind. It is a materialist view in the sense that the very foundations of mankind are to be found in the sphere of production in society, and that "the final causes of all social changes and political revolutions are to be sought, not in men's brains, not in man's better insight into eternal truth and justice, but in changes in the modes of production and exchange."[57] And it is historical in the sense that it is concerned with the nature of production and exchange in each of the major epochs of civilization. These epochs and their achievements create the

---

[55] See, for example, G.W.F. Hegel, *The Phenomenology of Mind* (New York: Harper & Row, Publishers, 1967). Also see the discussion of Hegel by Marx in such writings as Marx's *Contribution to the Critique of Hegel's Philosophy of Right* and in Marx's *The German Ideology*. Selections from both may be found in Tucker, *The Marx-Engels Reader*.

[56] Engels, "Socialism: Utopian and Scientific," p. 121.

[57] Engels, "Socialism: Utopian and Scientific," p. 125.

basis for the eventual, and natural, liberation of the working classes, and with them the emancipation of the rest of society as well.

Engels's other principal contributions to the body of Marxist theory are his analyses of the evolution of the family, and of the nature of the state—two topics about which Marx had written very little himself.[58] Drawing upon the ethnographic research of scientists such as Lewis Morgan, Engels seeks to trace the development of the family from its earliest recorded beginnings to its particular form under capitalism. His main points are to demonstrate that the family itself came to represent a type of oppression, and that the nature of this oppression was a reflection of the nature of property and of production in society. In prehistoric times, he argues, the family was constituted on a group basis, in which whole groups of men married whole groups of women—in effect, it represented a primitive form of communism in the family, itself. Somewhat later, during times he designates as those of barbarism, there came about the form of family known as pairing, in which single males and females became the basis of the family unit. Finally, there is monogamy, the modern form in which a single male and female become joined as the family unit for life, bounded together by contract.

The emergence of the patriarchic family, a particular phase of monogamy in which the husband becomes the central authority and the male forms the line of descent and inheritance, Engels insists, is related to the appearance of private property in society, and to the accumulation on the part of the male. The effect is to create within the confines of the family a setting analogous to that of societal class antagonisms and conflicts, in which the male represents the dominant force, reaping all the benefits of marriage, and the female the subordinate class, tied to the male exclusively and unable to exercise any rights or authority on her own. This arrangement is further elaborated with the development of modern bourgeois society. Here marriages between specific male and female partners are so planned as to enhance the wealth and property of the families to the marriage. Freedom for the males, and its denial to the females, grows ever more pronounced, the former, for example, having the luxury of engaging in extramarital affairs, while some of the latter in their turn occasionally are forced, by dint of poverty, to become prostitutes. Finally, Engels discovers the seeds of liberation for women, as for men, in the appearance of new family forms under modern capitalism. Within the working class more and more marriages occur freely, no longer on the basis of selection by parents, but on the basis of sex love, of what Engels conceives as equality. It is this form of marriage, in which both partners are free to choose one another on the basis of sex love, that heralds the coming of the new society, and with it the end to the oppressive bourgeois marital arrangement.

In this very same work, *The Origin of the Family, Private Property, and the State*, Engels also seeks to trace the historical evolution of the state, once again relying upon a form of evolutionary history, of the type which must have appealed to him in the writings of Darwin. He argues that the state did not always exist, but

[58] Engels, "The Origin of the Family, Private Property, and the State."

comes into being at a moment in history when it is required to secure the domination of the ruling class. It is not an entirely *de novo* institution, emerging suddenly, as it seemed to Hegel, to impose itself on society in order to secure a new level of order and harmony therein. Rather, the state emerges at a time when the conflicts among the classes in society are very substantial, arising as a means of holding these antagonisms in check. Yet, once established it eventually becomes the means whereby the dominant social classes are able to secure their rule over the other classes of society: "It is, as a rule, the state of the most powerful, economically dominant class, which, through the medium of the state, becomes also the politically dominant class, and thus acquires new means of holding down the oppressed class."[59] Moreover, Engels, in what appears to be a view entirely consistent with Marx, insists that at certain moments in history, such as that in the Second French Empire, when classes virtually are balancing one another off, the state may become an independent force, playing one class off against the others.

The writings of Engels, on the nature of the materialist philosophy and of the materialist view of history, on the nature of the family and of the state, have served since the death of Marx both to clarify and to somewhat distort the Marxist heritage. They have clarified Marx by extending his analysis to areas that he had not explained well himself, as in the case of the discussions of the family and the state; thus, later Marxists have found in the treatment of the family observations helpful to grasping the nature of the family in the twentieth century. But Engels seems also to have obscured Marx's intentions by extending dialectical materialism to the whole realm of nature. Thus, for instance, he seems to have rendered some of the basic concerns of Marx somewhat mute, taking away the special emphasis put upon production, particularly the role of labor and the laborer in erecting social institutions as well as the continuing historical importance of ideologies and consciousness. Engels's reading of Marx thus easily can give rise to those interpretations which reduce the nature of society and its evolution simply to the play of material forces, a reading whose parody is to be found in Nikolai Bukharin's *Historical Materialism*.[60] Only after Engels's own death did interpreters, particularly Lukács, act to restore—one might even venture to say, make more realistic—the balance between the role of material and of ideal forces in the Marxist version of history.

V. I. Lenin

While Engles contributed with his writings to providing the first extended articulation of the nature of dialectical materialism and of historical materialism, V. I. Lenin, born Vladimir Ilich Ulyanov in Russia in 1870, furnished important additions to the stream of the Marxist legacy in terms both of the meaning of revolutionary praxis and to the body of theory, itself. Above and beyond his

[59] Marx and Engels, *Selected Works in Two Volumes*, p. 290.

[60] Nikolai Bukharin, *Historical Materialism: A System of Sociology* (New York: International Publishers, 1928).

theoretical contributions, to which we shall turn shortly, Lenin and his collaborators, including Leon Trotsky, furnished a model for all subsequent revolutionaries.
By virtue of their success, they showed how a revolution could be made, particularly in a country that had skipped over the stage of capitalism, ousting the Russian
autocracy largely on the strength of a peasant revolution.[61] For under the regimes
of the Tsars, Russia had been a largely agricultural land, with a relatively small
working class; the dominant class had not been one of capitalists but rather one of
a nobility whose power lay in land, in nonproductive wealth, and in their heritage.
Thus, once revolution came to this backward country, one that had not been predicted by Marx to be the first site of a major socialist revolution in the world,
naturally all attention turned there. Much subsequent discussion and analysis thus
came to be devoted by Communist theoreticians, both within and outside Russia,
to the specific factors that contributed to the overthrow of the Tsar, and later the
government of Alexander Kerensky, and to the conditions required in order to
bring a socialist regime to full fruition. It was precisely on these points that Lenin
and Trotsky divided, and that later Stalin and Trotsky separated, leading ultimately
to the latter's death at the hands of an assassin in Mexico in 1941.

If Lenin's chief contribution to the Marxist legacy lay in his practical political
successes in Russia, so, too, therein lay his chief theoretical contributions as well. In
1903 he published a famous pamphlet, *What Is to Be Done?*[62] This document was
intended in part to be a polemic against his adversaries among the Social Democrats
in Russia—Plekhanov, in particular—as well as against those whom advocated
anarchy, a style of political action that had gained much enthusiasm in Russia during the latter half of the nineteenth century, particularly among the *narodniki*, or
Russian populists. Lenin in this pamphlet argues that the nature of the socialist
revolution had to be carried out on several fronts—a political and theoretical as well
as an economic one. One could not assume, he insists, that the trade-union efforts
on behalf of the working classes would by themselves produce liberation for the
workers. Such efforts, which he labels economism, were alone insufficient. They
were especially inadequate because they failed to cope with the existence of the
Tsarist autocracy—itself a political, not an economic, institution. In arguing against
simple efforts on behalf of better wages, and trade unions in general, Lenin was
arguing, too, against the reformist efforts which had occurred within various camps
of socialists, in Germany, in particular, by Eduard Bernstein. Lenin's point was that
those who sought revolution had to be prepared for it. The revolutionaries were
almost compelled to help to create and to mold the sentiments of the working
class, to elevate them to a true consciousness of the whole movement of history in
the doctrines of Marx and Engels. Thus, he believed, revolutionaries had to work

---

[61] Isaac Deutscher, ed., *The Age of Permanent Revolution: A Trotsky Anthology* (New
York: Dell Publishing, 1964), *passim*.

[62] V.I. Lenin, "What Is to Be Done? Burning Questions of Our Movement," in *The
Lenin Anthology,* ed. Robert C. Tucker (New York: W.W. Norton & Co., Inc., 1975), pp. 12-
114.

to achieve theoretical innovations and, at the same time, they had to devote themselves fully to the political effort—the effort of agitation against the government and of the preparation of a party to carry out the revolution.

For revolutionaries and for lay scholars alike, Lenin's analysis of the nature of the revolutionary party holds particular fascination. In contrast to many of his contemporaries, Lenin insists that the revolutionary party must consist of a cadre of full-time revolutionaries, people so completely devoted to the revolutionary cause that it absorbs their entire lives. Lenin's own life became an example of such dedication as he gave his energies over entirely to the revolutionary effort in Russia, even during those many years which he had to spend in exile abroad. It was such full-time revolutionaries as himself who would make the revolution. They would train themselves by becoming steeped in the doctrines of Marx and Engels, by devoting their entire attention to the nature of the actual situations they confronted, and by fostering the appropriate understanding of the current historical situation among the masses of people who would constitute the revolutionary movement. Such revolutionaries, Lenin further insisted, must necessarily engage in a tireless campaign of agitation, both in an attempt to arouse the enthusiasm of the mass of supporters, but also in the difficult effort to unseat the powerful regime they confronted. The success of the Bolsheviks in Russia inevitably led many other potential revolutionaries to seek the answer to their own form of revolution in Lenin's *What Is to Be Done?*

With considerable admiration Georg Lukács described Lenin as a person who was part theoretician, one who invents and elaborates the theories necessary to the success of the revolutionary party, and part politician, one who possesses a broad grasp of which tactics are to be used, and when and how to use them most effectively. Nowhere is this delicate blend between attention to theory and to actual fact more evident than in Lenin's constant demand that revolutionaries seek to interpret the current state of affairs in light *both* of the unique historical situation and of the stage of class conflict in a particular society. He condemned those so-called Marxists who blindly spoke of the working and bourgeois classes, and of class conflict in all societies, failing to take account of the special concatenation of circumstances within them. He believed that the nature of the class struggle was not everywhere the same in the modern world. Thus, he observed that "a Marxist must take cognizance of actual events, of the precise facts of *reality*, and must not cling to a theory of yesterday, which, like all theories, at best only outlines the main and general, and only *approximates* to an inclusive grasp of the complexities of life."[63] Lenin's insistence on an acknowledgment of the actual state of affairs, construed with the aid of the theory of historical materialism—rather than an unreflective application of those theories—has become recognized as yet another of his important contribu-

---

[63] V.I. Lenin, "Letters on Tactics," in Lenin, *Marx-Engels-Marxism* (Moscow: Foreign Languages Publishing House, n.d.), p. 400.

tions to the Marxist legacy, and has particularly influenced such scholars as Louis Althusser and Nicos Poulantzas.[64]

As with his other contributions to Marxist theory and practice, Lenin's contribution in *State and Revolution*, a document completed in August, 1917, but published after the October Revolution, took the form of political theory.[65] At length he explores the exact nature of a socialist or workers' state, something which, as we have learned, neither Marx nor Engels had been able to elaborate. It is here that Lenin seeks to discern the outlines of a revolutionary dictatorship of the proletariat, to determine how, in Engels's words, the state would ultimately "wither away." Lenin argues that in Russia the February Revolution, that which brought Alexander Kerensky to power but left the Parliament intact, was merely a preliminary step to the true socialist revolution. Indeed, he suggests, the February Revolution seemed to have all the characteristics of a bourgeois revolution, successfully overthrowing the Tsarist regime but, at the same moment, leaving the bourgeoisie in control of society. Thus, it was necessary that this regime, itself, be overthrown, and that it be overthrown in the name of the proletariat, the working classes of Russia. To do so, he further argues, required a joint effort on behalf of the peasants and the workers, the former largely outnumbering the latter save in a few urban places like Petrograd.

Once having overthrown the despised Kerensky regime, Lenin argued, the Bolsheviks then must turn to the task of constructing an appropriate workers' state in Russia. But what did it mean to say that such a state would be a revolutionary dictatorship of the proletariat? Was it not true, in the writings of Marx and Engels alike, that the state was conceived merely as an instrument for the oppression of the ruled by the ruling classes, and that with revolution it must necessarily disappear? On these issues Lenin had to struggle with the ambiguities found in the body of Marx's thought, to search for a way to remain consistent with the Marxist doctrine yet, at the same time, to develop novel principles to guide the workers' state in Russia. Hence, he came to argue that the workers' state had to take over the reigns of power on behalf of the working classes, and that it had to be occupied by people who, themselves, came from the working classes. But such a state also had to be used as a weapon against the previously dominant ruling classes, the remnants both of the bourgeoisie and the Tsarist regime. Here Lenin went beyond that which Marx and Engels proposed. He insisted that the workers' state could become a weapon in the struggle for the emancipation of the workers, and with them the rest of society. He further suggested, again on the basis of his reading and understanding of where Russian society stood in mid-1917, that the workers' state necessarily would entail a concentration of power in the hands of the representatives of the workers—an armed movement, in other words. In contrast to those

[64] See the discussion of Althusser, pp. 50-53. Two works by Poulantzas which are particularly valuable are *Classes in Contemporary Capitalism* (London: Verso, 1978), and *Political Power and Social Classes* (London: Verso, 1978). Both reveal the influence of Lenin's thought on Poulantzas's own work.

[65] V.I. Lenin, "The State and Revolution," in *The Lenin Anthology,* Tucker, pp. 311-98.

who proposed to implement a democratic republic, he claimed such a democracy would not be suitable for Russia, at least for a time, because the remnants of the past society still displayed pronounced social and economic inequities.

Lenin sought to use the Paris Commune of 1871 and, in particular, Marx's analysis of it, as a further device to furnish some sense of the socialist state. He found here support of his claim that the Russian state must be run on behalf of and entirely represent the workers rather than all citizens, as a simple reading of bourgeois democracy might suggest. And later, in the course of establishing a government on the heels of the Bolshevik Revolution of October, Lenin came to organize the new socialist regime on the basis of the soviets, the councils of workers who had helped to form the basis for the overthrow of the Kerensky government. The soviets, together with the development of the Communist Party apparatus, thus became the practical realization of the workers' state which Lenin sought to define in *State and Revolution.*

Lenin made one further, some even claim his most enduring, contribution to Marxist thought in the form of an analysis of imperialism. Imperialism, he argued, was the most advanced stage of capitalism.[66] In his writings about mature capitalism, particularly in *Capital,* Marx seemed to have failed to keep pace with historical events much beyond the middle of the nineteenth century. Yet it was at this time, if not somewhat later, that capitalism commenced to take on a novel appearance. Countries like Great Britain and France, for example, began to seek to extend their dominion over other parts of the world, particularly the lands of Asia and of Africa. In need of ever more abundant supplies of raw materials and of cheap labor for manufacture, not to mention larger markets for their goods, these more advanced capitalist nations sought to make permanent subjects of unsuspecting inhabitants of other lands. The net effect was to commence a deep and growing division in the world at large, between the richer, capitalist countries and the poorer, colonial, or subject, nations, a division that remains vividly alive today. (See chapter 11, on nation building, for further discussion of these issues.)

Lenin sought to clarify and to explain these developments in his pamphlet entitled *Imperialism: The Highest Stage of Capitalism.* Drawing upon historical developments in the last quarter of the nineteenth and early years of the twentieth centuries, together with the pioneering analyses of J. A. Hobson and Rudolph Hilferding, Lenin argued that modern imperialism entailed the development of handfuls of monopolies within capitalist countries alongside the rise of finance capital to a place of paramount significance.[67] In search for ever greater profit, the motive force of capitalism, the great industrialists in America, France, Germany, and the few other capitalist countries of the world turned to invest their capital in enterprises in the less developed lands, and to further secure their dominance over these countries through large loans. Ultimately, Lenin argues, the world by the

---

[66] V.I. Lenin, "Imperialism: The Highest Stage of Capitalism," in *The Lenin Anthology,* Tucker, pp. 204-74.

[67] Rudolph Hilferding, *Das Finanzkapital* (Vienna: I. Brand, 1910); and J.A. Hobson, *Imperialism* (Ann Arbor, Mich.: University of Michigan Press, 1965).

early twentieth century had become divided into the nations of owners, or capitalists, and nations of owned, or subjects. The division occurred in part at the initiation of the capitalist class, itself, in part by the cooperative efforts of government officials who sought to make lawful the control of monopoly capitalism in occupied colonies.

Lenin's analysis represented a novel twist to the Marxist legacy insofar as it emphasized the growth of monopoly capitalism as a new stage of capitalist development. Moreover, it was novel as well because of the way it portrayed the growing development of ties and alliances among the various countries of the world, and of the deepening polarization between those countries that one might regard as bourgeois—including segments even of the working classes, as in Great Britain—and those countries that were largely, if not exclusively, made up of masses of laborers. This division, Lenin seemed to sense, was so powerful that it could provide the basis for the worldwide proletarian revolution earlier anticipated by Marx.

Antonio Gramsci

As with Lenin, the Italian radical Antonio Gramsci had become deeply involved with socialist politics even as a young man; but unlike Lenin, Gramsci never succeeded in participating in the overthrow of a regime on behalf of the working class. In fact, as with so many other leftist radicals in the 1920s, Gramsci came to admire the Soviet regime for its great successes. Gramsci had taken up membership in the Italian Community Party in 1926, after many years of active political and intellectual involvement with the Italian left-wing groups. Only one year later, after flirting with capture for many years, Gramsci was seized by Benito Mussolini's police and put into prison. He remained there for the last decade of his life, subject to torture and to recurring physical ailments. This period also became the most intellectually creative of his life, a time when he attempted to deal with the possibility of proletarian revolution in Italy. In the course of his reflections he developed ideas that have had a profound influence over much subsequent Marxist thought.

One of Gramsci's principal ideas dealt with the role of the Communist Party in its efforts to oust the established powers. Departing from the seminal document of Niccolo Machiavelli, *The Prince*, composed in the sixteenth century while Machiavelli served as counselor to the House of the Medicis in Venice, Gramsci argued that in the modern world the prince actually represented not an individual person, but rather a corporate group, a collective will, to be quite specific, a party such as the Italian Communist Party.[68] If so understood, then there were many lessons that the Communists could learn from the reflections of Machiavelli. Just as the prince, the party must learn when the moment is right for the effort to take and to secure power. Just as the prince, the party must stand firm in its political convic-

[68] Antonio Gramsci, "The Modern Prince," in *Selections from the Prison Notebooks,* Antonio Gramsci, ed. and trans. Quintin Hoare and Geoffrey Nowell Smith (New York: International Publishers, 1971), pp. 123-205.

tions, committed to specific lines of action designed to acquire power for itself and for the working classes. Most importantly, just as the prince, the party must appear as the "centaur—half-animal and half-human."[69] That is, the party must exhibit a sympathy to the natural dialectics of the world, be able to engage in the use of force as necessary, but also be able to take advantage of the widespread convictions and sympathies of the public. It must seek, however delicately, to steer a course between imposing itself as a collective will on the people from without and regarding itself as a simple expression of the will of the people.

Gramsci's analysis of the role of the party displayed an unusually acute and complete grasp of the strategic problems that confronted revolutionary parties such as that of the Communists. This very same sensitivity also helps to account for the power of his insight into those conditions that sustained established regimes, an analysis of the conditions of *hegemony*.[70] Troubled by the failure of working-class parties to secure power on behalf of the working classes, particularly in Italy, Gramsci argued that no party could come to power unless such power rested upon the hegemony of their rule. As in the case of his analysis of the modern prince, this meant that the regime must be regarded by the public, not as an unsympathetic villain, but as the single, true expression of their wishes. The power of the State under its hegemony rested not on its force alone, but on a compliance more or less freely given by its subjects. Such a free and widespread public compliance, Gramsci reasoned, arose from the deep and complete entrenchment of a regime. Further, this entrenchment meant that a widespread loyalty must exist among the public for the regime, a loyalty that was manufactured by the panoply of social and cultural institutions.

The hegemony in the rule of a class thus came to rest on a highly complex and very diffuse set of sentiments within the public, sentiments virtually impervious to the occasional attacks of parties. "The superstructures of civil society," Gramsci wrote, "are like the trench-systems of modern warfare. In war it would sometimes happen that a fierce artillery attack seemed to have destroyed the enemy's entire defense system, whereas in fact it had only destroyed the outer perimeter; and at the moment of their advance and attack the assailants would find themselves confronted by a line of defense which was still effective."[71] Gramsci's analysis, of course, was extremely helpful to the effort to elaborate Marx's ideas in order to grasp the historic intransigence of regimes to the attempted radical penetration of them; at the same time it bore grave witness to the pessimism that overwhelmed him as he lay isolated and alone in prison.

Georg Lukács

The third of the figures who in the early twentieth century helped to widen the meaning of Marx and Engels's writings also was an active member of the Com-

[69] Gramsci, *Prison Notebooks*, p. 170.
[70] Gramsci, *Prison Notebooks*, p. 125 *et passim*.
[71] Gramsci, *Prison Notebooks*, p. 235.

munist Party. Georg Lukács had become a member of the Party in Hungary in the late teens, and was highly active in it until the late twenties when his work and ideas came under attack. Thereafter he remained on the periphery of Party thought and operations, continuing to be a member but one who was deeply engaged with other sorts of concerns as well. More so than his two fellow Communists, Lenin and Gramsci, Lukács had an extensive preparation and training as a scholar, becoming especially well-schooled in the writings of various philosophers. Indeed, it is one of the more interesting sidelights to his life that Lukács's first true acquaintance with the writings of Marx came by way of exposure to Georg Simmel and Max Weber, two men who possessed none of the deep revolutionary commitment and radical fervor of either a Marx or an Engels. By his own account, and from what one can tell through a close reading of his early writings, Lukács's major achievement was to reintroduce Hegelian dialectics into the interpretation of Marx's writings on classes and the class struggle. Moreover, he demonstrated a greater philosophical acuity than most other commentators, managing to decipher in those writings the precise philosophical nuances and novelties that seem to set them apart from all other philosophical discourse.[72]

Hegel, Lukács insisted, had correctly understood the true nature of the world and had formulated it in his doctrine of dialectical opposition and movement.[73] But, Lukács claimed, Hegel had mistakenly believed that dialectics took on a spiritual, or idealistic, form exclusively, and that the tensions of the world ultimately were to be resolved in the self-recognition of the Absolute Spirit. In fact, Marx had discovered the true basis of dialectical principles in his acknowledgment of the fundamental significance of productive activity, and of work. Drawing in part, then, upon Engels's discussion of the principles of historical materialism, Lukács claimed that the genuine subject-object of history was not the Absolute Spirit, as Hegel had maintained, but it was the proletariat or the working class. The working class, he argued, is the subject or entity that unbeknownst to itself evolves and develops over the course of history, reaching a point in the contemporary period when it could finally achieve a recognition of its goals and purpose, when it could finally overcome its state of alienation. And how does it achieve a full recognition of itself, how does it gain a sense of class consciousness? None other, Lukács cleverly insisted, than through the explanations and principles of Marx and Engels themselves, through ideas that provide the deep and subtle articulation of the purposes of the working class, that is, their class consciousness. This class consciousness of the proletariat is difficult to achieve, Lukács maintains, because it represents, at one and the same moment, the annulment of all past laws and institutions, and the creation of a whole new set of institutions to govern a world now free of oppression and inequality. Fifty years later, long after this interpretation of Marx and Engels was to have widespread and profound impact among Marxists

[72] See, for instance, Georg Lukács, "Reification and the Consciousness of the Proletariat," in Georg Lukács, *History and Class Consciousness: Studies in Marxist Dialectics* (Cambridge, Mass.: The MIT Press, 1971), pp. 83-222.

[73] Lukács, *History and Class Consciousness*, pp. 83 ff.

the world over, Lukács was to disclaim his early formulation, saying that he had "out-Hegeled" Hegel.[74]

Lukács's other main contribution to the Marxist heritage, which he also later disowned long after it had become a standard method for interpreting Marx, lay in his analysis of reification.[75] Once more, his exposition seemed to have been greatly colored by his grasp of Hegelian dialectics. Reification, according to Lukács, takes place when people come to believe that the objects they apprehend in the world beyond them are independent and foreign to them—even though they, or rather their ancestors, have in fact created these objects in the course of their productive activity. For instance, Lukács says, reification occurs when people believe that commodities are an immutable part of nature, and that the capitalist marketplace is governed by "natural" laws, such objects and their principles, he claims, are only indigenous to capitalism, and have been created by previous generations of mankind.

The mysterious creation of seemingly independent objects, Lukács goes on to claim, entities that seem to stand apart, even above mankind, is a puzzle that before Marx was not satisfactorily resolved. The great eighteenth-century philosopher, Immanuel Kant, had invented the puzzle, in effect, by claiming a difference to exist between things-in-appearance to us and things-in-themselves.[76] Later, Hegel pointed to the unsuitability of this distinction; but, Lukács argues, he, himself, did not solve it so much as he obscured and mystified it with his conception of an Absolute Spirit.[77] Only Marx truly settled the unsatisfactory dilemma posed by things-in-appearance to us and things-in-themselves by claiming that it was the condition of the alienation of mankind—or, to Lukács, the process of reification of man's own powers that led men to believe in a distinction between the two worlds of objects, appearances and essences. All objects, Lukács says in adhering to Marx, are the creation of people; only when mankind realizes this basic truth, in the form of the class consciousness of the proletariat, will reification as a fact of life disappear, and with it, of course, all the elements of mankind's alienation.

The Frankfurt School

Among contemporary Marxists there are few groups of scholars which can rival the influence of the Frankfurt School. Founded in 1934 in Germany by Theodor Adorno and Max Horkheimer, later temporarily transplanted to the United States during the reign of Adolf Hitler, the Frankfurt School's principals have interpreted Marx mainly as a philosopher rather than as a dedicated revolutionary thinker. In a sense, they have returned to the early, younger Marx as a means of drawing out the main insights they believe he contributed; at the same

[74] Lukács, *History and Class Consciousness*, pp. ix-xxxix.

[75] Lukács, "Reification and the Consciousness of the Proletariat."

[76] Immanuel Kant, *The Critique of Pure Reason*, trans. Norman Kemp Smith (New York: St. Martin's Press, 1965).

[77] G.W.F. Hegel, *The Phenomenology of Mind*.

time, they have added new elements to Marxist thought, introducing ideas such as sublimation and repression from Sigmund Freud, and rationality and legitimacy from Max Weber. Drawn toward a more philosophical rendering of the writings of Marx, they have fashioned a corpus of thought that almost is intellectually impenetrable, certainly a far remove from the needs of the working classes of the world today.

One of the main novelties of the Frankfurt School, particularly the writings of Herbert Marcuse and Jürgen Habermas, is the blending of ideas originally emphasized by Max Weber with the critical assessment of capitalism found in Marx. No longer concerned with the proletariat itself, or even with labor as productive activity, as in the classic Marxist formulations, Marcuse achieved great success and fame in the United States with his *One-Dimensional Man.*[78] He argues that modern civilization exhibits a radical divorce between the Reason sought after by the ancient Greeks, and the reason that displays itself throughout modern society. The Reason of the ancient Greeks was associated intimately with the search for Truth, and mind, itself, was not divorced from nature but was viewed as part and parcel of it. The Greek philosophers had assumed an intimate harmony between mind and nature, the one the part of the other, and Reason represented the working of the mind as it sought, by virtue of deep reflection, to discover those principles that were essential to nature and those that merely were ephemeral. What modern capitalist civilization has done, in the eyes of Marcuse, is to create a fundamental alienation of man from nature, of reason from Reason, and it has accomplished this by suppressing all those qualities which are fundamentally and essentially human— man's need to reflect deeply on the world as well as his sensual nature, his Eros, or love. In assuming this sort of perspective, Marcuse, just as Lukács before him, reintroduces dialectics into the nature of Marxist critical thought, so much so as virtually to disguise the essential Marxist twist to the thought, itself.

Marcuse's indictment of modern capitalist civilization, with America taken as the supreme instance of this civilization, draws a certain inspiration from Weber's emphasis upon the nature of rationality in the modern world.[79] Weber, as we shall soon learn in the next chapter, distinguished between technical rationality, that which seemed to characterize the essential element of modern capitalism, with a specific emphasis upon technique, efficiency, and calculability, and substantive rationality, that which was concerned with the ends, the goals, the values toward which action was targeted. That which is especially characteristic and, he implied, equally oppressive under modern capitalism, is that all action, in virtually every sphere of society, has become dominated by a concern with the quantitative and calculable assessment of the costs involved in reaching a particular end, any end, rather than with the substantive meaning of the end, itself. Marcuse compliments Weber upon this basic insight; yet, he then turns around immediately to condemn

[78] Herbert Marcuse, *One-Dimensional Man* (Boston: Beacon Press, 1964).

[79] Herbert Marcuse, "Industrialization and Capitalism in the Work of Max Weber," in *Negations: Essays in Critical Theory,* Herbert Marcuse (Boston: Beacon Press, 1968), pp. 201-26.

him for failing to carry through, in a true critical fashion, to ask why it is that technical and substantive rationality have become divorced.

To Marcuse, the answer lies, of course, in the fact that modern capitalist civilization displays the radical separation between the two forms of reason: technical reason becomes reason, substantive reason stands for the Greek conception of Reason. Again in a fashion strongly reminiscent of Hegel as well as of Lukács, Marcuse argues that the objects created by man thus came to stand apart from, and apparently above, him, at the same time as his own capacity for deep reflection, or imagination, was itself repressed. In effect, man no longer represents man, but something dehumanized; his own sense of himself was seen through the objects and bodies of thought to analyze objects he had created. Hence, man came to think of himself simply as a technical instrument, a worker on the assembly line divorced from a sense of self, owing to the scientific principles of management in modern civilization. His language took a form of some immediate connection between a concept and a thing rather than an imaginative connection empowered by his mind; even his sexual passions came to be reified, in the form of appeals to his prurient interests, and to his own body as a mere object of sexual passion rather than as a part of himself intimately involved in love. A good deal of this form of indictment of modern capitalism, it may be interesting to learn, found an even earlier expression in the very lucid and exceedingly insightful analysis of Antonio Gramsci.[80]

In perhaps his most well-known analysis, Jürgen Habermas, the current leading member of the Frankfurt School, too draws upon the work of Max Weber to critically understand the nature of modern capitalism. Taking up Weber's concern with the nature of legitimacy and legitimation, Habermas argues that the contradictions in modern society, in particular those engendered by the twin and paradoxical emphasis upon social welfare and upon mass democracy, have created a crisis in the assumed rightness and propriety of the decisions taken in modern capitalist nations. Both Weber and other scholars who shared with him an emphasis upon the legalistic nature of legitimacy, Habermas claims, were misled into believing that the very nature of legal decision making in modern society was, itself, sufficient to secure proof of the propriety of decisions. That, in fact, is incorrect, Habermas claims— there is a deeper, or different, level upon which legitimacy rests, one of validity based upon peoples' shared normative understandings of what is to be valued in the social world. But this level of understanding is obscure both in modern society itself, and in the theories about this society. Only a critical theory, he argues, one that holds as problematic the very foundations of modern capitalism, can penetrate to the truth of things in the world; and in this effort, Habermas proposes a program of "universal pragmatics," which seeks to expose the distortions and contradictions under modern capitalism through a detailed analysis for discursive language and communication. Habermas, unfortunately, is the most obscure and turgid author among all modern social theorists—not to say also the author of works that leave

[80] Antonio Gramsci, "Americanism and Fordism," in *Prison Notebooks,* Gramsci, pp. 277-318.

hosts of unanswered questions—and thereby perhaps has condemned his own theoretical efforts to be adopted by at most a handful of impassioned disciples.[81]

Louis Althusser

Finally, let us turn to the work of Louis Althusser, a French philosopher with long-established ties to the French Communist Party, someone who lately has made some of the more novel contributions to the Marxist legacy. Althusser has developed a profound and controversial reinterpretation of the writings of Marx, one that seeks to show that Marx did not merely invert the dialectics of Hegel, but that he, in fact, established the grounds for an entirely new form of philosophy and a new brand of science. In contrast to most other interpreters of Marx, among them, for example, Lukács and Marcuse, Althusser argues that Marx went through several stages in his development, and that it was not Hegel who influenced the young Marx so much as it was Ludwig Feuerbach, against whom Marx railed in his famous "Theses on Feuerbach."[82] Drawing upon the concept invented by Gaston Bachelard, Althusser further insists that Marx underwent a radical *epistemological rupture* in the course of his development, one that led him to invent an entirely new framework for the analyses that later became identified as historical materialism. The key to this epistemological rupture, Althusser notes, is to be found in certain passages in *Capital* where Marx suggests that Adam Smith and others of the classical school of political economy formulated their analysis of economics in such a way that they provided answers to questions they never even asked.[83] It was Marx, Althusser claims, who came to acknowledge the unasked question, in particular, who came to recognize the signal importance of the concept of *labor power*, instead merely of *labor*, and who thereby came to establish with this recognition the basis for his entirely new science.

In brief, Althusser claims, those who argue, using Marx's own words, that he turned Hegel on his head, fail to realize that what Marx really did was to shift entirely the frame of reference to be used in the analysis of capitalism. Hence, among other consequences, Marx's later work shows no continuity at all with his early efforts, and interpretations which claim that alienation is a theme that connects the writings of the young Marx to the old one, as Lukács insists, for example, are fundamentally wrong. Althusser's illuminating observations on how Marx seemed, in fact, to shift the frame of reference for the analysis of capitalism show a striking convergence with a pioneering work on the philosophy of science published in roughly the same period by the American philosopher of science Thomas Kuhn.

---

[81] See his various works, among them, Jürgen Habermas, *Legitimation Crisis* (Boston: Beacon Press, 1975); *Communication and the Evolution of Society* (Boston: Beacon Press, 1979); *Theory and Practice* (Boston: Beacon Press, 1973); and *Knowledge and Human Interests* (Boston: Beacon Press, 1971).

[82] Louis Althusser, "Feuerbach's 'Philosophical Manifestoes'," in *For Marx*, Louis Althusser, trans. Ben Brewser (London: Verso, 1979), pp. 43-48.

[83] Louis Althusser and Etienne Balibar, *Reading Capital*, 2nd ed., trans. Ben Brewster (London: NLB, 1977), Part I.

Kuhn argued that science can develop dramatically through a change in its frame of reference, or paradigm; hence, the revolution created by Einstein in physics, Kuhn suggests, came about, not because Einstein disproved the tenets of Newtonian physics, but because he changed the very grounds and questions that had been its major concerns.[84]

Somewhat later, in the manner of reflecting upon and providing philosophical foundations for Marx's epistemological rupture and his establishment of an entirely new science in the form of historical materialism, Althusser suggests that the science of historical materialism, since it operates on the assumption that all other science and philosophy is false, itself works on an entirely different set of principles.[85] It is established on the premise, following from Marx, himself, that there is an intimate link between theory and practice. Scientific knowledge is like any form of production, Althusser argues, in which human labor, in the form of mental thought, reworks and refashions raw materials into new products. Thus, the process whereby historical materialism arrives at new generalities is not to move from the absolutely concrete level to the level of abstract generalizations, in the manner of Frances Bacon's induction of *Novum Organum*, but instead to transform concepts already given to it—pregiven concepts—into statements about concrete objects, and then, having so transformed them, to create new and accurate scientific concepts.

Consider the notions of value and labor, Althusser suggests. The theory of the scientific process of historical materialism says that the practitioners of historical materialism begin by taking the ideologically tainted concepts of bourgeois thought, such as that of value, and stripping away all the ideological, or false, aspects of them. Then the practitioners of the science of historical materialism attempt to achieve insight into the true nature of the concrete by recognizing that the classical economists had failed to take account of the reality of the work of the laborer on the raw materials. Finally, having so recognized the concrete by moving from the false conception of the abstract, the historical materialist scientist creates a new generalization, that embodied in the concept of labor-power. What Althusser has done in effect with this scheme is to articulate the principles he believes Marx used in actually working within the mode of historical materialism he, himself, had discovered.

Althusser's other contributions to the Marxist legacy lie in seeking, as Lenin had done, to apply the science of historical materialism to concrete historical circumstances, and especially to take full account of why some historical sites, such as Russia, undergo a workers' revolution, whereas others, such as Germany, do not. Lenin, as we have learned, argued that capitalism is subject to the law of uneven development, by which he meant that the development of the form and manner of the class struggle is not everywhere the same, either among all the nations of the

---

[84] Thomas S. Kuhn, *The Structure of Scientific Revolutions* (Chicago: University of Chicago Press, 1962).

[85] Louis Althusser, "On the Materialistic Dialectic," in *For Marx,* Althusser, pp. 163-218.

world, nor even within the structure of a single nation.[86] Althusser further explores this issue.[87] Once more he introduces certain novel concepts to take account precisely of uneven development. Thus, he writes of *conjuncture,* by which he means the concrete realization of the stage of class struggle, including its basic contradictions, its diverse modes of production, at a particular historical moment. Russia in 1917, for instance, lay at a particular conjuncture, in terms of the nature of the struggle among the different classes, including the peasants and the workers along with the nobility, the character both of feudal institutions and of early capitalist ones, and the like. Althusser also introduces the concept of *social formation* to designate the actual social and historic site of the class struggle, and the various groups and classes that exist therein, along with recognition of the fact that in any particular country the contradictions owing to the basic contradiction between the forces and relations of production under capitalism can be found not only at the economic level of society, but also at the political and ideological levels, too. Again, Althusser seems to have had Russia in mind as a particular illustration of a social formation.

In seeking to clarify the nature of uneven development, and why, in particular, a seemingly backward country such as Russia also could be the most advanced in terms of the intensity of its contradictions, Althusser further advances the concept of *overdetermination,* borrowed from the French psychoanalytically oriented scholar Jacques Martin.[88] When he thus speaks of the overdetermination of the contradictions in a particular social formation, Althusser means that all contradictions act upon one another—that, specifically, the contradictions which occur in the practices at the economic level of a society also have ramifications for the contradictions at the level of politics, and that, in turn, those in politics have implications for those at the level of economics, and so on. In so embracing the concept of overdetermination, then, what Althusser seems to have done is to take account of the many complexities which Gramsci sought to explain with his concept of hegemony and, ultimately, acknowledge validity in Lenin's argument that the class struggle, hence the basic contradictions of a society, must occur at several levels, not that of the economic, alone.

Althusser's very novel contributions naturally have set off a storm of controversy among Marxists throughout the world, many of whom, particularly the philosophers, had insisted that Hegel was the immediate forebear, thus, the key in some sense to understanding Marx. Althusser's new interpretation of Marx rests, he shows, on a new reading of the works in the Marxist corpus, a reading of these texts not simply to imbibe them as literal truths nor to extract some essential kernel of truth, but rather to come to grips with their *problematique,* with the fundamental theoretical frame of reference that seems to underlie them. It is thus that he uses the illustration of Marx's reformulation of the issues addressed by

---

[86] See the discussion of Lenin, pp. 40-42.

[87] Louis Althusser, "On the Materialist Dialectic," pp. 178-79, *et passim.*

[88] See, for example, Louis Althusser, "Contradiction and Overdetermination," in *For Marx,* Althusser, pp. 89-128.

and Ricardo as the real key to understanding the issue that Marx, himself, had sought to examine. Besides creating controversy, Althusser's reassessment also has had a widespread influence on scholars, especially the French, and has had a notable impact on the recently deceased political sociologist Nicos Poulantzas.

There are many other scholars who, since the death of Marx in 1883, have greatly contributed to the legacy he has left us. Some of these we will learn more about in subsequent chapters of this book, such as the Marxist economists Paul Baran and Paul Sweezy, who claim to have found their own particular way of applying Marx to the contemporary world. But those individuals we have discussed here seem to have made among the most important and lasting contributions, ones which today have had profound influence over many people who seek to better understand what this very brilliant and controversial philosopher had to say about this world of ours.

CHAPTER THREE
The Vision
of Max Weber

The Puritan wanted to work in a calling; we are forced to do so. For when asceticism was carried out of monastic cells into everyday life, and began to dominate world morality, it did its part in building the tremendous cosmos of the modern economic order. This order is now bound to the technical and economic conditions of machine production which to-day determine the lives of all the individuals who are born into this mechanism, not only those directly concerned with economic acquisition, with irresistible force. Perhaps it will so determine them until the last ton of fossilized coal is burnt. In Baxter's view the care for external goods should only lie on the shoulders of the "saint like a light cloak, which can be thrown aside at any moment." But fate decreed that the cloak should become an iron cage.

MAX WEBER, *The Protestant Ethic and the Spirit of Capitalism*

MAX WEBER (1864-1920)

Max Weber was as complex a human being and as serious as scholar as Karl Marx.[1] An individual of remarkably vast resources of intellectual curiosity and strength, Weber was trained to become a lawyer and teacher of jurisprudence, but he later

[1] On Weber's personal life, see, for example, Marianne Weber, *Max Weber: Ein Lebensbild* (Tubingen: Mohr, 1926); or Arthur Mitzman, *The Iron Cage: An Historical Interpretation of Max Weber* (New York: Alfred A. Knopf, 1970). Marianne Weber was Weber's wife, and her account is a most thorough and insightful one; it clearly influenced the interpretation of Weber's life provided by Gerth and Mills in the introduction to their book. Mitzman's account is a good one as well but mainly cast in psychoanalytic terms.

developed an intense interest in a large number of other fields. History of all manner and kind represented a lifelong passion Within the field of sociology, a field much indebted to him for its beginnings, he carried out pioneering investigations of religious doctrines, economic life, law, urban settlements, and politics. He also maintained an interest in German politics, speaking and writing about the ways to improve its government and in particular helping to draft the constitution for the Weimar Republic in 1918.

Because of his many pursuits, Weber was compelled to engage in a delicate balancing act, seeking to sustain his work as a scholar and to continue with his active interest in everyday politics. Eventually he shaped a strategy for himself that has since become a model for many social scientists and historians. Above all else, he advocated, an intellectual must attempt to segregate his life as a scholar from that as a man of action.[2] The judgments involved in the two pursuits simply could not be mixed without endangering the effectiveness of each; as a scientist, in particular, one could not fairly or safely judge the proper course for the citizen. Along similar lines, the scholar, in his capacity as a teacher, should not engage in polemics in the classroom, particularly if such a strategy is designed to achieve popularity rather than to educate. "The task of the teacher," he wrote, "is to serve the students with his knowledge and scientific experience and not to imprint upon them his personal political views. . . . I am ready to prove from the works of our historians that whenever the man of science introduces his personal value judgment, a full understanding of the facts ceases."[3]

As serious scholarship and science make it imperative that polemics be removed from the setting of intellectual discourse, so the political arena is marked by its own special rules. Politics, in essence, represents a continuing conflict over the control of scarce material and symbolic (or ideal) resources. Any person who wishes to engage in this arena must be prepared to struggle, to compromise but eventually to emerge either on the side of the victors or on that of the vanquished. Thus, an ethics of ultimate ends, especially that of natural law that insists on the inherent rights and equality of all men, is doomed from the beginning to failure in politics.[4] Obviously Weber's view of politics, as of its connections to scholarship, differs greatly from that of Marx; Marx sought to achieve a unity among the seemingly independent pursuits. Nevertheless, Weber's perspective, like that of Marx, must be understood in the context of his vision of Western societies.

According to Weber, the nature of social and economic life in the West represents the heights of professionalism and routine activity. Each of the many and diverse kinds of activities is defined in the form of a profession, or vocation, thereby establishing a unique career path as well as a special set of rights and obligations. This theme, in turn, is part of a much broader and pervasive trend in the development of Western civilization; the theme is the rationalization of life. This, for

---

[2] See, for instance, Max Weber, "Science as a Vocation," in *From Max Weber: Essays in Sociology,* ed. Hans Gerth and C. Wright Mills (New York: Oxford University Press, 1958), pp. 129-56.

[3] Weber, "Science as a Vocation," in *From Max Weber,* Gerth and Mills, p. 146.

[4] Weber, "Politics as a Vocation," in *From Max Weber,* Gerth and Mills, pp. 122-27.

Weber, means that all life is subject to a common form of assessment, calculability—that is, the assessment of the most technically efficient means for attaining particular ends. Thus, in the marketplace the most efficient means for purchasing goods and services can be calculated with precision; in the courts the form of penalty or obligation incumbent on the lawbreaker can be made almost exactly; in war the strategy best designed to accomplish quick and efficient naval or land victories can easily be assessed.

These patterns are embodied in rational bureaucracy, the most dominant and striking feature of the West. This form of administration, Weber claimed, has both its advantages and its disadvantages. As the structural embodiment of the major themes of Western civilization, it represents major *technical* advances over all prior civilizations; it can accomplish tasks more quickly, precisely, and cheaply than any other form of organization. It also, however, invites the alienation of man; it represents the structural avenue through which modern life is administered, and the individual, lacking the personal ownership of this institution, is therefore unable to control the activities of his own life. Further, bureaucracy has become so pervasive an institution that the individual's options for action, and thus his freedom, have been reduced.

Although choice with regard to means has been reduced to a common measure of evaluation, it has not been similarly diminished with respect to ends. There are a finite number of values from among which men can choose to commit themselves. These become an integral part of Weber's sociology, finding their expression as objects that could provide the basis for distinctive social groups, status groups, as well as sources of competition and conflict in the political arena.

On balance, Weber's view of man is an extraordinarily pessimistic one.[5] Like Marx, he believed man is alienated, but from the means of administration rather than from those of material production. Unlike Marx, however, Weber was less hopeful that man could throw off the instruments of his alienation; he believed that virtually nothing can be done to reduce the encroachment of bureaucracies over the individual's life.

WEBER'S IMAGE OF THE SOCIAL ORDER

As with Marx, we discuss Weber's image of the social order in terms of three concepts: social stratification, social organization, and social system. To further maintain comparability among the scholars, we shall confine the discussion to Weber's writings about modern industrial societies in the West—Germany, France, Great Britain, and the United States in the late nineteenth and early twentieth centuries.

---

[5] On Weber's pessimism, see, for example, "Science as a Vocation," in *From Max Weber,* Gerth and Mills, as well as the brilliant introduction to that volume by the editors.

In so doing, the bulk of Weber's scholarship is neglected; interested readers may wish to consult Weber's *Economy and Society*.[6]

Social Stratification

There are two principal dimensions of the stratification system. The first, class, manifests itself along three different lines: property classes based on the differential distribution of property; commercial classes based on the differential distribution of goods and services in the marketplace; and social classes, which represent an emergent combination of the other two forms. In the case of classes based either on property or on the labor market, there are additional distinctions between those who possess positive privileges or negative privileges. For instance, the positively privileged among the commercial classes are generally entrepreneurs, in particular, bankers and financiers; the negatively privileged are laborers distinguished by their levels of skill, such as the semiskilled workers. Finally, Weber's four general social classes correspond to Marx's conceptions: the working class as a whole, the petty bourgeoisie, the propertyless intelligentsia and specialists, and those classes that gain privileges through property and education.

The other principal axis of the stratification system is based on status, or distinctions that can be measured by the level of esteem in which a group is held by the members of a society. (Many analysts have embraced the index as the substance of status groups, mistaking one for the other. A careful reading of Weber, however, suggests that esteem is only a trivial index at best and that the essence of status groups is to be found along the lines mentioned shortly.) Like the dimension of class, that of status is represented hierarchically in a society—some groups stand higher on the status ladder than others. Status groups are marked by their distinctive life styles, that is, a cluster of material advantages, such as property or liquid capital, and the monopoly of symbolic resources, such as habits of dress, religious beliefs, or codes of honor. In modern society there is an increasing tendency for such groups to have their origins in different fields of specialized training, such as law.

For Weber, class and status categories are somewhat complementary aspects of the stratification system of any society. In one sense, he remarked, "one might . . . say that classes are stratified according to their relations to the production and acquisition of goods; whereas status groups are stratified according to the principles of the *consumption* of goods as represented by special styles of life."[7] Accordingly, the two dimensions can be correlated with one another—special

---

[6]This is an extremely impressive work of scholarship on the part of the author, Weber, and the translators, Roth and Wittich. There are three large volumes; the most important for the reader's interests in political sociology are portions of volume I and virtually all of volume III. See Max Weber, *Economy and Society: An Outline of Interpretive Sociology,* trans. Guenther Roth and Claus Wittich (New York: Bedminster Press, 1968), I-III.

[7]Weber, *Economy and Society,* I, 937.

privileges in the marketplace or in the distribution of property provide a basis for a common life style, for example, among many laborers. Furthermore, societies tend to vary in the degree to which classes or status groups prevail in them; Weber observed that status groups in the United States seemed to be considerably more prevalent than in European countries.

The most important point about status groups and social classes in modern societies is that status groups are usually better able to create a common action for the protection and advancement of their material and ideal interests. This capacity stems mainly from the fact that these groups have their origins in interests that are individually and collectively meaningful, while classes are based on impersonal principles that reign in the economy. In this fashion, among others, Weber attempted to draw a major distinction between his image of social stratification and that of Marx.

Social Organization

For Weber, social organization in the West is bureaucracy, and its significance in his scheme of things cannot be too strongly emphasized:

> The development of modern forms of organization in all fields is nothing less than identical with the development and continual spread of bureaucratic administration. This is true of church and state, of armies, political parties, economic enterprises, interest groups, endowments, clubs and many others. Its development is, to take the most striking case, at the root of the modern Western State. . . . If bureaucratic administration is, other things being equal, always the most rational type from a technical point of view, the needs of mass administration make it today completely indispensable. The choice is only between bureaucracy and dilettantism in the field of administration.[8]

Several distinct things enter into the definition of bureaucracy—apart, of course, from its essential quality of employing the most technically efficient means for attaining its given goals. The characteristics of bureaucracy include the following: (1) its impersonal offices entail specific obligations and rights and are regarded as the property of the organization rather than of the officeholder; (2) its offices are organized in a hierarchy of authority; (3) each office has a sphere of jurisdiction; (4) each office is filled through competitive selection; (5) candidates for offices are chosen on the basis of technical and thus impersonal qualifications; (6) office-holders are remunerated by fixed salaries in money; and (7) the office constitutes a career, and there is the possibility of promotion through the hierarchy of offices on the basis of seniority and achievements.[9]

This conception, Weber went to great lengths to emphasize, is an abstract one made up of elements common to many forms of organization in modern society; in this regard, it is similar to many of Weber's other notions, for example, the

[8] Ibid., p. 223.
[9] These characteristics are a rough paraphrase of Weber's discussion in *Economy and Society*, I, 219-21.

Protestant Ethic.[10] Such conceptions are designed to further the efforts of scholars by enabling them to conduct comparative research on different forms of organization and allowing them to construct causal analyses of historical events—such as Weber himself had done with the Protestant Ethic. This sort of conception, with an emphasis on its rational and impersonal aspects, draws attention to its differences from other forms of organization, in particular the patrimonial form of administration in ancient China and the form of bureaucracy characteristic of ancient Egypt. In addition, it suggests possible causal preconditions for the emergence of the bureaucratic trend in modern society.

Social System

There is no general image of social system in Weber's writings; such an idea would be much too contrived to fit social reality. The sociological approach begins with the individual and involves an effort to understand the actions of that individual as a part of relatively small and clearly circumscribed groups, especially status groups. Thus, any attempt to impute actions or intentions to large collective bodies, such as social systems, radically distorts the fundamental aims and purposes of the sociological vision.[11] In large measure, this stance emerges from Weber's sociological intentions, namely, the effort to understand the past by abstracting from the records pertaining to its events and figures. This position places Weber squarely in opposition to those scholars who probe history with the aid of a highly formalized system of concepts, oftentimes conceived prior to an extensive immersion in historical realities; his general approach finds itself in the same intellectual camp as that of Alexis de Tocqueville, but on opposite fronts from those of Marx, Parsons, or Emile Durkheim.[12]

Notwithstanding a rejection of the systemic imagery, we can glean from Weber's writings some sense of his conceptual imagery of modern Western societies. At the highest level of abstraction, his vision encompasses the nation-state, within which there exist certain distinct institutional spheres, such as the economic, the political, and the religious. These settings possess certain common elements but not for analytical reasons—they are not integral parts of an abstract whole—so much as for historical ones. Economic and political institutions share a heritage founded upon rational law, a system of exchange based on a money economy, and, perhaps most important, a type of social organization that is fostered by the legal

---

[10]Weber's discussion of the ideal type is treated at length in his *Methodology of the Social Sciences,* trans. Edward Shils and Henry A. Finch (New York: The Free Press, 1949), pp. 40-44, 116-87. Reference in this paragraph to the Protestant Ethic concerns, of course, Weber's seminal monograph on the relationship between Protestantism and modern capitalism, *The Protestant Ethic and the Spirit of Capitalism,* trans. Talcott Parsons (New York: Charles Scribner's Sons, 1958).

[11]Reinhard Bendix, "Two Sociological Traditions," in *Scholarship and Partisanship: Essays on Max Weber,* ed. Reinhard Bendix and Guenther Roth (Berkeley, Calif.: University of California Press, 1971).

[12]Ibid.

system.[13] Beyond such common historical elements, however, institutions exist relatively independently of one another. Thus, with the exception of such analyses as that of the affinity between the Protestant Ethic and the spirit of capitalism, Weber rarely pursued institutional connections systematically or formally.

At a lower and more important level of abstraction, modern society is envisioned as an arena of social groups; the principal ones are status groups and bureaucracies. Status groups, whether based on common ties of ethnicity or of occupation, represent the settings in which men exist harmoniously, united by their shared material interests and beliefs. Bureaucracies, too, manifest an air of unity, but one founded upon distinctive relations of authority and power.[14]

Still, Weber was not so naive as to think that men were only cast into harmonious relations. To the contrary, the relationship *between* groups—as opposed to that within them—is essentially one of continuous conflict and struggle.[15] On the one hand, status groups in many different situations are opposed to the interests of one another and struggle either to monopolize limited material resources or to gain control over groups through the hegemony of their beliefs and ideals. On the other hand, in some contexts—particularly modern capitalism—the bureaucracies in different institutional spheres are themselves in competition with one another for the dominance of their interests; for Weber, this is preferable to control vested only in a state bureaucracy.[16]

Further, status groups often employ the power inherent in the bureaucratic apparatus to secure their superiority over other status groups; this is a particular application of Weber's more general observation about the importance of controlling the means of administration in society (see the section, "Weber's Image of Why Men Obey"). Among examples of this in his lifetime were the control of Tammany Hall and thus the Democratic Party in New York City by particular ethnic groups.[17] One status group in a particularly favorable position to secure its dominance over other groups through the control of the bureaucratic means of administration is upper-echelon bureaucratic functionaries. On one occasion Weber remarked:

> The bureaucracy seeks to secure the official's position, his orderly advancement, and his provision for old age. In this, it is supported by the "demo-

[13] Max Weber, *General Economic History* (New York: Collier Books, 1961).

[14] It is important to recognize that this represented an "air" of harmony only; any form of administration, bureaucratic, patrimonial, or otherwise, involves a latent form of conflict between the chief, or administrative heads, and staff. For further explanation, see the section, "Weber's Image of Why Men Obey."

[15] Randall Collins, "A Comparative Approach to Political Sociology," in *State and Society: A Reader in Comparative Political Sociology,* ed. Reinhard Bendix et al. (Boston: Little, Brown and Co., 1968), pp. 42-67. This essay is excellent and represents the best brief introduction to Weber's political sociology.

[16] Weber, *Economy and Society,* III, 1401.

[17] Although Weber does not make this analysis explicit, it is possible he had it in mind in his discussion of Tammany Hall in "Politics as a Vocation," in *From Max Weber,* Gerth and Mills, pp. 109-10.

cratic" sentiment of the governed which demands that domination be minimized; those who hold this attitude believe themselves able to discern a weakening of authority itself in every weakening of the lord's arbitrary disposition over the officials. *To this extent bureaucracy, both in business offices and in public service, promotes the rise of a specific status group, just as did the quite different officeholders of the past.*[18]

Apart from these conclusions, little more can be claimed about Weber's conception of modern society without doing him a serious injustice.

WEBER'S IMAGE OF THE POLITICAL ORDER

Before discussing Weber's image of the political order, it is appropriate to make several general observations concerning his view. First, the political order, like society in general, is characterized by constant struggle among groups. Sometimes the conflict involves status groups contending for control of the political institutions, but just as often it means conflicts between political agencies and figures, such as the head of state and the occupants of prominent civil service positions. Thus, in contrast to Marx, Weber did not conceive of the political order as all of a piece acting mainly as the instrument of the ruling class or classes.

Second, the state and its institutions did not come under the control of a single class or status group, but many of the positions in the modern state are likely to be occupied by lawyers because they possess the requisite education and technical skills for understanding complicated legal aspects of politics and for engaging in political oratory.[19] To the extent that lawyers and related professional experts represent a separate status group, they are by implication in a position to secure special material and ideal privileges for themselves.

Third, in accordance with Weber's more general conclusions, those who come into control of the major positions of authority in the various political agencies can exercise a decisive impact on other social institutions and groups. Resisting highly abstract generalizations, Weber declined to offer this as a general rule; yet it is evident from his analysis of such political leaders as Bismarck and Napoleon Bonaparte that those who hold political power can succeed in shaping social development and in aiding the emergence of the nation-state. Again, such a view stands in contrast to that of Marx who believed political institutions were no more than mere tools in the struggle for the monopolization of material resources.

[18]Weber, *Economy and Society*, III, 1001. In this regard, Weber's conclusions and speculations antedate those of scholars who claim that the technical experts in modern society are the major power holders, such as John Kenneth Galbraith, and those who claim that the occupants of the highest positions in bureaucracies are likely to emerge as an elite group bent on maintaining their positions, such as Robert Michels. In fact, Weber's close association with Michels suggests that the latter's view was substantially influenced by the former. On this theme, see Guenther Roth's introduction to *Economy and Society*, I, lxv.

[19]Weber, "Politics as a Vocation," in *From Max Weber*, Gerth and Mills, pp. 94-95.

Finally, Weber was personally committed to a democratic form of govern-ment—particularly of the plebiscite form—in which there are capable and respon-sible political leaders. Without such leaders, democratic government is a sham government, left either in the hands of technical experts in the civil bureaucracy or of party bosses who exercise their will over political machines. This orientation lies at the heart of Weber's admiration for the democratic forms of government in the United States and Great Britain and of his revulsion over the German constitutional monarchy between the reign of Bismarck and the inception of the Weimar Republic in 1919.

Political Rulers

For Weber, talented and responsible political rulers are the most important element for effective democratic government. From the direct democracy of ancient Greece to the mass democracy of the modern state, the best government is that under control of the few—a sort of "democratic elitist" perspective later en-larged upon by Joseph Schumpeter.[20]

> Nowhere in the world, not even in England, can the parliamentary body as such govern and determine policies. The broad mass of deputies functions only as a following for the leader or the few leaders who form the govern-ment, and it blindly follows them *as long as* they are successful. . . . Political action is always determined by the 'principle of small numbers,' that means, the superior political maneuverability of small leading groups. In mass states, this caesarist element is ineradicable.[21]

In modern societies, in particular, the most effective governments are those that are administered by single individuals and their counselors, such as the prime minister and his cabinet in Great Britain; the least effective are those that provide little, if any, opportunity for the rule of capable individuals, such as those in Germany after the fall of Bismarck.

There are two principal devices through which capable political leadership can be selected. In countries with popular elections, such as the United States, strong political parties represent the most successful method for securing capable leaders. In contrast, where the political leader is chosen from within parliament, Weber noted a variety of alternative strategies:

> Administrative heads must be recruited from [parliament's] midst—the *parlia-mentary system* proper—or . . . they need the express confidence of its majority for holding office or must at least resign upon losing its confidence—the *parliamentary selection* of the leaders: . . . they must account for their actions exhaustively to parliament, subject to verification by that body or its committees—*parliamentary accountability* of the leaders: further, . . . they

[20] Joseph Schumpeter, *Capitalism, Socialism, and Democracy,* 3rd ed. (New York: Harper & Row, Publishers, 1962).

[21] Weber, *Economy and Society,* III, 1414.

must run the administration according to the guidelines approved by parliament—*parliamentary control* of the administration. Then the leaders of the dominant parties have a positive share in government.[22]

It is in situations in which these principles are absent altogether, such as in post-Bismarckian Germany, that decisive political leadership is likewise missing.

State Machinery

The main parts of the modern state's machinery are the parliament or congress, the political parties, the military, and the civil service bureaucracy. The significance of each of these, Weber thought, varies from nation to nation. For instance, in the United States Weber found that the Congress and political parties were most prominent, while in Germany he observed (repeatedly and with acerbity) that in the absence of effective leadership, the civil service bureaucracy represented the most significant element of the state. England, too, was a nation in which the Parliament and the political parties were the most significant forces.

There are, moreover, two major types of political parties—a patronage party and an ideological one. Nations vary in the prevalence of these forms, just as they vary in the significance of particular elements of the state machinery. In the United States, Weber thought, parties were mainly of the patronage type due to the system of direct elections and to the authority vested in the presidency; in Germany, he believed, parties tended to be ideological. Those that are ideological tend to render their governments ineffective because their clashes over principles make it difficult to achieve compromises, particularly in the selection of parliamentary leaders.

Among the different wings of government, there are none more villainous, in Weber's eyes at least, than the civil service bureaucracy. The concentration of expertise and technical knowledge among the ranks of the bureaucrats give them and, by implication, their institution an inordinate amount of power. Consequently, the authority of the monarch can be diminished, as in Germany, or the politicians in the parliament rendered ineffective, especially in such specialized areas of decision making as fiscal policy. The tragedy of it all for Weber is that bureaucrats are only technical experts and can provide no political leadership whatsoever.

Political System

For Weber as for Marx, the political system is the state, comprising the head of state and the machinery of the state. The central feature of this institution is its possession of the "monopoly of the legitimate use of physical force within a given territory."[23] Accordingly, this institution occupies a prominent place in modern societies and, thus, furnishes important grounds for many groups to seek its control. However, as noted earlier, the state does not represent an instrument of

---

[22] Ibid., p. 1408.
[23] Weber, "Politics as a Vocation," in *From Max Weber,* Gerth and Mills, p. 78.

oppression to be wielded by a particular class or status group. Rather, it is an arena of constant conflict and involves the representatives of a variety of different status groups. In addition, it also represents an arena that can involve conflict among the separate agencies of the state.

There are several potentially separate lines of combat within the state. The first engages the political ruler, or head of state, and the parliament-civil service bureaucracy coalition. Despite some admiration for certain aspects of Bismarck's leadership in Germany, Weber thought that this kind of leadership ultimately reduced the chances for achieving democratic rule. The second struggle is a contest between the parliament and the civil service bureaucracy; Weber thought this conflict should be decided in favor of the parliament, again so that the necessary direction for democracy could be provided. The third battle pits the head of state and the parliament against the civil service bureaucracy. Here, again, Weber believed that democratic government required political leadership, not technical expertise alone; thus, he offered a strategy that would decrease the power of the bureaucracy and at the same time enhance that of the head of state and the parliament.

In the final analysis, the principal contest in the modern state is between the political leader and the civil service bureaucracy—a particular application of Weber's general observation that political leaders and their staffs are constantly engaged in a struggle for domination. Weber argued that political leaders are essential for democratic politics and urged the German government, in particular, to take the necessary steps to choose such leaders. Yet, in the end, he equivocated about who would ultimately prevail as the genuine ruler: "In a modern state the actual ruler is necessarily and unavoidably the bureaucracy, since power is exercised neither through parliamentary speeches nor monarchical enunciation but through the routines of administration."[24]

WEBER'S IMAGE OF WHY MEN OBEY

The matter of why one group of men obey another group, in modern nations as well as ancient societies, was of fundamental concern for Weber. The dominance relationship in its most abstract and essential form involves a ruler who gives commands and followers who obey them. The question is then, Why do the followers obey? First of all, in the daily operations of any organized form of domination—whether it be a bureaucracy or a feudal manor—habit or custom is the first principle securing obedience. It also is the weakest, as there is usually a latent conflict between the ruler and his followers. Thus, there have to be additional principles to secure the bond.[25]

---

[24]Weber, *Economy and Society,* III, 1393.

[25]Differences of opinion exist among interpreters of Weber's views about the weight he assigned to such matters as custom, material advantage, and legitimacy in the bond between ruler and ruled. Some, such as Roth, argue persuasively that Weber believed all these elements to figure almost equally into the bond, whereas others claim Weber stressed the importance of legitimacy.

coercive remunerative authority

The next principle is that of an administrative apparatus. This helps to enforce the obedience of people to the ruler by providing punishment for non compliance with commands, by levying and collecting taxes, by carrying on war, and by attending to related matters. "Organized domination," Weber remarked, "requires the control of those material goods which in a given case are necessary for the use of physical violence . . . [as well as] control of the executive staff and the material implements of administration."[26] Administration entails its own problems because major struggles for the position of dominance always occur between the ruler and his staff. To lessen the threat of usurpation of the ruler's power, there must also be a solidarity of interest between the ruler and the staff; the burden for establishing such solidarity falls on the shoulders of the ruler. As in similar instances, such solidarity is insured through the provision of material and ideal rewards by the ruler: "The fear of losing [material reward and social honor] is the *final* and *decisive* basis for solidarity between the executive staff and the power-holder."[27]

not

Still, even an administrative and military force, together with the associated material implements, is sufficient for sustaining the continued dominance of the ruler over his subjects, particularly during times of crisis and of threats about the ruler's right to hold power. There has to be a third and final principle that acts to furnish the *ultimate guarantee* of obedience by the followers—namely the follower's belief in the legitimacy of the ruler. When it comes to the crunch, when custom melts and administration weakens, the principle of legitimacy always upholds the ruler; the followers believe that a particular figure (or figures) has a right to command them, and they, on their part, have a duty to obey him.[28]

340

Our interpretation here highlights legitimacy as the final guarantee; it rests on such passages as the following from Weber:

> The members of the administrative staff [of a superior] may be bound to obedience to their superior [or superiors] by custom, by affectual ties, by a purely material complex of interests, or by ideal [*wertrationale*] motives. The quality of these motives largely determines the type of domination. *Purely* material interests and calculations of advantages as the basis of solidarity between the chief and his administrative staff result, in this as in other connections, in a relatively unstable situation. Normally other elements, affectual and ideal, supplement such interests. In certain exceptional cases the former alone may be decisive. In everyday life these relationships, like others, are governed by custom and material calculation of advantage. But custom, personal advantage, purely affectual or ideal motives of solidarity, do not form a sufficiently reliable basis for a given domination. In addition there is normally a further element, the belief in legitimacy.
>   Experience shows that in no instance does domination voluntarily limit itself to the appeal to material or affectual or ideal motives as a basis for its continuance. In addition *every such system attempts to establish and cultivate the belief in legitimacy* [my italics]. (Weber, *Economy and Society,* I, 213.)

[26]Weber, "Politics as a Vocation," in *From Max Weber,* Gerth and Mills, p. 80. For a similar statement, see also Weber, *Economy and Society,* I, 264.

[27]Weber, "Politics as a Vocation," in *From Max Weber,* Gerth and Mills, p. 80.

[28]For an excellent discussion of Weber's conception of legitimacy, see Reinhard Bendix, *Max Weber: An Intellectual Portrait* (Garden City, N.Y.: Doubleday and Co., Inc., 1962), chapter 9. The discussion here is much indebted to Bendix's analysis.

Using the principle of legitimacy as an abstraction, an ideal type, Weber proceeded to distinguish among three separate forms: legitimacy based on traditional grounds, legitimacy based on charismatic appeal, and legitimacy based on rational-legal standards. In the first case, individuals obey a leader, often regarded as the patriarch, out of time-honored devotion. The leader is thought to possess power because he and his ancestors have always held the position of dominance. The patriarchic household and the patrimonial estate represent the specific settings in which such domination is evident. Charismatic domination, the most unstable and transitory of the three, is characterized by feelings of awe and complete devotion on the part of followers. The leader is presumed to possess some uncommon talents—sometimes magical ones—and to be capable of carrying out miracles. Such leadership arises especially during times of societal stress and acts as the glue to bind men together in dominance relations when other principles of legitimacy, traditional or rational-legal, have been eroded. The last form of legitimate domination, rational-legal, involves a relationship between a superior and his subordinates. The underlying principles that justify the dominance of the superior in this case are those of written laws. These serve to establish the precise limits to the leader's authority and the subordinates' obedience. Moreover, the followers under these conditions obey the leader because he holds a particular office, not because of his own qualities as a person; the essence of the form, then, is impersonal.

In the modern state, as throughout history, concrete cases of domination actually involve mixtures of the three principles. The leadership of a monarch, for example, might rest on a combination of charismatic and traditional legitimacy. The leadership of the president of the United States often seems to combine all three forms. Such combinations notwithstanding, Weber thought that empirical analysis would be furthered if a concrete form of domination were to be characterized as one of the pure types.

This image of domination has had far-flung consequences and resulted in widespread applications to a number of different circumstances. The notion of traditional domination, for instance, has been used to examine leadership in the developing nations, while that of charismatic domination has frequently been used to explore the nature of leadership in political movements.[29]

As lucid as this analysis of domination is, it does have some flaws. The major one concerns the idea of legitimacy. The problem with legitimacy as a concept is that it appears to exist only in the minds of the followers—in their beliefs and opinions. For instance, Weber asserted, charismatic leaders do not possess charisma but rather it is bestowed on them by their followers: "It is recognition on the part of those subject to authority which is decisive for the validity of charisma."[30] Though such a notion is in keeping with Weber's injunction that sociology should concern itself mainly with the subjective interest of individuals—their intentions—its use means that observers of society actually possess no independent and objective

[29] See, for example, Guenther Roth, "Personal Rulership, Patrimonialism, and Empire-Building," in *Scholarship and Partisanship,* Bendix and Roth, chapter 8.

[30] Weber, *Economy and Society,* I, 242.

basis for determining the presence of legitimacy—other than their own imaginative interpretations. Consequently, those who examine the nature of domination are left to conclude that leaders are continuously obeyed because followers believe they, the leaders, are legitimate holders of power, and the holders of power must be legitimate for they are continuously obeyed. There are ways to escape this circularity; some are suggested by those scholars who have elaborated on Weber's notion.[31]

But Weber says people obey for other reasons too, fear a calculation. . . .

WEBER'S IMAGE OF CHANGE

This discussion of Weber's writings about change involves a more discursive treatment than the appraisal of Marx's writings. Perhaps because of his premature death at the age of fifty-six, Weber was unable to develop in a formal and systematic fashion a single, comprehensive vision of change. He, of course, concerned himself throughout his work with rationalization of the Western societies, but this is not to say that he possessed a clear theoretical image of it, as Marx possessed of revolution and class conflict or Parsons possessed of evolution. Hence, an effort to grasp and appraise his images of change must rely on the bits and pieces of vision Weber left.

In its most pervasive fashion, change represents the development of rationality in the West and is manifested in all major institutional spheres. Rationality represents a novel form of belief, thought, and organization. The essence of rationality lies in the employment of the most technically efficient strategy for attaining goals. The process that gives rise to it, that helps to mold and to give life to it, occurs at a gradual pace and comprises the incremental growth of societies as a whole, as well as of their distinctive institutional spheres. Such developments come about, moreover, not as the product of a single, dramatic turning point in history, but as the culmination of many separate themes. In a phrase, Weber's conception of the development of rationality, or of rationalization, might be regarded as *change by convergence*; separate and independent elements emerge at different points in time, become woven together over a period of indefinite magnitude, and in combination, create the new social form.

To be more exact, let us illustrate this perspective by using Weber's analysis of the specific origins of the modern state bureaucracy, the most prominent structural embodiment of rationality. Weber's discussion involves a historical description of the preconditions required for the rise of the modern state. These include rational law, a money economy, the concentration and sophistication of the means of communication and transportation, and the concentration of the means of civil

---

[31] See, among others, Peter M. Blau, "Critical Remarks on Weber's Theory of Authority," *American Political Science Review,* vol. 57, no. 2 (June 1963), 305-16; and Martin E. Spencer, "Weber on Legitimate Norms and Authority," *British Journal of Sociology,* 21 (June 1970), 123-34.

and military administration. For Weber, none of these conditions are particularly decisive; all are equally necessary.

On close scrutiny, however, this sort of analysis turns out to be inadequate on several grounds. First, it remains extremely close to the historical details that Weber examined in tracing the rise of rationalization or its particular embodiment, the modern state bureaucracy. Weber did not attempt to develop a theory cast on a higher plane of abstraction, as did Marx, for example. Hence, his image proves useful for subsequent generations of sociologists only insofar as they wish to correct his historiography, but it does not provide a clear basis for examining contemporary bureaucratization. Because the discussion is framed in historical terms, moreover, the causal analysis for the growth of the modern state bureaucracy proves to have a logical flaw. In particular, Weber's analysis suggests that most of the preconditions for the rise of the modern state bureaucracy are none other than the same elements that enter into its definition. Roman law, for example, permitted the rise of the state bureaucracy, but at the same time, the distinctive feature of this bureaucracy was calculability achieved through Roman law. This analytical procedure stands in vivid distinction to the more valid practice of attempting to explain phenomenon A by phenomenon B, presuming the two are not comprised of the selfsame elements—for example, the state bureaucracy by growth in the number of eligible citizens.[32] Parsons, dealing with precisely the same kind of change and many of the same elements as Weber, solves the problem by invoking a highly subtle and complex vision of evolution. A last difficulty with Weber's vision is that the presumed preconditions of rationality in the West are so general and broad as to skirt the issue of the factors essential and necessary to the emergence of the state bureaucracy, particularly under contemporary circumstances.

Notwithstanding Weber's failure to provide an unflawed portrait of the origins of rationality in the West, many piecemeal efforts to examine change are scattered throughout his writings. One significant example is his dialectical analysis of the place of bureaucracies in democratic nations. Mass democracy encourages the rise of modern bureaucracies because it, like the bureaucracies themselves, is based on equal justice and representation under law. As the development of bureaucracy produces a status group with special expertise, however, it may give rise to inequities that can subvert the very foundations of democratic government. Further, bureaucracy, because of its requirements of specialized training for employees, also elevates formal education as a new basis for social stratification, thereby producing additional inequalities within mass democracies.[33] Another approach to change is that certain institutions evolve in response to pressures in their environments. This

[32] Weber may have intended that the state bureaucracy represent an emergent phenomenon, something qualitatively different from the individual components that went into its manufacture. This, of course, serves as an appropriate analytical strategy similar, for example, to Neil Smelser's use of the value-added method to explore the dynamics of collective behavior (chapter 12 contains a detailed explanation of Smelser's approach). Nevertheless, a close reading of Weber does not really suggest he had this in mind, in part because on these matters he was more an attentive historian than a sociological analyst. I am grateful to Kenneth Wilson for bringing this possibility to my attention.

[33] Weber, *Economy and Society,* III, 999-1001.

is a form of analysis comparable to that used extensively by Parsons and one in which the analyst asserts that institutions (or systems) evolve to accommodate tensions. Weber remarked that the growth of the modern state bureaucracy occurred because "the bureaucratic tendency has been promoted by *needs* arising from the creation of standing armies, determined by power politics, and from the related development of public finances [my italics] ."[34]

Of all the ideas that Weber uses to study change, none are more useful than those of the three types of domination. These may be used to explore the existence of additional forms of domination as well as to specify the precise circumstances that lead to change from one form to another. Patrimonial authority, a form of traditional authority that includes a staff of administrators, often leads to the overthrow of the leader and subsequently to a change in the type of domination. Similarly, the transition to the modern state was fostered by the expropriation of the power of the subfeudal lords by the feudal lord.

To use these concepts of domination for a formal analysis of change would create a theory that is fundamentally cyclical. The core of the theory would be the stability of domination or its obverse, erosion. In barest outlines, the theory might claim that when the erosion of domination does occur, and a vacuum of leadership appears, then charismatic domination arises to fill the void. However, owing to its unstable character, charismatic rule would soon be overtaken and routinized into rational-legal, or traditional, domination, and the cycle would repeat itself.

Attention might also be focused on the interplay between the possession of material advantages or symbolic privileges held by the leader and the bestowal of the right to lead possessed by the administrative staffs and subjects. Obviously the leader is unable to lead unless he possesses enough in the way of rewards to satisfy the demands of his followers. The demise of Richard Nixon as president of the United States is a case in which, among other things, the leader simply lost all ability to summon forth the prestige of his office and to bestow it on the American people and the Congress; consequently he was compelled to resign. Even if the followers fail to grant the right to lead, they may have no choice but to obey commands, particularly when the leader possesses absolute control over the military and civil forces of a nation. Analysts employing this imagery might further study those conditions under which the interplay between the rewards possessed by the leader and the granting of legitimacy by followers is weighted toward one side or the other.

The notions of the three forms of domination inspire additional inquiries. Some of these leads have been pursued by scholars interested in topics as diverse as the changing nature of social movements and their leadership and the forms of rule that have recently emerged in the developing nations of Asia and Africa.[35] (Chap-

[34]Weber, *Economy and Society*, III, 972.

[35]See, for example: Mayer Zald and Roberta Ash, "Social Movement Organizations: Growth, Decay, and Change," *Social Forces*, 44, (March 1966), 327-40; Roth, "Personal Rulership, Patrimonialism, and Empire-Building," in *Scholarship and Partisanship*, Bendix and Roth; and Reinhard Bendix, "Charismatic Leadership," in *Scholarship and Partisanship*, chapter 9.

ters 11 and 12 provide more materials on these matters.) In the end, it is unfortunate that Weber did not live long enough to be able to develop and pursue the ideas that he bequeathed to us.

MARX AND WEBER:
COMMON EMPHASES

Marx and Weber provide some common points of reference, notwithstanding their very important and considerable differences (see table 3-1). However, their points of convergence more often than their points of difference provide political sociology with its broad directions.

Broadly, Marx and Weber agree; first, that the social and the political orders penetrate one another and that events and phenomena in the one influence events and phenomena in the other. This point, made in chapter 1, is one of the essential premises of political sociology. Of course, the two differ somewhat in how they view the penetration; Marx takes the more abstract approach but sees the social order as primary, whereas Weber focuses on separate institutional spheres and sees happenings in political institutions as often radically affecting events in social ones. Marx and Weber also agree that a key element of the social order that can influence outcomes in the political arena is the system of stratification; for Marx, this, in the form of social classes, is the only element, and for Weber, this, in the form of status groups, is one of two—the other being, for example, the bureaucratic form of organization prevailing in the economy. Third, Marx and Weber view the political process, as opposed to the political structure, as the same. Groups—whether classes, status groups, or bureaucracies—are engaged in a constant battle with one another; sometimes it is latent, but it always exists. Each of the groups is after dominance and each believes that such dominance can be assured through control of the political institutions. For Marx, such control is part of a larger pattern of the ideological hegemony of the ruling class; for Weber, occupancy of the political institutions does not assure control as there are conflicts as well within the realm of the state— for example, between rulers and their staffs of administrators.

Each theorist, of course, has his own separate ideas that have independently cast light on the political and social horizons. In this regard, Marx has proven to have had considerably more effect on the intellectual orientations of many sociologists interested in politics because he deals with change in such an inventive manner. Weber has also had an impact among sociologists in general, because of his attention to the nature and origins of social status and to the growth of bureaucracies in the modern world.

Marx and Weber illuminate the political world in ways that their intellectual predecessors failed to do. They went so far beyond their predecessors that their insights continue to shape the outlook of those who are their self-selected heirs.

Table 3-1 Comparisons of Marx and Weber

Dimension	Marx	Weber
Main principles of stratification	Social class based on ownership of means of production	Social status based on differential levels of social honor and material rewards
Main principles of social organization	Social classes	Bureaucracy
Conception of the social system	Social classes in competition for control of means of production and material rewards	Status groups and bureaucracies in competition for material and symbolic benefits
Main principles of the political system	Both the rulers and the state machinery act to enhance the interests of the ruling class, the bourgeoisie	Status groups compete for positions of control in the state machinery, but no one group is dominant; state bureaucracy promotes emergence of social inequalities and status groups and exerts influence on national development; struggles within the state, principal one between ruler and state bureaucracy
Conception of obedience	Bourgeoisie dominate proletariat through control of means of production and communication	Rulers dominate citizenry through control of means of administration and war, and dominate their staffs through control of material and symbolic rewards
Conception of change	Qualitative, abrupt, and assumes form of political, then social revolution	Qualitative, gradual, and takes the form of the erosion of authority
Logical principles	Dialectical change	Change in cycles

Antecedents	Economic:
	  Centralization of capital
	  Proletarianization
	  Immiserization
	Social:
	  Urban concentrations
	  Communication
	  Politicization
	  Class consciousness
		No specific ones

[handwritten margin notes: "state action.", "Legit", "Value auton"]

CHAPTER FOUR
The Vision
of Talcott Parsons

*The United States' new type of societal community, more than any other
single factor, justifies our assigning it the lead in the latest phase of
modernization. We have suggested that it synthesizes to a high degree the
equality of opportunity stressed in socialism. It presupposes a market system,
a strong legal order relatively independent of government, and a "nation-
state" emancipated from specific religious and ethnic control. The
educational revolution has been considered as a crucial innovation, especially
with regard to the emphasis on the associational pattern, as well as on
openness of opportunity. Above all, American society has gone farther than
any comparable large-scale society in its dissociation from the older ascriptive
inequalities and the institutionalization of a basically egalitarian pattern.
Contrary to the opinion among many intellectuals, American society—and
most modern societies without dictatorial regimes—has institutionalized a far
broader range of freedoms than . . . any previous society. This range is
perhaps not greater than that sometimes enjoyed by such small privileged
groups as eighteenth-century European aristocracy, but it is certainly broader
than ever before for large masses of people.*

TALCOTT PARSONS, *The System of Modern Societies*

TALCOTT PARSONS (1902-1979)

Among contemporary sociologists there are few who have had as great an impact as
Talcott Parsons. Beginning in the 1930s, when he became one of a small number of
people to join the newly established Department of Sociology at Harvard, Parsons

exercised an influence over sociology and the social sciences generally that was profound. He helped to train a large number of students who have gone on to achieve considerable fame and success in the academic world, among them Robert Merton, Kingsley Davis, Wilbert Moore, Robert Bellah, Clifford Geertz, and Neil Smelser. Moreover, he produced more written work during this time than almost any of his peers, having written dozens of articles and a large number of books. But it is neither the number and distinction of his students nor the vast number of publications that account for Parsons's reputation and influence among modern scholars. Like Marx and Weber before him, Parsons created a grand theory of society—a broad and expansive design to help us explore and understand the mysteries of the social universe.[1]

To understand the theoretical vision of Parsons, it is necessary to understand something about Parsons himself, his intellectual aims, his relationship to his intellectual forebears, and his actual achievements. Let us begin with his intellectual goals and ambitions. He published—usually with associates—works intended not only to guide us in the study of societies and of other social groups but also to advise us in the examination of cultures and of personalities. He was successful in creating a comprehensive scheme for the study of several different layers of human life and showed us how these different spheres are analytically distinct and empirically joined. He groped to articulate this scheme first in his earliest book, *The Structure of Social Action*, wherein he argued that the social nature of human action meant that such action should be construed both as subjective and voluntary and thus as a realm of study independent of both biological and environmental circumstances.[2] Later, in *Toward a General Theory of Action*, published in 1951, he and several colleagues articulated these thoughts and schemes far more clearly and presented a comprehensive and sophisticated method for both conceiving and studying the nature of societies, of cultures, and of personalities.[3] In his later works he continued his effort to create a science of human action; he concentrated not only on the nature and development of societies but also on cultures, personalities, and even biological conditions to show how these forces stimulate and condition social ones.[4]

In his effort to create a comprehensive vision of the life of man, Parsons clarified a number of issues and provoked a number of original questions. For example, observing the analytical distinction between the sociological and psy-

---

[1] The special danger associated with the discussion and analysis of contemporary great figures is that they will not be regarded equally magnificently by future generations. At present, Parson's reputation among many sociologists, particularly younger ones, is on the decline for a variety of reasons; hence, there is some possibility that his influence will not be felt nearly so strongly on future generations of social scientists as it has been felt among his contemporaries.

[2] Talcott Parsons, *The Structure of Social Action* (New York: The Free Press, 1968), I and II. Originally published in 1937, reprinted in 1939.

[3] Talcott Parsons and Edward A. Shils, eds., *Toward a General Theory of Action* (New York: Harper & Row, Publishers, 1951).

[4] Talcott Parsons, *Societies: Evolutionary and Comparative Perspectives* (Englewood Cliffs, N.J.: Prentice-Hall, Inc., 1966); and Talcott Parsons, *The System of Modern Societies* (Englewood Cliffs, N.J.: Prentice-Hall, Inc., 1971).

chological frames of reference, Parsons found that these perspectives converged and traced the implications of their convergence. In several writings he remarked that Emile Durkheim, a sociologist, and Sigmund Freud, the father of modern psychoanalysis, each invented different names for somewhat similar insights.[5] In particular, Parsons observed, Durkheim and Freud each insisted that societies acted to constrain the insatiable desires and appetites of human beings; Durkheim spoke of this phenomenon in terms of the social constraints, such as the *collective conscience*, and Freud wrote of it in terms of the *superego*. The recognition of this parallel enabled Parsons to distinguish clearly between the sociological frame of reference, which emphasizes the externality of rules, and the psychological frame of reference, which stresses the internalization of such rules. Moreover, it also enabled him to identify one of the ways in which the subject matter of sociology and that of psychology intersect. This, together with a number of other penetrating insights into parallel concerns of nineteenth and twentieth century students of humanity, allowed Parsons to move beyond his self-selected forebears in many important and imaginative respects.

In addition to creating a comprehensive view of man, Parsons self-consciously drew upon several of the ideas found in the writings of earlier students of humanity. Two of the themes that characterized many of his writings, those of rationalization and of the emergent nature of social life, were deliberately selected from the visions of Weber and Durkheim respectively.[6] Parsons, however, gave them his own special twist. Thus, in his attempt to explain the differences between societies of the past and of the present as well as to account for variations among contemporary societies, Parsons elaborated on Weber's conception of rationalization. In particular, he decomposed the idea into elements that could account for the social action of men and interpreted such action as though it represented a dilemma between a ratonal course, and a nonrational, or better, a prerational, course.[7] He also used Weber's conceptions as a guiding principle in his work on the evolutionary development of societies, speaking of evolution as if it were a gradual and continuous rationalization of social life.[8] Perhaps the main clue to Parsons's devotion to this idea is found in his first major work, wherein he observed that "in any concrete system of [social] action a process of change . . . can proceed only in the direction . . . of . . . rational norms [that are] binding on the actors in the system."[9]

The second theme, the emergent character of social life, occupied Parsons's attention as much, if not more, than the first. Obviously the effort that he devoted

[5] See Parsons and Shils, *Toward a General Theory of Action,* p. 22; and Parsons, *The Structure of Social Action,* I, xi.

[6] Parsons, *The Structure of Social Action,* I and II. For further insight into the part that these themes played in Parsons's intellectual career, see Talcott Parsons, "On Building Social System Theory: A Personal History," *Daedalus,* vol. 99, no. 4 (Fall, 1970), 826-81.

[7] These are the notions of the pattern-variables, mostly clearly explained in Parsons and Shils, *Toward a General Theory of Action,* pp. 76-91.

[8] Parsons, *Societies: Evolutionary and Comparative Perspectives* and *The System of Modern Societies.*

[9] Parsons, *The Structure of Social Action,* II, 751.

to clarifying and exploring the connections among several different layers of human life represents a major reflection of this theme. An even more prominent one is to be found in his singularly creative contribution to the social sciences, that is, his particular conception of the social system. Drawing upon the ideas of system in classical mechanics as well as in biology, Parsons maintained that social reality must first be conceived as a system. The insistence on this conception results in less emphasis on the human and personal side to social life, for which Parsons was roundly castigated, and at the same time, it produces innumerable insights into the mysteries of this life. It is safe to say, in fact, that the intellectual reputation of Parsons will mainly rest on how well he is thought to have exploited this single conception and on the judgment of future generations concerning this pursuit.

Parsons also possessed a special image of the nature of man and man's relationship to society that informs us greatly about his social theory. Like Sigmund Freud, with whom he claimed close affinities, Parsons took a dim view of the basic nature of man, believing that if men were left to their own primitive and natural devices they would ultimately destroy one another. Man to Parsons is not the noble savage of Jean Jacques Rousseau but the nasty, mean, and ill-tempered animal of Thomas Hobbes. To become fit to live with one another, men must be subject to external constraints; otherwise their unruly passions get the best of them. For Parsons, these constraints are distinctively social—in fact, for him they are moral. They are conceptions of the good, the just, and the beautiful that men arrive at through mutual consent and enforce through a variety of social sanctions. Parsons solves the age-old Hobbesian problem of the potential war of all against all by substituting one set of constraints over men—moral—for another—force. In the context of his view of man, his solution is considerably less interesting than his assumption that men are inherently unruly and must be controlled.[10]

This particular philosophical premise about the nature of man, especially man in society, is by no means the only alternative open to the student of human action. Some, among them Abraham Maslow and Jean Piaget, do not insist that men are inherently base and primitive creatures but instead see them as possessing the potential for self-initiated forms of growth and development.[11] Even students of social action, such as Karl Marx, do not necessarily adopt such a dismal perspective on man; Marx maintained that social institutions, those of capitalist societies specifically, poisoned the otherwise generous and sociable nature of man and left him alienated. While both Parsons and Weber agree on the basic tendencies for rationalization inherent in modern society, Weber constantly emphasized the personal costs that result from this process, whereas Parsons emphasized the enhancement of man's freedom. Parsons, in brief, firmly believed that the social order—*any* social order—serves not to debase man but to civilize him, not to strangle him but to liberate him. For instance, in an essay on the political analysis of American

[10] For Parsons's initial discussion of the Hobbesian problem of order, see Parsons, *The Structure of Social Action*, I, 89-94.

[11] Jean Piaget, *The Moral Judgment of the Child*, trans. M. Gabain (London: Routledge and Kegan Paul, Ltd., 1926).

society by C. Wright Mills, Parsons wrote of the significance of "positive social organization," and maintained that "power, while of course subject to abuses and in need of many controls, is an *essential* and *desirable* component of a highly organized society [my italics] ."[12] Certainly neither Marx, Weber, nor many other social theorists conceive any and every social fabric through such rose-colored concepts.

PARSONS'S IMAGE OF THE SOCIAL ORDER

Our discussion of Parsons's image of the social and political orders of society essentially parallels the treatment both of Marx and Weber. This treatment is a means of providing a fuller understanding of the nature of a theorist's work and thought. Among other things, the parallel treatment permits a better appreciation of the different and often unique emphases in the way a theorist approaches the task of creating a vision of the social world. There is one slight change in the strategy for Parsons, however. Because his conception of the social system occupies a prominent part in his view of the social world, other of his images, in particular those of social stratification and of social organization, cannot be fully understood without reference first to Parsons's vision of the social system. Thus, the discussion of social order begins with Parsons's notion of the social system, then moves to his visions of social stratification and of social organization. The discussion also focuses on Parsons's analysis of the nature of very advanced, or differentiated, societies—those societies with which he concerned himself most often in his wealth of publications.

Social System

The concept of social system, which is the master theme of Parsons's theoretical analyses, is so broad an idea that it can be applied virtually to any setting of social action, ranging from a small group of friends to an entire society. There are a number of criteria that go into its definition.

At its simplest and most basic, Parsons defines a social system as a setting in which social roles exist and in which interaction occurs among the occupants (people) of these roles. Normative rules of conduct guide the interaction, specifically socially recognized and shared rights and obligations associated with each role. In turn, the broader cultural setting of the social system defines the rights and obligations, those definitions of the permitted and unpermitted forms of action. For example, in the terms laid out by Parsons, American society can qualify as a social system for it contains social roles—citizen, husband, worker—and interaction proceeds among the members of corresponding roles—citizen and official, husband and wife, worker and employer. There are also normative guidelines that define

[12]Talcott Parsons, *Politics and Social Structure* (New York: The Free Press, 1969), p. 202.

both rights and obligations of roles, for example, the rights and obligations of the citizen vis à vis the government. Moreover, the normative guidelines receive their definition, their very validity, from broad cultural traditions—traditions that in the case of citizenship are articulated in the Bill of Rights and the Constitution.

Parsons further insists that a social system, like any system whether mechanical or biological, has boundaries and an environment beyond the boundaries. The boundaries of the social system can be conceived conceptually as the borders between it and other social systems as well as between it and other spheres in the system of human action. There are three other such systems, two of which Parsons and his colleagues examined at length: the cultural system, which involves symbols and ideas; the personality system, which involves individual "need-disposition" and motivation; and the behavioral organism, which concerns biological systems.[13] Though pictures render a certain injustice to some of the conceptual subtlety of these matters, figure 4-1 may aid our understanding of the features of the social system and its environment. The social system is simply one of four separate systems in Parsons's overall scheme of human action. Its environment consists of the three other systems—the cultural, the personality, and the behavioral organism— with which it is contiguous.

The arrows that lead from the social system into the other systems and from these back into the social system indicate that the boundaries of the social system are permeable, that is, that there are things that pass between the social system and its environment. The social system is an "open" system, open to and dependent for

FIGURE 4-1   The social system and its environment

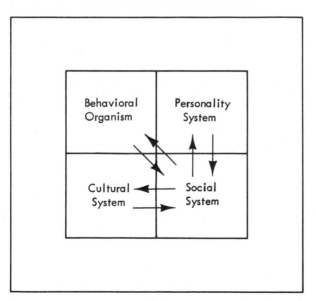

---

[13]Parsons and Shils, *Toward a General Theory of Action*, part 2.

its survival on exchange of resources and products with its environment.[14] What does it exchange? Consider first the arrow leading from the cultural system into the social system. This indicates that from the cultural system the social system receives the religious values, like brotherhood and charity, that serve to legitimize the interaction among people in roles. In the case of the arrows leading between the social system and the personality system, the social system receives from the personality system an infinite number and variety of persons who will occupy the roles and fill the organizations that make up the settings of social interaction of the social system—the children as well as the adults who literally give life to the skeletal framework of social interaction.[15] At the same time, the social system reciprocates on this exchange and provides the personality system with a number of diverse roles and settings of interaction that help to create personalities; the roles of infant, child, student, and others help to lay the foundations for the mature person.[16] Similar exchanges take place between the social system and the behavioral organism, as well as among the other systems. All systems are contiguous with one another, and all are dependent for their survival on such exchanges with their environments.

A social system also has its inner workings, and Parsons devotes much theoretical analysis to describing and clarifying these parts. Basically there are two sorts of internal parts: those that can be conceived as structures, analogous to the organs of a human body, and those that can be conceived as processes, analogous to the firing of pistons in an internal combustion engine.[17] Every social system, Parsons maintains, has a social structure comprised of several distinctive elements; altogether there are four of them. A hierarchical arrangement loosely connects all of these elements with one another; the contents of one are likely to correspond to the contents of the others, change in one is apt to create a tendency for change in the others. Values, which are the most general and important of the four elements, define normative expectations for the proper and improper actions in any social system. They represent the desirable qualities of social action toward which people aspire, and ultimately their contents can be traced to the religious doctrines of a cultural system. Norms, next in the hierarchy of the social structural elements, provide more specific guidelines for social action; they are the specific rules that translate values into action. The third element of the social structure is represented by collectivities and furnishes the organizational setting within which the values and the norms of a social system are specified. Finally, there are roles, the most concrete and fundamental elements of any structure; roles occur within the boundaries

---

[14] Talcott Parsons, "An Outline of the Social System," in *Theories of Society: Foundations of Modern Sociological Theory,* ed. Talcott Parsons (New York: The Free Press, 1961), I, 36.

[15] Ibid., pp. 62-63.

[16] Ibid.

[17] As with pictures, these analogies should only be seen as devices for helping to comprehend better the workings of the system. Neither the structures nor the processes of the social system are exactly like those of biological or mechanical systems, and any effort to construe them as such seriously distorts Parsons's conception of the social system.

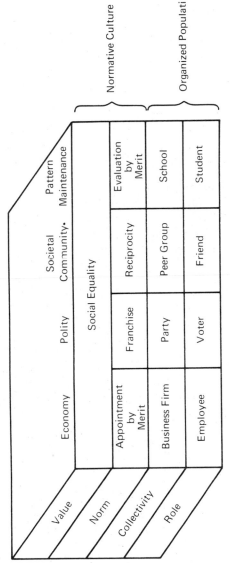

FIGURE 4-2 The components of social structure

of collectivities, and the action of their occupants is guided by the normative expectations of a social system, that is, the values and norms.

Again, it is useful to rely upon an illustration of these ideas for clarification and to take American society as the example. Figure 4-2 portrays some of the elements of the social structure in this setting and is based upon Parsons's own analyses.[18] Four separate sectors distinguish each of the elements: the economy, the polity, the societal community, and the pattern-maintenance (these sectors are defined shortly). The economy, like every sector, possesses social equality as a value. The value owes its origins to the Christian heritage of the United States and is articulated in various ways in many American official documents. Below this in the hierarchical arrangement of the elements of structure is a norm, appointment by merit; this refers to the method whereby appointments are conventionally made in economic institutions and is obviously consistent with an emphasis on the value of social equality. Business firms, typical collectivities in the economy, are the settings in which both the value and the norm are applied, and within these settings, the application is made to people who occupy the role of employee.

Thus, this example illustrates each of the four elements of social structure in American society, the hierarchical arrangement of these elements, from the most general to the most concrete, and the way in which the four are interconnected. Similar inspection of the elements of social structure within each of the other major sectors of American society furnishes identical sorts of patterns. In the polity, for instance, the franchise represents the specific norm that translates the value of social equality into a guide for social action, while the party represents the setting within which this norm is applied, and the role of voter is that specific role to which the value and norm are applied. The same patterns of definition and of specification hold true as well for the sectors of societal community and of pattern-maintenance.

(In passing it should be noted that while the structural elements of any social system can be spelled out in this manner, there are few such systems among societies in which this degree of consistency among the various elements is observed. Some societies, for example, emphasize the value of social equality but apply it only to the polity or to the societal community; others possess the value but are also comprised of roles that are not clearly defined, such as that of voter or of employee. There are many such societies in the world today, and these sorts of inconsistencies in the elements of their social structures create strains that often manifest themselves in social protest and other forms of discontent.[19] The United States, in this regard, is for Parsons an exception—it is a contemporary setting in which the greatest advances have been made in achieving a degree of integrity among the contents of the various values, norms, collectivities, and roles that comprise it.[20])

[18] Parsons, *The System of Modern Societies,* chapter 6.

[19] Parsons et al., *Theories of Society,* pp. 71-72.

[20] Parsons, *The System of Modern Societies,* chapter 6.

Besides the structural elements of any social system, there also exist definite processes that maintain and sometimes even alter the system. Parsons identifies several of the important processes, but only the most significant concern us here.[21] There are four basic processes in any social system; these processes may be considered as functions crucial to the survival of the system. They may also be conceived as loosely analogous to—but *only loosely analogous to, and not identical to*—such functions as respiration or digestion, without which the system that characterizes human beings, as a biological species, could not survive. All four, moreover, are further construed by Parsons as subsystems of the social system. The first of these processes is that of latency, or pattern-maintenance, and refers to the function whereby the patterns of social organization and interaction that are characteristic of a social system are sustained over time. Integration is the second major process of any social system and is that process whereby the diverse sets of structures in a system are regulated and coordinated in a fashion that prevents any serious strains or inconsistencies from disrupting the system. The process of goal-attainment, that of the formulation and establishment of priorities among systemic goals, is equally important to the survival of any social system and represents the third major process. Finally, there is the process of adaptation that refers to the allocation of technical resources and role-opportunities to the individuals and the groups that comprise a social system—an allocation accomplished in the pursuit of the system's goals.

At this level of generality, of course, the processes are abstract. Figure 4-3 presents a simple diagram of the four processes, as defined and specified for an advanced society such as that of the United States or of France. Each of the four processes, or functions, can be identified with some broad sector or institutions. The process of adaptation, identified with the upper left-hand cell, is carried on within the economy of a society, a societal sector that, as our own observations must suggest, is associated with the allocation of resources and opportunities in every advance society. Even more specifically, the function of adaptation can be attributed to industrial organizations, or industries, within the economy. The adjacent cell, that of the polity, involves the process of goal-attainment, the formulation and establishment of priorities among different goals in a society. Again, the association of this function with the polity verifies our own everyday observations about advanced societies. Within the polity it is the institutions of government, in particular, that are concerned with the function of goal-attainment.

The cell immediately below the polity is integration, which is identified with the subsystem labeled societal community. Although this designation is not immediately obvious, the sort of institution principally concerned with integration, namely law, is perhaps more plausible. Legal organizations and institutions appear to act as devices that coordinate and regulate diverse, sometimes even conflicting, settings in a society, precisely the meaning of the process of integration. Finally, the cell designated as pattern-maintenance covers the process of latency and is

---

[21] For other processes, see the articles on influence and value-commitments in Parsons, *Politics and Social Structure*, part 4.

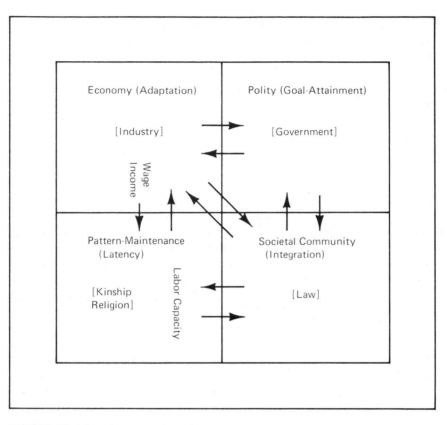

FIGURE 4-3 The subsystems of a society

specifically represented in the kinship and religious institutions of a society. Institutions like families or churches act in ways that serve to establish and to maintain the basic value patterns of a society—the family acts to lay down these value patterns principally through the formation of personalities amenable to filling roles in a social system, while churches, or their functional equivalents, secure value patterns through their regular promulgation of the highest, the penultimate, beliefs of a society.

A few comments are in order about this portrait of the basic processes, or subsystems, of a society. First, returning to figure 4-2, the sectors there now have meaning; they are the basic processes, or subsystems, of a society, and within them are the various elements of social structure. Next, these four basic processes possess all the fundamental elements of a social system—they are settings within which interaction occurs; they are comprised of the basic elements of social structure; and they have boundaries as well as an environment. It is obvious from the diagram, in fact, that there exist boundaries of these subsystems and that these boundaries, like those of the social system, are permeable, allowing the exchange of resources to occur with other parts of the system. For example, the economy provides certain products to the polity and receives certain resources in return. To be even more specific, the exchange between the economy and the pattern-maintenance subsystem partly involves two things that confirm our expectations. The economy provides wages as a resource to the pattern-maintenance subsystem; in return, it receives labor services from this subsystem—wages are exchanged for labor.[22] Similar resources are exchanged across the borders of the other subsystems and prove vital to the maintenance of each of the subsystems as well as to the social system.

One final principle that is critical to Parsons's vision of the social system is "cybernetic hierarchy," which Parsons adopts from the brilliant mathematician Norbert Weiner who invented the science of cybernetics in the late 1940s.[23] The fundamental meaning of this principle is that in any hierarchy of elements those that stand higher control the operation, in fact the very meaning, of those that stand lower. Parsons makes special use of the principle and asserts that, in general, those elements that stand highest in a hierarchy, whether it be one of systems or structures, are the normative elements. Parsons maintains that they are the values, or the religious ideas, that act as the ultimate sources of the definitions of that which is good, just, or beautiful.[24]

Consider how Parsons applies this principle to the elements of social structure. Referring once again to figure 4-2, there is a particular arrangement among the structural elements such that values stand highest, with norms just beneath them, followed by collectivities and roles, respectively. As applied to these elements of social structure, the principle of cybernetic hierarchy means that values provide the broad set of conditions within which collectivities must be compatible, and that collectivities provide the broad set of conditions within which roles must be compatible. In figure 4-3, the hierarchy of basic processes, or subsystems, of the social system begins with the pattern-maintenance subsystem, as we might expect since it contains religious institutions, and it moves counterclockwise in the diagram from the societal community, to the polity, and finally, to the economy. Here the meaning of the cybernetic hierarchy is that in any given society, the value patterns within the pattern-maintenance system establish the broad conditions within which the other subsystems must be compatible or, generally, that each of the subsystems establishes broad conditions *necessary* to the operation of those processes below it in the cybernetic hierarchy.

Using this principle and its specific applications to the general action system (figure 4-1), to the social system (figure 4-3), and to social structure (figure 4-2), Parsons examines and explains a great variety and number of different empirical events. In the case of broad change, he uses the principle to argue that the Christian heritage of the West furnished a broad set of conditions within which other events, such as the extension of the franchise, eventually could take place and achieve stability (or what he calls "institutionalization"). As applied, in fact, the principle

[22] For further details on these processes, see Talcott Parsons and Neil J. Smelser, *Economy and Society* (New York: The Free Press, 1956), chapter 2 especially.

[23] Norbert Weiner, *Cybernetics* (Cambridge, Mass.: The M.I.T. Press, 1961).

[24] Parsons, *Societies: Evolutionary and Comparative Perspectives,* chapter 1.

of cybernetic hierarchy comes to mean that higher-level conditions *must* occur and *must* achieve regularity if the lower-level circumstances are to achieve stability.[25]

This, then, is Parsons's vision of the social system. At its simplest, it is a setting of social interaction comprised of roles and governed by norms. It possesses an environment consisting of other social systems as well as the three broad systems of the culture, the personality and the behavioral organism. Internally it consists of social structure, which is comprised of values, norms, collectivities, and roles. Like any such system, moreover, it also involves basic processes; in its special case it involves those of pattern-maintenance, integration, goal-attainment, and adaptation. The arrangement of its various parts is defined by the principle of cybernetic hierarchy, a principle that accounts for the control of the lower-level elements by higher-level ones and that, in Parsons's unique application, maintains that values, religious beliefs, or generally, normative elements represent the very highest levels of human action.[26]

It is evident, of course, that this vision of the social world differs markedly from that of Marx and Weber and that it has its own special implications. These matters are dealt with at the end of the chapter.

Social Stratification

Social stratification occupies almost a peripheral element in Parsons's scheme of the social world. Its moment of greatest importance comes early in the evolutionary development of societies; it assists in the movement from the most primitive stage to a somewhat more advanced one. In highly developed societies, such as that of the contemporary United States, Parsons thinks that stratification becomes so complex as to lose its significance as a major instrument of stability or of change. In this respect, Parsons's vision differs dramatically from that of either Marx or Weber.

Within a highly advanced society, stratification is thought of in terms of the symbolic media through which it works, those of prestige and influence, and of

---

[25]Parsons occasionally refers to this matter of stability in the contents of social structure or social system as that of "institutionalization." By this he means the manner in which normative definitions at the highest levels filter down and influence patterns at the lower levels. See, for example, Talcott Parsons, *The Social System* (New York: The Free Press, 1951), pp. 36-45; and Parsons and Shils, *Toward a General Theory of Action, p. 20*.

[26]Of course, it is difficult to visualize this system no matter what aid our diagrams might provide. Another helpful trick is to conduct a small experiment. Suppose that American society, or perhaps your immediate community, were threatened with extinction. Under these circumstances, the various parameters and pieces of these entities, as social systems, would become visible. Thus, under such a threat it is exceedingly likely that individuals, as American citizens, would be called upon to give great sacrifice; hence, some institution would attempt to integrate the society. Similarly, the goal-attainment processes would likely be highly visible, with various leaders and organizations acting in a concerted manner to provide direction for the society. So, too, the economic institutions quite suddenly would appear in their full detail, and we would realize the special nature of the economic process and how it articulates, especially under such severe circumstances, with the political process. And on and on, we would discover, with the use of this very simple mental experiment, that the conception of the social system as used by Parsons comes very close to describing much of social reality, even though under normal circumstances such reality is never completely disclosed to us.

Explain p. 340;
draw on Davis-Moore

the function it fulfills, that of integration. It represents the ranking of individuals and families on a scale of prestige; those who occupy roles of greater importance also hold the higher ranks. Social importance conveys two meanings—a sense that some individuals and groups occupy roles that are crucial to the survival of society, and a connotation that some individuals and groups hold roles that are especially compatible with the general societal values. Naturally the two forms of importance can overlap, but such convergence is not necessary.[27] Stratification fulfills the function of integration in two major respects. The differential distribution of prestige and influence through which it operates enables positions of greatest social importance to mobilize the resources necessary to their operation and hence to the survival of society. Those in positions of leadership and of greatest influence in any advanced society routinely seem able to attract the greatest amounts of power and money and thus to reach their goals; this, Parsons believes, is a symptom of stratification. Stratification is integrative in this regard because it acts to link the pattern-maintenance subsystem in which societal importance is defined to the polity and the economy in which the goals as well as the resources are located (see figure 4-3).

Stratification proves to be integrative in another way as well. Although it represents the provision of unusual amounts of prestige to some positions rather than others, it also furnishes an explanation for the legitimacy of this inequity. There are some roles that receive more prestige, influence, and other privileges than other roles; these positions are also the ones of greatest significance to our society; hence, your small reward (or large, as it may be) can be justified by the minor (or major) importance of your role to society. In this way, social stratification attempts to integrate society, dampening the inevitable discontent and envy by calling upon the commitments of individuals to society as a whole.[28]

Social Organization

The elements of social organization, in contrast to those of stratification, occupy a very central place in Parsons's image of the social world. Broadly conceived, social roles and collectivities are two of the major components of social structure.[29] Social roles represent the most elementary particles of social organization; they are the normative expectations of action for such distinct positions as student, child, teacher, and worker.[30] Roles exist in every possible setting of social interaction, although a major feature of social change, or evolution, is the gradual increase and diversification of roles.[31] Collectivities, on the other hand, represent a higher order of social organization; they are clusters of roles systemati-

---

[27]Talcott Parsons, "A Revised Analytical Approach to the Theory of Social Stratification," in *Essays in Sociological Theory*, ed. Talcott Parsons (New York: The Free Press, 1964), pp. 386-439.

[28]For further details on this form of integration, see Parsons, *Politics and Social Structure*, pp. 405-38.

[29]Parsons, *Societies: Evolutionary and Comparative Perspectives*, p. 18.

[30]Parsons, *The Social System*, chapters 2 and 3.

[31]See, for example, Parsons, *The System of Modern Societies*.

cally organized for specific societal functions.[32] While the kinship units of primitive societies represent a type of collectivity as a special form of structure, collectivities take on their greatest societal significance in the later stages of evolution.[33] One that becomes most significant is bureaucracy.[34] Adopting the fundamental insight of Weber, Parsons argues that bureaucracies become vital to the evolution of societies at a certain stage and furnish a form of social organization within which power is concentrated and the function of goal-attainment is focused. They also represent the societal settings within which authority occurs and is legitimized by the values and norms of a society.[35]

Two additional forms of social organization that are also characteristic of the later stages of social evolution are democratic associations and professional organizations.[36] Democratic associations that, like modern bureaucracies, tended to emerge throughout Western Europe and the United States in the eighteenth and nineteenth centuries were equally vital to the sequence of evolutionary development. Professional associations have become prominent with the rise of specialized and diversified roles, especially in the legal, medical, and academic professions. They, too, represent a form of social organization within which the roles that are typical of advanced societies may be organized in a stable and regular fashion and in which the broader normative patterns of structural and systemic evolution can be secured. (Further discussion of the nature and patterns of social evolution and of its connections to the emergence of the several special forms of social organization is contained in the section entitled "Parsons's Image of Change.")

PARSONS'S IMAGE OF THE POLITICAL ORDER

The strategy for examining Parsons's vision of the political order is similar to that used in discussing social order. His notion of the political system brings into sharp focus all other political elements.

Political System

The political system is that part of a social system exclusively concerned with the function of goal-attainment. Like any such system, it possesses the elements of structure—values, norms, collectivities, and roles—as well as boundaries that it continually seeks to define and to maintain. The most important parts of its environment are the other subsystems of a society: the pattern-maintenance, the societal

[32] Parsons et al., *Theories of Society,* pp. 41-42.

[33] Talcott Parsons, *Sociological Theory and Modern Society* (New York: The Free Press, 1967), pp. 503-7.

[34] Ibid.

[35] Talcott Parsons, *Structure and Process in Modern Societies* (New York: The Free Press, 1960), pp. 170-98.

[36] Parsons, *Sociological Theory and Modern Society,* pp. 503-7.

community, and the economy. For its own survival, it depends on an exchange of resources with these other subsystems. (Again the reader may want to consult the diagrams in figures 4-2 and 4-3 to refresh his or her sense of these various facets of the social system, particularly the polity.)

Parsons believes that in a highly evolved society, one like modern France or the Soviet Union, the processes of the political system assume a crucial significance.[37] Power represents the most important of these processes. Introducing an extremely novel idea, Parsons asserts that power, like money, is a generalized and circulating symbolic medium that permits advanced societies to perform their basic functions in a more efficient and effective fashion than primitive societies.[38] Power is "the capacity of a social system to mobilize resources to attain collective goals."[39] Power, in other words, is a medium that acts on behalf of all the members of a society and that carries with it the obligation that those who are subject to its exercise must act accordingly. Ultimately the obligation to act on behalf of societal goals in the exercise of power is supported by the highest values of a society. In an advanced society, moreover, virtually every adult possesses power. Thus the voter, like the president, possesses power; at elections the former exchanges his or her right to use power to the president who acts on the voter's behalf in the formulation of policies.[40]

The successful and continuous performance of the political system and, by implication, the society as a whole depends in highly evolved societies on the processes of boundary-interchange. These help to determine, among other things, the amount of power in a society. In particular, the exercise of power is contingent on the amount of material resources, the strength of citizens' loyalties, and the commitment of individuals to the highest values of a society. Or, the amount of the symbolic medium of the polity (power) is dependent upon the amount of similar media in other spheres—in the economy (money or resources), in the societal community (loyalties), and in the pattern-maintenance subsystem (value-commitments.)[41] To examine the manner of the exchanges that permit this logical equivalence, the diagram in figure 4-4 provides a more detailed inventory of patterns shown in figure 4-3.

The patterns of exchange in figure 4-4 provide a crisp method for portraying processes that are belabored by other scholars with more descriptive techniques. In the case of the boundary-interchanges between the societal community (lower right-hand cell) and the polity (upper right-hand cell), individuals in their capacity as citizens, role-occupants of the societal community, act in two principal respects with regard to the polity. As voters, they provide support for the polity and its principal occupants, officials; and as members of interest groups, they furnish demands for special policies of concern to them. Looking at the same process from

[37] Parsons, *Politics and Social Structure*, pp. 317-51.
[38] Ibid., pp. 352-404.
[39] Ibid., p. 206.
[40] Ibid., pp. 204-40.
[41] Ibid., p. 205.

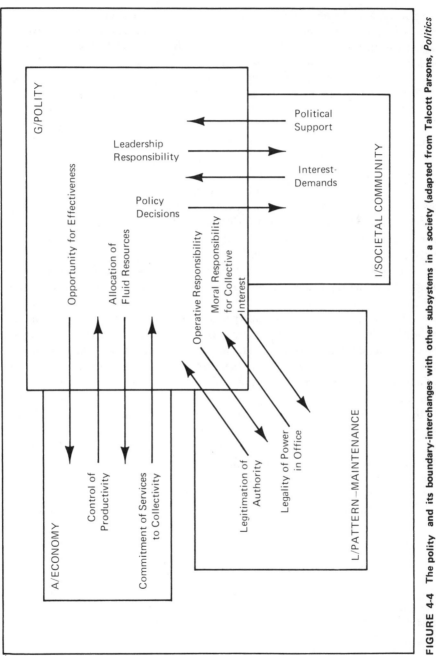

FIGURE 4-4 The polity and its boundary-interchanges with other subsystems in a society (adapted from Talcott Parsons, *Politics and Social Structure* [New York: The Free Press, 1969])

the other side, officials appear to act in a reciprocal fashion. In return for the articulation of demands by citizens, officials provide binding policy decisions; likewise, in exchange for political support they assume responsibility for leadership in a society.[42]

Studied closely, Parsons's processes of boundary-interchange neatly capture the fundamental operations of any highly evolved political system, especially those in democratic societies. The same neatness and balance of process is also evident in the interchanges between the economy and the polity and between the pattern-maintenance subsystem and the polity. In the latter case, the pattern-maintenance subsystem buttresses political process through its provision of basic legitimacy; simultaneously, the polity furnishes the responsibility for actions taken on behalf of the entire society.

Parsons's conceptions of the political system are strikingly original and powerful tools for the analysis of politics. He provides entirely new sets of ideas that are considerably different from those of Marx, Weber, and most other analysts of politics. A few of these differences need to be further highlighted. Most, if not all, analysts have envisioned power as a scarce commodity. If held by one group in a society, it is therefore unavailable to another group; this is the portrait that Marx paints and many others paint (see chapter 6). Parsons claims that power is a positive commodity in a society; it is employed on behalf of the entire society to accomplish societal goals. Thus, everyone gains from the use of power, not simply special groups.[43] At the same time, however, power like money, can introduce certain inequities into a society. Power is provided to the occupants of political offices, but some individuals may take advantage of their positions and attempt to hoard or to enlarge their power. This action presumably could continue for a long time and might include the suspension of mechanisms through which public support is granted, namely elections. In Parsons's imagery of things, however, it cannot continue indefinitely without rendering society impotent. Power ultimately depends upon the loyalties of citizens to the societal community and to the fundamental values of the society; loyalties and values provide the ultimate checks on misuse of power.

Reconsidering the principle of the cybernetic hierarchy and its application to the social system of a society, other important implications of Parsons's view of politics are also evident. The principle of the cybernetic hierarchy asserts that there exists an order of control in the social system such that each subsystem, beginning with the pattern-maintenance, controls the operations of those below it. In the case of the political system, this means that the societal community, in its many parts, controls the operations of the political system. Thus, we can deduce from Parsons's vision that power within the polity and those who exercise it are ultimately beholden to the citizens of society. Further, the same principle implies that power, generally, and government, in particular, are under the control of law in a society,

---

[42] Ibid., pp. 204-40.
[43] Ibid., pp. 352-404, 185-203.

and law acts as the principle integrative mechanism. These, as well as other similar empirical deductions, make it evident why, for example, the claim can be made in a society like the United States that no person stands above the law, or why, to be even more specific, a president who attempts to usurp the power of his office must eventually relinquish that office because of the application of law and the loss of public support.

They cybernetic principle also discloses an unexpected deduction—namely, the political system controls the operations of the economic system. In Parsons's imagery, it is not the leaders of the economy, those individuals of enormous wealth or managerial expertise, who control the leaders as well as the processes of government; to the contrary, it is the leaders of government, acting on behalf of the public, who control the operations of the economy.[44] In some settings, for example, the Soviet Union, this deduction seems to fit the empirical facts; yet in other settings, for instance in the United States, it runs contrary to much of the evidence (see chapter 6). Nonetheless, Parsons maintains that government in the final analysis acts to manipulate and shape the operations of the economy through its fiscal policy as well as through its own control of more significant devices, such as the agencies of law enforcement.[45] In any event, this particular implication calls into question many of the conclusions of Marxists and other scholars about the links between government and business; more than that, it is a deduction deserving of more systematic inquiry.

Political Rulers

Political rulers, in Parsons's special vision, represent those roles from which the leadership is exercised in a social system. As such they are the locations within which the initiative for the formulation and implementation of collective goals is concentrated.[46] A more detailed examination of the functional features of the polity in an advanced society, as shown in figure 4-5, further illuminates the special qualities of rulers, or leaders. Leadership performs the function of goal-attainment within the polity; as a subsystem, leadership is even further differentiated in an advanced society, with the executive wing of a government focused primarily on the attainment of the general societal goals.

State Machinery and Ancillary Organizations

Most of the details of the political order, including those of the nature of the state machinery and organizations like parties, do not attract probing examinations from Parsons. His most important observation is that such institutions fulfill specific and critical functions in the polity of an advanced society. Reexamination of figure 4-5, for instance, reveals that the state machinery, the bureaucracy, acts to

[44] Parsons, *Politics and Social Structure,* pp. 473-522, 190-91; and Parsons et al., *Theories of Society,* p. 68.

[45] Parsons, *The System of Modern Societies,* p. 18.

[46] Parsons, *Structure and Process in Modern Societies,* pp. 149-51.

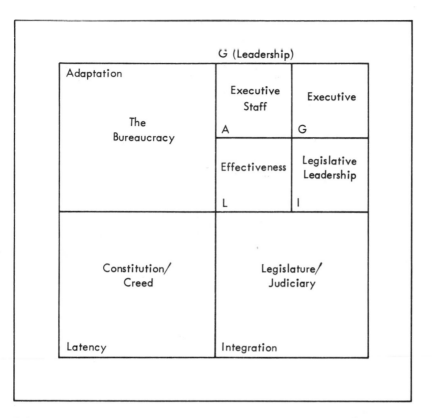

FIGURE 4-5   Details of the functional organization of the polity (adapted from Talcott Parsons, *Politics and Social Structure* [New York: The Free Press, 1969])

perform the function of adaptation, while the legislature and the judiciary act to fulfill the function of integration. Incidentally, Parsons's lack of concern with the details of these processes and organizations appears to be a reflection of his greater interest in establishing a breadth to his vision of society and politics than in providing it a depth.

PARSONS'S IMAGE OF WHY MEN OBEY

The response of a theorist to the issue of men's obedience in society frequently helps us to comprehend better the theorist's images of power and authority. Marx and Weber provided seminal and illuminating answers. Parsons might claim that the powerless comply with the commands of the powerful because the powerful exercise the capacity to make binding decisions on behalf of the entire society. However, why do some men make decisions that are *binding* over the actions of other men? In what sense are the decisions taken on behalf of the *entire society*? The answers to these questions disclose Parsons's vision of the fundamental nature of obedience and of power as well.

To uncover Parsons's image of the nature of obedience, let us assume that the roles of powerful and powerless exist in any collectivity. As a generic case such an example is perfectly compatible with Parsons's view because he believes power to be distributed in such a way that the decision taken by some roles in a collectivity take precedence over decisions taken by other positions, or, in more conventional terms, that some positions hold more power than others.[47] This illustration obviously oversimplifies matters; in Parsons's full vision of the social world no one can truly divide positions, or individuals, into the powerful and the powerless. For one thing, Parsons conceives power to be widely distributed among all individuals, particularly in an advanced society. For another, he makes no claims about the existence of two sorts of roles, the powerful and the powerless; at best, there may exist roles that approximate the conditions of holding power, or holding no power—those of an elected official ànd its counterpart, a voter, for instance.

Those individuals who occupy the roles of powerless are compliant with the commands of those who occupy the roles of powerful for several reasons. First and foremost, they are compliant by virtue of the roles they occupy, not because of qualities that they possess as individuals. Certain roles simply assert that their occupants must obey the instructions of other roles. For example, the role of citizen in a society claims that its occupant must act in accordance with the instructions of public officials. In view of such demands, why does an individual choose to occupy such a role? Because, Parsons's imagery suggests, all such roles, in an advanced society at least, also contain significant privileges or rights. The role of citizen, for example, entitles its occupant to expect protection from elected officials, in addition to many other benefits. Thus, the first source of obedience is that *those individuals who obey the commands of other individuals do so because they have freely selected to occupy such roles, based upon the privileges those roles provide.*

The obedience of some individuals to others by virtue of the roles they hold cannot by itself be sufficient to motivate individuals to be compliant over a long period of time, however. The roles must also entail certain specific mechanisms to insure the obedience of occupants. There are two such devices, though in fact they are but mirror images of one another—it is the obligation of the role of the powerless to obey the commands of those who occupy the role of the powerful, and it is the right of the powerful to expect the compliance of those who hold the role of the powerless. For instance, it is the obligation of the citizen to comply with the commands of the official and the right of the official to expect the compliance of the citizen. Thus, the second source of compliance is that *those individuals who obey the commands of other individuals do so because of the obligation of their roles.*

Even the obligations of a role, however, are insufficient to command automatic and indefinite compliance. Individuals do not find the roles they occupy

---

[47]Parsons, *Politics and Social Structure*, pp. 369-71.

continuously satisfying but occasionally find such roles to be highly restrictive. When individuals find the duty associated with their roles unbearable and when they are inclined to disengage from the role and its obligations, other mechanisms must come into play. These are the sanctions—the negative sanctions in particular, such as the application or threatened application of force—that those who occupy the roles of the powerful can use to secure the compliance of those who hold the roles of the powerless. They are the devices that seem to make the actions of the powerful truly *binding* over the actions of the powerless. The government, for instance, may apply or threaten to apply various forms and degrees of force—including imprisonment—if the citizen fails to comply with its commands. Hence, the third basis for compliance is that *those individuals who obey the commands of other individuals do so because to do otherwise would elicit the application of force.*[48]

Is it true that force is an important, indeed perhaps the ultimate, means that may be used to secure the compliance of the powerless to the powerful, of the citizen to the government? Is Parsons, in fact, in league with Thomas Hobbes, maintaining that individuals are compliant because the sovereign authority under which they live would apply the instruments of coercion if they act otherwise?[49] Nothing could be further from the truth. To understand the role of force in society, Parsons asks, What gives individuals who occupy specific roles the *right* to use the means of force? What gives the government in a society, for instance, the *legitimate* monopoly over the application of the means of physical force in cases of noncompliance with its commands? To know the foundations of the right to use such means of force? What gives the government in a society, for instance, the legitimate imagery.

The final source is the values and the norms, the definitions of the rights and obligations in any society. These normative elements are such that through a complex and long process they become translated into the very expectations of the roles of the powerful and of the powerless in a society.[50] It is a process that begins at birth, in the form of socialization by parents, and continues throughout life as one encounters increasingly more specialized collectivities and roles.[51] The normative elements for Parsons, like ideology for Marx, are pervasive throughout the various structures of a society. Thus, for example, the Constitution of the United States assigns to the president as well as to the Congress the capacity to make decisions on behalf of the entire nation; at the same time, it defines the norms and articulates the values, which in this particular and important instance assert that the

[48] Ibid., pp. 365-66.

[49] Hobbes as well as his alleged "problem of order" had been a favorite target of Parsons's criticism throughout the latter's career. To get a sense of this, see Parsons, "On Building Social System Theory," pp. 869-70 especially.

[50] Parsons, *The Social System,* pp. 36-45.

[51] Parsons, *The Social System,* chapters 6 and 7; and Parsons et al., *Theories of Society,* pp. 62-66. Antonio Gramsci, a Marxist, also emphasizes the key role of moral authority with his conception of hegemony. See our earlier discussion of Gramsci's ideas in chapter 2, on the Marxists.

occupants of some roles, citizens, must comply with the actions of the occupants of other roles, the president and the Congress. Thus, the last and most significant of the sources of obedience is that *those individuals who obey the commands of other individuals do so because those commands are buttressed by the very highest values of a society.*

PARSONS'S IMAGE OF CHANGE

For the greatest part of his career Talcott Parsons was the target of critics who reviled him for failing to build a viable theory of social change.[52] They argued that Parsons created a vision of the world that, because of its emphasis on the needs and the survival of the social system, conveyed a static rather than a dynamic portrait of societies, or, if not a static one, then surely one that was sympathetic to the status quo. Until his writings of the 1960s, when he was in his seventh decade, Parsons's critics were right; only briefly did he attempt to develop notions about social change.[53] However, Parsons abruptly shifted his emphasis and began to devote almost exclusive attention to social change and, more generally, to the processes characteristic of social systems. His work during these years developed this relatively neglected angle of his vision. This section reviews a few of its highlights. Incidentally, the polity, and its structures, do not figure prominently in Parsons's analysis of change; the discussion here is intended to show where they do fit in and to provide a description of his logical principles of change—principles that might well become the basis for much future research in political sociology.

Breadth and Depth of Change

Defining change broadly as a special type of process characteristic of social systems, there are three types of change to which Parsons directed his attention.[54] The first he refers to as circular process, adapting a notion from economics; it is the way in which the polity, for example, continues to fulfill the function of goal-attainment under the usual conditions of uncertain and scarce resources. Thus, the polity partly sustains its supply of power by drawing on the resource of political support from the societal community and, at the same time, by replenishing that support with its provision of policy decisions. The second sort of change is growth; in the case of the polity this represents the ways in which the amount of power is increased or diminished. For instance, it might involve the steps that political leaders take to incorporate new groups of citizens into a society. Although the

---

[52] For the single most devastating critique in recent years, see Alvin W. Gouldner, *The Coming Crisis of Western Sociology* (New York: Basic Books, Inc., 1970), part 2 especially.

[53] See, for example, Parsons, *The Social System*, chapter 11; Parsons and Smelser, *Economy and Society,* chapters 4 and 5; and Talcott Parsons and Robert F. Bales, *Family, Socialization and Interaction Process* (Glencoe: The Free Press, 1955), chapter 1.

[54] Parsons, *Politics and Social Structure*, pp. 342-50.

political support originally allocated to leaders does not typically call for such action, the action can enhance the capacity of a society to pursue its goals and thereby create more power. Simultaneously, it has important consequences for the amounts of resources in other subsystems of the society, increasing, for example, the supply of manpower for the economy. Finally, the third type of change identified by Parsons is that of fundamental structural change. This is the sort of change examined for both Marx and Weber. It is examined here from the special perspective of evolution that Parsons used in some of his last writings on the subject.

The vision of structural change created by Parsons is extraordinarily sweeping.[55] It seeks to explain how today's world was fashioned and the great diversity among contemporary societies by investigating its primeval structural and systemic forms. This journey in search of the origins of today's world takes Parsons on several paths, including studies of seminal structural patterns in ancient Greece and Israel and examinations of a vast array of materials assembled by anthropologists on primitive societies. It is a vision that is often subtle, frequently complex, and ambitious in its scope. In the end, it is a view that is deliberately the parallel of Darwin's view of change in biological forms; it is a view of social change as evolution.

At root, the evolution of societies means the improvement of their capacity to adapt to the environment about them.[56] This environment includes the cultural system, the personality system, the biological system, and the physical realities that societies encounter. A society that is successful in making evolutionary progress is one that can handle the demands placed upon it by its environment in ways that represent a more efficient and effective use of societal resources. The essence of this greater effectiveness lies in the creation of more specialized and focused structures that perform the basic functions of the social system—adaptation, goal-attainment, integration, and latency—with greater speed and precision. Parsons observes:

> If differentiation [change] is to yield a balanced, more evolved system, each newly differentiated sub-structure . . . must have increased adaptive capacity for performing its *primary* function, as compared to that function in the previous, more diffuse structure. Thus economic production *is* typically more efficient in factories than in households. . . . This change applies to both role and collectivity levels; the participating people, as well as the collectivity as a whole, must become more productive than before. . . . These changes do not imply that the older "residual" unit will have "lost function" in all contexts of its operations. The household is no longer an important economic producer, but it may well perform its other functions better than in its earlier form.[57]

Evolution, in other words, is the increasing rationalization of societies.

It is notable that all societies do not manage to make the great leap forward into a higher stage of adaptation. Some fail and die out; others remain in existence

[55] Parsons, *Societies: Evolutionary and Comparative Perspectives* and *The System of Modern Societies.*
[56] Parsons, *Societies: Evolutionary and Comparative Perspectives,* especially pp. 21-24.
[57] Ibid., p. 22.

but often in a dependent relationship to more advanced societies. Those societies that succeed in making advances do so for two reasons. Some achieve an evolutionary breakthrough—the manufacture from within their own bowels of an element vital to evolution; others fail to create a novel element from within but are in sufficiently close social proximity to an advanced society that they become the recipients of a diffused element.[58] The varying degrees of success in the evolutionary process contribute to much of the diversity of cultural and social patterns, both at present and throughout recorded history.

Logic of Change

In Parsons's view, every major structural change in a society, whether it proves of evolutionary significance or not, involves three phenomena: differentiation, integration, and strain. These do not necessarily occur in a particular sequence, but all must take place in order for genuine structural change to happen. As will be evident, they also represent a special application of the dialectical principles of change and thus furnish an important point of agreement in the visions of Parsons and of Marx.

Differentiation is a concept that is used in the accounts of social change, particularly evolutionary change, by such theorists as Herbert Spencer. In Parsons's hands it represents the process whereby a single element of a system, or of its structure, becomes divided into at least two new elements, and each becomes more exclusively concerned with performing single, or at least distinctive, functions. Moreover, the process of differentiation never seems to take place in only one subsystem, or at one level of structure, but occurs at multiple points; as Parsons observed, "we would expect this process of differentiation at the level of the general action system to stimulate and be stimulated by similar processes internal to the society as a system."[59] One excellent illustration of the process of differentiation is provided by Parsons, who relies on the analysis by his student Neil Smelser of change during the Industrial Revolution:

> Perhaps the best example is the differentiation of occupational roles . . . from embeddedness in kinship structures. . . . On the role [level] the change means that what has been one role of an individual in a single kinship collectivity . . . becomes differentiated into two roles in two distinctive collectivities, the kinship group and the employing organization. . . . The outcome of [this change in Great Britain] was the incorporation of a very large new group of the working-class labor force into the factory system, in fully differentiated occupational roles, with the concomitant loss of most of the function of family economic production. Working in factory premises, for an individual wage and under factory rather than kinship discipline, was a main structural feature of the outcome. Smelser makes it clear that this was not a simple matter of attracting workers by better wages than could be offered else-

---

[58] Parsons, *Sociological Theory and Modern Society,* p. 494.

[59] Parsons, *Societies: Evolutionary and Comparative Perspectives,* p. 25.

where; it was only possible through a major restructuring of the working-class kinship system.[60]

Observe here how differentiation has become evident at several points. It is evident in the division of functions, the adaptive (or productive) from the pattern-maintenance (or kinship); in the division of roles, that of occupational (or worker) from that of kinship (or relative); and in the division of collectivities, that of the adaptive (factory) from that of the pattern-maintenance (family).

In order for new patterns to become firmly institutionalized in a society, differentiation must be complemented by a second process, integration. Integration is the process whereby the new patterns are refashioned in a way that allows a society to maintain its integrity, as a social system, and also permits it to move to a higher level of adaptive capacity. Like differentiation, integration may occur at any of a number of points in the systems and structures of a society; obviously, if structural change is to be realized, integration must necessarily occur at those points where the new, differentiated patterns have been introduced. Above all else, integration involves a society in seeking out new and more general bases for unity where differentiated patterns may, and often do, create the foundations for social conflict. Naturally, in Parsons's vision of the social world, these threads of unity lie at the very highest cybernetic levels of the social system and of the social structure—in values and norms in particular. Thus, the establishment of the new patterns of collectivities and roles in Great Britain, of structural change, was greatly facilitated by the broader system of values and norms that served to legitimize them:

> As Smelser shows, it was very important in the British case that the structural changes in the role-organization of the labor force of the late eighteenth century were preceded, and for some time, accompanied, by a marked revival, in precisely the geographical section and population groups involved, of the Puritan religion. According to the famous Weber hypothesis, Puritanism has legitimated both profit-making and more broadly effective contribution. . . . More immediately, the main justification of the factory system was its greater productive effectiveness. In the typical working-class household, there was promise of both realistic opportunity to organize work in a new way, and legitimation of that way in terms of a family institutionalized religious tradition. A steady pattern of sanctions operated to reinforce the change.[61]

Structural change, in short, involves the process of differentiation, which promotes the division and introduction of new structural patterns, and integration under a broad, if not new, system of values and norms that serves to give the patterns integrity with previously existing patterns in a society.

Almost universally the processes of differentiation and integration, if they are to result in genuine structural change, are necessarily accompanied by tensions

[60] Parsons et al., *Theories of Society,* I, 76-77. For Smelser's original materials, see Neil J. Smelser, *Social Change in the Industrial Revolution* (Chicago: University of Chicago Press, 1959).

[61] Parsons et al., *Theories of Society,* I, 77.

and conflicts in a society. Parsons conceptualizes such tensions and conflicts as structural strain, a condition in which a society as a social system cannot meet the demands made on the operation of its structures and its processes. Everywhere such strain becomes evident in the anxieties and dissatisfactions it arouses among individuals; indeed, "only when strain impinges on and involves this level . . . can structural change ... become possible."[62] As strain becomes more pervasive throughout a society, conflicts may erupt in more violent form among collectivities as well as among persons who occupy particular roles. The result can be a society divided into opposing camps. On the one side are those groups that choose to resist the establishment of the new structural patterns and that are engaged in the support of old patterns, or "fundamentalism"; often such groups include the most powerful and established collectivities in a society. On the other side stand those groups that favor the establishment of the new structural patterns and that are engaged in support of the newer and more general principles, those of "inclusion." The successful introduction and institutionalization of structural innovations often hangs in balance indefinitely as the forces of fundamentalism battle those of inclusion. One vivid illustration of this condition of conflict occurred in the French Revolution. On the one side stood those who represented the forces of fundamentalism, the landed classes and the crown; on the other side stood those who represented the new structural patterns of inclusion—those of democracy *(Liberté, Egalité, Fraternité)*—the bourgeoisie and their cohorts. Moreover, as this particular example well illustrates, the forces of fundamentalism often hold the upper hand in conflict because they exercise the existing rights to use the means of social control, including laws and physical weaponry, over their opponents.[63]

Sequence and Pattern
of Evolutionary Change

In the long and often circuitous process that takes a single society along the route from a primitive to an advanced stage of development, there are a number of innovations that must occur. These are crucial to adaptation; their incorporation permits a society virtually to leap ahead in its adaptive capabilities. Both their particular contents and the sequence in which they have been introduced in the evolutionary process reflect the fundamental patterns of elements in Parsons's vision of the social order—those of the cybernetic hierarchies among the elements of the social system and of its social structure. The sequential pattern of their introduction, hence the resulting levels of societal evolution, is an analytical rather than chronological one; namely, some structural elements may be historically pre-

---

[62] Ibid., 75.

[63] The analysis here relies on two sources: Parsons et al., *Theories of Society,* I, 75; and Parsons, *Societies: Evolutionary and Comparative Perspectives,* pp. 22-23. For further insight into the involvement of strain and social control in structural change, see the discussion of Smelser's theory of collective behavior in chapter 12, "Social and Political Movements." This highly original theory departs from and employs many of these elements of Parsons's vision of social change.

sent in a society before others, but unless they are combined in the sequential and logical order of evolutionary innovations, they will not actually become firmly institutionalized as regularized patterns of a society. (The reader might wish at this point to refresh himself or herself on these elements by briefly rereading the discussion of the social system.)

First in the sequence is that of social stratification. This evolutionary development, Parsons claims, is critical because it enables the most primitive of societies, that in which there exists a "seamless web" of social relations, to take the initial and possibly the most difficult step away from traditional patterns. It involves, in particular, the emergence of a primitive class system in which a segment of society becomes differentiated from the group as a whole and in whose hands the capacity to mobilize societal resources and to define societal goals is placed. The appearance of a leadership class with its special privileges and rewards in a previously homogenous social setting must necessarily arouse envy and hostility among other inhabitants. To counter such possible opposition and to permit a society to move to an even higher level of adaptation, a system of values and norms, however elementary, must arise to provide legitimacy to the differential distribution of rewards. The content of such a system, strictly speaking a cultural system, varies enormously among specific societies; "a 'God-King,' " Parsons observes, "may be the primary vehicle of legitimation of his own political regime, or the political 'ruler' may be dependent on a priestly class that is in some degree structurally independent of his regime."[64] These first two structural innovations, in Parsons's vision of evolution, are in a very general fashion logically deducible from Parsons's broader vision of the social order; they lie at the very highest levels of the cybernetic hierarchies, those of the cultural system, and within the social system, those of the latency and of the integrative subsystems. Small wonder that Parsons believes them to be so critical and so controlling of the process of societal evolution.

The next major feature that permits a society to move into higher levels of adaptation is that of bureaucratic organization. Everywhere bureaucratic organizations have been introduced they have provided—as Max Weber first acknowledged— a technical and administrative means for conducting the business of a society in a more efficient and effective fashion. Thus, in some of the most ancient of societies, such as those of Egypt and China, there were full-fledged bureaucratic developments that, to all appearances, allowed a degree of development unsurpassed by their contemporary societal counterparts. Likewise, the next structural innovation, or rather set of innovations, those of a market system and a money complex, also permit considerable improvement in the adaptive capabilities of societies. Even with the presence of a leadership class, a widespread system of cultural values, and bureaucratic organizations, societies can adapt only so well to the exigencies imposed upon them by the everyday requirements for survival. To become even more effective in the adaptive process and to meet the needs required by a more differentiated and complex economic subsystem, a market system must emerge that is

[64] Parsons, *Sociological Theory and Modern Society*, p. 502.

capable of handling the problems created by the differentiation between the production and consumption of goods. Likewise, to facilitate the economic exchanges across such differentiated patterns, there must arise a medium that is symbolic insofar as it represents, but is not actually, the ownership of property and that can readily change hands; that medium, throughout all societies at this stage of evolution, is none other than some form of money. Both these structural developments in the evolutionary process take place at somewhat lower rungs on the cybernetic ladders, specifically at the levels of the goal-attainment and the adaptive subsystems, respectively.   *because govts permit n print them*

There are two other major features that occur universally in the evolutionary development of societies; historically, these can be traced to even more recent times than those of the market system or money. Universal norms represent the first of these features and can perhaps be most easily identified with comparatively recent developments in Western European societies, for example, England and France. Such norms allow a society to move to adaptive capabilities even beyond those permitted by the introduction of money and represent the necessary response, if a society is to operate effectively, to the increasing diversity of structures and processes—of roles and collectivities—found among those societies in which all other evolutionary developments have taken place. Such norms, which are threads of integration, permit a clearer and more precise definition of the rights and obligations of roles vis à vis one another and are clearly required as societies advance beyond the stage in which roles and persons become differentiated from one another. The last, and most historically immediate, element to appear in the evolution of societies is that of democratic associations. Like universal norms, such associations meet the exigencies that arise as societies become increasingly diverse in their structures and as such systems become differentiated from the individuals who, as personalities, inhabit them. This increasing complexity and diversity produces such a rich mixture of societal opportunities and of individual persons that inevitably no simple patterns of stratification and of the concentration of power can sustain it. Consequently, virtually a society of equals is created, demanding radically new patterns of integration. Democratic associations arise to meet precisely such a need and permit the widespread distribution of power and new forms of social relationships to occur.

This repesents Parsons's most general vision of change in societies. It is equally as sweeping in its scope as Weber's vision of the inevitable rationalization of societies and equally as vigorous in its conception of change as Marx's vision of class conflict and revolution. It is a vision that, in its broad outlines, Parsons applied to interpret the entire course of Western history.

AN EVALUATION OF THE PARSONIAN VISION

Parsons's vision is one that, because of its complexity and logical rigor, is difficult to evaluate. Moreover, there is not a body of critical literature to assist an evaluation, as there exists for Marx's writings, since the Parsonian vision is too new to have provoked extended controversy or to assess its intellectual durability. Even the literature that it has stimulated often turns out to misconstrue the major points of Parsons's writings.[65] Yet Parsons, as much as anyone else, must be held to blame for these misinterpretations for he often failed to take the pains necessary to communicate clearly and easily with his readers.

The appraisal of Parsons begins with a note of the strengths of his vision. To assist in this task table 4-1 contains the material from table 3-1 that compared Marx and Weber, as well as the principles from Parsons. Parsons's vision is, to begin with, comprehensive in its scope, accounting for the form and mechanics of several different layers of human life. It seeks to draw attention not only to the social but also to the biological, the psychological, and the cultural dimensions. It identifies these as analytical dimensions and then explains how they intersect; how, for instance, the cultural and social layers of life are joined in real, empirical circumstances. Compared with its major alternative, the Marxist vision, it has several strengths. In its emphasis on values, it seems able to account for a much greater diversity of historical settings and cultural variations. Also, its emphasis on the abstract configurations of norms, collectivities, and roles enables it to move away from an exclusive, sometimes parochial, concern with social classes—those of the bourgeoisie and proletariat in particular. These terms are awkward and graceless as compared to that of social class, but they permit a wider vision to operate in the analysis of social reality. Again in comparison with the Marxist vision, the writings of Parsons provide a more detailed and comprehensive analysis of social change, particularly the social rather than economic elements of this process.

A careful study of Parsons reveals a large number of concepts that possess reasonably clear definitions. Unlike Weber, who often failed to construct clear concepts and to apply them to his interpretation of history, Parsons goes to great lengths to provide the necessary conceptual boundaries and contents. One major illustration of this, and of the difference between Weber and Parsons, occurs in the concept of legitimacy. Weber's conception of legitimacy is vague and diffuse, leading to the sort of logical difficulties noted in chapter 3; Parsons's conception is clear and explicit, and though we may disagree with it, we certainly cannot disdain it for its ambiguity.

The Parsonian vision also has other weaknesses, besides those noted at the outset of this chapter. Parsons's conceptions of efficiency and effectiveness as the criteria of adaptive capability are inadequate. Applied to many social institutions, they fail to capture the heart and essence of these settings. For example, Parsons claims that the nuclear family now prevalent in many Western nations represents a more highly evolved system than the extended family—that it performs its functions with greater efficiency. How can this observation possibly be correct in light of the high and increasing rates of divorce among such families, the appearance of large numbers of runaways, and other similar problems that are characteristic of this form of the family? Efficiency and effectiveness, in other words, are properties

---

[65] See, for example, Gouldner, *The Coming Crisis of Western Sociology.*

Table 4–1 Comparisons of Marx, Weber, and Parsons

Dimension	Marx	Weber	Parsons
Main principles of stratification	Social class based on ownership of means of production	Social status based on differential levels of social honor and material rewards	Ranks of individuals and families on prestige scale based on social importance of roles
Main principles of social organization	Social classes	Bureaucracy	Collectivities and roles (social structure)
Conception of the social system	Social classes in competition for control of means of production and material rewards	Status groups and bureaucracies in competition for material and symbolic benefits	A setting of interaction carefully circumscribed by boundaries, comprised of a social structure and maintained by four major functions—adaptation, goal-attainment, integration, and pattern-maintenance; action within setting is defined and sustained ultimately by values
Main principles of the political system	Both the rulers and the state machinery act to enhance the interests of the ruling class, the bourgeoisie	Status groups compete for positions of control in the state machinery, but no one group is dominant; state bureaucracy promotes emergence of social inequalities and status groups and exerts influence on national development; struggles within the state, principal one between ruler and state bureaucracy	Subsystem that performs the function of goal-attainment; it employs power to achieve goals and maintains a careful exchange of resources with other subsystems

Conception of obedience	Bourgeoisie dominate proletariat through control of means of production and communication	Rulers dominate citizenry through control of means of administration and war and dominate their staffs through control of material and symbolic rewards	Roles of powerful dominate roles of powerless through the rights and obligations that bind each role; obligation of powerless to obey is supported ultimately by force that is legitimated by the highest societal values.
Conception of change	Qualitative, abrupt; assumes form of political, then social revolution	Qualitative, gradual; takes the form of the erosion of authority	Qualitative, gradual, evolutionary; change is enhancement in the adaptation of social system to environment
Logical principles of change	Dialectical change	Change in cycles	Differentiation, integration, strain; a form of dialectical change
Antecedents	Economic: Centralization of capital / Proletarianization / Immiserization / Social: Urban concentrations / Communications / Politicization / Class consciousness	No specific ones	Evolutionary advances require sequential addition of / Social stratification / Cultural system / Bureaucracy / Market system and money / Universal norms / Democratic associations

of the social system, but they obscure many real and meaningful occurrences in the social world.

Along somewhat related lines, the Parsonian vision embodies a number of ideas that may easily be construed as bound by culture and time. The notions of efficiency, egalitarianism, and democracy, together with his assertion in *The System of Modern Societies* that the United States now represents the societal location in which the greatest advances have been made in the achievement of these qualities, are much too vulnerable to the charge that they represent ideological chauvinism. Parsons's assertion, in the same work, that the Soviet Union represents an instance of dedifferentiation, of a less highly evolved society than the United States, adds credence to the view that he is merely a spokesman, however sophisticated, for the interests of the United States. Surely such criticisms are not completely justified, particularly in view of the seriousness of purpose and rigor of mind with which Parsons has pursued his vision of the world; still his ideas can be, and have been, dismissed on just such grounds.[66] Ultimately, however, it will not be these kinds of criticisms that truly test the viability of the Parsonian world view so much as it will be the fundamental ideas that give rise to them—his interpretations of rationalization and of the social system.

In the appraisal of Parsons's writings it is important to note two sorts of observations that represent nothing more than red herrings. One involves an alleged polarity between conflict and consensus theories; Marx and Weber are assumed to illustrate the former perspective, and Parsons to serve as an example of the latter one.[67] This opposition is at most one of emphasis. No careful student can fail to find important elements of agreement, in values and attitudes for instance, in Marx or to locate important elements of conflict in Parsons. The central issue in this alleged debate comes down to this. Are the values that prevail in a society manipulated by one group, the capitalist class, or are they somehow mutually agreed upon? Examined closely this matter inevitably is one that cannot be answered in any definitive fashion, at least not by science; therefore, it must remain a moot point. The second red herring is the contention that the Parsonian vision is not a theory but simply a frame of reference or a set of conceptual schemes.[68] True, the Parsonian vision is not a theory, but then neither are the views of Marx or Weber. What these three scholars have done is to provide us with vantage points from which to view the world, but they have not provided testable propositions, certainly not in the sense of the contemporary social sciences.

After reviewing the strengths and weaknesses of the Parsonian vision, there are still a number of dilemmas. These arise in a comparison of this vision with its

---

[66] One of many such critiques is José F. Ocampo and Dale L. Johnson, "The Concept of Political Development," in *Dependence and Underdevelopment: Latin America's Political Economy,* ed. James D. Cockcroft, André Gunder Frank, and Dale L. Johnson (Garden City, N.Y.: Doubleday and Company, 1972), pp. 399-424.

[67] Ralf Dahrendorf, *Class and Class Conflict in Industrial Society* (Stanford, Calif.: Stanford University Press, 1959).

[68] Max Black, "Some Questions About Parsons's Theories," in *The Social Theories of Talcott Parsons,* ed. Max Black (Englewood Cliffs, N.J.: Prentice-Hall, Inc., 1961), pp. 268-88.

major alternative, that of Marx. A confrontation between the two leaves a number of questions that cannot be resolved by a body of evidence, indeed, this is perhaps the mark of a vision rather than of a scientific theory. The easiest way to highlight this dilemma is to observe that while Marx and Parsons agree on the significance of normative ideas in social life, they reverse the priority assigned them. Parsons accords major emphasis to these elements and believes that religious ideas and cultural systems, among others, are the controlling mechanisms in the social world:

> The longer the time perspective, and the broader the system involved, the greater is the *relative* importance of higher, rather than lower, factors in the control hierarchy. . . . This level is cultural rather than social and, within the cultural category, religious rather than secular. Within the social category, values and norms, especially legal norms, stand higher than political and economic interests.[69]

Marx's vision is an alternative point of view; such elements merely represent ideology and are, therefore, only a reflection of the major forces of society that lie in the economy. This issue is such, however, that there is as much evidence to support Parsons as Marx. In the final analysis it comes down to a matter of faith not of science and to a fundamental dilemma—whether we believe that ideas are so powerful as to shape material realities, or whether we believe that material conditions constrain the contents of our ideas.

[69] Parsons, *Societies: Evolutionary and Comparative Perspectives,* pp. 113-14.

CHAPTER FIVE
Basic Forms of Political Rule: Democracy and Oligarchy in the Modern World

If there were a people of gods, it would govern itself democratically. Such a perfect government is not suited to men.

JEAN JACQUES ROUSSEAU, *The Social Contract*

So a prince need not have all the . . . good qualities, but it is most essential that he appear to have them. Indeed, I should go so far as to say that having them and always practising them is harmful, while seeming to have them is useful. It is good to appear clement, trustworthy, humane, religious and honest, and also to be so, but always with the mind so disposed that, when the occasion arises not to be so, you can become the opposite. It must be understood that a prince and particularly a new prince cannot practice all the virtues for which men are accounted good, for the necessity of preserving the state often compels him to take actions which are opposed to loyalty, charity, humanity, and religion. Hence he must have a spirit ready to adapt itself as the varying winds of fortune command him. As I have said, so far as he is able a prince should stick to the path of good, but, if the necessity arises, he should know how to follow evil.

NICCOLO MACHIAVELLI, *The Prince*

Our current thinking about the nature of politics has been shaped as much by the writings of ancient Greek philosophy as by those of any other civilization or time. We are indebted to the Greeks, particularly Plato and Aristotle, for helping us to conceive the setting of politics and of the rules that regulate it—in their words, the *polis* and the laws. Politics today is still thought to be how those people who are the members of a given community or society act, and should act, as members of its body politic. Politics continues to provoke the questions first raised and probed by the ancient Greeks: the questions of the rights of people to become involved in the body politic; of the beliefs people possess about their ability to act effectively in the body politic; of the willingness of those who occupy center stage—the aristocrats, the oligarchs, or whoever—to permit the great majority of people to enter into the deliberations that go on in the body politic.

This chapter considers some of the basic features of the political arena in modern societies as well as some of the variations that exist from one arena to another. Among other things, the discussion deals with the character of modern democratic societies—societies that are focused on throughout this book. It is most appropriate that the discussion depart from ancient roots, and thus, it begins with a review of the classical Greek conception of the *polis*.

BASIC TYPES OF POLITICAL RULE: THE CLASSICAL GREEK CONCEPTIONS

Aristotle's conception of the Greek body politic, the *polis*, rested on two features: the qualities of its residents and the nature of its rules.[1] First, the *polis* was made up only of the body of citizens in a city-state; citizens were those who were governed and who could exercise the privilege of governance. Lower classes, including mechanics, artisans, and the large number of slaves, were not included among the people who qualified as citizens and hence as members of the *polis*. Second, the rules of the *polis* consisted of the laws and traditions of the Greek city-state; the laws were for Aristotle the most sovereign feature of the city-state. The governance of the citizens of the *polis* meant the "rightly constituted laws . . . and personal rule, whether it be exercised by a single person or a body of persons, should be sovereign only in those matters on which law is unable, owing to the difficulty of framing general rules for all contingencies, to make an exact pronouncement."[2]

There were, Aristotle further thought, two broad sets of political arenas: those in which men achieved all the prime moral virtues—wisdom, goodness, beauty, justice—and those in which men lived in more debased, if not more "real," circumstances.[3] Within each of these two sets were three subsets of *polis*: the moral set

---

[1] Aristotle, *The Politics of Aristotle*, trans. Ernest Barker (London: Oxford University Press, 1975), III, IV, and V.

[2] Aristotle, *Politics*, p. 127.

[3] The reader must remember that Aristotle, like other Greek philosophers, did not make a distinction between idealized visions constructed for the purposes of realizing a certain moral aim and idealized visions constructed to achieve certain analytical goals. In other words, Aristotle drew a distinction only between the ideal and the real, whereas today we distinguish between the ideal in moral terms, the ideal in analytical terms—for example, Weber's notion of the Protestant Ethic and Marx's notion of capitalism—and the real. Thus, when Aristotle wrote of the ideal set of constitutional orders, he wrote of a moral vision; when he described the debased set, he spoke both of an unjust and a more realistic portrait of the character. This may explain why Aristotle spent so much more of his effort in *Politics* writing of the nonideal polities; he simply meant to concede that they represented those forms more likely to achieve realization in ancient Greece.

contained kingship, aristocracy, and polity; the other comprised tyranny, oligarchy, and democracy. Each of the three also possessed its counterpart in the other set. Thus, kingship had tyranny as its counterpart; aristocracy had oligarchy as its counterpart; and polity possessed democracy as its counterpart. The chief element that the three pairs held in common was the number of rulers in the *polis*; in kingship and tyranny there was only a single ruler, in aristocracy and oligarchy there existed several rulers, and in polity and democracy the large majority of citizens were their own rulers. There were other differences among the several forms, but Aristotle reserved most of his attention for democracy, oligarchy, and polity.

Oligarchy was thought to represent the perversion of the aristocratic form of rule. Aristotle believed that under the rule of oligarchy those individuals who held property, a minority of the population, limited the exercise of governance to themselves and ruled in ways that would advance their own interests exclusively. Democracy represented the perversion of rule in polity—a *polis* in which the large majority of people had become sovereign but in so doing violated the rights of the minority, the property holders. Each of the two forms violated the sense of justice that should prevail in the ideal community. Instead of adhering to the principle of distributive justice—the contribution of an individual to a society's well-being is rewarded in an amount commensurate to his contribution—democracy and oligarchy rewarded citizens on the basis of special qualities having nothing to do with their contributions to the vitality of the community. Hence, a democracy held all citizens to be equal although not all of them contributed equally to the well-being of the *polis*; an oligarchy insisted that all citizens are unequal although such inequality existed only by virtue of their disproportionate property holdings, not by the degree of their contribution to the well-being of the *polis*.[4]

In contrast to Plato, Aristotle maintained that in principle a democracy could possess certain desirable traits. For one thing, he believed the people as a whole possessed a better combination of qualities of judgment and good sense than any small number of individuals. "Each of the [people]," he wrote, "may not be of a good . . . quality; but when they all come together it is possible that they may surpass—collectively and as a body, although not individually—the quality of the few best."[5] He further claimed that the governance of the *polis* by the people, or by their elected magistrates, could be justified on the grounds that the people represent the best judges of their own interests.

Polity and tyranny appeared to him as the best and the worst of political arenas. Although at first polity seemed to be only the virtuous counterpart of democracy, on further analysis it appeared as a mixed form of government, incorporating features of democracy and oligarchy. Citing the examples of Sparta, Aristotle claimed that polity ought to be construed by some observers as an oligarchy, by others as a democracy. He remarked:

[4] Aristotle, *Politics*, II, chapter 9.
[5] Ibid., p. 123.

There are many who would describe [Sparta] as a democracy, on the ground that its organization has a number of democratic features. In the first place, and so far as concerns the bringing up of the young, the children of the rich have the same fare as the children of the poor, and they are educated on a standard which the children of the poor can also attain. . . . No difference is made between the rich and the poor: the food at the common mess is the same for all, and the dress of the rich is such as any of the poor could also provide for themselves. . . . A second ground for describing Sparta as a democracy is the right of the people to elect to one of the two great institutions, the Senate, and to be eligible themselves for the other, the Ephorate. On the other hand there are some who describe the Spartan constitution as an oligarchy, on the ground that it has many oligarchical factors. For example, the magistrates are all appointed by vote, and none by lot; again, the power of inflicting the penalty of death or banishment rests in the hands of a few persons; and there are many other similar features. *A properly mixed "polity" should look as if it contained both democratic and oligarchical elements—and as if it contained neither* [my italics].[6]

Moreover, polity, if properly planned, corrected for the extremes of democracy, rule by the many, and of oligarchy, rule by the few, by basing its form of rule upon the majority, the middle class. Asserting his preference for moderation in all things, Aristotle argued that polity, by being based upon a large middle class, assisted in eliminating the conflicts and tensions evident in democracies and in oligarchies. Yet, he noted, the establishment of polities was unlikely, for in most Greek city-states the middle class was very small and disputes inevitably arose between the very rich and the very poor. Tyranny, in contrast to polity, represented the very worst sort of government. It was a base type of rule because it benefitted the smallest possible number of citizens in a *polis*. Also it represented a form of government in which the rule of the person replaced the rule of law; lawlessness for Aristotle was the most perverse form of governance.

To complete this brief portrait of the Greek view of politics, it is important that we remind ourselves that in actual practice the constitutional orders of ancient Greece comprised many different features, including magistrates, councils, and sometimes, assemblies of the entire body politic. Still, the differences between democracy and oligarchy pervaded the entire *polis*. Leonard Whibley, a close student of the Aristotelian conceptions of the *polis* and of the actual practices of the ancient Greek constitutional orders, summarily observed some of these differences between the two types of *polis:*

In the fully developed democracy the people wanted to exercise their powers directly, they were jealous of all institutions in the state other than the assembly, and both council and magistrates were rendered in every way subordinate agents of the popular power. The duties of government were divided amongst a great number of magistrates whose authority was restricted as far as possible: the lot secured that ordinary men would be chosen

---

[6]Ibid., p. 178.

Would have been better to introduce Greek concepts of justice and reason.

(so that it was impossible to leave much to their discretion): their tenure was short, reelection was usually forbidden, offices were intended to rotate and all who exercised the smallest authority did so with a full responsibility to the governing body.

In the oligarchies almost every one of these conditions is reversed. The functions of government were not so thoroughly divided, the magistrates had larger independent powers, they were appointed by and from a small privileged body, the same men might be reelected.[7]

In sum, the basic principles that Aristotle revealed through his analysis of the nature of democracies and oligarchies—in particular, the size of the ruling group, their social foundations in property, and the interests on behalf of which their leaders ruled—were in practice found to be operating down to the very smallest details in the Greek city-states.

How useful are these conceptions to the analysis of contemporary political orders? Can we transport them across 2,500 years of time and use them to illuminate the features of current political realities? They are useful in isolating some of the basic outlines of the political order and some of the fundamental differences that exist among such orders. But there are at least two reasons why they cannot be transplanted unchanged from Aristotle and the Greek world to the contemporary world. First, the Aristotelian conceptions are useful primarily for the study of social groups no larger than the common city-states of ancient Greece—communities typically numbering in the tens of thousands. Many twentieth-century nations number in the tens, if not hundreds, of millions of people; simply by virtue of the difference in magnitude of population there is a less than perfect fit between the Aristotelian notions and contemporary circumstances.[8] Second, the revolution in industry and technology that in the eighteenth and nineteenth centuries helped to lay the economic foundations for the modern world brought about a number of changes of great political consequence—changes in our conception of citizenship, changes in our sense of the legitimate boundaries between public concerns and private interests, and transformations in the technical means that rulers may employ in cultivating the obedience of those whom they rule. One simple reflection of this feature of the modern world is that both Marx and Weber wrote of bourgeois or capitalist democracies, not simply democracies, suggesting that to them this form represented something unique. Thus, it is unwise to apply the Aristotelian conceptions to social and economic circumstances that are so very different from those of 2,500 years ago. The classical Greek conceptions, therefore, are broad guidelines on the nature of the body politic. More recent reflections and writings are more useful for the most significant features of current political orders.

[7]Leonard Whibley, *Greek Oligarchies: Their Character and Organization* (New York: G. P. Putnam's Sons, 1896), p. 144.

[8]For interesting observations on the matter of size and the character of the body politic, see Robert A. Dahl and Edward R. Tufte, *Size and Democracy* (Stanford: Stanford University Press, 1973).

TYPES OF POLITICAL RULE
IN THE MODERN WORLD

In the twentieth century, there are two pure species of political rule and many intermediate forms, or subspecies. First, there is modern democracy, a form that retains the ancient name because it shares certain features with the Greek *polis* of the same description—for instance, an emphasis upon widespread and voluntary citizen involvement in public life. Second, there is a new form, one that has elements of the ancient tyranny to which Aristotle referred but that also has a number of unique features; this is totalitarianism, represented in its purest respects in the Soviet Union and in Germany under the rule of Adolf Hitler. Other varieties are discussed, or at least attention is drawn to some of their more prominent features.

Democracy: The Utopian Vision and the Empirical Reality

"Utopian" is a loaded term; why not "normative"? traditional?

There are two different sets of ideas about modern democracy. The first, similar to that of the ancient Greeks, envisions the shape of democratic rule in utopian terms and thus seeks after the very best and the most just form of political rule under which citizens may live. In somewhat different fashion, this vision of a democratic society was shaped by political philosophers such as Jean Jacques Rousseau, John Locke, Montesquieu, and John Stuart Mill in the eighteenth and nineteenth centuries, and assisted by the writings of John Dewey and Robert MacIver, among others, in the twentieth century.[9]

At heart, the utopian vision of a democratic society claims that individuals are the best judges of their own interests. Eschewing a society sustained by a small number of rulers, a group of oligarchs in other words, this vision insists that individuals can exercise the faculties of sound judgment and wisdom required to maintain the well-being of the body politic. The authors of these ideas, moreover, believe that the political capacities of individuals, their skills as well as their actual comprehension of the mechanics of politics, are capable of improvement through self-governance. Even those individuals without sound judgment on politics benefit from engagement in the institutions and processes of the political arena. These premises suggest to some of the authors of the utopian vision that all persons should be permitted an equal opportunity to participate in politics, and to secure protection from political institutions. "The very fact of natural and psychological inequality," Dewey wrote, "is all the more reason for establishment by law of equality of opportunity, since otherwise the former becomes a means of oppression of the less gifted."[10]

[9]For writings that illustrate these themes, see Jean Jacques Rousseau, "The Social Contract," in *The Essential Rousseau*, trans. Lowell Bair (New York: New American Library, 1974), pp. 1-124, and John Stuart Mill, "On Liberty" and "Representative Government," in *Utilitarianism, Liberty, and Representative Government*, John Stuart Mill (New York: E. P. Dutton and Co., 1951), pp. 81-229, 231-532.

[10]John Dewey, "Democracy as a Way of Life," in *Frontiers of Democratic Theory*, ed. Henry Kariel (New York: Random House, Inc., 1970), p. 15.

Last, the utopian vision of a democratic society insists that the very involvement of individuals in the process of self-governance is a desirable goal in and of itself. Writing of the American experiment in democracy begun at the end of the eighteenth century, Hannah Arendt observed that the fundamental assumption underlying popular political participation "was that no one could be called happy without his share in public happiness, that no one could be called free without his experience in public freedom, and that no one could be called either happy or free without participating, and having a share, in public power."[11]

There is a second body of thought that considers the substance of modern democratic societies; it seeks the creation of a theory of democracy inductively, based upon the study of current political realities. It is this stream of scholarship that furnishes many of the ideas and facts for the discussion in this book; this theory, for instance, in one way or another incorporates views described in the chapters on power in the United States, power in communities, and citizen participation in politics. The general set of notions embodied in this empirical view of democracy are found in some of the writings of Bernard Berelson, Robert A. Dahl, Giovanni Sartori, and Joseph Schumpeter, among many others.[12]

At its root the empirical conception of democracy shifts attention from the qualities of individual citizens and their fundamental rights of self-government to the rulers and the public competition that has brought them into office. In particular, this conception lays claim to the premise that modern democracy consists of institutions that furnish contenders for public office; typically, if not invariably, these institutions are political parties. The empirical theory holds, moreover, that there usually exist rival claimants for the opportunity to occupy the highest public offices. It incorporates the notion of citizen into its purview by asserting that

[11] Hannah Arendt, "On Public Happiness," in *The Frontiers of Democratic Theory*, ed. Kariel, p. 5.

This very short condensation of the utopian vision, in addition to having been based upon the writings of Rousseau and Mill, was aided in its formulation by several important secondary analyses of these matters. In particular, the reader is urged to examine the following excellent studies: Graeme Duncan and Steven Lukes, "The New Democracy," *Political Studies*, II (1963), 156-77; Lane Davis, "The Cost of Realism: Contemporary Restatements of Democracy," *Western Political Quarterly*, 17 (1964), 37-46; Kariel, *Frontiers of Democratic Theory*; Carole Pateman, *Participation and Democratic Theory* (Cambridge: Cambridge University Press, 1970), chapter 2 especially; and Dennis F. Thompson, *The Democratic Citizen* (Cambridge: Cambridge University Press, 1970). Although each one of these works is good, the book by Thompson is particularly outstanding; his two concepts of individual autonomy and improvability helped to furnish much of the intellectual groundwork for the summary here. One reference on the moral vision of democracy that is wise to avoid is found in Joseph Schumpeter, *Capitalism, Socialism and Democracy*, 3rd ed. (New York: Harper & Row, Publishers, 1962), chapter 21.

[12] Bernard Berelson, "Democratic Practice and Democratic Theory," in *Voting*, ed. Bernard Berelson, Paul Lazarsfeld, and William McPhee. (Chicago: University of Chicago Press, 1954), pp. 305-23; Robert A. Dahl, *Who Governs? Democracy and Power in an American City* (New Haven, Conn.: Yale University Press, 1961); Robert A. Dahl, *Polyarchy: Participation and Opposition* (New Haven, Conn.: Yale University Press, 1971), chapter 1; Giovanni Sartori, *Democratic Theory* (New York: Frederick A. Praeger, 1965); and Schumpeter, *Capitalism, Socialism, and Democracy*, 3rd ed., chapter 13.

citizens have the right to select among the rival sets of leaders those who they believe best represent their interests. A now classic quotation from Joseph Schumpeter succinctly serves to portray these features of the empirical theory by asserting that the democratic method is "that institutional arrangement for arriving at political decisions in which individuals acquire the power to decide by means of a competitive struggle for the people's vote."[13]

Having transferred the emphasis from citizens to leaders in democratic societies, the empirical theory further reduces the necessary role of citizens in their own self-governance. It asserts that in order for a society to lay claim to the label "democratic," its leaders merely need to be responsive to the wishes of the majority of citizens. This is accomplished in two ways: first, through the medium of elections—if the candidates for public office fail to respond to the wishes of a majority of citizens, the candidates would fail to be elected; and second, through the development of policies in office that are supposed to anticipate the wishes of the citizens. In other words, it is not necessary for citizens to engage *actively* in the process of politics. In fact, the widespread active and continuous engagement of the citizenry in the body politic constitutes for some empirical theorists a greater danger than benefit to a democracy—a claim that echoes Alexis de Tocqueville's fear of the "tyranny of the majority."[14] Berelson, for example, makes the following observation:

> How would a mass democracy work if all the people were deeply involved in politics? Lack of interest by some people is not without its benefits, too. True, the highly interested voters vote more, and know more about the campaign, and read and listen more, and participate more; however, they are also less open to persuasion and less likely to change [*sic*]. Extreme interest goes with extreme fanaticism that could destroy democratic processes if generalized throughout the community . . . [whereas low] interest provides maneuvering room for political shifts necessary for a complex society in a period of rapid change.[15]

Thus, the empirical conception virtually transforms the root meaning of democracy —whether defined in Aristotelian terms as rule by many citizens or in those of the modern political philosophers. Democracy is no longer a body politic in which the engagement of citizens exists as its *sine qua non*, but one in which active involvement may be unnecessary, even undesirable.

Since these two perspectives, the utopian vision and the empirical theory, exist as countervailing views of the nature of modern democratic societies, it is important that the reader carefully scrutinize and compare them to search for similarities as well as advantages and disadvantages of each. The utopian vision is founded upon both ancient and modern ideals, and represents a set of prescriptive

[13] Schumpeter, *Capitalism, Socialism, and Democracy*, 3rd ed., p. 269.

[14] Alexis de Tocqueville, *Democracy in America*, trans. Henry Reeve (New York: Random House, 1945), I, pp. 269-72.

[15] Berelson et al., *Voting*, pp. 318-19.

statements about the conditions necessary for the well-being of a democratic society. The empirical theory, on the other hand, is grounded in a set of facts uncovered in societies conventionally thought to be democratic, and constitutes a set of descriptive statements about the actual conditions of governments. One obvious danger in the facile adoption of the utopian vision is that one might fail to understand the actual workings of a democracy by not attending to their realities.[16] The dangers of an easy acceptance of the empirical theory might prove more harmful, however. First, the empirical view too readily accepts the conventional definition of societies as "democratic," and this definition is sometimes more myth than reality.[17] After a review of many facts, it is possible to draw the conclusion that the United States more nearly resembles an oligarchy than a democracy (see chapter 6).[18] Second, adoption of the empirical theory can lead to an ideological justification of existing political forms. Berelson's previously cited observations, for instance, are couched within a broader analysis that implies not only that democracy *actually* performs in a certain manner but that it also *should* perform in this fashion. Last, by abandoning a commitment to the utopian ideal of widespread citizen participation in the body politic, the empirical view dismisses, perhaps unwittingly, a rich heritage of political thought and tradition; more importantly, it relinquishes a position it could serve in the modern world of revealing how modern democratic societies could be refashioned in ways to approximate more closely the ancient ideal of a democratic society.

Regardless of this dispute—a dispute to remain unresolved—a few of the more salient details of modern democratic societies may be sketched. These introduce the nature of these societies as well as provide a benchmark for a comparison with totalitarian orders.

1) Constitutional and Procedural Foundations. Democratic societies invariably are based upon a tradition of law with an emphasis upon broad civil rights for the citizens, including, among others, the right of dissent. There is a separation of functions among the various branches of government, producing three separate organs, an executive, a legislative, and a judicial branch; the actual functions of each of these varies from one democratic society to another. The process of governance is carried out through a system of representatives; the institution in which the representatives serve is variously called the parliament or the congress. Suffrage is widespread, and elections occur frequently. The occupants of the executive branch are elected either directly, as in the presidential democracy in the United States, or indirectly, as in the parliamentary democracy in Great Britain.

---

[16] However, see Thompson, *The Democratic Citizen*, for an excellent method of incorporating current empirical findings into the corpus of the utopian vision of democracy.

[17] Robert Dahl overcomes this difficulty by an ingenious ploy, the reconceptualization of the forms of the state. Thus, for example, conventional democratic societies become polyarchies, while conventional totalitarian societies become hegemonies. See Dahl, *Polyarchy: Participation and Opposition.*

[18] For similar observations on the character of political rule in the United States, see, for example, Thomas R. Dye and L. Harmon Zeigler, *The Irony of Democracy*, 2nd ed. (Belmont, Calif.: Wadsworth Publishing Company, 1972).

In the twentieth century these constitutional and procedural foundations have been supplemented through the continued or new growth of a large bureaucratic apparatus. The scope of the operations of this bureaucracy, initially designed to aid and to protect the constitutional rights of the citizenry, have begun to encroach seriously upon these rights in places such as the United States.

2) Ideological Foundations. [19]   Modern democracies are founded upon beliefs in equality of individual citizens, in widespread public liberties, and in the desirability of citizen involvement in politics.

3) Social Foundations.   Fundamental to the social foundations of modern democratic societies is a widespread plurality of groups and diversity of interests. A large number of voluntary organizations have been developed for citizen membership and involvement and serve as an infrastructure or a buffer zone between the lives of individual citizens and the political control exercised by the rulers. Chief among these many groups are political parties and factions within a single party that serve, among other things, as means for organizing and expressing citizen concerns and for attaining the constitutional right to exercise power.

4) Economic Foundations.   Modern democratic societies, Great Britain and the United States in particular, developed concomitantly with the growth of capitalist institutions. Thus, their fate is inextricably linked to the fate of these institutions. General conditions of affluence seem to have been most favorable to the growth of democratic governments, as in the United States, and the governments themselves have acted in important respects to further the conditions of affluence. However, even in settings of pervasive poverty, as in India, modified forms of democracy exist or have existed. In the twentieth century especially, the institutions of the state have increasingly assumed widespread welfare responsibilities for the citizenry; the extent of such responsibilities varies from extensive, as in Sweden, to only moderate, as in the United States.

This description of the principal features of modern democratic societies should provide at least a general impression of them; details of their composition are etched more sharply in later chapters. In addition, this capsule portrait helps to distinguish between democratic and nondemocratic societies in the modern world.[20]

---

[19] Ideology here as well as in the following discussion of totalitarian regimes does not refer to the Marxian concept of ideology, but rather to the all-embracing symbolic, or cultural, foundations of a regime. Later in this book, in chapter 10, we shall go into considerably more detail on the nature of beliefs, or thought, and politics. At that point we shall invent a frame of reference that embraces both the notion of symbols, or culture, in the Parsonian sense, and the notion of ideology in the Marxist one. For the time being, let us assume that the ideological foundations are accepted as true and natural by the members of those regimes or, in Weber's sense, as legitimate.

[20] This capsule portrait of democratic societies is based upon a large number and wide variety of documents—too many, in fact, to be able to cite here easily. Some of the broader treatments that figured into this presentation include Robert A. Dahl, ed., *Political Oppositions in Western Democracies* (New Haven, Conn.: Yale University Press, 1966); Robert A. Dahl, *Polyarchy: Participation and Opposition*; Leon D. Epstein, *Political Parties in Western Democracies* (New York: Frederick A. Praeger, Publishers, 1967), chapters 1-4; and Edward Shils, *Political Development in the New States* (The Hague: Mouton, 1962).

Totalitarianism

The idea of totalitarianism, or totalitarian dictatorship, is meant to convey the absolute domination of a nation and its people by a single political party as well as by those who control the party. Totalitarian rule seeks to obliterate the social ties and groups typical of democratic societies, for instance the ties of the nuclear family, and to substitute for them new forms of social ties that are intended to absorb the individual completely as a member of the society. Between the party and its leaders, no groups or individuals are permitted to intervene and to replace the party as the single object of the individual's loyalty and commitment.[21] The concept has been used primarily to describe two different historical regimes in the twentieth century, those of the Soviet Union, especially under the rule of Joseph Stalin, and Nazi Germany. The combination of these two historical forms under a single rubric overshadows certain differences between them, in particular the distinction between the nature of communism and of Nazism. For many purposes this does not seem to create too much distortion, though some observers regard the dissimilarities between the two as more substantial than their common features.[22]

Carl J. Friedrich and Zbigniew K. Brzezinski, two scholars who have contributed greatly to our understanding of totalitarian societies, claim that such societies can be singled out for six distinctive qualities: (1) an elaborate ideology that covers each and every phase of an individual's life; (2) a single political party that typically is led by one individual, the "dictator"; (3) a widespread system of terror, channeled both through state and party institutions and directed alike against external and internal enemies of the regime; (4) a virtually complete control of the apparatus of mass communication that is unique because of its technological sophistication and complexity; (5) a monopoly over the weaponry and men associated with the armed forces; and (6) the direction of the entire economy, or at least its most significant sectors, by the state bureaucracy.[23] Alone, however, these six characteristics of totalitarian societies do not sufficiently convey the true nature of such regimes. Thus, as a counterpart of the capsule analysis of modern democratic societies, the features of totalitarian ones are briefly elaborated. Nazi Germany is discussed in particular, but many of the very same features describe equally as well the general characteristics of the Soviet Union.

[21] For somewhat different definitions of this concept, compare the following works: Hannah Arendt, *The Origins of Totalitarianism* (Cleveland, Ohio: World Publishing Co., 1958); Benjamin R. Barber, "Conceptual Foundations of Totalitarianism," in *Totalitarianism in Perspective: Three Views*, ed. Carl J. Friedrich, Michael Curtis, and Benjamin R. Barber (New York: Praeger Publishers, 1969), pp. 3-39; and Carl J. Friedrich and Zbigniew K. Brzezinski, *Totalitarian Dictatorship and Autocracy*, 2nd ed. rev. by Carl J. Friedrich (Cambridge, Mass.: Harvard University Press, 1965), chapter 1 especially.

[22] For one intelligent observer who does find the difference to be highly significant, see Barrington Moore, Jr., *Social Origins of Dictatorship and Democracy: Lord and Peasant in the Making of the Modern World* (Boston: Beacon Press, 1967), chapters 7-9 especially.

[23] Carl J. Friedrich and Zbigniew K. Brzezinski, *Totalitarian Dictatorship and Autocracy*, chapter 2.

¹⁾ Constitutional and Procedural Foundations.   One of the principal features of Germany under the reign of Adolf Hitler and the National Socialist Party was the absence of constitutional and legal foundations; the only procedural foundations were those established through the auspices of the party. To all outward appearances, however, Nazi Germany seemed to constitute an extension of the government inaugurated as the Weimar Republic in 1918. Actually the National Socialist Party committed a legal revolution, overturning the Weimar's Constitution by employing that Constitution's very own provisions. Among the means used to achieve this end were a series of decrees and enabling acts passed in 1933 and 1934 that placed all power in the hands of Hitler as Chancellor and, later, President of Germany. In addition, the regime represented a virtual morass of offices and rules; Hitler fashioned a regime in which the National Socialist Party and the state bureaucracy seemed to share equal power—though the party and Hitler ultimately were dominant—and in which for each office in the state bureaucracy there existed a parallel and competing one in the National Socialist Party. From Hitler's point of view, of course, the result of this morass was to create rule through *divide et impera*; the competition among occupants of parallel offices secured the effectiveness of his own leadership. Apart from Hitler, only key members of his immediate coterie—Martin Bormann, Joseph Goebbels, and Heinrich Himmler mainly—were able to exercise reasonably free and unrestrained rule; yet even they were not entirely free, for they remained in positions of unquestioning obedience to the commands of Hitler. During the early years of the Third Reich, there was also a facade of apparently democratic procedures that were consistent with the provisions of the Weimar Constitution. Thus, for example, there were several nationwide elections, but despite the large turnout of voters and the overwhelming support for the National Socialist Party, these elections were thoroughly manipulated by Hitler and his staff through their exclusive command of the radio and most newspapers, and their ability to assemble at a moment's notice large rallies of supporters.

An important part of the Nazi regime in Germany were the organs of the party and the state that were designed to combat the internal enemies; these agencies included the Gestapo, or secret police, and the S.S. troops under the authority of Heinrich Himmler. Both agencies were employed as means for combatting dissent and for eliminating the enemies of the state, particularly Jews. The S.S. troops, in particular, assumed responsibility for the administration of the death camps.

Ideological Foundations.   One of the most visible and unique features of Hitler's totalitarian dictatorship was its ideology, an assortment of myths that were transplanted, in toto, from the declarations Hitler had earlier set out in his autobiography, *Mein Kampf.* Hitler and the National Socialists dispensed a doctrine of racial and national dogma that established the myth of the Aryan race as world saviors and made Jews appear as the scum of the earth; moreover, they sought and gained widespread popular acceptance of this doctrine. After 1938 these principles became transformed into actual practices of the Nazi regime, first through random terror committed against Jews inside Germany—as, for example, during *Kristall-nacht*—and later through the terror organized under the auspices of the concentration camps and the wartime hostilities undertaken against many nations.

Not exactly; rather merely atomize populace they seek control of all secondary groups latter needed to facilitate mobilization

Social Foundations.   In their effort to secure total commitment and obedience from the people, totalitarian regimes literally seek to declassify citizens. Upon their accession to the positions of leadership in the German government, for example, the National Socialist Party leaders, through their practices of terror, tried to eliminate the many diverse social groups that existed during the Weimar Republic. Trade unions, for one, were eliminated and replaced by the Labor Front, which simply became an organized means for the National Socialist Party to manipulate the interests and lives of the workers. Except in a few instances, independent news media were either destroyed or taken over by the party. The churches remained more or less institutionally intact, but priests became the object of intense and unremitting attacks by members of the Nazi regime. In place of older organizations, new ones arose under the management of the National Socialist Party; thus, for instance, Nazi youth groups designed to socialize young Germans in the new, official system of thought were developed in large numbers. Symbolic of this gigantic program to design German society anew were the mass rallies that took place in the early years of the Third Reich; in those that occurred in Nuremberg, for example, thousands of people were arrayed across the floor of the arena—attentive, obedient, and absolutely mesmerized by Hitler.

Economic Foundations.   Many analysts characterize the totalitarian economy as a command economy, noting such particulars about its structure as the regular plans for its expansion—five-year programs in the Soviet Union, four-year plans in Nazi Germany—the regimentation of the labor force, the special organization of the industrial plants, and the centralized form of planning concerning the budget and industrial output. These characteristics, like others, have matured more fully in the Soviet Union than they did in Nazi Germany; moreover, it is difficult to know precisely how the German economy might have performed under extended peacetime circumstances, since Germany went to war in 1939, only six years after the inception of Nazi rule. During its brief existence, however, the German economy actually comprised two different sectors: one, the command sector that was controlled through the National Socialist Party and state administrations; two, the large private sector that comprised many cartels in manufacturing and other forms of industry.[24]

[24] This very brief portrait of the totalitarian society, with special attention to the Third Reich, is based upon the following sources: Hannah Arendt, *The Origins of Totalitarianism,* part 3 especially; Lucy S. Dawidowicz, *The War against the Jews: 1933-1945* (New York: Holt, Rinehart and Winston, 1975), part 1; Joachim C. Fest, *Hitler,* trans. Richard and Clara Winston (New York: Avon Books, 1971), parts 5-8 especially; Carl J. Friedrich and Zbigniew K. Brzezinski, *Totalitarian Dictatorship and Autocracy;* Adolf Hitler, *Mein Kampf,* trans. Ralph Manheim

Paper comparing model to reality, even on just one of Orum's foundations — social, e.g. (using s

This brief description naturally cannot do full justice to the range and the depth of the features of totalitarian societies; hence, the reader is urged to consult other materials on Nazi Germany as well as to consult discussions in later chapters of such nations as the Soviet Union. Nonetheless, the overview here helps to introduce two of the most prominent features of totalitarian regimes—the complete and total absorption of the individual into society, thus leaving the distinction between the public and private realms absolutely meaningless, and the genuine dominance of the party, its leaders and ideology, over all other institutions of the society. This last point, in particular, seems to render Marxist interpretations of Nazi Germany fundamentally incorrect; Hitler's dictatorship effectively supplanted all of the conventional features and processes of a capitalist economy with an administration less driven by economic doctrines than by national and racial dogma. These latter doctrines represented the motive force behind the establishment and short-lived reign of the Third Reich.

As one final caveat to the analysis here of totalitarian regimes, it is imperative that the reader—particularly he or she who is new to these materials—recognize the very transitory and somewhat controversial features associated with the concept of totalitarianism. As a result of events in the Soviet Union since the death of Joseph Stalin in 1953 and of developments in such Communist nations as Yugoslavia, scholars are increasingly coming to realize that the concept of totalitarianism incorporates some elements no longer pertinent to nondemocratic regimes. First, neither extensive terror nor a single leader is universally characteristic of totalitarian regimes in the 1980s, though that is not to say that such elements may not reappear in the future.[25] Second the image of power as limited and concentrated in the hands of a very few members of the party also appears to some observers as a distorted view of the nature of totalitarian regimes by deflecting attention away from the origins and bases of conflict in such regimes.[26] Third, the notion of totalitarianism, like that of democracy, has become something of a special symbol employed in the ideological struggles of the cold war and has been tinged to no small degree with highly emotional overtones.[27] For all these reasons, then, the

(Boston: Houghton Mifflin Company, 1971), vol. 1, chapter 11 especially; Helmut Krausnick et al., *Anatomy of the SS State*, trans. Richard Barry et al. (Collins: London, 1968), especially chapters 2-3; Franz Neumann, *Behemoth* (New York: Oxford University Press, 1942); and Albert Speer, *Inside the Third Reich*, trans. Richard and Clara Winston (New York: Avon Books, 1971), parts 2-3 especially.

[25] For a discussion of the transformation of the role of terror in communist regimes, see Alexander Dallin and George W. Breslauer, *Political Terror in Communist Systems* (Stanford, Calif.: Stanford University Press, 1970), chapters 7-8 particularly.

[26] On the renewed interest in the various forms of conflict in communist regimes, see the excellent set of readings in Lenard J. Cohen and Jane P. Shapiro, eds., *Communist Systems in Comparative Perspective* (Garden City, N.Y.: Anchor, 1974), especially the articles by Roman Kolkowicz, Michel Oksenberg, and Andrzej Korbonski. Fairly early recognition by scholars of these forms of conflict, at least in reasonably mature communist systems, is evident in Zbigniew Brzezinski and Samuel P. Huntington, *Political Power: USA/USSR* (New York: The Viking Press, 1965), chapters 5-8 especially.

[27] See, in particular, Michael Curtis, "Retreat from Totalitarianism," in *Totalitarianism in Perspective*, ed. Friedrich et al., pp. 53-121.

reader is urged to view the concept with healthy skepticism, using it as an analytical device that may well hide almost as much as it discloses.

THE VARIETIES BETWEEN DEMOCRACY
AND TOTALITARIANISM

If the conception of political rule in the modern world were restricted to the
purest forms of democracy and totalitarianism, very few actual societies would
qualify as pure democratic forms or pure totalitarian forms. There are many different such schemes to classify all of the other, indeed the great majority of, societies
that presently exist, and no one scheme proves satisfactory for all purposes. Robert
Dahl, for example, develops a conception of polyarchy—a conception that resembles pure democracy on such important criteria as existence of political opposition but differs in other ways—into a finely calibrated scale, thereby classifying
many societies on the extent to which they approximate polyarchy.[28] Those
societies more closely approximating democracy rank higher on the polyarchy
scale, whereas those more closely approximating totalitarian regimes rank lower
on the scale. Such a method is unsatisfactory, if for no reason other than it renders
qualitative differences invalid by fitting all societies into a quantitative continuum;
for many problems such a continuum is a valid tool, but on this matter it is not
entirely satisfactory. Juan Linz proceeds in a somewhat different manner and invents a new category of classification, the authoritarian regime, that is different
from a democratic society and a totalitarian one, and that claims the following as
its distinctive elements:

> . . . limited, not responsible, political pluralism—without elaborate and
> guiding ideology (but with distinctive mentalities); without intensive nor
> extensive political mobilization (except at some points in their development);
> and in which a leader (or occasionally a small group) exercises power within
> formally ill-defined limits but actually quite predictable ones.[29]

Despite the clear advantages of such a definition, it, too, becomes ambiguous.
In Linz's later work, he stretches the conception to incorporate an incredibly large
number of different societies and thus renders the category almost useless.[30] A
useful and appropriate scheme of classification should be simple and clear, adhere

[28] Robert A. Dahl, Richard Norling, and Mary Frase Williams, "Appendix A," in *Polyarchy: Participation and Opposition*, ed. Dahl, pp. 231-35.

[29] Juan J. Linz, "An Authoritarian Regime: Spain," in *Cleavages, Ideologies and Party
Systems: Contributions to Comparative Political Sociology*, ed. Erik Allardt and Yrjo Littunen
(Helsinki: The Academic Bookstore, 1964), p. 297.

[30] Compare Linz, "An Authoritarian Regime: Spain," in *Cleavages, Ideologies and Party
Systems*, ed. Allardt and Littunen, pp. 291-341, and Linz, "Totalitarian and Authoritarian
Regimes," in *Handbook of Political Science: Macropolitical Theory*, ed. Fred I. Greenstein
and Nelson W. Polsby (Reading, Mass.: Addison-Wesley Publishing Company, Inc., 1974), III,
pp. 264-357.

to the ancient classifications but supplement these categories with new ones that represent modern realities and be both analytically insightful and descriptively useful. One such classification scheme is provided by Edward Shils, who developed such a scheme years ago as a means of highlighting the alternative courses of development that might be pursued by countries of the Third World, the developing nations.[31]

Shils retains the elegant Greek distinction between democracy and oligarchy but supplements it with descriptive terms that help to identify various shades of democracy and oligarchy. The developing countries of the world, he argues, are caught in a dilemma. Their leaders often admire the liberalism of the West and hence seek to emulate the democratic forms of the United States and Great Britain; yet at the same time, they frequently feel more comfortable with the more tightly controlled and disciplined politics of the Soviet Union and thus seek to model themselves after such totalitarian regimes.[32] Between these two poles, they often strike a balance—between the parliamentarism of the West and the centralized authority of the Soviet Union and the People's Republic of China. There emerge in consequence three other sorts of rule. The first, Shils claims, is tutelary democracy; this retains the essential institutions of democratic societies, for example an independent judiciary, but it permits a greater concentration of power in the executive branch of government. The ruling group of such societies is more stable, more tightly controlled, and less subject to the influx of new elements than that of typical democratic societies. Moreover, public opinion is weaker than in pure democratic societies, and political opposition is permitted but carefully prevented from securing power through the use of clever strategies. A competent civil service is allowed to exist and to remain stable, and other institutions of pure democratic societies, such as widespread elementary education and mass communications, are also allowed to operate. Shils observes, however, that this intermediary form of political rule may be the most unstable because of the intense concentration of power among the top leaders; it is more likely to shift into a form of oligarchy rather than to make the transition to democracy.

A second intermediary form between pure democracy and pure totalitarian rule is the modernizing oligarchy, toward which tutelary democracy can shift. This form reduces the freedom of opposition that exists under tutelary democracy, fashioning an even more manipulative ruling group. There is no independent judiciary, and the role of the parliament is one of accommodation and ratification. The ruling group, moreover, controls all mechanisms of public opinion, and it cultivates an enthusiastic, obedient response from the public—both of which are necessary if it is to be successful in its effort to undertake large-scale industrial development. This portrait of a form of political rule seems to fit the circumstances of many contemporary African nations, and because of the wisdom and intelligence with which it was formulated, it also outlines the situation of many

---

[31] Edward Shils, *Political Development in the New States.*

[32] On this matter also see Samuel P. Huntington, *Political Order in Changing Societies* (New Haven, Conn.: Yale University Press, 1968), pp. 334-43.

currently industrialized nations of the world at an earlier point in their history, for instance, Germany under the Bismarck regime, particularly after 1870.

A last form of political rule identified by Shils is traditional oligarchy, which tends neither toward modern democratic nor modern totalitarian rule. This is the form that characterized many of the African countries at a point prior to their independence. The ruling group, Shils observes, makes little effort actually to develop the various attributes of the more heavily industrialized nations of the world and relies upon the various traditional forms of administration, for instance the tribal councils, to solve conflict with opposition groups. There are few, if any, of the institutions associated with the more fully industrialized countries of the world, including no form of systematic education. Moreover, local kinship groups and ethnic clans continue to exercise a considerable amount of power and to hinder the possibility of attaining a widespread sense of "nationhood." Saudi Arabia at the present time comes close to this type of political regime.

In summary, the use of Shils's categories of various forms of political rule along with the purer forms previously described provides a helpful battery of concepts with which to begin the analysis of the social and political realities of many modern nations. However, they represent only a beginning and must be supplemented with more intensive and thorough investigation of the features of the state and society in these nations.

COMPARING DEMOCRATIC
AND TOTALITARIAN RULE

There are several key similarities and differences between modern democratic and totalitarian regimes. First, both forms of political rule exhibit complex and widespread bureaucratic machinery that is particularly concentrated in the administration of government. This specific similarity has come to be emphasized increasingly in recent years, in particular by observers of the United States and the Soviet Union. They stress that the common factor of bureaucracy in both societies is so striking that it might even be preferable to abandon the emphasis on the distinctions between democratic and totalitarian forms of rule in favor of concentrating on the types of conflict and control likely to be produced in both societies as a result of bureaucratic administrations.[33] Second, both forms of government display a set of ideological beliefs, myths if you will, that proclaim

---

[33] For a treatment of this and other contemporary issues in the analysis of democratic and totalitarian regimes, see Jerry F. Hough, "The Soviet System: Petrification or Pluralism?" in *Communist Systems in Comparative Perspective*, ed. Cohen and Shapiro, pp. 449-86. Also see the introduction by Cohen and Shapiro in the same book; among other things, this includes a brief but excellent treatment of some of the criticisms of the concept of "totalitarianism" and some of the other analytical schemes that may be used to examine differences and similarities between the communist and noncommunist countries. An extensive recent examination of politics and a wide variety of other matters in the Soviet Union may also be found in Robert J. Osborn, *The Evolution of Soviet Politics* (Homewood, Ill.: The Dorsey Press, 1974).

freedom and equality for their citizens; indeed, the myth of equality, even to some degree that of freedom, is no more the unique possession of modern democracy than it is of modern totalitarian rule. Third, both types of society are similar insofar as they exhibit a common foundation in large-scale industrial enterprise, even though the control of the enterprise varies considerably between the two—one controlled by the party and the state, the other controlled chiefly by private bureaucracies and individuals.

Finally, there are present under both types of rule some very profound social and economic inequalities whose existence stands out for many observers as the chief similarity between democratic and totalitarian regimes. In the United States, the privileged groups originate chiefly in the industrial sector and the federal government. In Nazi Germany they resulted from wealth and advantage in the private economy as well as from special advantages given to the higher echelons of the National Socialist Party, including Hitler, members of his coterie, and the *Gauleitern*—National Socialist Party members who were responsible for the political administration of the districts set up by the Nazi regime. Similarly, in the Soviet Union individuals of special privilege and wealth have emerged as a result of the special role they have assumed on behalf of the fulfillment of the Communist Party's goals. Evidence of these disproportionate advantages in both sets of nations, incidentally, has led some observers to suggest that the United States and the Soviet Union are moving toward a common destiny, through a convergence in their broad social, economic, and political outlines.[34]

Any such claim overlooks some crucial differences between the two sets of countries; these differences become more evident in later chapters of this book. In particular, political dissent can emerge freely under democratic forms of rule, partly through the competitive political parties and through the large number of different interest groups. Totalitarian societies disallow spontaneous articulate opposition and replace it with organized and polemical forms of opposition that merely reflect the current thinking of party leaders.[35] In addition, totalitarian societies systematically attempt to isolate and single out dissenters; the control over personal freedom is so complete as to render such a concept virtually null and void. Democratic societies cannot escape criticism on these grounds; as is evident in recent years, such societies, in particular the United States, have begun to threaten the personal freedom of their citizens. Nevertheless, the forms as well as the extent of political control evident in the Soviet Union far surpass that found in the United States. It seems fair to conclude that there may exist as wide a gap between the utopian vision of democracy and the democratic reality of the twentieth century as there exists between this latter reality and its counterpart in modern totalitarian societies.

[34] For relevant data see, for example, Milovan Djilas, *The New Class* (New York: Frederick A. Praeger, 1957). A thoughtful discussion of the thesis of convergence also may be found in Brzezinski and Huntington, *Political Power: USA/USSR,* pp. 9-14, 419-36.

[35] On the different forms of opposition evident in the Soviet Union, see Brzezinski and Huntington, *Political Power: USA/USSR,* pp. 104-21.

CONCLUSION

The analysis of modern political regimes is very difficult and must be approached with considerable caution, particularly in view of the emotion with which the terms *democracy* and *totalitarianism* are charged. Moreover, as recent events in countries like the Soviet Union, the People's Republic of China, Cuba, Yugoslavia, and Poland show, there is likely to be as much variation in politics among regimes that all are identified as totalitarian as there is between the politics of such regimes and their democratic counterparts. At best these sorts of theoretical classifications can only provide an initial point of departure.

CHAPTER SIX
Patterns of Power and Influence under Contemporary Capitalism: The Case of the United States

I am of the opinion, on the whole, that the manufacturing aristocracy which is growing up under our eyes is one of the harshest that ever existed in the world; but at the same time it is one of the most confined and least dangerous. Nevertheless, the friends of democracy should keep their eyes anxiously fixed in this direction; for if ever a permanent inequality of conditions and aristocracy again penetrates into the world, it may be predicted that this is the gate by which they will enter.

ALEXIS DE TOCQUEVILLE, *Democracy in America*

The business of America is business.

CALVIN COOLIDGE

This conjunction of an immense military establishment and a large arms industry is now in the American experience. The total influence—economic, political, even spiritual—is felt in every city, every state house, every office of the Federal government. We recognize the imperative need for this development. Yet we must not fail to comprehend its grave implications. Our toil, resources, and livelihood are involved; so is the very structure of our society. In the councils of government, we must guard against the acquisition of unwarranted influence, whether sought or unsought, by the military-industrial complex. The potential for the disastrous rise of misplaced power exists and will persist. We must never let the weight of this combination endanger our liberties or democratic processes. We should take nothing for granted.

DWIGHT D. EISENHOWER

We have discovered in previous chapters some of the ways that social theorists attempt to uncover the nature of politics both in modern societies and in more primitive ones. Marx taught us that the forces that operate in modern societies are, at root, economic ones, and that if we wish to understand the nature of the modern polity, then we must understand the nature of the modern economy as well. Weber instructed us to look not simply at the nature of economic forces in modern society, but to look at the operations of large-scale organizations, bureaucracies, as well as at the organizations that work on behalf of special occupational groups, and at political parties. And Parsons directed our attention to the very complex character of modern societies, to the interdependence between the political and the other sectors, or subsystems, of these societies.

Now we shall turn from these very abstract theories to consider the nature of politics in the United States. Once we do that we, naturally, confront something of a problem, for we are faced with different points of view about the concrete circumstances of American politics, some of which come directly from the writings of Marx, Weber, and Parsons. Here, instead of forcing the rich facts of American politics into a tight and neat theoretical framework, based upon the writings of only one of the theorists, we shall instead use the insights of these theorists together with the facts as they present themselves in recent American political history, and identify some major tendencies of American politics. That is, we shall seek to steer a course somewhat midway between the highly abstract generalizations provided by Marx or by Parsons, and the very specific, daily sets of facts that we confront about the rich display of American political institutions and events. In that way, we shall come to see both how the theories can be applied to the occurrences of modern politics in the United States and, at the same time, we shall be able to put the many and diverse facts of these politics into better perspective for ourselves.

Thus, in this chapter we shall examine some of the major and minor tendencies of politics in the United States. To limit ourselves, and to provide the basis for making some sensible statements, we shall concentrate on political history in the twentieth century. However, before we turn to discuss these matters let us consider the nature of power in a general sense.

The Concept of Power

To appreciate the substance of power in American society it is necessary that we begin with a clear definition of it. Such a definition ought to recognize some of the variety of interpretations that exist and incorporate such diversity.

A Definition of Power

Adhering to the spirit of the definitions of Marx, Weber, Parsons, and several others, power is defined as the *social capacity to make binding decisions that have far-reaching consequences for a society (or community)*. There are several key features of this definition. First, power is defined as a *social capacity*. This means

Isn't this power reducing to auth ?

that individuals as members of groups rather than as personalities possess power; it means that power must be associated with a social position in a society—a role, in Parsons's terms—and with a social organization, such as a university or a factory. This phrase also incorporates those cases in which power may be exercised, not by a single role occupant, but by a number of them, as voters collectively do at the polls or as the cabinet of a president often does. The notion of *capacity* emphasizes the fact that power is something that may be used by an occupant of a position but need not necessarily be employed; it represents a potential rather than an actual phenomenon.

Second, there is the phrase *make binding decisions* that is crucial to the definition. Making of decisions is a quality that most contemporary students of power adopt, largely because it allows them to examine real instances of power in the world; it focuses attention on decision making that is more or less observable and suggests that analyses of this process—its origins, its participants—tells us much about the nature of power. *Binding* is a strategic part of this definition, too. It means that those who wield power expect their decisions to have consequences for the actions of other individuals and groups and that, in turn, those who are subject to the exercise of power carry out the decisions. Both those who exercise power and those who are subject to its exercise regard the action as legitimate, as right or proper. This particular element of the definition skirts a knotty problem that some observers, including Weber, have raised—whether the exercise of power does not, in fact, encounter resistance or refusal on the part of those who are subject to its exercise.[1] Weber overcame this difficulty by distinguishing between power and authority; authority assumed a legitimacy to the exercise of commands, and power did not. For our purposes, this distinction is unnecessary. Nevertheless, the bindingness of a decision is problematic and is considered at some length in chapter 12 on organized resistance in the form of social and political movements.[2]

Finally, there is the last element of the definition, *far-reaching consequences for a society.* Equally critical as the other elements, this is intended to suggest that to study power as decision making, the crucial consequences that follow its exercise must be studied. Often such consequences are immediate, as when individuals in a society collectively vote in a new leader of government or when they rebel and topple the current regime. Sometimes such consequences are less obvious and immediate, as when Franklin Roosevelt reshaped the nature of the American presidency during his years in office—a restructuring that some claim has led to a marked concentration of power in the hands of the president.[3] Therefore, the

---

[1] A thoroughgoing discussion of the various nuances to the concept of power can be found in Marvin E. Olsen, ed., *Power in Societies* (New York: The Macmillan Company, 1970), section I particularly. Also, see Dennis Wrong, *Power: Its Form, Bases and Uses* (New York: Harper & Row, Publishers, 1979).

[2] One of the best analyses of the problematic nature of the issue of bindingness is in William A. Gamson, *Power and Discontent* (Homewood, Ill.: The Dorsey Press, 1968), chapter 2.

[3] Among many other sources on this, see Emmet John Hughes, *The Living Presidency: Resources and Dilemmas of the American Presidential Office* (Baltimore, Md.: Penguin Books, Inc., 1974), chapter 6.

indirect and long-term consequences of the making of decisions are at least as significant as the immediate and obvious consequences.[4]

Further Refinements in the Definition

There are several other elements that are critical to the definition of power. The *range* of power refers to the variety of issues over which decisions may be exercised.[5] Thus, some occupants of particular social positions may be able to make decisions on a great many different issues, for instance, the mayor of a city, whereas other individuals may make decisions within a more limited domain, as the head of the transportation department in a municipal government. Thus, there is a greater range of power to the office of the mayor than there is to that of the head of the transportation department. *Resources* for power are equally important, indeed even more so in the eyes of some analysts.[6] This means that power is always grounded in other phenomena and that such other phenomena often, but not always, can be converted into power. Thus, votes, as Parsons noted, are one resource of power, just as skill may be; plain and simple wealth can be a resource for power, although it may operate less often in this way than many of us think. Perhaps the most critical aspect of resources is that those who exercise considerable power are often able to count on considerably more resources, and resources that are more easily convertible into power, than those who do not. The next chapter on power in communities considers some of the ways in which individuals with very little power attempt to mobilize and to assemble their resources to exercise binding decisions of far-reaching consequence.

A third feature of power is its *expandability*. This notion, following the insightful discussions of Parsons (chapter 4), simply means that power can be enlarged or reduced in any community or society and also that the power associated with any single social capacity (or position) may expand or contract. Thus, if the resources that underlie the power of a particular position grow, for instance, with the extension of suffrage to greater numbers of people, then the power of that position has expanded; if the occupant of a particular social position manages to make a greater number and variety of binding decisions, then the power of his position has expanded.[7] It is important to include such an element in any

---

[4]To examine such consequences in even further and more subtle fashion, sociologists often engage in the analysis of both the latent and manifest functions of a phenomenon, such as power, as well as its dysfunctions. See Robert K. Merton, *Social Theory and Social Structure* (Glencoe, Ill.: The Free Press, 1957), chapter 1.

[5]This notion is adapted from Robert A. Dahl, "The Concept of Power," *Behavioral Science,* II (July 1957), 201-15.

[6]Resources for power, long a significant idea, plays an especially prominent part in the analyses of the resource-management school of thought. For further discussion of this perspective, see chapter 12, and Gamson, *Power and Discontent,* chapter 5.

[7]This is only in absolute terms. If the amount of power in a society has expanded to a greater degree than that of a position within the society, then the relative amount of power of the position has been reduced, not enlarged. Speaking only in the most broad and general terms, such comparisons are precise but not especially germane.

definition of power; otherwise the analysis that uses such a definition unrealistically assumes that power remains constant over time in a given group. However, such an assumption, as Parsons points out, seems to be quite invalid. Finally, *distribution of* power refers to its dispersion among the members of a community or society, that is, the number of individuals or, strictly speaking, social positions that possess power in a given social setting. Usually students of politics find most power to be concentrated mainly among a small handful of individuals; the major resources for power as well as its actual employment over fateful decisions rests in the hands of an elite (or, equivalently, oligarchy), perhaps even several elites. Always lurking behind this finding is a contrast-conception that considerable power could be distributed in the hands of a large number of individuals and groups and that the society could then be represented as one in which the masses share in the daily exercise of power.

These several features of power tap a more general quality—amount. Instead of defining this attribute in some very vague and ambiguous terms, it can be defined most precisely in terms of its *range*, its *resources*, its *expandability*, and its *distribution*. There is frequently good reason, for instance, to distinguish especially between the range and resources of power; resources may sometimes increase, as the skill an individual brings to occupancy of an office, without at all advancing the range of issues over which decisions can be made. Moreover, these several elements distinguish what is meant when someone has more power than another—it can mean that an individual possesses a greater range to his decisions or that he possesses more resources.

Power and Other Things

Writers often go to great lengths to consider how power differs from other conceptions within the same family of ideas. These points are not belabored here for they are covered satisfactorily elsewhere.[8] For purposes of our analysis of power, however, it is important to define one other conception, influence, for the two ideas are often confused. Influence is simply the *social capacity to affect the exercise of power by decision makers.* This straightforward definition does not get into the niggling details of influence, such as the supposed difference between it and force. Rather, it gets to the heart of power as decision making; some individuals hold positions, as friends or professional co-workers for instance, that enable them to affect the decisions made by those who exercise power.[9] This conception helps to clarify some of the debates over the nature of power and influence in the United States, and it suggests an important additional notion that circles and networks of people often operate in the exercise of power. That very vivid notion from American politics, "influence-peddler," seems to convey quite precisely the meaning of influence suggested here.

Where does Jerry Falwell fit into this scheme?

[8] See Olsen, *Power in Societies.*

[9] See, for instance, Robert Bierstedt, "An Analysis of Social Power," in *Power in Societies,* Olsen, p. 12; and Gamson, *Power and Discontent.*

POWER IN THE AMERICAN PAST

The lessons of the past, we are told, tell us something of the present. They may tell us how far a society has come from times past, or they may tell us how much a society retains of its traditions, but the lessons always provide us with a clearer perspective on a particular society.

There are several major lessons from the history of power in America. First, those who made the great decisions of the past represented only a handful of the citizens of the United States—power was concentrated in a few hands rather than dispersed among many. For example, the Constitutional Convention was an instance in which decisions of lasting importance in American history were made by a few men who took part in the deliberations. The same, of course, was true at the signing of the Declaration of Independence. In the nineteenth century, there was little reason to conclude that power became much more widely dispersed, at least in terms of the number of individuals who exercised it. Political decisions continued to be made at the national level by a few individuals, as in the case of the decision to embark on the Civil War. Certainly decisions of great consequence in the economy, particularly at the end of the nineteenth century, were essentially made by a few prominent individuals and families, among them the Morgans, the Rockefellers, and the du Ponts.

Second, those who made the great decisions at the founding of the republic represented a relatively clear and seemingly comfortable convergence of interests. In their religious beliefs, they were mainly Congregationalist; in their economic interests, they were mainly traders, financiers, or great landholders; and in party politics, they were committed to the Federalist platform. They represented a small and coherent ruling class—in Marxist terms, an aristocracy of privilege and manner—moved apparently coequally by the same concerns and purposes.[10]

Third, with the rise of great industry at the end of the nineteenth century, the cohesiveness of the early ruling class had been broken, and the locus of major decisions moved essentially out of its hands and away from the political order into the economy. The captains of industry in America appeared to be the captains of virtually everything else as well; their decisions over markets and goods, over expansion, over oil and railroads, and over many other things were ones of major consequence in the United States.[11] Moreover, the political decision makers were often willing to stand idly by, if not to cooperate wholeheartedly, and to allow the captains of industry to take the initiative. Commenting on the attitudes of the dominant political party at the time, the Republican Party, E. E. Schattschneider has remarked that "the Republican party . . . did have a well-defined and well-

[10] For this history, see any of the following: Robert Dahl, *Who Governs?* (New Haven, Conn.: Yale University Press, 1961), chapters 2 and 3 especially; C. Wright Mills, *The Power Elite* (New York: Oxford University Press, 1959), pp. 269-72; and David Riesman, *The Lonley Crowd* (New Haven, Conn.: Yale University Press, 1961), pp. 206-8.

[11] This sort of perspective takes its inspiration from the writings of Charles and Mary Beard on American history. Of their many writings on the subject, see Charles and Mary Beard, *A Basic History of the United States* (New York: Doubleday, Doran & Co., 1952).

established policy—the policy of giving business a free hand to exploit the economy with a minimum of governmental interference. This indeed was a policy; it was general, and it was comprehensively and effectively imposed on the whole national government by a powerful party."[12]

Fourth, despite the shift away from the easy convergence of diverse interests at the end of the eighteenth century to the clear dominance of the great economic decision makers at the end of the nineteenth century, it is evident in the eyes of various historians of the American experience that there always has been some degree of community of interest among the major economic and political decision makers in the United States.[13] At times in the past, the government has had the upper hand in this community, promoting its goals over those of business enterprise or agriculture. Alexander Hamilton, himself a mercantilist, attempted to foster at the very beginning of the republic a close alliance between the interests of the wealthy traders and holders of securities and the national government. He believed that the purposes of the large moneyed interests and those of the national government were one and the same, and thus he acted to implement the former by his designs for the latter, including among them a private bank of the United States, excise taxes, and tariffs on goods manufactured within the United States.[14] At other times, business has been the more active member of this community of interest, as in the case of the disputed election of 1876 in which the Republican Rutherford B. Hayes ultimately secured the presidency with the aid of Southerners. This historical record reveals that the compromise that led to the selection of Hayes was largely the work of some representatives of railroad interests in the United States who were intent on the expansion of railroad networks into the South and thus assisted in the effort to reunite it with the North.[15]

These observations accord with important interpretations of the historical evidence on the nature of decision making, or power, in the American past. In general, they reveal a shifting social base of power in terms of the social backgrounds and institutional settings of major decision makers; they also portray a more or less continuous concentration of power in a relatively small number of hands. This image of an elite or ruling class that holds the reins of power must be tempered with two other observations that are somewhat more speculative but equally plausible. In terms of the *expandability* of power, it is undoubtedly the case that the amount of power in the United States has grown absolutely since the founding of the republic, largely because of the increase in the resources that

---

[12] E. E. Schattschneider, "United States: The Functional Approach to Party Government," in *Modern Political Parties: Approach to Comparative Politics,* ed. Sigmund Neumann (Chicago: University of Chicago Press, 1956), p. 199.

[13] Beard and Beard, *A Basic History of the United States.* For apt criticisms of this view, see Lee Benson, *Turner and Beard: American Historical Writing Reconsidered* (Glencoe, Ill.: The Free Press, 1960).

[14] William Nisbet Chambers, *Political Parties in a New Nation: The American Experience, 1776-1809* (New York: Oxford University Press, 1963), chapters 2 and 3.

[15] C. Vann Woodward, *Reunion and Reaction: The Compromise of 1877 and the End of Reconstruction* (Garden City, N.Y.: Doubleday & Co., Inc., 1956).

can be converted into power. Historian David Potter points out that the very abundance of resources on which wealth is based contributes to amounts of power widespread among the citizens of the United States.[16] Other resources that are convertible into power, such as the votes of individuals as well as the number of citizen organizations in existence, have also increased. Another tendency that affects the *range* of power held by any single individual is differentiation and specialization of social positions and organizations, in Parsons's apt terms. Since the founding of the republic, there has been a widespread growth of new organizations and occupational roles as well as a continuing differentiation in the functions of both organizations and roles; these make it increasingly likely that the range of power exercised by the occupant of any single position has narrowed. Thus, the range of power has diminished. Whereas an Alexander Hamilton, for example, once could initiate decisions with major consequences both for the government and the economy, today's treasury secretary possesses a considerably narrower range of power. The same must hold for virtually most, if not all, other positions that wield power in the United States.

These two admittedly speculative conclusions must be weighed against recorded historical evidence and the interpretations of that evidence. While interpretations obviously suggest a relatively high concentration of power in a few hands and institutions, the evidence suggests that this concentration may well be a historical mirage. First, there is generally more power at present than in the past (based upon resources), and second, the range of power for the occupant of any particular social position is considerably narrower than in the past. Is power as concentrated now as it has been in the past in the United States? Has there always been something resembling a cohesive elite or a ruling class? Finer measurements of power, perhaps forthcoming in future research in political sociology, may ultimately help to settle this matter with greater precision.

POWER AND INFLUENCE IN THE AMERICAN PRESENT: MAJOR THEMES

There are four principal themes that are peculiarly characteristic of the nature and evolution of American politics during the course of the twentieth century, motifs that we shall examine in some detail. These are as follows: the growth in power and influence of the modern corporation; the growth in the power and influence of the federal government; the growth in the rationalization and routinization of work for many, if not most, Americans; and, lastly, the spread and growing awareness

---

[16] David M. Potter, *People of Plenty: Economic Abundance and the American Character* (Chicago: The University of Chicago Press, 1958). Actually Potter's argument is that the abundance of resources has permitted a democratic system of government to remain in effect in the United States, contributing to the reigning myths of widespread equality, and so on. The interpretation here casts his argument in a somewhat different light, but one consistent with the overall themes of his analysis.

among Americans of the democratic ethos—of the claims that they, as citizens, are entitled to be free in the course of their lives, and to be treated as equal to their fellow citizens. These major themes, though they capture the diversity of American politics today, are not entirely consistent with one another. In fact, it is their very incongruity which contributes, at least in part, to various forms of tension and conflict evident in the American polity itself. Moreover, they are to be regarded only as the major themes, giving life, as we shall later observe, to some minor variations as well.

The Expansion of the Modern Corporation

The growth in power and influence of the modern corporation is a phenomenon which has been recognized by any number and all kinds of observers of the American polity. One of the more important and famous statements about it comes from C. Wright Mills, an eminent and, especially after his premature death at the age of forty-six in 1962, an immensely influential figure. It was Mills who helped to alert our modern sensibilities to the conception of a military-industrial complex—almost as much as President Dwight D. Eisenhower's pronouncement on his departure from office—for it was Mills who first drew attention to an alliance among the leaders of business, of the military, and of the federal government.[17] American society in the twentieth century, Mills insisted, is a considerably different setting than it was in the nineteenth century, much transformed from the vision with which liberals had imbued it.[18] With the consolidation of businesses during the teens and twenties, the modern corporation emerged. No longer was the small businessman, epitomized in the mom and pop stores on Main Street, the principal character of the American economy; rather it was the company official, the corporate manager, neatly attired in his blue pin-stripe suit, who came to epitomize the nature of the modern American economy.

Mills argued that the corporation has grown in power and influence owing to certain structural developments in the broader American society. The nature of business practices and enterprises relies much on the principles of efficiency and profit—and, in the course of seeking to achieve both goals, businesses naturally tend to become larger, to consolidate as well as to extend themselves. Form follows function, in effect, and as the markets of the businesses expand, taking in new customers and new clients, so too the offices of the businesses must enlarge. Drawing to a degree upon the earlier insights of Weber, Mills insisted that the growth of business into the modern corporation entails the growth of the organization of the business enterprise into the modern bureaucracy. Numbers of people in the business enterprise become subject to the authority of the office place and, in turn, come under the control of their superiors. And, Mills believed, this control over the lives of many hundreds, if not thousands, of individuals within the company itself,

---

[17]C. Wright Mills, *The Power Elite* (New York: Oxford University Press, 1959).

[18]C. Wright Mills, "Liberal Values in the Modern World," in C. Wright Mills, *Power, Politics and People* (New York: Ballantine Books, n.d.).

coupled with the obvious effect marketplace decisions by large firms could have, thus put into the hands of the managers and owners of large corporations an unprecedented ability to affect, if not directly to make, decisions of national significance in America.

But Mills is not the only scholar to turn our attention to the nature of the modern corporation. Marxist and neo-Marxist scholars, too, have found in the modern corporation the location of extraordinary power and influence. Two such scholars, Paul Baran and Paul Sweezy, published a highly influential work in the mid-1960s in which they insisted, just as Mills had, that the American economy consists of a number of sectors in which a small handful of enterprises (an oligopoly) could effectively regulate the prices clients had to pay.[19] Terming this the stage of "monopoly capitalism," Baran and Sweezy claimed that the emergence of the modern corporation has somewhat changed the shape of the American economy, although it retains the fundamental contradictions and irrationalities so observed by Marx in his famous analyses. They argue, for example, that while the modern corporation has given birth to the disjunction between the management of the corporation and its ownership and, in consequence, to the emergence of what appears to be two separate social groups, if not classes, in actual fact the owners and the managers are basically one and the same group. Thus, Baran and Sweezy note, for instance, that the managers of the large corporations often are the very largest stockholders of them, so that it is foolish to claim, as some scholars have done, that managers effectively control the large corporations and run them more or less free from the day-to-day interference by the large shareholders.[20]

Baran and Sweezy also were among the first of the neo-Marxist scholars to reemphasize the fundamental contradictions and inconsistencies inherent in the nature of the modern American corporate economy. Pointing out that the large corporation had become the vehicle for securing ever more surplus value, roughly the equivalent of profit in common parlance, they argue that one evident contradiction in the nature of the modern American economy is that corporations are securing more and more profit yet are faced with diminishing demand and declining domestic markets.[21] Thus, in America, Baran and Sweezy argue, the corporations are compelled to rid themselves of this excess surplus value, gained at the expense of the sweat and toil of the workers in the United States, through a variety of dubious, if not entirely nonsensical, outlets. One of these is to expend consider-

[19] Paul Baran and Paul Sweezy, *Monopoly Capital: An Essay on the American Economic and Social Order* (New York: Monthly Review Press, 1968).

[20] For related materials on this discussion see the following: Michael Patrick Allen, "The Structure of Interorganizational Elite Cooptation: Interlocking Corporate Directorates," *American Sociological Review,* 39 (June 1974), 393-406; Michael Patrick Allen, "Management Control in the Large Corporation: Comment on Zeitlin," *American Journal of Sociology,* 81 (January 1976), 885-94; Maurice Zeitlin, "Corporate Ownership and Control: The Large Corporation and the Capitalist Class," *American Journal of Sociology,* 79 (March 1974), 1073-1119; and Maurice Zeitlin, "On Class Theory of the Large Corporation: Response to Allen," *American Journal of Sociology,* 81 (January 1976), 894-903.

[21] For the original conception Marx held of the nature of surplus value, see Karl Marx, *Capital* (Moscow: Foreign Languages Publishing House, 1961), I, Parts III, IV, V, *et passim.*

See also J. Coleman,

able monies on advertising, thus seeking to attract ever increasing demand for goods among the workers, as consumers. Another is to expend monies in the pursuit of new markets abroad. This means that money often will be spent needlessly on the defense industries as well as in a variety of foreign engagements, wars and the military overthrows of regimes deemed unpopular to the economic interests of the United States. Moreover, Baran and Sweezy laid bare a fundamental contradiction that most Marxist analysts since Marx have proclaimed—namely, the contradiction between an economic system that is based upon capitalism and a political system that is based upon democracy.[22] "In the United States, as in all other capitalist countries," they write, "the propertyless masses have never been in a position to determine the conditions of their lives or the policies of the nation's government. Nevertheless, as long as democracy meant the overthrow of monarchial despotism and the ascent to power of a relatively numerous bourgeoisie, the term focussed attention on a major change in the life of society. But what is left of this truth content in a society in which a tiny oligarchy resting on vast economic power and in full control of society's political and cultural apparatus makes all the important political decisions?"[23]

These observations of C. Wright Mills as well as Paul Baran and Paul Sweezy, along with those of other scholars, clearly reveal a genuine and important pattern of development in the American economy over the course of the twentieth century. And it is a pattern that apparently has been a long time coming, though initially it was little recognized and little appreciated. In what has since become a classic statement, Adolph Berle and Gardiner Means in 1932 published a book entitled *The Modern Corporation and Private Property*.[24] They took note of a startling fact— that much of the business conducted in the American marketplace was done at the time by very large firms, and that, in fact, a comparatively small number of such firms actually controlled a disproportionate amount of the assets in each of several fields. For instance, they noted that, in 1929, shortly before the crash on Wall Street, 130 of 573 companies that did business on the New York Stock Exchange could be classified as corporations, and further, that these 130 companies controlled fully 80 percent of the assets in the market.[25] Berle and Means went on to argue that the emergence of the large corporation had ramifications of the most severe sort. It meant, for example, that the whole conception of property had fundamentally changed in America, that those who actually owned the corporations, the stockholders, were a large and dispersed lot of people, whereas those who actually ran the corporations, the managers, were a very small number of people actively involved in the day-to-day corporation operations. Property under condi-

[22] See also our discussion of Lenin's writings on bourgeois democracy, pp. 43-44; Ralph Miliband, *The State in Capitalist Society* (London: Quartet Books, 1973); and Alan Wolfe, *The Limits of Legitimacy: Political Contradictions of Contemporary Capitalism* (New York: The Free Press, 1977).

[23] Baran and Sweezy, *Monopoly Capital*, p. 339.

[24] Adolph A. Berle and Gardiner C. Means, *The Modern Corporation and Private Property*, rev. ed. (New York: Harcourt Brace Jovanovich, Inc., 1968).

[25] Berle and Means, *The Modern Corporation and Private Property*, p. 29.

tions of private enterprise, then, had been silently transformed from that of an active entity into that of a passive one in which the owners, while theoretically in control of what they owned, actively played little part in how their property was employed, manipulated, invested, or divested.

Berle and Means were the first students of the American economy to draw attention, in the sharpest terms possible, to the emergence of the corporation as the vehicle through which a considerable amount of business was transacted. Yet their claim that management had become divorced from ownership can be more easily contested. For while it is true that, with the growth of the large corporation, single families, on the order of the Mellons, the Carnegies, and the du Ponts, tend to represent the exception rather than the rule, at the same time it also is the case that ownership is not so widely dispersed as Berle and Means would have us think. Information assembled on the distribution of wealth in the United States by Robert J. Lampman, and later by James Smith and Stephen Franklin, show the considerable concentration of wealth in the United States.[26] In 1953, for instance, the richest 1 percent of the population held 27.5 percent of the net worth of all individual Americans; that figure remained more or less constant until it declined somewhat to 24.9 percent in 1969. Moreover, this same 1 percent of the population in 1969 held fully half of all corporate stock in the United States. Moreover, as Baran and Sweezy observe, many times the managers of corporations, themselves, are among the largest stockholders, granted sizable numbers of shares in stock and other perquisites of ownership as part of the financial compensation for their official responsibilities in the corporation. Still, Berle and Means drew what seems to be the major conclusion from the earlier developments in the twentieth century, that of the startling growth of the corporation. And in so doing they posed a problem for American society in the future, one especially interesting because Berle and Means wrote not as radical thinkers but rather as conventional observers. "The rise of the modern corporation," they wrote, "has brought a concentration of economic power which can compete on equal terms with the modern state—economic power versus political power, each strong in its own field. . . . Where its own interests are concerned, (the modern corporation) even attempts to dominate the state. The future may see the economic organism, typified by the corporation, not only on an equal plane with the state, but possibly even superseding it as the dominant form of social organization."[27]

Those of us alive today surely can attest to the great wisdom evident in this forecast by Berle and Means, made almost half a century ago. The corporation remains a fact of business life in the United States. Indeed, with the activities of the large economic conglomerates, such as Transamerica, International Telephone and Telegraph, Gulf Oil, and many others like them, it seems that the corporation, more than ever before, is the true representative of the American economy. Just as Berle

---

[26] Robert J. Lampman, *The Share of Top Wealth-Holders in National Wealth* (Princeton: Princeton University Press, 1962); and James D. Smith and Stephen D. Franklin, "Concentration of Personal Wealth, 1922-1969," *American Economic Review,* 86 (May 1974), 162-67.

[27] Berle and Means, *The Modern Corporation and Private Property.*

and Means found a considerable concentration of economic power in the hands of a comparatively small number of firms, so, too, today we can observe a similar concentration of marketplace wealth. For example, in 1976 there were roughly 212,000 manufacturing firms in the United States. A bare handful of these firms, 482, held almost three-quarters of all the assets of manufacturing corporations.[28] Similarly, in 1979 the fifty largest commercial banks in the United States held 36 percent of the assets of all commercial banks.[29] There even appears to be a growing increase, though slight to be sure, in the concentration of economic power in the hands of the largest corporations. Thus, in 1950, the 200 largest manufacturing corporations in America held 47.7 percent of the assets of all manufacturing firms; in 1965 the 200 largest held 56.7 percent of all assets, and in 1979 the figure was 59.0 percent.[30] Quite plainly, then, a relative handful of firms now actively manage the American marketplace.

But the modern corporation has gone beyond the boundaries of the American marketplace, as Baran and Sweezy observed, to rival the American state enterprise, as Berle and Means had claimed. Sometime in the 1960s, social and economic analysts began to take a special interest in the large firms, those with major offices located in more than one country. These firms, variously called transnational, multinational, or even global, corporations, and exemplified especially by firms like Exxon, the General Motors Corporation (GM), International Telephone and Telegraph (IT&T), and International Business Machines Corporation (IBM), introduced an even more novel phenomenon, but one entirely consistent with the forecast by Berle and Means—if not by Marx![31] Operating in more than one nation, they not only rivaled the economic resources of some nation-states—for instance, Richard Barnet and Ronald Müller claim that in terms of gross national product in 1973 Goodyear Tire Company was larger than Saudi Arabia—but it seems they could operate free of any meaningful sanctions or penalties of the nation-states themselves. Barnet and Müller, coauthors of the definitive treatment of these organizations, thus quote the president of the IBM World Trade Corporation who declared that

> For business purposes the boundaries that separate one nation from another are no more real than the equator. They are merely convenient demarcations of ethnic, linguistic, and cultural entities. They do not define business requirements or consumer trends. Once management understands and accepts this world economy, its view of the marketplace—and its planning—necessarily expand.

[28]*Statistical Abstract of the United States,* United States Department of Commerce, Bureau of the Census, Washington, D.C., 1980, Table 950.

[29]*Statistical Abstract of the United States,* 1980, Table 882.

[30]*Statistical Abstract of the United States,* 1980, Table 952.

[31]Richard J. Barnet and Ronald E. Müller, *Global Reach: The Power of the Multinational Corporations* (New York: Simon and Schuster, 1974), see also Michael Barrat-Brown, *The Economics of Imperialism* (London: Penguin Books, 1974).

And, the same gentleman concludes by remarking that the "world outside the home country is no longer viewed as a series of disconnected customers and prospects for its products, but as an extension of a single market."[32]

Not a well settled case

If, indeed, there is a major threat that business poses to the well-being of people, it is embodied now in the operations and the goals of these great worldwide corporations. Managed by people whose primary aim is to maximize profits, the worldwide corporations act as if the nation-state represented an anachronism, seeking to locate new markets and cheap labor whenever and wherever they can. Such firms can be run more freely, and yet also more authoritatively, than can democratic governments because they do not rest on public consent or public surveillance. Since they are based on profit and the accumulation of wealth, they seem to advance civilization with every new plant they open and every new worker they employ. But since they serve to the advantage of some people, such as their managers and major stockholders, more than others, such as their customers, they may also serve to accentuate the division between the rich and the poor nations of the world. Moreover, in their very effort to expand, they often recklessly seek to circumvent the integrity of the nation-state, one of the major and most tragic illustrations being the role of IT&T and its chairman, Harold Geneen, in the over- throw and subsequent assassination of Salvador Allende and his Marxist regime in Chile in 1973.

The Expansion of the Modern American State

Whereas once one might have thought of the mayor, the local congressman, even the president as, in some sense, a representative of the people, the very size and great complexity of political operations in the late twentieth century make of such an image a romantic illusion. Instead of people who represent and articulate the views of citizens, forming policies in their name and on their behalf, the modern state has grown to be one of the large and often apparently very distant and indifferent institutions. Moreover, such institutions seem to exercise a profound influence over our daily lives, affecting our health care, the lives of our retired citizens, the nature of our education in public schools, the amount we pay in taxes, to mention but a few things. In brief, all the institutions that comprise today's state—the government, the courts, the police force, and the military—have expanded in size and scope to an enormous degree, and now exercise unprecedented influence over the daily lives of each and everyone of us. Once again, it happens, it was C. Wright Mills who helped to direct much of contemporary thought and analysis to the emerging role of the modern state, particularly to the role of the federal government and the military in modern America.[33] Drawing upon political history in the nineteenth and early twentieth centuries, as well as upon the rich insights of Max Weber, Mills argued that the federal government has grown to wield

[32] Barnet and Müller, *Global Reach,* pp. 14-15.
[33] C. Wright Mills, *The Power Elite.*

enormous power. He insisted, in particular, that the executive branch of the federal government, meaning the president and his various advisors and counselors, have come in the last half of the twentieth century to have a control over the lives of American citizens unmatched in earlier history. How did this come about? And what particular form has it assumed in various presidential administrations? Briefly let us review some of the most salient facts that Mills, and many others echoing his view, have used to document the claim of the power of the presidency.

The Executive Branch and Its Power.   With the administration of Franklin Delano Roosevelt there came into the presidential office a figure of enormous charisma and equally unbounded ambition. He managed during his tenure in office to initiate a number of federal programs that eventually served to reshape the links between the federal government, the world of business, and the broader public. Under his administration, for example, there came into existence the Social Security Program, in 1935, the Tennessee Valley Authority, in 1933, and a host of general welfare programs designed to extricate the United States from the depths of the Great Depression. Under Roosevelt, too, owing both to the circumstances of the depression as well as to the Second World War, the Congress seemed to become less and less an equal partner in the operations of the federal government. Roosevelt's influence, because of his special gifts of communication, extended well beyond the confines of 1600 Pennsylvania Avenue. Thus, during the 1930s he managed to fashion a structure of partisan loyalties and identities in the United States that would not disappear for, at least, another forty years.

Yet, Roosevelt was not the only president to have succeeded in expanding the power and influence of the presidency, though he surely was one of the most skillful. Owing in part to the more aggressive role the United States sought in world affairs during as well as after World War II, the incumbents of the presidency came increasingly to make decisions that had worldwide, not to say historic, significance. Harry Truman made the decision to drop the atomic bombs both on Hiroshima and Nagasaki, acts that set into motion an entirely new understanding of the meaning of war and human violence. John Foster Dulles, Dwight Eisenhower's secretary of state, made decisions that reshaped the nature of the balance of power in the Middle East, and with it the relations between the United States and the Soviet Union as well.

However, it was during the presidential administrations of Kennedy, Johnson, and Nixon, observers agree, that the power of the presidency truly came into its own. During this period, which began with Kennedy's administration in 1960, the United States government sought to extend its influence abroad, creating new alliances in Asia, Africa, as well as the Latin American nations. In 1960, for example, the Organization of American States was created under the initiative of the Kennedy administration. Ostensibly designed to furnish American aid to the Latin American countries and to solidify the American alliance in the north and south, many observers saw the OAS in truth merely as a device to extend and to protect

American political and economic interests in Latin America.[34] The Peace Corps, too, was an innovation of the Kennedy administration, apparently created to furnish aid to citizens of other countries with no strings attached; yet, once more, from another angle observers saw it as simply a means of extending the hegemony of American political power abroad.[35] And, of course, there was the abortive Bay of Pigs invasion of 1962, taken under the initiative of the Kennedy administration, and carried out with the cooperation of the Central Intelligence Agency (CIA), that marked still another attempt by the American president and his counselors to extend American influence beyond the shores of the United States.[36]

The major effect that contributed to the growth in the power and influence of the president and his counselors, to the development, in the words of Arthur Schlesinger, Jr., of an "imperial Presidency," was the Vietnam War.[37] To all outward appearances, the United States government should have had very little interest in Vietnam. Here, after all, was a country in the midst of an internal conflict, a war that had only a decade earlier led to the humiliating defeat of the French. It was a country thousands of miles from the shores of the United States, moreover; yet, for some reasons only later to be clarified, the president and his counselors believed it necessary to introduce American troops into the struggle. Hence, in 1963 the United States commenced to increase aid to the tottering Diem regime in South Vietnam. With the assassination of President Kennedy, and after winning election on a platform in which he condemned his opponent for his trigger-happy intentions in Vietnam, Lyndon Johnson presided over a major escalation of the United States' effort. He did so, moreover, through actions, such as the Gulf of Tonkin incident in 1965, that seemed to be strategically designed to force the United States into ever greater participation; and he did so, most significantly, without the free and ready advice and consent of the American Congress.

Why should the United States have become involved in such a war? And why did the president and his advisors, particularly the members of the National Security Council under the leadership of Walt Rostow and McGeorge Bundy, seek to assert American influence in this far-flung region of the world? Those who have examined carefully documents of these administrators, and reflected on them at length, argue that American advisors believed the national interest was at stake, in fact that the Communist nations posed a major threat to American democracy. Hence, they reasoned, it was important for the United States to put up an aggressive front, in the words of Richard Barnet, to display a macho and aggressive style, as a means of protecting the national interests of the United States.[38] If Vietnam

[34] See Julio Cotler and Richard R. Fagen, eds., *Latin America and the United States: The Changing Political Realities* (Stanford: Stanford University Press, 1974).

[35] Cotler and Fagen, eds., *Latin America and the United States,* pp. 350-57, *passim.*

[36] On this matter see, for example, David Wise and Thomas B. Ross, *The Invisible Government* (New York: Random House, 1974), pp. 8-90.

[37] Arthur M. Schlesinger, Jr., *The Imperial Presidency* (New York: Popular Library, 1974).

[38] Richard J. Barnet, *Roots of War* (Baltimore, Md.: Penguin Books, Inc., 1972).

fell, it was assumed in terms of the so-called domino theory, so, too, would other nations in the region, leading eventually to the dominance of the Communists in that part of the world and thereby shifting the balance of power between the Communist and non-Communist countries. Such an event, the Kennedy and the Johnson administrations both believed, must be avoided, and thus they engaged in an almost reckless use, and sacrifice, of American troops and weaponry.

The "imperial Presidency" may, or may not, have come to an end with the exposure of criminal abuse of presidential power in the Watergate scandal. Quite obviously, the Nixon administration simply was the culmination of all those tendencies for power to accumulate in the executive branch, tendencies first set into motion with the actions of Roosevelt in the 1930s. As Marx is reported once to have written, events occur in history twice, the first time as tragedy and the second as comedy. If Johnson's presidency displayed the tragedy of imperial presidential power, surely Nixon's revealed its comedy. The very recent successes of Ronald Reagan, along with his advisors on the budget, David Stockman in particular, bear witness, it seems, to the continuing enormous power of the presidency. At the same time they contain an irony of major proportions—that it will take the very power and influence which have accumulated in the hands of the president to diminish that very same power over the lives of American citizens.

The Military, the Central Intelligence Agency (CIA), and the Federal Bureau of Investigation (FBI).   Besides the executive branch of government, Mills and those who have adopted his position on the nature of power and influence in twentieth-century America argue that power has accumulated as well in the hands of other agencies of the federal government—the military, the CIA, and the FBI in particular. Mills was particularly insistent that with the close of World War II the military principals of the government had come to assume an enormous impact on the making of public policy, not so much because of the frequency of battles, but because of the threat that nuclear war with the Soviet Union posed. In fact, in the past thirty-five years more and more individuals with experience in the American military have come to occupy high positions in the government. A favorite example for Mills, of course, was Dwight Eisenhower who moved from being the commander of allied forces in Europe to become president for two terms, beginning in 1952. Other military figures who have become important in the shaping of American foreign and domestic policies in the years since the close of World War II include General Maxwell Taylor, who during the Vietnam War furnished key advice to the Kennedy and Johnson administrations.

More recently, there has been the figure of General Alexander Haig. Haig first rose to prominence as chairman of the Joint Chiefs of Staff of the armed forces, later became a personal and controversial counselor to Richard Nixon and, it was said, played a large role in the final days of Nixon's presidency.[39] In the admin-

---

[39] Bob Woodward and Carl Bernstein, *The Final Days* (New York: Simon and Schuster, 1976).

istration of Ronald Reagan, Haig has achieved the penultimate position, perhaps, for a military figure, apart from the presidency itself, serving as secretary of state. His influence undoubtedly is part of the reason for the Reagan administration's highly aggressive stance on foreign policy, not to say the recommended increases for spending on defense. Defense spending, in fact, in the past several decades has further displayed the importance of the military, and of the military mentality, in the imagery of Mills, in American politics. Thus, in 1980, $130.4 billion was directed to the Department of Defense, about one-quarter of the national budget. And in 1970, at the height of the United States' involvement in the Vietnam War, the federal budget targeted $78.7 billion for defense, fully 40 percent of the entire federal budget at the time.[40]

Besides the military, there are other agencies of the federal government which since the end of World War II have come to exercise considerable influence over American foreign and domestic policies. The two most significant are the CIA and the FBI. In a country that proclaims itself to be a democracy, what proves to be so especially foreboding about the activities of these agencies is that until very recently they have been free of any surveillance either by the Congress or by informal representatives of the general public. Let us consider the case of the CIA, first of all.

The CIA came into being as a result of the National Security Act of 1947, the same act which had created the Department of Defense and had established the National Security Council.[41] Originally it had been the intention of its creators that the CIA remain under the control of the National Security Council, and that it operate explicitly to gather intelligence overseas. But after its establishment, and particularly under the leadership of Allen Dulles, brother of Eisenhower's secretary of state, the role of the CIA expanded considerably. It began to initiate various clandestine activities abroad, among them efforts to overthrow governments perceived to be unsympathetic to American national interests. Ever since the enlargement of its role under the tutelage of Dulles, the CIA has acted in important ways to shape and to direct American foreign policy. Most recently, in the case of Iran, for example, it is clear that it helped to support the forces of the late shah as well as undermining any attempts to overthrow his regime. Indeed, efforts to create regimes in Iran sympathetic to American interests date back to 1953, when the CIA participated in the overthrow of Premier Mohammed Mossadegh, who was thought to be far more sympathetic to Moscow than to Washington.

There appear, in fact, to have been countless instances of foreign conflicts and episodes in which the CIA somehow has been involved, including of course the major fiasco, the Bay of Pigs, in which the CIA virtually sponsored an effort to oust Fidel Castro and his regime. There also was the famous U-2 spy plane incident of 1960, when Francis Gary Powers was shot down while flying over Russia. Later it was discovered that his mission was under the supervision of the CIA. The CIA also

---

[40] *Statistical Abstract of the United States,* 1980, Tables 432 and 436.

[41] This and the next few sentences of discussion about the CIA are based upon Wise and Ross, *The Invisible Government.*

has participated in the overthrow of the Guatemalan regime in 1954, another government claimed to be unfriendly to American interests; and it is reported as well to have assisted in undermining the Marxist government of Premier Salvador Allende in Chile in 1973. To the chagrin of many people, officials and public alike, the CIA has not overstepped the tacit limits of national sovereignty on foreign soil exclusively. In the early 1970s, for instance, it was learned that the CIA had for a period of time provided financial support to certain members of the National Student Association in return for their help in collecting information on alleged radical students. Elsewhere, on campuses and in research laboratories throughout the United States, it has been reported, the CIA has also provided financial support to people who were willing to inform on the activities of their colleagues and friends.[42]

Even today as Bates of Bowdoin

All such acts, and many other foreign engagements abroad, have been done in complete secrecy, conceived and produced by an inner council within the CIA, known as the Special Group. Moreover, the budget of the CIA, although artfully disguised from the curious eyes of wary congressmen, is reported to rival in size that of its Russian counterpart, the KGB. In short, as David Wise and Thomas Ross tersely claim in their important analysis, the CIA has during the years of its existence operated almost as an "invisible government" in the United States.[43]

With the death of J. Edgar Hoover in 1970, the influence of the FBI declined in importance, aided in no small part by investigations of its activities by the Congress. Yet, during the reign of Hoover the FBI represented a very powerful agency of the federal government; presidents, themselves, even occasionally seemed to reverse the Constitutional relationship between the president and his subordinates, showing enormous respect and deference toward Hoover. Over the years the FBI has limited its own intelligence work to American soil, but it has ranged far and wide in the pursuit of information on alleged dissidents. During the late 1940s and into the 1950s, the FBI played a major part in collecting information on so-called Communist agents or sympathizers in the United States, helping to feed American political paranoia in that decade.[44] Where the FBI began to overstep itself, in terms simply of gathering intelligence, was in the fabrication of information that could be used to discredit otherwise important and respected Americans.[45] For instance, it has been reported that the FBI fabricated stories about alleged sexual liasons of the Reverend Martin Luther King, Jr., during the mid-1960s in an attempt to diminish his influence as a spokesman for black civil rights. And, in even more controversial operations, in 1980 the FBI undertook the ABSCAM effort, an intelligence operation in which an FBI agent who posed as an Arab oil magnate tried to bribe various

---

[42] Wise and Ross, *The Invisible Government*, pp. 247-48.

[43] Wise and Ross, *The Invisible Government*.

[44] See, for example, Gary T. Marx, "Thoughts on a Neglected Category of Social Movement Participants: The Agent Provocateur and the Informant," *American Journal of Sociology,* 80 (September 1974), 402-42; and James Rule, Douglas McAdam, Linda Stearns, and David Uglow, *The Politics of Privacy* (New York: New American Library, 1980).

[45] Gary Marx, "The Agent Provocateur and the Informant."

congressmen. Defense attorneys for several of the congressmen indicted for accepting such bribes have tried to show that the FBI did not merely "gather" information, as is its mandate from the government, but tried to create it instead.

In summary then, it seems clear that by any standard of judgment, but particularly in terms of the policies fashioned and numbers of lives influenced, the modern state has come to wield enormous power in the late twentieth century. In particular, the president and his advisors, along with high officials of the military, and officials of the CIA and FBI, have come to play a role in American democracy far beyond that originally envisioned by those who framed the American Constitution. Moreover, it is a role whose only contemporary counterpart is to be found in the equally large hand played in the shaping of policies by the very largest corporations.

The Rationalization of Work

The two themes we have discussed so far—the growth of the modern corporation and the growth of the modern state—each concern broad historic trends in the twentieth century which have modified the structure of how Americans work and consume, and how they are governed. These tendencies, we have learned, greatly promoted the power and influence of certain key positions and certain key individuals, elevating them far above the average American citizen. Now we shall turn to look at these same developments from another angle, to examine how they have had an impact on the everyday lives of Americans. We shall look first at the nature of work in modern American society.

Karl Marx and Max Weber each had something significant to say about the nature of work in modern society, especially insofar as its character arose out of the broad historical and structural patterns they perceived. To Marx, the divorce of the worker from the implements with which he had fashioned products entailed something very degrading and dehumanizing. It meant essentially that the worker was deprived of the capacity to be creative and to retain the fruits of his own creative activities; it meant, in more technical Marxian imagery, the alienation of man's *species-being* from itself.[46] Until such alienation was eliminated from the conditions of work in modern society, men and women, indeed the whole of society, would be subject to considerable social and personal turmoil. Weber, himself, was much impressed with Marx's conclusions, of course. But he came to believe that the discontent of workers would arise not so much from a somewhat mysterious condition of human alienation as from the very technical imperatives of work itself.[47] To Weber, the development of modern society and of modern work meant the rationalization of the way in which work was to be performed.

---

[46] Karl Marx, "The Economic and Philosophic Manuscripts of 1844," in *The Marx-Engels Reader,* ed. Robert C. Tucker (New York: W.W. Norton Co., Inc., 1972).

[47] See the brilliant analysis of Weber's writings on this point in Hans Gerth and C. Wright Mills, eds., *From Max Weber: Essays in Sociology* (New York: Oxford University Press, 1958), chapter 3.

This entailed, as we earlier discovered, a growing emphasis on the nature of efficiency in the workplace and, at the same time, a growing stress on the general conduct of work, particularly the clarity of the rules according to which labor was to be performed. Out of the emphasis on technical efficiency, or what we might call the technical imperative of work, labor would come to involve more and more precision which meant, in effect, that the worker would become subject increasingly to rules of a technical nature and to a work staff, itself, that would be designed to implement and to carry out such rules. Workplace authority eventually would come to reign supreme over the work of modern laborers, producing among them, Weber believed, a profound sense of estrangement and discontent.

This theme, of the rationalization of worklife in modern societies, the United States in particular, became the leitmotif of the writings of Herbert Marcuse, who until his death was a central figure of the Frankfurt School of critical social theory.[48] Marcuse insisted that in some sense Weber had been correct in observing that a major feature of modern capitalist societies was the growing rationalization so characteristic of the workplace and of work. But Marcuse, a philosopher persuaded by the writings both of Hegel and Marx, went beyond Weber's claims. He argued that Weber misapprehended the full and true impact of rationalization in modern society and that he had done so because he failed to be thoroughly critical of the character of modern capitalism. Had Weber sought to be fully critical of the way in which formal rationality—an emphasis on the purely formal and technical features of reason through efficiency, calculability, and quantification—had become separated from substantive rationality—a consideration of the ends, particularly the human ends toward which reason strives—Marcuse argued, he would have better appreciated the nature of modern capitalism, especially its various foibles.

As it is, Marcuse insisted, under modern capitalism reason succeeds in form alone, taking over in many realms, including that of contemporary philosophy, in which it has produced a body of thought largely concerned with the bare abstractions of facts and logic, and of modern science, in which it is equally obsessed with matters of form and of number, and very little concerned with the substantive world which lies beyond, or behind, such forms. In the modern workplace, he adds, where the critical use of reason would lead men and women to employ their intelligence as a means of liberating themselves from the toil and hardship of labor, there one finds instead that reason continues to parade in form and abstraction only, with an emphasis upon efficiency, and an ever growing production of new technological devices. In the modern workplace especially, Marcuse claims, human beings have become truly the captives of their own creations, that of the technical means intended to attain for corporations ever greater profits. Thus, the technical apparatus and the administrative mechanisms of workplace authority, rather than easing the everyday worklife of the laborer, have come instead to oppress the laborer.

That the nature of work for many men and women in modern America has come to approximate this Marcusian imagery seems highly plausible, though the

---

[48] See our discussion in chapter 2 on the writings of Herbert Marcuse, pp. 48-49.

Odd neglect of Braverman here.

evidence required to support this argument is elusive and of the most diverse sorts— and some, quite frankly, is even conflicting. To begin with, if one assumes that people who work in the largest firms in the United States are especially subject to the technical imperative of modern work along with the impersonal form of super- vision so characteristic of American factories, then a sizable and gradually increas- ing sector of the labor force thus is exposed to the modern forces of rationalized work. In 1980, for instance, the largest 500 industrial corporations in America, according to the *Fortune Directory*, employed 15.9 million workers or more; this represented fully 15 percent of the entire American work force. Moreover, this figure represented an increase over twenty years earlier, when one of every eight American workers was employed by the top 500 industrial firms, or roughly 12 percent of the work force.[49] General Motors Corporation, alone, employed 746,000 employees, almost 1 percent of the entire labor force. Or, to look at the issue another way, the number of people who are self-employed has declined steadily in recent years. Among whites, for example, the proportion of the labor force that is self-employed has declined from 5.8 percent in 1960 to 3.0 percent in 1970, and to 2.0 percent in 1979.[50]

Above and beyond the fact that more and more people are becoming em- ployees of the large firms, there is the sense of meaning to work that, itself, appears to suffer with its growing rationalization. Here it is the divorce of form from con- tent, of the rules according to which work is performed and the products created through work, to which Marx, Weber, and Marcuse all pointed in offering their respective critiques. For, under the conditions of work in the large corporate or factory system, the sense of control, indeed of creativity, which the worker might come to possess, is instead increasingly divorced from him. Studies of worker dissatisfaction are suggestive in this respect, though by no means definitive. For instance, Norval Glenn and Charles Weaver recently examined survey responses given in 1955 and in 1980 to the question, "Do you enjoy your work so much that you have a hard time putting it aside?" Among men they found that 52.6 percent responded affirmatively to the question in 1955 and only 34.1 percent in 1980. Likewise, among women they found that 48.9 percent responded affirmatively in 1955, only 32.4 percent in 1980. Glenn and Weaver suggest that the differences may reflect a changed orientation toward work among the younger cohorts in 1980. Regardless, the data clearly suggest that work itself simply is no longer as comparatively satisfying to Americans as it once was.[51]

There are special personal vignettes we occasionally come across as well that in the intimacy of their detail and human sympathy strike us as especially sympto-

---

[49] *The Fortune Directory, The 500 Largest Industrial Corporations* (New York: Fortune, Time-Life, Inc., August 1961 and May 1981).

[50] *Statistical Abstract of the United States,* 1980, Table 698.

[51] Norval D. Glenn and Charles N. Weaver, "Enjoyment of Work by Fulltime Workers in the United States, 1955 and 1980," n.d. Data furnished here with permission of Norval Glenn. But cf. *Cumulative Codebook for the NORC General Social Surveys, 1972-1980* (Chicago: NORC, University of Chicago, July 1980), Question 133, p. 135.

matic of the often harsh and cruel character of technical work in modern society. Take the case of airplane controllers who must amass a host of technical information quickly in order to guide accurately and safely airplanes on their flight paths. Such persons, who seem subject to uncommon stress because of the excruciating agony posed by the tension between sophisticated apparatus and the lives of hundreds, if not thousands, of people, burn out rapidly. Jim Westerman of Detroit had been an air-traffic controller for ten years. He collapsed under the mounting pressure of the job after an incident which took the lives of two policemen who had been flying a police helicopter. The accident was no fault of Westerman's, as reports later confirmed; yet, the responsibility that lay in his hands was too much for him. He burned out because daily he had had to reduce the "fate of thousands of lives to tiny dots on a glass screen." To recover his sense of self-esteem, "to save his soul," Westerman subsequently took up a simple trade—constructing a forty-foot wooden boat in his backyard. He did it alone; and he, alone, was responsible for the final product.[52]

In order perhaps to truly appreciate the possible consequences of the increasing rationalization of work, one has only to turn to current discussions in the United States of the declining productivity of the work force. The United States has ranked first among industrialized nations in worker productivity since the end of World War II. But between 1960 and 1972 the increase in the output per man-hour of workers was the lowest among the work forces of the major industrialized nations in the world, with the highest rate of annual change in such productivity registered in Japan.[53] Moreover, in the period between 1973 and 1978 United States industry recorded lower average annual gains in productivity than it had in the preceding twenty-five-year period, another sign of the diminishing rate of productivity among American workers.[54] Businesspersons in the United States increasingly are becoming agitated over this trend, tracing the lower rates of productivity, in some part at least, to the very way in which work in the United States is rationalized—made formal and, most importantly, made impersonal. For the first time in this century at least, American businesspeople now look elsewhere to find models of the right way in which to perform work under conditions of advanced capitalism, with many of them coming to envy the system of productivity that has emerged in Japan since the end of World War II. Japan seems to have succeeded precisely in those ways in which American business has failed, seeking, in other words, to treat workers with respect and human concern. As Robert Cole observes in his important comparative analysis of Japanese and American industrial practices, "the Japanese manager views his employees as having socio-psychological needs, which, if nurtured, will yield economic returns to the firm."[55]

[52] *Austin American-Statesman*, August 22, 1979, p. F10.

[53] "Productivity: An International Perspective," Bulletin 1811 (Washington, D.C.: U.S. Department of Labor, Bureau of Labor Statistics, 1974).

[54] "Productivity Indexes for Selected Industries," Bulletin 2054 (Washington, D.C.: U.S. Department of Labor, Bureau of Labor Statistics, 1979).

[55] Robert E. Cole, *Work, Mobility and Participation: A Comparative Study of American and Japanese Industry* (Berkeley, Calif.: University of California Press, 1979), p. 223.

At first glance, it might seem that the growth of rationalization of work and of the workplace in modern America has little, if anything, to do with the exercise of power and influence. Still, just as it is the growth of the modern corporation that has propelled certain firms and groups of people into positions of unparalleled power and influence, so it is these same corporations, and particularly the nature of work within them, which has influenced the way the common man and woman act and think about their exercise of power. Subject to the technical and impersonal strictures of rational authority on their jobs, they may come to feel humbled, even powerless, in seeking to voice their concerns within the larger American polity— quite apart from the fact that they simply do not possess either the position or the resources for such exercise granted to those who stand at the top of the corporate hierarchies. These effects of the rationalization of work and authority in the workplace often go unrecognized by students of politics. And yet, as Marx and Weber informed us, the nature and character of work is part and parcel of modern life; hence, how it affects human beings as workers unquestionably will shape their lives as citizens, too.

The Extension of Citizenship

If the rationalization as well as routinization of work in modern America represents the other side of the growth of corporate power—indeed, almost an inevitable byproduct of it—so we might expect that in the same fashion the expansion of the obligations or, generally, the impotence, of the citizen would stand as the parallel to the growth of the modern state. Nothing could be further from the truth; it is, in fact, the precise opposite circumstance that seems so characteristic of the American polity now, rights having proliferated at a faster rate than obligations. Specifically, a greater proportion of the population now can claim the right to receive equal and just treatment in America, the very cornerstones of the liberal democratic ethos, than ever before. And, at the same time, the whole meaning of citizenship seems to have become enlarged in the twentieth century, deepening from citizenship in the most superficial sense, the right simply to be a member of the polity and to vote, to citizenship in the most profound fashion, the right to expect equal treatment and opportunity in any and all sectors of society. No one, of course, ever would deny that the rights of citizenship are important; yet the proliferation of such rights alongside the increase in the display of technical and administrative authority in the workplace conceivably could engender a contradiction of the most severe magnitude in American institutions. Toward the close of this chapter we shall explore the nature and implications of this contradiction more completely.

The meaning of citizenship in the United States has almost from the very first been defined in terms of equality. The Declaration of Independence proclaimed that all men are created equal, and that they are by nature free to pursue ends of their own choice. Just decades later, the perspicacious French aristocrat

Alexis de Tocqueville devoted volumes to the conditions of equality in America.[56] Americans, he argued, seem to feel themselves the social equal of one another, and this has come about, he further insisted, because America has not had to wrestle with the obstacles inherited from a feudal past. The very same theme was articulated a century later by the great Swedish economist Gunnar Myrdal. He claimed that the central foundations of American society had been erected on the fundamental notion that all people were created equal. Yet, he went on to observe that while true in principle, in fact there was considerable inequality in the United States, particularly between the races.[57]

Myrdal in some sense turned out to be the more accurate observer. Even while Tocqueville was claiming evidence for the presence of considerable social and political equality in the United States, numbers of people did not share in it. In the mid-nineteenth century, slavery still remained widespread, and only men could exercise the principal right of citizenship, that of suffrage. Not until the twentieth century did the idea of equality come to be extended to the great majority of people, and it happened because they were claimed to be citizens, thereby entitled to exercise certain basic Constitutional rights.

Citizenship in the twentieth century has become expanded in the first instance through the extension of certain fundamental rights to ever larger and more varied types of people. The passage in 1918, for example, of the nineteenth amendment to the Constitution meant the guarantee that women now could exercise the right to vote, and thus join their male counterparts after being so deprived for almost one hundred and fifty years. In 1948, the armed forces became integrated by a presidential order, putting black and white combat troops on an equal social footing for the first time in American history. Yet, it seems, the major breakthrough so far as the extension of citizenship rights was concerned, took place with the Supreme Court decision in the case of *Brown* v. *Topeka* in 1954, the famous ruling on school desegregation. Under the guiding hand of Earl Warren, the Court decided that no black Americans should be denied the right to an education the equivalent of that of whites, and it thus declared that public schools should become desegregated "with all deliberate speed." The decision of the Court proved historic in more than one sense, for by overturning the earlier ruling in the case of *Plessy* v. *Ferguson*, the case in which the Court decided in 1896 that Plessy, a black man, was not entitled to travel in the same public accommodations as whites, it proclaimed that black Americans were entitled to equal treatment before the law *simply* and *primarily* because they were citizens of the United States. That legal interpretation, together with subsequent Congressional decisions in the Civil Rights Acts of 1964 and 1965, served to shore up the extension of citizenship to black

---

[56] Alexis de Tocqueville, *Democracy in America,* Vols. I and II, trans. Henry Reeve (New York: Vintage Books, 1945).

[57] Gunnar Myrdal, *An American Dilemma,* Vol. I (New York: McGraw-Hill Book Company, 1964), chapter 1.

Americans. At the same time, the implications of those actions were that no citizens could be deprived of equal and fair treatment in education, politics, or even in such public domains as housing and public accommodations on the basis of their race, color, or creed. By implication, then, other non-Anglo groups, such as Hispanic Americans and native Americans, fell under the rule of these new laws and the new interpretation of the Constitution; thus, like blacks, they too came to benefit from the extension of citizenship to all groups that previously lay beyond the pale.

Soon, the movements inspired by these historic legal and Congressional decisions worked to the advantage of the largest numerical minority in America—women. Working hard and long hours, many women together with their male supporters managed to get an Equal Rights Amendment passed by the Congress. This further ensured that the rights of citizenship would be extended to women much along the same lines they had been expanded for religious and racial minorities; that, in particular, women, too, could not be subject to any type of occupational discrimination based simply upon their sex. Yet, the battle for full and complete citizenship for women may prove to be the longest and most difficult, with the adoption of the Equal Rights Amendment now dependent on the actions of several state legislatures. On balance, however, a greater variety of people, including women, in late twentieth-century America can enjoy the benefits of citizenship, and the implementation of the Constitutional provisions for equal treatment and opportunity, than in times past.

The extension of citizenship in the twentieth century took another, one must say, greatly more profound, turn. For until the 1954 Supreme Court decision, citizenship only included the most minimal kinds of rights. In the case of women, for example, it only meant the right to vote; even in the case of black Americans, until the 1954 Court ruling, citizenship only covered, in a limited fashion, suffrage. The more significant meaning, then, of the 1954 decision was that citizenship now came to take on a new meaning—people regarded as citizens of the United States were now to be further guaranteed, as part of their Constitutional heritage, a right to receive the same education as one another. The philosophy of "separate but equal" claimed legitimate in 1896 now was deemed to be invalid; true citizenship meant the full and complete implementation of the notion of equality, taking in the widest possible spectrum of the social domain. In light of this reinterpretation, and fundamental extension, of the meaning of citizenship, it only could be a matter of time that citizenship actually took on a more substantial form. It is in this regard, then, that the Congressional acts of the 1960s served simply to secure the 1954 Supreme Court ruling. Moreover, this very same period, of the 1950s and 1960s, witnessed additional elaboration upon the basic redefinition of the meaning of citizenship. Thus, with the passage of the various welfare measures in the 1960s, the Johnson administration was not merely creating a dependent population, as some social critics have claimed.[58] In fact, the administration was saying, in effect, that

[58] Frances Fox Piven and Richard A. Cloward, *Regulating the Poor* (New York: Pantheon, 1971).

citizenship in the United States now furnished one not merely with the chance to live, to work, and to be educated—by themselves extraordinary extensions of rights—but it also guaranteed a certain minimum standard of living to those people, who for whatever reasons, were unable to secure one for themselves. A very minimal interpretation, thus, of citizenship at the beginning of the twentieth century has, by the end of it, turned out to be an extraordinarily broad one.

The effects of the extension of citizenship in the United States over the long duration of the twentieth century, of what we might consider from another angle as the implementation of the liberal democratic ethos, often are overlooked by students of American politics, so intent are they on simply uncovering demons. Yet, even the slightest reflection on this obvious tendency suggests it to be a very profound and even disquieting one. For, when coupled with other tendencies, such as the growing dissatisfaction of Americans with their political institutions, one wonders whether the expansion of citizenship is necessarily a good thing for a polity after all.

Themes and Their Variations

Besides the principal themes we have discussed here, there are several other patterns that today are especially characteristic of power and influence in the United States. Three of them deserve our special attention: the alliances and divisions among the holders of high corporate and political office; the growth in the organized resistance to power lodged in the corporations and federal government; and the conflict between the imperatives of rationalization and the claims to equal treatment as citizens.

The Corporation and the State:
Alliances and Divisions

Certainly one of the most important observations advanced by social theorists who have studied modern politics is that there exists some sort of link between the exercise of power by the state and its exercise by the business firm. Karl Marx put the presumed connection most plainly. Political agents, such as the president, and political agencies, such as the government, are likely to act in ways that will further the interests of the ruling class, the capitalists in modern society. More recent analysts have taken up the same point of view. Thus, Ralph Miliband has claimed that in all modern capitalist countries the institutions of the state play a major role in securing and advancing the interests of large-scale capitalism.[59] This happens, he insists, in different respects. Those who occupy the major positions of state—for example, those who occupy the executive branch of the federal government, those who hold major judicial posts, even those who hold positions in Departments such

[59] Miliband, *The State in Capitalist Society.*

as that of State—all these individuals, among many others, are themselves people of considerable income and wealth, hence members of the capitalist class. But more than that, Miliband argues, the decisions of the leaders of state generally tend to favor the interests of private property, and to militate against those of the working class. He even insists that such favoritism has happened under the regimes of the Labour Party in Great Britain and of the Socialist Party in France, despite the fact that both parties represented themselves as advocates for the interests of workers.

Miliband's observations, however much they were shaped by it, were not exclusively intended to echo the ruling class thesis of Marx. For they also were designed to elaborate upon another wrinkle in the argument advanced by C. Wright Mills twenty-five years ago.[60] Mills claimed, in his thesis of the power elite, that in modern America the exercise of power within the corporate and governmental realms was greatly facilitated through an alliance among their top leaders. The leaders of state did not merely run the affairs of politics so as to secure ever more profits for capitalists. Rather, the leaders of state and those of the corporate realm essentially occupied the very same world, holding fast to many of the same ideals and values. They have been raised, Mills observed, in the same circumstances of great privilege, they have attended the same elite educational institutions, they belong as adults to many of the same social clubs; hence, it is not in the least surprising that they have come to hold corresponding outlooks on the way the world works. In other words, those who occupy the offices of great power and influence in the United States represent a fairly small and cohesive group of people; even if they do not meet or talk on a regular basis, they still act more or less in concert, committed to the same basic conception of the American national purpose.

Although they come from somewhat different theoretical angles, Miliband assuming essentially the thesis of a ruling class, Mills taking the position of cohesive elite groups, both scholars still reach agreement on a basic point—that between the officials of state and those of the corporation there is an alliance, leading in modern America to an unprecedented concentration of power and influence. Among many contemporary students of these matters, the difference between the claim that a ruling class exists and the argument that there simply are groups of elite figures is thought to be extremely crucial. Here, however, we shall overlook this difference, and concentrate simply on the basic features of this high-level alliance.[61]

During the past fifteen years a growing body of evidence has confirmed the existence of some kind of alliance among leading figures in politics and business, and also provided details about its main features. Thomas Dye and his associates,

---

[60] Mills, *The Power Elite.*

[61] On materials relevant to this disagreement among scholars, see, for example, David A. Gold, Y.H. Lo, and Erik Olin Wright, "Recent Developments in Marxist Theories of the Capitalist State, Part I," *Monthly Review,* 27 (October 1975), 29-43; "Recent Developments in Marxist Theories of the Capitalist State, Part II," *Monthly Review,* 27 (November 1975), 36-51; Nicos Poulantzas, *Political Power and Social Classes* (London: Verso, 1978); and Göran Therborn, *What Does the Ruling Class Do When It Rules?* (London: NCB, 1978).

for instance, assembled materials on the leading figures in each of several institutional sectors in the United States, among them the corporate and governmental realms.[62] They concluded that a group of people, comprised roughly of four thousand persons, represent something of a governing class in America. These are the people who occupy the top policy-making positions in industry and in government, positions from which are formulated decisions on key political and economic issues. Altogether Dye and his colleagues found that these four thousand individuals occupy about five thousand positions of great importance in the nation's institutions. Thus, they further claimed that power is rather intensely concentrated among this group of people. As we would expect, those individuals who make up this group often are figures whose names are very familiar to us. Among them are David Rockefeller, until recently the chairman of the board of Chase Manhattan Bank, and Henry Ford III, chairman of the board of the Ford Motor Company.

Research by Gwen Moore and by Michael Useem, each, further confirms claims of the existence of a high-level alliance among political and business figures in the United States. Moore and her associates conducted a survey of the leaders of a number of different institutional sectors, including the federal government, in 1971-72.[63] The results showed evidence of communications among a number of leaders in each sector, along with the presence of over thirty social cliques, consisting on the average of three members, each. Most importantly, Moore uncovered evidence of a large inner circle within the sample of leaders, itself consisting of 227 men and women, all of whom possessed relationships with one another, as well as crucial links to other cliques. This inner circle, drawn largely from the members of Congress, political appointments and business circles, possessed not only common social ties to one another, Moore found, but in some cases certain of its members belonged to the same social clubs, thereby further contributing to a common sense of purpose.

Michael Useem, in a series of articles designed to explore the structure of the capitalist class in America, has uncovered evidence of an inner circle within the capitalist class, itself, consisting again of a small number of people, on the order of sixteen hundred individuals.[64] Drawing upon materials collected about the lives of figures who held directorships of the 797 largest United States firms in 1969, Useem finds that those who possess the largest number of such directorships—who, to him, seem to constitute the inner circle of the capitalist class—generally are more likely than their fellow businesspeople to exercise governance over institutions outside the world of business. They are, specifically, more apt to serve in some

[62] Thomas R. Dye, Eugene R. Declerq, and John W. Pickering, "Concentration, Specialization, and Interlocking among Institutional Elites," *Social Science Quarterly,* 54 (June 1973), 17-19; and Thomas R. Dye, *Who's Running America? Institutional Leadership in the United States* (Englewood Cliffs, N.J.: Prentice-Hall, Inc., 1976).

[63] Gwen Moore, "The Structure of a National Elite Network," *American Sociological Review,* 44 (October 1979), 673-92; and Michael Useem, "The Social Organization of the American Business Elite," *American Sociological Review,* 44 (August 1979), 553-72.

[64] Useem, "The Social Organization of the American Business Elite."

Table 6-1 Individuals holding the highest number of multiple positions

David Rockefeller. Chairman and Chief Executive Officer, Chase Manhattan Bank. He is a director or trustee of the Rockefeller Foundation, Museum of Modern Art, Harvard University, University of Chicago, Council of Foreign Relations. He is also a Director of Chase International Investment Corporation, Morningside Heights, Inc., Rockefeller Center, Inc., Downtown Lower Manhattan Association. He is a centi-millionaire and a heavy political contributor.

Richard King Mellon. Chairman of the Board of Mellon National Bank and Trust Company; President, Mellon and Sons, director of the Aluminum Company of America, General Motors Corporation, Gulf Oil Corporation, Koppers Company, Pennsylvania Company, and the Pennsylvania Railroad. He is a centi-millionaire. He is a lieutenant general in the Reserves, a trustee of the Carnegie Institute of Technology, the Mellon Institute, and the University of Pittsburgh.

Crawford H. Greenewalt. Chairman of the Board of Directors E. I. duPont de Nemours; a director of the Equitable Trust Company, Boeing Aircraft Corporation, Christiana Securities Company, and Morgan Guaranty Trust Company; a trustee of Massachusetts Institute of Technology, Wilmington General Hospital, Philadelphia Academy of Natural Sciences, Philadelphia Orchestra Association, American Museum of Natural History, Carnegie Institute of Technology, and the Smithsonian Institute.

Arthur A. Houghton. President and Chairman of the Board of Directors of Corning Glass Works; a director of Steuben Glass Company, Erie-Lakawanna Railroad Company, New York Life Insurance Company, and the United States Steel Corporation; a trustee of the Corning Museum of Glass, J. Pierpont Morgan Library, Philharmonic Symphony Society of New York, Fund for the Advancement of Education, Lincoln Center of Performing Arts, Cooper Union, Metropolitan Museum of Art, New York Public Library, Rockefeller Foundation, and Institute for Contemporary Art of Boston. He is a centi-millionaire.

Amory Houghton. Chairman of the Board of First National Bank of New York City (First National City Corporation); a director of Metropolitan Life Insurance Co., Dow Corning Corporation, Pittsburgh Corning Corporation, Boy Scouts of America, Eisenhower College. He is a former Ambassador to France, and a trustee of the International Chamber of Commerce. He is a centi-millionaire.

Stewart R. Mott. Son of Charles S. Mott, former President and Director of General Motors Corporation, former Chairman of the Board of U.S. Sugar Corporation, and former mayor of Flint, Michigan. He is a director of Michigan National Bank, U.S. Sugar Corporation, Combo Industries, Rubin Realty, Planned Parenthood, Center for the Study of Democratic Institutions, National Committee for an Effective Congress, and the Urban League. He is a centi-millionaire, and a large political finance contributor.

Grayson L. Kirk. President and trustee of Columbia University. He is Director of Mobil Oil Co., IBM Corporation, Nation-Wide Securities Co., Dividend Shares, Inc., Consolidated Edison Co., Greenwich Savings Bank, Morningside Heights, Inc., and for Carnegie Foundation. He is also Bryce Professor of History and International Relations at Columbia University.

James Stillman Rockefeller. Former Chairman and current director of First National City Bank of New York; a director of the International Banking Corporation, National City Foundation, First New York Corporation, First National City Trust Company, Mercantile Bank of Canada, National City Realty Corporation, Kimberly-Clark Corporation, Northern Pacific Railway Company, National Cash Register Company, Pan-American World Airways, and Monsanto Company.

Table 6-1 (Continued)

C. Douglas Dillon. Chairman of the Board of Dillon, Read & Co., Inc., member of New York Stock Exchange, and Director of Chase Manhattan Bank. He was formerly Secretary of Treasury, and Undersecretary of State. He is a trustee of Metropolitan Museum of Art, Brookings Institution, The American Assembly, and Harvard University. He is a large political contributor, and his wife is a trustee of the Museum of Modern Art.

Cyrus B. Vance. Senior Partner, Simpson, Thacher & Bartlett. He is a director of Pan-American World Airways, Aetna Life Insurance Co., IBM Corporation, Council of Foreign Relations, American Red Cross, University of Chicago, and the Rockefeller Foundation. He was formerly Secretary of the Army, and Undersecretary of Defense. He was chief U.S. Negotiator at the Paris Peace Talks on Vietnam under President Lyndon Johnson.

G. Keith Funston. Former President of the New York Stock Exchange. He is Chairman of the Board of Olin Mathieson Corporation, a director of Illinois Central Industries, Chemical Bank of New York, IBM Corporation, Metropolitan Life Insurance Co., Ford Motor Co., Republic Steel Corporation, AVCO Corporation, and National Aviation Corporation. He is a trustee of Trinity College and a director of the American Cancer Society. He was Chairman of the War Production Board during World War II.

Harold Holmes Helm. Chairman of the Board of Chemical Bank of New York. He is a Director of Equitable Life Assurance Co., McDonald Douglas Aircraft Corporation, Uniroyal, Western Electric, Bethlehem Steel, Colgate-Palmolive Co., F. W. Woolworth Co., Cumm Engine Co., and Lord and Taylor. He is a trustee of Princeton University, National Industrial Conference Board, and the Woodrow Wilson Foundation.

H. L. Romnes. Chairman of the Board and Chief Executive Officer, American Telephone and Telegraph Company. He is a director of United States Steel Corporation, Chemical Bank of New York, Colgate-Palmolive Co., Cities Service Co., Mutual Life Insurance and Co. He is also active at the national level in the United Negro College Fund, the Urban League, and the Salvation Army. He is a trustee of M.I.T., the National Safety Council, and the Committee on Economic Development.

Henry Ford, II. Chairman and Chief Executive Officer, Ford Motor Company. He is a Director of General Foods Corporation and a trustee of the Ford Foundation. His brother, Benson Ford, is also a director of Ford Motor Company and the Ford Foundation, as well as a director of the American Safety Council and United Community Funds of America. Another brother, William Clay Ford, is President of the Detroit Lions Professional Football Club and a director of the Girl Scouts of America, Thomas A. Edison Foundation, and the Henry Ford Hospital. These Fords are centi-millionaires and heavy political contributors.

Richard S. Perkin. President and Chairman of Board of Perkin-Elmer Corporation. He is a director of Ford Motor Co., International Telephone and Telegraph, New York Life Insurance, Consolidated Edison, Southern Pacific Railroad, Aetna Life Insurance, New England Telephone Co., U.S. Trust Co. of New York. He is a trustee of Metropolitan Museum of Art, American Museum of Natural History and Pratt Institute.

Robert V. Roosa. Partner, Brown Brothers, Harriman & Co. (investments). He is a director of American Express Co., Anaconda Copper Co., and Texaco. He is a trustee of the Rockefeller Foundation, The Rye County Day School, Council on Foreign Relations, and the National Bureau of Economic Research. He was formerly Undersecretary of the Treasury. He holds an earned Ph.D. from the University of Michigan.

Arthur H. Dean. Senior Partner, Sullivan and Cromwell; Chairman of the U.S. Delegation on Nuclear Test Ban Treaty, chief U.S. negotiator of the Korean Armistice Agreement; a director of American Metal Climax, American Bank Note Company, National Union Electric Corporation, El Paso Natural Gas Company, Crown Zellerbach Corporation, Campbell Soup Company, Northwest Production Corporation, Lazard Fund, Inc., and the Bank of New

Table 6-1 (Continued)

Source: Adapted from Thomas R. Dye, Eugene R. Declerq, and John W. Pickering, "Concentration, Specialization, and Interlocking Among Institutional Elites," *Social Science Quarterly*, vol. 54, no. 1 (June 1973), 17–19.

policy-making capacity in philanthropic organizations, scientific and research firms, organizations exclusively concerned with world economic development, and colleges or universities. They also are more apt to hold advisory positions with the federal government. Thus, Useem believes, the members of the business elite, or inner circle of the capitalist class, come to wield great power and influence outside their own sphere of immediate competence through securing positions of strategic policy-making significance elsewhere.

Possibly the most telling evidence of an alliance among the leading figures comes from studies of the membership and workings of certain policy-making groups that seem to operate on the fringes of American business and government. G. William Domhoff, who has done as much as anyone to reveal the various facts of an alliance, finds that several groups have been particularly critical to the formation of domestic and foreign policy in America.[65] Among them are the Council on Foreign Relations (CFR), the Committee for Economic Development (CED), and the Business Advisory Council (BAC). The CFR, founded in 1921, has over the years provided a meeting place for members of the academic, business, and political

[65]See, for instance, G. William Domhoff, *The Higher Circles: The Governing Class in America* (New York: Vintage Books, 1971); G. W. Domhoff, *Who Rules America?* (Englewood Cliffs, N.J.: Prentice-Hall, 1967); and G. W. Domhoff, *Who Really Rules? New Haven and Community Power Reexamined* (Santa Monica, Calif.: Goodyear Publishing Company, Inc., 1978).

worlds. It publishes various reports and pamphlets, including the widely influential quarterly, *Foreign Affairs*, along with holding frequent seminars and conferences on special topics. It also has provided some individuals with means for achieving their first form of public recognition, among them former Secretary of State Henry Kissinger. And in recent decades its membership often has furnished much of the talent for the occupants of major governmental positions.[66]

The CED and the BAC each have been comprised of prominent persons in the business and political worlds, and have shaped economic policy much as the CFR has molded explicitly foreign policy.[67] Both groups generally have adopted the economic premises of John Maynard Keynes, namely, that the federal government should play a very active part in the regulation of the economy. Since 1932, members of both organizations have had a significant impact on the making of economic policy at the very highest governmental levels. Philip Burch, for example, reports that members of these groups were decisive in the formulation of the Marshall Plan in 1947, the program that eventually helped to rescue Western Europe from possible financial disaster. Among those people who helped to create this plan, and who later served to implement its provisions, were Averell Harriman, long a prominent figure in both corporate and diplomatic circles, Paul Hoffman, the president of the Studebaker Corporation, and Robert Sproul, former president of the University of California.[68]

Although none of this documentation fully demonstrates the precise operations of a high-level alliance, it still seems sufficient to suggest the outlines of cooperative policy-making and policy-shaping groups in the United States. Yet, we must not embrace the notion of some deep alliance too hastily for, in some respects, there exist as many indications of important divisions among the leading circles as alliances. One obvious division within this world has occurred on a territorial basis, though territory here probably is simply symptomatic of a deeper discord over economic interests. The division first came to light with the election in 1964 of Lyndon Johnson, the first time in a century that a Southerner was elected as president. By and large, however, Johnson's advisors were many of the same figures as those of his predecessor, John Kennedy, a group of men bred and nurtured in the Northeast. Richard Nixon, first elected to the presidency in 1968, brought with him a group of Southern Californians, headed by John Mitchell, Robert Haldeman, and John Ehrlichman, all of whom came from outside the circles that for several decades have provided Washington its top leaders. The shift away from the councils of the Northeast to the South and Southwest continued with the administration of Jimmy Carter, even in a somewhat more pronounced fashion. It has been argued by some, in fact, that Carter's failures as president lay precisely

[66] Domhoff, *The Higher Circles*, pp. 112-23.

[67] Domhoff, *The Higher Circles*. Also see Philip H. Burch, Jr., *Elites in American History: The New Deal to the Carter Administration* (New York: Holmes & Meier Publishers, Inc., 1980).

[68] Burch, *Elites in American History*, pp. 97-101.

in his almost exclusive reliance on the so-called "Georgia Mafia," a group of counselors typically unfamiliar with the routines of the Congress and, especially, with knowledge of the various behind-the-scenes figures so crucial to the shaping of policy in earlier Democratic administrations.

Yet, to date the sharpest division among the higher business and political circles in America has occurred with the election of Ronald Reagan to the presidency. For Reagan's election means not simply a host of new faces, and backgrounds, in Washington, it also portends a broad and deep shift in the policies of the federal government. Reagan's "kitchen cabinet" is composed of men and women associated with the Hoover Institute of Stanford University, a think tank notable for its highly conservative orientation. It includes on its roster Milton Friedman, chief spokesman for classical economics in America over the past several decades. These men and women, generally, are highly disdainful of the economic theories of Keynes. They claim that the federal government, beginning with the presidential tenure of Franklin Delano Roosevelt, has come to meddle far too much in the workings of business enterprise in America, and that a healthy economy can only be realized if the principles of a free market are permitted to work their special magic. Thus, during his first few months in office Reagan has demanded, and received, congressional approval for a major cutback in federal spending, the most severe reductions to take place in the sorts of social welfare and service programs initiated with the Roosevelt administration. If the Reagan program does indeed bear fruit, especially if it helps to stem the rate of inflation in America, it will at the same time serve to deepen a division among the higher circles of leaders.

To sum up, then, the power of the corporations and of the federal government in twentieth-century America has been solidified in the form of a social alliance among leading figures of both spheres. Sometimes these alliances are construed as evidence of a ruling class, other times as evidence merely of elites. Whatever the interpretation, however, it surely is the case that some kind of active cooperation takes place, leading to a shared view of the national purpose. But this alliance, which over the past decade and one-half has received ever more attention from the probing eyes of social scientists, faces its most severe test in the near future. The division between the liberal and conservative segments among the leading circles appears to have grown ever sharper, and to have displayed itself most markedly in the actions of the Reagan administration. If, as Reagan and his advisors hope, this administration proves to undo the whole complex syndrome of policies enacted since the Roosevelt presidency, and at the same time is able to cope successfully with the urgent problems facing America, such success could deeply divide American leaders and make an illusion of claims of close alliance at the top.

Organized Resistance
to Corporate and Governmental Power

A second variation on the themes of power and influence in contemporary America concerns the resistance to power organized among different groups of citizens. Federal and state government have gone a long way toward achieving the extension of citizenship in the twentieth century. Black Americans, native Americans, Hispanic Americans, and women, among other minorities, have gained privileges previously denied to them, and they thus have come to enter the political arena in a very substantial manner. But therein hangs a paradox. For, the very extension of citizenship, of the right to be equal in America, has meant that ever increasing numbers of citizens now believe it proper to seek to shape the policies that will be decisive over their destinies. The creation of a new and fuller form of citizenship in the polity, in other words, has led more people to press the claims ever more urgently for even added expansion of such rights. *or benefits*

Among those sectors of the population who have sought to take advantage of the new climate of democracy which has descended upon America are women, in particular. While they have been the beneficiaries of the new interpretations of citizenship in the 1950s and 1960s, at the same time such an extension appears to have fueled their efforts—or, at least, the efforts of many of them—to gain equality with men in a decisive and consummate fashion. The National Organization for Women (NOW), founded in 1965, represents a leader among women's groups in the effort to attain full citizenship for women. It has pressed more and more vigorously for complete citizenship for women, and has been the principal sponsor of those efforts in various states across the land to secure passage of the Equal Rights Amendment. Women, however, are not the only group to take advantage of the new climate in America. At the very opposite end of the political spectrum, among the Moral Majority and the National Conservative Political Action Committee (NCPAC), one discovers a similar degree of enthusiasm for pressing the rights of citizenship in America. In this case, however, demands are made for a new, if not broader, tolerance of religion in the United States, as well as for a willingness to put up with a deeper and more secure connection between the realm of religious faith and that of political action. Both the Reverend Jerry Falwell, and Terry Dolan, the leaders respectively of the Moral Majority and NCPAC, each seem to have assembled an enormous amount of support for their cause, in terms either of active partisan backers and/or in terms of substantial financial underwriting. Opposed to the policies taken by the federal government during the past forty years, deeply set against the welfare statism of the Democrats, these groups would like to reinstate certain basic religious and political ideals in America, such as the sacredness of the nuclear family, and probably would very much like to roll back the broadened conception of equality that has developed in recent years. Of course, there is great irony in the fact that the success of their programs to mobilize public opinion, however widespread, is due, in some measure at least, to the very gains they wish to eliminate.

The federal government is not the only target of public criticism nowadays. So, too, the power of the corporation has come under heavy attack, led by the consumer crusader Ralph Nader. Nader first achieved nationwide fame in 1967 as the author of a stinging critique of the American automobile industry, *Unsafe at Any Speed*.[69] He claimed that Detroit manufactured cars that were vulnerable to various

---

[69] Ralph Nader, *Unsafe at Any Speed* (New York: Grossman, 1965).

mechanical and structural defects, and that it did so often fully aware of the dangers involved for passengers. As a result of this book and his testimony before congressional committees, the automobile industry was compelled to make ever more careful examinations of the products they manufactured; this has led to the periodic recall of American automobiles for defects uncovered by their creators. Nader also broadened his attack to take in other areas of industry, among them clothing and foodstuffs. Because of these efforts, along with those of other groups such as Common Cause and the Sierra Club, the whole character of consumer rights and expectations has become changed in recent years, leading to stricter standards on the manufacture of products.

These, and other examples of organized resistance to federal and corporate power in America—for example, resistance in the form of the tax revolts—seem to signify a different character to the nature of resistance than existed earlier in this century. The Moral Majority, NOW, Nader's Raiders, among others, make demands not so much to be admitted as citizens into the political arena as to be permitted more opportunity to have a decisive voice over policies now that they are in the arena. Almost everybody now is a citizen, as a result of decisions taken in the 1960s; the issue now is, How far do rights extend? But it is not simply the changed milieu of politics, owing to the spread of the democratic ethos, which signifies a difference between the politics of today and the politics of yesterday. The dissident groups today are better organized, and strategically more clever, than their ancestors of the past. The Moral Majority, for example, has employed the mass media in such a way as to reach larger numbers of people than dissidents ever could reach in the early part of this century. Likewise, they, as well as the NCPAC, and even some of the groups organized on behalf of traditionally liberal concerns, have come to rely not on stampeding bodies alone, but on certain financial resources to get their respective messages across to the public.[70] In short, these various forms of organized resistance to federal and to corporate power nowadays offer hopeful signs that somehow the tide might be turned, however so slightly, in favor of citizens. At the very least, they suggest that power and politics in twentieth-century America consists not merely in the actions of big government and big business. In this climate of the 1980s, it also consists of people who wish to take advantage of their newly won sense of citizenship and equality.

The Obligation to Obey vs. the Right to Be Equal

Among philosophers there seems to have been a selective attention to the nature of obligations and rights in the human condition. Immanuel Kant, the great eighteenth-century German philosopher, tended to emphasize obligations involved

---

[70]This change in the character of contemporary movements has been identified and analyzed at length by John McCarthy and Mayer N. Zald, *The Trend of Social Movements in America: Professionalization and Resource Mobilization* (Morristown, N.J.: General Learning Corporation, 1973).

in moral action more so than rights, arguing that in his capacity as a rational human being a person had an obligation to act on the basis of certain moral imperatives, in particular, the categorical imperative.[71] To Kant, a person, as a rational human being, was moral insofar as he acted from a sense of duty—both to himself, as a creature possessed of the capacity to reason, and to others, to whom he perforce must admit the same basic capacities and moral senses as himself. Yet other philosophers, such as Jean Jacques Rousseau and John Locke, have emphasized the rights that attach to the human condition more so than the obligations, arguing that in his capacity as a human being a person is possessed of certain fundamental and inalienable rights, among them, in effect, the right to property and the right to have his interests expressed.[72] Both to Rousseau and to Locke alike, it would be a denial of human nature if an individual was not permitted to exercise these rights. Thus, between these two sorts of philosophical positions—those who consider man as moral if he fulfills certain obligations, and those who consider him moral should he act on the basis of certain rights—man, himself, is suspended, caught between an inevitable and indissoluble tension.

This very tension, between the individual in his capacity as someone who remains obedient to higher authority, and the person who at the same time is free to exercise inalienable rights, is a tension peculiarly characteristic of the circumstances of men and women in late twentieth-century America. For men and women have been urged, especially in the course of their workaday lives, to fulfill certain technical and administrative imperatives in the nature of their work. As work and industry themselves have grown ever more technically advanced, as the operations of plants have become expanded, as firms have become enlarged, all these have meant the growing reliance upon certain technical and administrative procedures in the workplace. Specifically, people increasingly have come under the firm and omnipresent hand of workplace authority, instructed in the nature of their work, in the routines they must follow, and in the very fashion in which they must produce. It is in this sense that the authority of the workplace has come to supplant, even possibly to suppress, as Marcuse claimed, the full and rich fashion through which men and women might otherwise be free to create products of their own choice.

The dilemma arises for people when they confront an opposing tendency in the late twentieth century, namely, that which we have called variously the expansion of citizenship, or the extension of the democratic ethos. While in the workplace they are urged to adhere to the claims of industrial authority, yet in the political arena people are aware of the extension of the privileges of citizenship, particularly that which entails and permits them to be treated as the equal of one another. And while they themselves may often not be directly confronted with this

[71] Immanuel Kant, *Critique of Practical Reason,* trans. Lewis White Beck (Indianapolis, Ind.: Bobbs-Merrill, 1956).

[72] John Locke, *Two Treatises of Government* (New York: New American Library, 1963); Jean Jacques Rousseau, "The Social Contract," in *The Essential Rousseau,* trans. Lowell Bair (New York: New American Library, 1974).

dilemma—between the obligation to obey and the right to be free, as let us say working women are—nevertheless, it is likely that many citizens have come to sense the blatant contradiction here. They are caught and suspended on the horns of a major dilemma.

For many Americans, especially those who have not become actively engaged in the effort at organized resistance to federal and corporate power, this very dilemma, and its ensuing tension, might well account for the continuing decline in Americans' satisfaction with the operations of their institutions. Social scientists who have attended to these matters have discovered, since the late 1950s, that a greater and greater percentage of Americans claim themselves to be unhappy with the running of major firms and with government itself. Consider, for example, the survey data assembled in table 6-2. These materials, which come from sample surveys conducted by the Louis Harris organization, show that the confidence of Americans in all their institutions has shown a steady drop between 1966 and 1976. No doubt, there are different reasons that could be held to account for these attitudes. Yet, surely some of the most important spring precisely from the growing contradiction between the demands of occupational authority and those of political equality.

Along such lines, there are observers who write of the current condition in America, especially in the political arena, claiming there to be a decline in responsible citizenship and effective authority. They argue, in effect, that the current atmosphere of the American polity—one in which there seems more confusion than clarity, more voices raised in dissent than clarion calls to high ideals—springs from the decline in a shared set of norms and the exercise of social control within the

Table 6-2   Assessment of the leadership of key institutions (Harris poll data)

	percentages of the public stating they have "a great deal of confidence" in certain institutions						
	1976	*1975*	*1974*	*1973*	*1972*	*1971*	*1966*
Medicine	42%	43%	50%	57%	48%	61%	73%
Higher education	31	36	40	44	33	37	61
Organized religion	24	32	32	36	30	27	62
The military	23	24	33	40	35	27	62
The U.S. Supreme Court	22	28	40	33	28	23	50
The press	20	26	25	30	18	18	29
Major companies	16	19	21	29	27	27	55
Executive branch of the federal government	11	13	28	19	27	23	41
Organized labor	10	14	18	20	15	14	22
Congress	9	13	18	29	21	19	42

Source: Adapted from Everett Carll Ladd, Jr., "The Polls: The Question of Confidence," *Public Opinion Quarterly,* vol. 40, no. 4 (Winter, 1976-77), 545.

society.[73] But such a judgment is far too shortsighted; indeed, it appears to mis-apprehend the situation altogether. For what, in fact, has occurred is that American institutions, especially those of the workplace, have tried in the name of higher profits to exercise increasing authority over human beings while, at the same time, political institutions have extended the right to dissent on the basis of equality. It should be more than obvious that if these two claims upon the life of individual human beings are both to be effective, then they must be suitably balanced, if not by the individual, then surely by the institutions themselves. And yet, with the exception of a few experiments in certain industries, such as those in which laborers share in the profits of their firms as well as in the decisions over production, the nature of American society at present is such that the claims to obedience and those for equal treatment are viewed as opposing, rather than as complementary.

Perhaps the difficulties which philosophers have confronted in trying to reveal the fundamental moral character of humankind should alert us to how difficult it may be for any society to mix easily both duties and rights. Yet it remains evident that one of the major characteristics of the American polity now, at the close of the twentieth century, is this very dilemma posed between rights and obligations. And, assuming that workplace authority becomes ever more extensive, and political equality ever more embracing, it is a dilemma not soon to disappear.

CONCLUSIONS

In this chapter we have considered some of the major and minor themes of power and influence in American society over the course of the twentieth century. Two great developments—the expansion of the corporation and the growth of the state—each have led to a concentration of power, and of wealth, in the hands of a very small number of men and women. Used unwisely such power could seriously endanger the lives of millions of citizens; employed toward the attainment of humanitarian goals, it could do much to relieve the misery of peoples the world over. Whether the good uses of such power can emerge from a society, if not a world, dominated by an overriding interest in profit, is an issue that concerns many scholars, not to say citizens.

These two great tendencies, as we also have seen, seem to have certain parallels in their effects on the common man and woman in modern America. Like Marcuse, we have argued here that a certain discontent in modern America emanates from the formalization and routinization of work. We also have claimed that the twentieth century has witnessed an ever greater extension of citizenship rights to the American population. These two tendencies, themselves, when seen

[73] See, for example, the analyses by Janowitz. Morris Janowitz, *The Last Half Century: Societal Change and Politics in America* (Chicago: University of Chicago Press, 1978); and Morris Janowitz, "Observations on the Sociology of Citizenship: Obligations and Rights," *Social Forces,* 59 (September 1980), 1-24.

in conjunction with one another, lead to a potential danger—the obvious dilemma between the demands on the worker to follow authority and to work in a precise, formal fashion, and the rights granted the same individual, to be free and to receive equal treatment as any other human being. This clash is one that lies deep in the fabric of modern American life, and necessarily affects the sense that individuals have about their own public power and influence.

To appreciate, then, the nature of power and influence in modern America is to recognize some of the complexities that exist, along with the various tensions and dilemmas woven into the character of this society. Such an acknowledgment might help us to deal better with the issues of power and influence in the future.

CHAPTER SEVEN

Patterns of Power and Politics in Communities

Now, the city is the great center of political force, of intellectual force, of money force. Its influence upon National politics is immense, if not decisive. The question of Good City Government is in effect the question of Good National Government.

HERBERT WELSH, *The Movement for Good City Government*
in the United States (date)

Areas where large numbers of people congregate and settle have been places of vitality throughout history—the very seats of civilization and learning. Sites such as Athens, Sparta, Rome, Venice, Florence, Paris, London, Moscow, and New York seem to harbor the very best that a particular civilization has to offer. The great ideas of humankind issue forth from such centers. New forms of social organization and economic production, such as that in Rome or in the great cities of the Middle Ages, are instituted in them. These are centers of learning, such as Athens in ancient times or London in modern times. Great works of art and other forms of creativity are achieved in these centers, such as in Florence or Venice during the Middle Ages or in New York and Paris now. The list is endless, but such centers do not retain their elegance and vitality indefinitely. Rome turned from the seat of a civilization into the first site of its crumble and decay; Bruges turned from a first-rate center of finance and trade in the Middle Ages into a minor place of residence in the age of great industry; London was transformed from one of the two or three most active centers in the West in the eighteenth and nineteenth centuries to a mere doormat of civilization in the latter part of the twentieth century; and New

York, once regarded as the fountain of American life, becomes as the twentieth century closes a "behavioral sink" and an "unheavenly city," to use two current epithets.[1]

Seeking to unlock the secrets of social life and social behavior, it is small wonder that philosophers and journalists, scientists and novelists have looked to the rise and fall of cities for the answers to the persistent questions about the human condition: Where is this society heading? What is the nature of the relations among people? What are the evils that this civilization perpetrates on human beings? How may the good life be secured? Many among those who helped to create a sociological point of view on the world and a body of knowledge about it sought answers to these and other questions in turning their attention to the areas where large masses of people assembled and lived. The penetrating and insightful German social philosopher Georg Simmel saw in the city many of the evils that would come to burden modern man—the cash nexus as a substitute for the social bond; the anonymity of men instead of their intimacy; and the quick and disquieting tempo of social life as opposed to the restful one.[2] Somewhat later, other sociologists including Robert Park, a student of Simmel's, evoked a similar interest in the character of urban life, focusing on the personal ills and social disruptions and creating an entire brand of social scientists whose interest lay exclusively in the dynamic qualities of urban life.[3]

Urban life continues to arouse the interest and spark the probing imaginations of students of social life. Of special interest to students of politics are the appraisals of those scholars who seek to understand the nature of the polity in communities. Urban settings for them appear not only as the wellsprings upon which much of modern life draws but also as an accessible and convenient location in which to examine many of the larger questions about power in modern society. Over the course of the past four decades, observers of politics in urban settings have turned their attention to such matters as the form of leadership, the level of mass participation, and the extent of disaffection as manifest in political forms. Answers to these matters are taken, in part at least, as offering wisdom and insight on the quality of leadership in modern society and the form and level of disaffections within it. Despite the encroachments of the nation-state and national governments on virtually every center of life in modern societies, many of these scholars appear to remain firm in their belief that, as Welsh observed, "the question of Good City Government is in effect the question of Good National Government."

This chapter examines recent inquiries into the character of politics in community settings. As in other portions of this book, the focus is chiefly upon the United States.

---

[1] Edward Banfield, *The Unheavenly City Revisited*, rev. ed. (Boston: Little, Brown and Company, 1974).

[2] Georg Simmel, "The Metropolis and Mental Life," in *Georg Simmel on Individuality and Social Forms*, ed. Donald N. Levine (Chicago: University of Chicago Press, 1971), pp. 324-39.

[3] For a discussion of Simmel's influence on Park and other American sociologists, see Levine, *Georg Simmel*, pp. liv-lxv.

THE STRUCTURE OF POWER
IN COMMUNITIES

The previous chapter devoted some attention to identifying the most salient dimensions of power. However, one additional element of power that is important is an element that refers to a further characteristic of the dispersion of power among the members of a social setting. This is the *structure* of power, a concept that refers to the social relations and organizations through which the holders of power in a social setting are linked and through which their power becomes exercised. Students of community politics are extremely sensitive to the nuances in the structures of power, and collectively have arrived at several basic shapes to the power structures of communities. Figure 7-1 presents diagrams of each of the major forms and community sites to which those patterns conform. Type A, the simple pyramid, consists of an individual, or a small number of individuals, who exercise virtually all the power in a community; Middletown, a community studied in the 1930s by Robert and Helen Lynd, best illustrates it.[4] In type B, there again is a small handful of individuals at the top of the structure, but their power over the masses is exercised through mediating instruments or organizations that are somewhat hierarchically organized. Each of the organizations, moreover, exercises control over separate domains of activity within the community, for example, the economic or the political; Atlanta as revealed in Floyd Hunter's study of the 1950s is an illustration of this shape.[5] Type C, like type B, has multiple centers. In this case, the integration of their aims and purposes comes through the existence of another center possessing roughly the same amount of power; the pattern probably is best described as that of "first among equals." The findings from Robert Dahl's study of New Haven most closely conform to this shape.[6] Multiple centers of power are also found in the type D pattern, but in contrast to types B and C, there is no point of control or integration of these centers. Moreover, the boundaries of domains over which the centers exercise their power are often not very sharply defined, and hence conflicts can and do arise among these centers in their attempts to extend their power into other domains. The studies of New York by Wallace Sayre and Herbert Kaufman and of Chicago by Edward Banfield present pictures most closely resembling the type D shape.[7] Type E is amorphous, representing no discernible shape to the structure of power in communities. Although some observers claim to have identified such patterns, there are no available case studies of communities whose results actually conform to this pattern. The types of structures are clarified in discussions of these studies later in this chapter.

---

[4] Robert S. Lynd and Helen Merrell Lynd, *Middletown in Transition: A Study in Cultural Conflicts* (New York: Harcourt Brace Jovanovich, 1937), chapters 3 and 9 especially.

[5] Floyd Hunter, *Community Power Structure: A Study of Decision Makers* (New York: Doubleday and Company, 1963).

[6] Robert Dahl, *Who Governs? Democracy and Power in an American City* (New Haven: Yale University Press, 1964).

[7] Wallace S. Sayre and Herbert Kaufman, *Governing New York City* (New York: Russell Sage Foundation, 1960); and Edward Banfield, *Political Influence* (New York: Free Press of Glencoe, 1961).

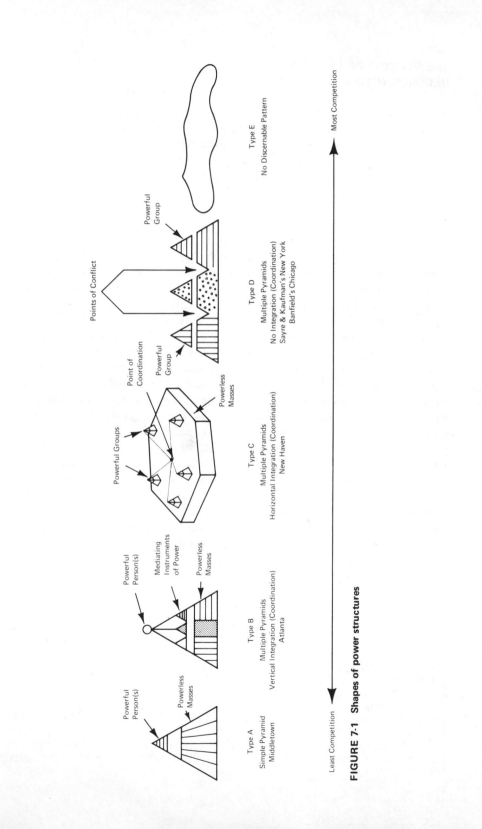

FIGURE 7-1 Shapes of power structures

CURRENT PATTERNS OF POWER
AND POLITICS IN COMMUNITIES

Who actually has the power to run things in the communities of modern America? Is it a small handful of businesspersons sitting in the backrooms of smoke-filled clubs who make the major decisions that control our lives in rural or urban America? Is it, instead, the people down at city hall, the mayor and his or her associates, who effectively act to control our public goods, such as parks, streets, and schools? Or is it groups of individuals, representing our various interests and concerns, who run our lives, sometimes simply through the compromise victories achieved in battle among themselves? The question of who runs things now and the different answers appear to be simple and straightforward. Yet, this query is by no means simple, and it often generates opposing answers and opposing frameworks for analysis.

There are two different points of view about who runs things in modern American communities. One, the elitist, uses certain distinctive methods to arrive at the answer that the public life of American communities is controlled by a small handful of people whose resources for power are mainly economic. The other, the pluralist, uses its own strategies to reach the conclusion that modern communities consist of different sectors, for example, the economic and the political; each sector appears to be dominated by separate handfuls of individuals battling among themselves for supremacy, and the victory often goes to those who sit in the principal seats of political power in the community. To understand each point of view more fully, let us briefly review the exemplary studies from each genre.

Elitist Patterns

Floyd Hunter's study of Atlanta, Georgia, was published in the early 1950s. His theoretical point of view is clear from the outset; like Dahl, Weber, and many others, he believes that power is an aspect of a social relationship and, in particular, that it is the act of men who get other men to do things for them. Hunter further asserts that the effectiveness of an individual's power rests on the strength of the social structure and social relations in which he is located: "Power of the individual must be structured into associational, clique, or institutional patterns to be effective."[8] This notion is part of his broad, implicit assumption that the ongoing life of communities is largely the life of their organizations and institutions, not of the individuals qua individuals who reside within them.

Hunter identified the men of power and the networks within which they resided in Atlanta. As a first approximation, he employed a technique called the reputational method. To identify the power holders, he first drew up a large list of names of people who occupy important positions in each of the four sectors of Atlanta; individuals were put on the list who represent civic leaders, governmental leaders, business leaders, and social leaders. These names were provided by organi-

---

[8] Hunter, *Community Power Structure*, p. 6.

169

zations within each of the sectors of the community that Hunter considered important. For instance, the Community Council helped to assemble the early lists of civic leaders, while the Chamber of Commerce provided those of business leaders. Leaders in society and individuals who were wealthy were given by newspaper editors and other civic leaders. Hunter assembled an initial list of one hundred seventy-five leaders in the community. His next step, the heart of the reputational method, involved the collective judgment of a panel of experts. Hunter selected a group of fourteen people from within Atlanta who, he claimed, represented expert informants on the nature of the community, particularly the character of its politics. Hunter asked these fourteen people to select the names of the ten most influential people within each of the four major sectors of the community. Specifically, he asked of them:

> Place in rank order, one through ten, ten persons from each list of personnel—who in your opinion are the most influential persons in the field designated—influential from the point of view of ability to lead others.[9]

Using the opinions of the expert panel, who ranked individuals according to their reputations for influence in the community, Hunter arrived at a list of the forty most influential leaders in the community.

The forty individuals were then interviewed with a battery of questions; twenty-seven of them, those who apparently turned out to rank as the most influential, were questioned extensively. The questions were designed in part to give further rankings of power and influence in the community. For instance, one of the questions that Hunter employed to identify the top leadership segments of the community was, "If a project were before the community that required *decision* by a group of leaders—leaders that nearly everyone would accept—which *ten* on the list of forty would you choose?" Also, the questions were employed to identify friendship and associational networks among the forty individuals. Thus, the men were asked which of the other forty individuals they knew on the list, how well they knew each other, whether they attended clubs together, and about the existence of cliques and crowds—in short, a whole variety of both qualitative and quantitative devices designed to reveal the existence and strength of relations that tied leaders to one another. Finally, the questions asked of the forty men were also employed to reveal how specific decisions, most within the recent memory of participants, had been initiated and implemented in the community. Through this device, Hunter tried to verify evidence gathered on the general reputations for power and influence possessed by individuals on his list of leaders. Hunter clearly employed a most comprehensive and thorough strategy in attempting to detect the main threads of power in Atlanta.

Taking all of his evidence, Hunter comes up with several striking conclusions about the nature of power in Atlanta. First, he suggests that the power structure of Atlanta consists of two major segments, the policy-makers and the policy-

9 Ibid., p. 258.

executors. The first group represents the top echelon of influentials in Atlanta; they are the ones who are ranked the highest in terms of their influence and the ones who, from the discussion of the course of policy decisions, appear to create the materials for decisions. Moreover, each of the policy-makers comes from the pinnacle of power within the separate sectors of major concern in Atlanta. They are not bound through formal organizational ties or affiliations but rather appear to assemble on an informal basis as the need for policy formation arises. Just below them is the group of policy-executors; they represent the men who effectively carry out the policy once it has been formulated, and they are the ones most visible to the public. Most often they represent the second level of power within each of the major institutional spheres in Atlanta and are brought into the arena of policy execution by the most influential figures in their own respective spheres. Figure 7-2 illustrates these patterns in Atlanta.

Second, there are strong social ties and shared perceptions of influence that unite the men of power. The policy makers, for example, appear to strongly agree among themselves that they represent the major source and fund of influence in Atlanta; on the basis of sociograms, they more often choose one another as influentials than they select men in the undergroup of policy executors.[10] In addi-

FIGURE 7-2   Generalized pattern of policy committee formation utilizing institutional and associational structures (adapted from Floyd Hunter, *Community Power Structure* [New York: Doubleday and Company, 1963])

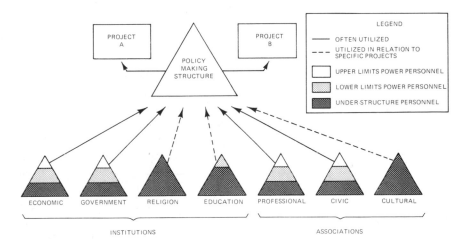

[10] A sociogram is a method that enables researchers to diagrammatically portray the social relationships that exist among people. There actually are a variety of special methods, all of which parade under the label of sociogram and some of which are exceedingly mathematically sophisticated. Hunter's own sociograms were fairly elementary, but they did convey several important features about the relationships among individuals, particularly which individuals appeared to represent a cohesive social group.

tion, Hunter shows that some of the leaders are united through interlocking corporate directorships, suggesting to him that the goals and interests of the leaders are apt to be cohesive rather than disparate. The leaders are also bound together through membership in social groups that often meet together, and dine together, and they belong to the same clubs. The existence of these crowds is commonly agreed upon by leaders. As one of them noted:

> I simply mean that there are "crowds" in Regional City [Hunter's fictitious name for Atlanta] —several of them—that pretty well make the big decisions. There is the crowd I belong to [the Homer Chemical crowd]; then there is the First State Bank crowd—the Regional Gas Heat crowd—the Mercantile crowd—the Growers Bank crowd—and the like.[11]

Although Hunter fails to make this point clear, it seems that the crowds through which the interests and goals of leaders are united in Atlanta are mainly composed of the men who represent the pinnacles of power in the community and their underlings, the policy makers and the policy executors.

Third, after inquiring into the occupations and affiliations of the forty leaders in Atlanta, Hunter comes away convinced that wealth and business leadership represent the main resources for power in the community. He observes:

> Each man mentioned as belonging to a crowd also belongs to a major business enterprise within the community—at least the clique leader does. His position within the bureaucratic structure of his business almost automatically makes him a community leader, if he wishes to become one. The test for admission to this circle of decision-makers is almost wholly a man's position in the business community in Regional City.[12]

This is not to suggest that leaders are only drawn from the business community; Hunter notes that some leaders represent leadership in terms of social standing in the community and others, such as the mayor, leadership in terms of the operation of government. The business leaders, however, appear to exercise predominant influence; they are disproportionately the policy makers, not the policy executors.

Finally, Hunter's research reveals that the process of making policy and arriving at decisions on major issues facing the community is rarely, if ever, open to the public. The policy makers get together on an informal basis, perhaps at lunch or at a local club, and discuss one or several of the major issues they believe confronts the community. If any dissent arises—and it usually does not—it does so within the confines of the meetings of the influential figures. They always seek for unanimity of opinion, and then they introduce the policy to the public, employing the various instruments they control, such as government and the press, to mobilize opinion in favor of the policy. As one respondent noted:

---

[11] Hunter, *Community Power Structure*, p. 77.
[12] Ibid., p. 78.

The public doesn't know anything about the project until it reaches the stage I've been talking about. After the matter is financially sound, then we go to the newspapers and say there is a proposal for consideration. Of course, it is not news to a lot of people by then, but the Chamber committees and other civic organizations are brought in on the idea. They all think it's a good idea. They help to get the Council located and established.[13]

The entire procedure of arriving at policy is one of avoiding the surfacing of issues by the influentials and of always acting as a cohesive group, a united front. Among the forty leaders, only one, the mayor, is reported to have sought to raise issues before the community, and he rarely engaged in the practice.

Though Hunter's study of Atlanta best represents the general perspective and specific results labeled as elitist, there are other inquiries that in one way or another validate his effort. The broad study by Robert and Helen Lynd of Muncie, Indiana, published as *Middletown in Transition*, found that one family exercised inordinate control in the community—over the newspaper, the mayor, and others—a control that appeared to be based upon their widespread economic holdings and interests in the community.[14] Robert Presthus's highly sophisticated comparative inquiry, employing several different techniques for isolating the distribution and structure of power, into the nature of power in two communities reveals that in one of the communities power tends to be concentrated in the hands of a comparatively small number of people and that in most of the major battles facing the community, the economic leaders often come away victorious.[15] In perhaps the richest and most insightful of community studies, *Small Town in Mass Society*, Arthur Vidich and Joseph Bensman report that the flavor of decision making is roughly the same as Hunter found in Atlanta; hardly any issues ever arise, for the decision makers always seek unanimity of opinion:

> There is the continuous effort to seek the formula by which unanimity can be achieved. Until unanimity is reached, there is a tacit agreement to discuss the proposal and to postpone the decision until the time comes when either by wearing down, time limitations or accident a formula is found.[16]

There are criticisms of the elitist approach; these are commonly addressed to the theoretical premises and empirical strategies that Hunter used. One criticism coming from such pluralist proponents as Dahl and Polsby is that Hunter presumed too much about the distribution and structure of power in Atlanta. Instead of asking about members of the power structure, they suggest that Hunter should have queried, Does anyone hold power here? "The first and perhaps most basic

---

[13] Ibid., p. 172.

[14] Lynd and Lynd, *Middletown in Transition*. (first citation)

[15] Robert Presthus, *Men at the Top: A Study in Community Power* (New York: Oxford University Press, 1964).

[16] Arthur J. Vidich and Joseph Bensman, *Small Town in Mass Society: Class, Power and Religion in a Rural Community* (Princeton, N.J.: Princeton University Press, 1968), p. 131.

presupposition of the pluralist approach is that nothing categorical can be assumed about power in any community. It rejects the [stratification] thesis that *some* group necessarily dominates a community."[17] If one were to take Hunter's critics on their word on this matter, they would appear as nothing short of psychological reductionists let loose upon the analysis of politics, whose own results would presumably reveal the number of great and small men in communities but nothing of their social ties, position in the stratification system, or other social and economic facts that social scientists have found to be so crucial to understanding politics. However, careful consideration of Dahl's own analyses reveals that the assertions of the pluralist critics must not be taken too literally.[18] Instead they simply mean that one must not automatically assume that those who are rich or high in prestige also possess the most clout in politics.

A second criticism of Hunter, again originating in the pluralist camp, is that he failed to actually study power, but studied associated dimensions of it—that is, the resources that people possess, for example, wealth or position, or the perceptions of those in power. This is a partly accurate criticism, for much of Hunter's case rests simply on these dimensions, not on the actual exercise of power. Still, the mere possession of resources such as wealth gives individuals a clear advantage in attempting to exercise power over others who do not possess wealth, and perceptions that someone is influential, like perceptions generally, can become transformed into behavior so that individuals who simply are thought to be powerful can induce compliance in other individuals.[19] Furthermore, this criticism fails to give credit to Hunter's extensive analysis of the origins and development of specific policy decisions in Atlanta, an analysis that provides both additional insight into and some validation of the workings of the power structure in Atlanta.

A last, and perhaps the most valid, criticism of Hunter's work is that he relied upon the reputational method for initially isolating the individuals who were thought to be leaders in Atlanta.[20] This method, it is claimed, is faulty when used alone because it does not reveal the numbers and kinds of people who are actually involved in determining policy on the major questions and controversies facing a community. Decision-making studies, these critics further argue, should focus on the decision-making process, not simply those people reputed to have influence upon the process. Regardless of whether Hunter's additional evidence and analysis truly uncovers the character of power in Atlanta, this criticism, it seems, is wholly justified. As a technique, the reputational method is liable to produce answers about power that are contaminated with other notions in the respondents' minds. For instance, asking people to select the ten top names in

---

[17]Nelson W. Polsby, *Community Power and Political Theory* (New Haven, Conn.: Yale University Press, 1963), p. 113.

[18]Dahl, *Who Governs?*

[19]William A. Gamson, "Reputation and Resources in Community Politics," *American Journal of Sociology*, 72 (September 1966), 121-31.

[20]Raymond E. Wolfinger, "Reputation and Reality in the Study of 'Community Power,'" *American Sociological Review*, 25 (October 1960), 636-44.

terms of their influence could result in nothing more than a list of the ten people held in highest esteem in the community; Hunter's top forty leaders could be nothing more than the forty most esteemed people in Atlanta. Although they may well have been involved in policy making in the community, it is evident that a number of other people—perhaps a large number of other people—also could have been implicated in the process, having been omitted simply because they were not so highly regarded. To correct for this fault in Hunter's research, later investigators either abandon the reputational approach and attempt to use alternative methods, for example, a focus on the history and outcome of decision making, or use it in tandem with other methods to isolate different kinds of leadership.

Pluralist Patterns

Robert Dahl's study of New Haven, published in 1961, in many respects provides one of the most masterful and elegant analyses of politics in modern America.[21] Although the study was addressed to an examination of the character of politics and power in New Haven, it became the platform for Dahl to present a general theory of American politics, a theory of pluralist democracy. There are several salient aspects of Dahl's perspective. First, he believes that life in New Haven, like that in modern America, can best be seen in terms of dominant institutional sectors, such as the economic, the political, the arts, and the religious. Within each of these major institutional sectors, there are special organizations and groups that act to produce for, and demand the special talents of, members of the general public. Second, he claims that the ongoing character of each of the institutional sectors and, of course, the organizations within them operates through the accumulation and investment of basic resources. Moreover, the operations of each sphere tend to require specialized forms of resources; the economic sphere deals in the accumulation and investment of material wealth, the sphere of high society in the accumulation and investment of prestige, and the political sphere in the accumulation and investment of political power.[22] Third, he asserts that the influence of individuals within each of the major spheres—their ability to get things done by making decisions and getting other people to do things for them—depends upon their capacity to mobilize and amass the special resources of their sphere. Thus, the influence of the businessperson rests on an ability to amass and later to wisely invest wealth, while that of the politician rests on an ability to amass and later to wisely invest political power.

These first three premises clearly distinguish Dahl's approach from that of elitists like Hunter, particularly insofar as they reveal Dahl's belief in the existence in modern society of institutional barriers to the transfer of resources, hence,

---

[21] Dahl, *Who Governs?*

[22] Dahl, it would appear, seems to have drawn upon Max Weber's classic distinction among the three institutions of modern society, classes, status groups, and parties. See Max Weber, "Class, Status and Party," in *From Max Weber: Essays in Sociology,* eds. Hans Gerth and C. Wright Mills (New York: Oxford University Press), 180-95.

power and influence; in other words, he assumes that money in the bank cannot very easily be transformed into power down at city hall even though it may help to purchase some politicians and to acquire political nominations. Dahl then asserts, as his fourth point, that the major amount of influence within each of the institutional sectors of New Haven, like that of communities and societies generally, is exercised chiefly by two groups—leaders, who exercise the greatest amount of influence, and their subordinates, subleaders. By and large, the only influence that most people in communities exercise is of an indirect form. For example, leaders of industry or the polity wish to keep their constituents—the consumers or voters—happy; therefore they anticipate the wishes of their constituents by formulating policies on their behalf. Fifth, Dahl claims that within New Haven's political system, again as in political systems generally, there is a distinct political stratum of people who are more active and interested in politics than other people. This stratum comprises those people who act as leaders and subleaders of political organizations, such as the parties, as well as a small number of others who take an active role in political organizations. Most people, he further asserts, do not care about politics, and they give it little of their attention and time. Moreover, he claims that in the political sphere, as in all others, there is a pervasive inertia among people—that is, they simply will not take action on most matters, so that decisions are left in the hands of the leaders and subleaders.

Finally, Dahl assumes that everyone—leaders, subleaders, and the public—shares a common set of values and goals. In the political sector these are the norms of the democratic creed, for example, the particular beliefs that make political competition legitimate and support the idea of political equality. Disputes over these beliefs, Dahl maintains, normally just involve questions about how they will be applied to practical matters and, thus, can be resolved in routine fashion. Disagreements of more major proportions may engage different political leaders, such as the heads of the Democratic and Republican parties, in battle, but even these disagreements do not become so large as to involve the public in their resolution. Only rarely, in fact, are disputes over the basic norms governing the polity brought before the public, and then it occurs when disagreements cannot be handled by the political leaders. Such matters, Dahl further suggests, are taken to the voters by members of the competing factions simply as a way of settling policy on particular issues. Never, to Dahl's way of thinking, is it conceivable that the disagreements within the political stratum, or between the political stratum and the electorate, will assume such large proportions as to produce widespread grievances with the nature of the polity or the norms governing its operation.

Dahl's social canvas is a broad one, and both the details and overall portrait he paints of pluralist democracy are exceedingly elegant. Using this portrait as a kind of general image, he then proceeds to inquire into the accuracy of its fine points by examining the nature of politics in New Haven. Like that of Hunter, his method to determine who governs New Haven is somewhat distinctive. Instead of inquiring into the reputations people have for influence and attempting to fit individuals into a hierarchal pattern as Hunter had done, Dahl and his associates selected three critical issues in which the general public seemed to have a stake: the selection of candidates by the political parties, policies governing urban renewal in the community, and policies governing public education in the town. Dahl maintained that these three issue areas were truly of concern to the community as a whole; therefore those who exercised power to make policies in these areas exercised genuine community power. Within each of the three areas, he gathered evidence on who participated in the decisions arrived at with regard to policies and on the special roles played by these individuals. The materials on decision making were supplemented with others as well. With the aid of various documents, Dahl was able to identify specifically members of the social and economic elite in New Haven. Members of the economic elite, or "notables" as Dahl refers to them, were identified through determining the largest individual property owners in the town and consulting such standard indices as city directories and business listings. Also, he assembled some general sample survey data on members of the community to help identify the rates of political activity and the interest of groups of people with different access to resources. Besides all this, one associate of Dahl's spent a full year in city hall observing the movements of the major officials and other individuals.

Dahl's investigations of New Haven politics led to several major conclusions, most (but not all) of which are at variance with those of Hunter. First, the New Haven research reveals that only a small handful of individuals exercise direct influence over the establishment of major policies. Some exercise indirect influence —the policies are tailored to their expected wishes—and most seem to exercise no influence whatsoever.

Second, the different issue areas in New Haven tend to recruit separate sets of individuals whose recruitment is largely determined by an interest in the substance of the issues under discussion. On the matter of political party nominations, for example, a few leaders and subleaders within each of the two political parties decided upon the choice of candidates. In the area of urban redevelopment programs, the research materials of Dahl revealed that the mayor of New Haven, together with a group of his own urban experts, exercised the most influence over the establishment of policies, mainly through initiating the basic policy proposals. Moreover, an examination of the large number of individuals who participate in one form or another in decision making within each of the three areas reveals that few people participate in decision making in more than one of the areas.

Third, the New Haven data reveal that the social and economic notables of the community rarely, if ever, play a part in the decision-making process. One wealthy individual did take part in the decisions of the political parties, but his participation occurred less because of his material wealth and social standing than because of his active involvement in Democratic Party politics.

Last, the results of the New Haven study suggest that if one wished to single out an individual or group as having disproportionate influence over decision making in all three issue areas, then the mayor and one or two associates would come closest to fitting this description. Moreover, Dahl discovered that this particular mayor, Richard Lee, had effected a highly successful technique of gaining the cooperation of the numerous factions in the New Haven community, acting in effect as a chief executive who often manipulated the interests of the different factions to suit his own interests in areas of policy such as urban redevelopment.

Dahl's research in New Haven has not been the only case to reveal such patterns as the specialization of influence and interest in particular areas and the dominant authority of the mayor. Wallace Sayre and Herbert Kaufman employed the decision-making approach to study patterns of power and found that New York City exhibited a pattern of political pluralism comparable to that which Dahl found in New Haven.[23] In particular, they observe:

> The city government is most accurately visualized as a series of semiautonomous little worlds, each of which brings forth official programs and policies through the interaction of its own inhabitants. There are commentators who assert that Tammany, or Wall Street, or the Cathedral, or the labor czars, or the bureaucracy, or even the underworld rules New York. Some of these, it is true, are especially influenced in shaping some decisions in some specialized areas. Taking the system over-all, however, none, nor all combined, can be said to be in command. . . . New York's huge and diverse system of government and politics is a loose-knit and multi-centered network in which decisions are reached by ceaseless bargaining and fluctuating alliances . . . and in which the centers are partially but strikingly isolated from one another. . . .[24]

Edward Banfield, in a study of Chicago politics conducted in the late 1950s, also employed the decision-making strategy to uncover patterns of power and influence.[25] Like Dahl, he found that the major actors on matters of policy tended to shift from one issue area to another. He also discovered that the major influence lay with the mayor who acted to cope with the formal pattern of decentralization of influence—in effect, formal pluralism—by informally centralizing power in his own hands through his control of the Democratic Party in Chicago and through taking special advantage of his office as mayor.

Like the research of Hunter, the investigations by Dahl and other pluralists have come in for a heavy barrage of criticism. One criticism, directed specifically at Dahl, is that his general theoretical perspective foreshadowed the kind of patterns of influence he uncovered. This criticism is most valid as it is applied to Dahl's discoveries about the disproportionate amount of influence wielded by the mayor. Dissenters argue that Dahl's notion of influence over the public sphere of New Haven's community life dictated that he focus his attention on the role of the mayor to the exclusion of the role of corporate magnates or large property owners.[26] What would Dahl have uncovered, they suggest, if he had assigned

[23] Sayre and Kaufman, *Governing New York City.*
[24] Ibid., p. 716.
[25] Banfield, *Political Influence.*
[26] Thomas J. Anton, "Power, Pluralism and Local Politics," *Administrative Science Quarterly,* 7 (March, 1963), 448-57.

research associates to spend an entire year observing the movements of singularly prominent social or economic notables?

A second criticism of Dahl's research and that of other investigators such as Banfield is that the issue-oriented, decision-making methodological strategy has various defects, some of which can produce results that show a pluralist pattern of influence with its different and seemingly coequal factions. The research of Walton, for instance, reveals that studies of community politics that employ the issue-oriented approach by and large tend to produce a pluralist pattern of influence; correspondingly, those that use the reputational strategy tend to result in an elitist pattern.[27] Moreover, two of Dahl's severest critics, Peter Bachrach and Morton Baratz, claim that his use of the issue-oriented strategy only allows him to get at one side of power, its visible component.[28] They argue, quite rightly, that power is often exercised by individuals through the avoidance of the public sur-   340 facing of issues, that is, through the "non-decision-making" process; evidence of this can be found in Vidich and Bensman's research as well as in that of Hunter. To the degree that Dahl has failed to explore the number and kind of individuals who exert influence in this manner, Bachrach and Baratz suggest, he has failed to reveal the full picture of power in New Haven. Moreover they also observe that Dahl provides no firm criteria for distinguishing between *important* and *unimportant* issues, implying that the three issues—party nominations, urban redevelopment and public education—that Dahl selected in New Haven may or may not have been significant to the members of the community as a whole. Only significant issues, they further suggest, actually will bring out the true dimensions of power and powerlessness in a community.

Finally, there is the criticism that Dahl's observations about indirect influence in New Haven politics represent more wishful thinking than scientifically observed facts. Although Dahl may have believed that the authors of policies in New Haven were in some way attempting to anticipate the wishes of their constituents through formulating specific policies, he failed to support his beliefs through inquiries of the perceptions of the authors of policy, or of the affected citizens. Moreover, he also failed to explore the various sanctions that the authors of policy had at their disposal to enforce their commands—sanctions that might well have prevented grievances from arising among the body of citizens.

Beyond Elitism and Pluralism

Among students of community politics, the elitist-pluralist controversy has raged on for more than a decade. It has probably reached the end of its course, for it has proven to be more of an obstacle than an aid to enlightenment on the nature

[27]John Walton, "Substance and Artifact: The Current Status of Research on Community Power Structure," *American Journal of Sociology*, 71 (January 1966), 430-38. Also see the lucid discussion of these matters in Presthus, *Men at the Top*, chapter 2.

[28]Peter Bachrach and Morton S. Baratz, "Two Faces of Power," *American Political Science Review*, 51 (December 1962), 947-52.

of community political patterns. Of course, the debate can be dismissed by simply observing that the researchers of elitist persuasion and those of the pluralist have been interested in somewhat different problems—the former in the question of who sits in the power structure, the latter in the problem of who governs; it is to be expected that they will arrive at different conclusions. However, for a full and comprehensive picture of how things are really run in a community it is probably necessary to attempt to select the best from both the theory and methods of the elitists and pluralists, and to apply them systematically to an inquiry into the nature of power and politics in any given community. On occasion, however, the use of the different strategies for locating leaders merely seems to produce different sets of leaders in communities with little overlap among them.[29] In the hands of a sensitive and skilled investigator, however, the synthesis of the theoretical underpinnings and methodological devices of the two schools can achieve insights unavailable from each approach used alone.

An exemplary study along these lines is that of Robert Presthus, who investigated community politics in two small towns in upper New York State.[30] Using both the techniques of the elitists and those of the pluralists, Presthus found that the distribution and structure of power varied between the two communities. In the one, the economic leaders tended to be the most influential even though they encountered frequent opposition from the political leaders; in the other, he discovered that the political leaders exercised the most power and that the economic leaders had withdrawn from the arena of public battles to tend to their own pastures. In part the differences in the character of power in the two communities sprang from the economic resources they possessed. The town in which the economic leaders exercised the most power also possessed the more fertile economic situation, while a poor economic base in the other town prompted the political leaders to become more powerful as a means of recruiting outside resources to the community. Presthus explicitly noted that the research strategies of the elitists and pluralists acted in tandem better than they would have alone; for instance, one very powerful figure did not emerge as a leader in one of the communities through use of the decision-making approach, but did emerge as one through the reputational technique. Presthus claimed that this result, among others, provided a fuller picture of the way power worked.

To get beyond the elitist-pluralist debate does not simply mean achieving a synthesis of their approaches, however. Both approaches neglect some vital issues about the nature of community politics that require sharper and more complete inquiries. First, in some form, the power residing within communities rests mainly in the hands of elite groups. Whether these groups are grounded in political resources or in economic ones seems to be a less significant matter than the cohesiveness of the members of the groups. Although Hunter comes considerably closer to dealing with this question than Dahl, neither scholar addresses it

[29]Linton C. Freeman et al., "Locating Leaders in Local Communities: A Comparison of Some Alternative Approaches," *American Sociological Review*, 27 (October 1963), 791-98.

[30]Presthus, *Men at the Top*. (1964)

fully. A second important matter is how the exercise of power can be maximized among the nonelite groups. What are the special resources that the nonelite groups possess, and how can these be employed to maximize their influence over the political process? A useful study by Michael Lipsky of rent strikes and other forms of political protest during the 1960s provides some initial answers to these questions by suggesting that the most valuable resources of nonelite groups with grievances are public opinion in general and the influence of third parties who possess ties to the elite groups in communities.[31] Third, inquiries into the politics of communities could greatly profit from more extensive employment of a systems approach, perhaps along the lines of Talcott Parsons as Terry Clark has suggested.[32] Among other insights offered by this perspective is a clearer distinction in the nature of resources for power, especially the distinction between the resources of the community as a whole—literally the public resources—and those of individuals and groups such as business people in the community. Only when such a distinction is clearly made is it possible to draw fair conclusions about who controls the ultimate well-being of a community.

Finally, researchers on community politics, on the whole, have paid too little attention to the links between the resources and politics within the community and those at the level of the state and, especially, the federal government. It is something of a paradox that the very nature of the federal system in the United States is partly responsible for the great concern with the nature of community power and that those studies that focus on community power neglect the bearing of the federal structures on communities! Encouraged by such specific experiences as that of the Roosevelt administration in the 1930s, both the resources and the exercise of power in America have shifted in importance over the past several decades from the local to the federal level. There exists, however, a continual tension between the two levels—that of the local and the federal—and at present the mood in Washington seems to favor a relocation of important financial resources from federal jurisdiction to local. Tensions between these levels and the historical shifts in the locus of power remain important issues that clearly deserve greater appreciation by students of community politics.

Before leaving these matters it is important for us to note that in the past several years an entirely new, and different, brand of investigation into the nature of power in urban areas has arisen under the banner of neo-Marxism. Among the more prominent figures in this field are Manuel Castells, a European sociologist, and David Harvey, a British geographer; both now teach in the United States.[33]

[31] Michael Lipsky, "Protest as a Political Resource," *American Political Science Review*, 62 (December, 1968), 1144-58, and Michael Lipsky, *Protest in City Politics* (Chicago: Rand McNally, 1970).

[32] Terry N. Clark, "Community Structure and Decision Making," in *Community Structure and Decision Making: Comparative Analyses*, ed. Terry N. Clark (San Francisco: Chandler Publishing Company, 1968), pp. 91-126.

[33] See, for example, Manuel Castells, *The Urban Question* (London: Arnold, 1977); and Manuel Castells, *City, Class and Power* (London: Macmillan, 1978). And, on Harvey's work, see David Harvey, *Social Justice and the City* (Baltimore, Md.: The Johns Hopkins University Press, 1973).

This new approach is rather diffuse at present, the result of the innovations of a number of different researchers; but essentially it seeks to explain the nature of power differences, and of the origins of popular protest, in urban areas through emphasizing the role of capital accumulation and the nature of class struggles. Among the more interesting work in this area, especially to Americans, are the recent efforts of David Perry and Alfred Watkins, who seek to explain the rise of the new cities in the Sunbelt by speaking, at the same time, of the decline of urban areas in the Snowbelt.[34] It is the thesis of Perry and Watkins that the birth and death of different cities are intimately related to one another, and that both, in some part, are the result of shifts as well as transformations in the nature of capital. It seems evident that all the new work in this area, tailored along the lines of a radical political economy, is destined to infuse the study of community power with a vigor it has lacked for some time.[35]

MAJOR ANTECEDENTS AND CONSEQUENCES OF THE DISTRIBUTION AND STRUCTURE OF POWER IN COMMUNITIES

Despite the debate between the pluralists and the elitists, some social scientists have managed to address other critical issues in the study of community politics. One of these lies at the heart of the scientific enterprise. It is the effort to forecast the kinds of social and economic conditions in communities that seem to go along with distinct patterns in the distribution or structure of power, as well as the kinds and numbers of public policies that seem to be produced by certain kinds of political arrangements. Does a more centralized political structure in a community result in more or fewer policies designed to benefit the community as a whole? Or, as Presthus suggests, does a community rich in economic resources tend to produce leadership centralized in the hands of economic leaders? Unfortunately analysis of these kinds of questions has not yet proceeded very far, but this section tries to convey some of the principal generalizations that social scientists have thus far drawn both about the antecedents and consequences of the character of power in communities.

[34] See, especially, the joint essays by Perry and Watkins in David C. Perry and Alfred J. Watkins, eds., *The Rise of the Sunbelt Cities*, Urban Affairs Annual Reviews, vol. 14 (Beverly Hills, Calif.: Sage Publications, 1977).

[35] I am much indebted to my friend and colleague Joe Feagin for providing me the information and insights found in this paragraph. Other works that include writings in this area are as follows: Michael Dear and Allen J. Scott, eds., *Urbanization and Urban Planning in Capitalist Society* (London: Methuen, 1981); C. C. Pickvance, ed., *Urban Sociology: Critical Essays* (London: Tavistock Publications, 1976); and William K. Tabb and Larry Sawers, eds., *Marxism and the Metropolis: New Perspectives in Urban Political Economy* (New York: Oxford University Press, 1978). Also see the new work, Joe R. Feagin, *Building Capitalist Cities: Developers, Bankers, and Consumers* (Englewood Cliffs, N.J.: Prentice-Hall, forthcoming).

Antecedents

One of the major dimensions along which communities vary is the number of their residents. A whole range of consequences, from greater specialization of occupations to a variety of traumatic psychological reactions, is thought to flow simply from increases in the numbers and the density of people living in areas.[36] Those who inquire into the nature of community are equally taken with the idea that the numbers of people may have some consequences for the character of power; in particular, it is thought that larger populations with their typically greater specialization of roles and greater variety of social and economic resources are likely to produce more fragmented and specialized power structures—similar to the patterns that Sayre and Kaufman observed in New York City and Banfield found in Chicago. Although his evidence is by no means definitive, Presthus reports findings that tend to confirm intuitive expectations. Comparing the extent to which the influence of individuals overlaps from one issue area to another among a wide variety of communities—that is, the extent to which influence is, or is not, specialized—Presthus shows that overlap tends to decline among larger communities.[37] Thus, influence appears to become more specialized the larger the size of the community.[38] Presthus further suggests that this very pattern might well explain the specialization of influence Dahl uncovered in New Haven compared with the relative concentration that he found in his two communities, Riverview and Edgewood.

Obviously size cannot fully account for variations in the distribution and structure of power. Hunter's Atlanta, for example, was a sizable community at the time of his study, yet his research revealed it to have a small and fairly cohesive group of leaders, not specialized persons of power. Thus, another possible source for variations in the patterns of power in communities is their underlying industrial structure, or the degree to which they are industrialized. Not only does Presthus's research hint at the apparent importance of this factor, but historical trends in America suggest that elite rule in communities becomes more specialized as industrialization proceeds and that the ruling groups become more fragmented and divided. The research of Terry Clark casts some light on this aspect of communities.[39] Clark hypothesizes that more diverse economic structures in communities

---

[36] For a view counter to the conventional one of the trauma induced by city living, see Claude S. Fischer, "Toward a Subcultural Theory of Urbanism," *American Journal of Sociology*, 80 (May 1975), 1319-41, and the various references cited therein by Fischer to his own writings. Also see Claude Fischer, *The Urban Experience* (New York: Harcourt Brace Jovanovich, Inc., 1976).

[37] Presthus, *Men at the Top*, p. 95.

[38] Also see Claire Gilbert, "Community Power and Decision Making: A Quantitative Examination of Previous Research," in *Community Structure and Decision Making*, Clark, pp. 139-56.

[39] Terry N. Clark, "Community Structure, Decision Making, Budget Expenditures, and Urban Renewal in 51 American Communities," in *Community Politics: A Behavioral Approach*, eds. Charles M. Bonjean, Terry N. Clark, and Robert L. Lineberry (New York: The Free Press, 1971), pp. 293-313.

tend to be associated with more decentralized decision-making structures, that is, more specialized and fragmented structures. His results, based upon an extensive comparative study of fifty-one communities, support this hypothesis.[40] (It is noteworthy, yet difficult to explain, that Clark's research also reveals that industrial activity is *negatively* associated with the decentralization of decision making, and that greater activity leads to greater centralization. It is entirely possible that the amount of industrial activity is simply a reflection of the vigor of the industrial elites in a community rather than of pressures to specialize and diversify; where they are more vigorous, both industrial activity is higher and their attempts to exercise leadership in the community are more effective, the latter leading to a greater centralization of the power structure.)

The most conceptually sophisticated effort to isolate some of the antecedents of power in communities is that of John Walton, who sought to link the dependence of communities on state and national institutions to the centralization of power within the community.[41] In one of the few empirical efforts, in the United States at least, to seriously explore the impact of extracommunity conditions on power within them, Walton argues that as communities become increasingly dependent on outside institutions and agents—economic, governmental, and otherwise—the tight and homogenous fabric of their normative order is likely to be disrupted, leading to a more competitive (fragmented or pluralistic) power structure. In particular, he has in mind the idea that as powerful outside groups enter the community, they attempt to exercise their power and influence, to control local industry perhaps or to control the local parties; as a result, they disrupt the homogenous patterns previously secured within the community. They may precipitate struggles among local groups; or outside groups from different institutional sectors, such as the economic and the political, may become engaged in a struggle for local hegemony. In any event, the product, Walton suggests, is more fragmented leadership in the community. Several results tend to support his general perspectives on the effects of extracommunity forces; specifically, communities with absentee ownership of industry (versus those with local ownership), with competitive local parties (versus those with noncompetitive), and that are suburban or satellite communities (versus independent) exhibit the more decentralized power structure.

Although there are a few other conditions that appear to be associated with the degree to which the power is centralized in communities—for example, the average level of education of residents—none seem to be as significant in their impact or to stand as clearly in the role of causal agents as those previously cited. Further research will probably uncover additional forces and, perhaps, even reveal general patterns under which these forces can be subsumed.

[40] For parallel results, see Gilbert, "Community Power and Decision Making."

[41] John Walton, "The Vertical Axis of Community Organization and the Structure of Power," [Southwestern] *Social Science Quarterly*, 48 (December 1967), 353-68.

Consequences: Policies

If we ask ourselves what community power can do, surely one of our first answers would be that power can get things done on behalf of the community. Translating this rather intuitive notion (intuitive, and yet it conforms to the earlier discussion of power) into its more formal counterpart, power in communities should lead to the creation of policies that would act to further the growth of the communities. This notion, in fact, is roughly the same as Talcott Parsons's principal assertion that power enables a social system—whether a community or a society—to get things done that help to further its development (see chapter 4). Carrying this logic a step further, communities that put their power (or the resources upon which it is based) to its most effective use ought to be more capable of creating and implementing policies on behalf of themselves than communities that are not as effective in deploying their power (or resources upon which it is based).

One of the most imaginative and provocative studies of communities develops these ideas linking power and policies and, in so doing, furnishes the main hypothesis that now guides work on the determinants of public policies in communities. The particular study, the product of Amos Hawley, a distinguished student of the community, presented the following as its guiding hypothesis: "The greater the concentration of power in a community, the greater the probability of success in any collective action affecting the welfare of the whole."[12] Hawley's next step was to develop operational indices of his two principal variables, that is, of the concentration of power in communities, and of success in collective actions affecting the welfare of the whole. His measures of each were ingenious. The concentration of power was measured as the ratio of the number of managers, proprietors, and officials in the labor force of a community to the number of people in the entire employed labor force, or as

$$\frac{\text{Number of managers, officials, and proprietors}}{\text{Number of people in the employed labor force}}$$

According to Hawley, as the ratio—formally known as the MPO ratio—became smaller, the concentration of power in a community became higher, and conversely, as it became greater, the concentration of power in a community grew weaker (see table 7-1). His reasoning was that a smaller ratio meant there were fewer managerial functions in a community relative to the labor force; therefore as a group, the managers, officials, and proprietors would likely be more cohesive and would certainly possess more unilateral power to get things done. His measures of the policy outputs were whether communities had become involved and later executed urban renewal programs; Hawley assumed that such programs acted to promote the welfare of the community as a whole.

[12] Amos H. Hawley, "Community Power and Urban Renewal Success," *American Journal of Sociology*, 68 (January 1963), 422-31.

Table 7-1 Number and MPO ratios, cities by size class and by urban renewal status

Urban Renewal Status	All Cities of 15,000 Population and Over		Cities of 50,000 Population and Over		Cities of 15,000–50,000 Population	
	No.	MPO Ratio	No.	MPO Ratio	No.	MPO Ratio
Execution stage	136	9.0	95	9.0	41	9.1
Dropout	79	10.0	38	10.1	41	9.8
Never in program	402	11.0	61	10.8	341	11.1
Total	617	10.4	194	9.5	423	10.7

Quintile distribution of cities (MPO ratios), by urban renewal status[a]

Urban Renewal Status	1st (Under 7.7)	2d (7.8– 8.9)	3d (9.0– 9.9)	4th (10.0– 11.7)	5th (11.8 and Over)
Execution stage	27	22	21	17	9
Dropout	3	9	8	8	7
Never in program	9	9	8	13	22

Source: Adapted from Amos H. Hawley, "Community Power and Urban Renewal Success," *American Journal of Sociology,* 68 (January 1963), 426.

[a] $\chi^2 = 23.516$, $C = .330$, $P < .01$.

Thus, the specific hypothesis Hawley tested, which derived from his more abstract proposition linking power and policy outputs, was that in communities where the MPO ratio was smaller, there should also be a greater likelihood of execution of urban renewal programs. Since a number of other factors naturally could affect involvement in urban renewal programs, Hawley had to control systematically for these; having done so, however, he still found a clear relationship between the MPO ratio and execution of urban renewal programs that conformed to his hypothesis.

Hawley's pathfinding research has not been free of criticism; indeed, the follow-up research of Straits suggests he may have been wrong.[43] There has also been other research to take up where Hawley left off, and this, too, has made different findings. Starting from a somewhat similar hypothesis that the greater the centralization of power in a community, the higher the policy outputs, Clark investigated to see whether the centralization of power and the amount of expenditures on urban renewal programs and on the general budget were related in a comparative study of fifty-one different communities in the United States.[44] Using the number of leadership roles and the amount of overlap in leadership roles from

[43] Bruce C. Straits, "Community Adoption and Implementation of Urban Renewal," *American Journal of Sociology*, 71 (July 1965), 77-82. In that same issue, also see the reply by Hawley.

[44] Clark, "Community Structure, Decision Making, Budget Expenditures, and Urban Renewal in 51 American Communities."

one issue area to another as his measure of centralization, Clark found quite the opposite of Hawley. The greater the decentralization of power in a community, he discovered, the larger the amounts of money the community spent both on urban renewal and on its general budget.

Were Clark's results possibly idiosyncratic or were those of Hawley? The weight of the evidence appears to favor Clark's findings. In the most exhaustive examination of all, Michael Aiken investigated the effects of the centralization of power on several different forms of community policy—public housing programs, urban renewal programs, the poverty programs of the 1960s, and the model cities programs of the same decade—all of which required a large investment of funds from the federal government.[45] Employing a slightly different but equally valid measure of centralization of power, roughly comparable to the ranking of structures of power presented in figure 7-1, Aiken found that the more decentralized the structure of power in a community, the more successful communities were in attracting the federal funds required for each of the several different types of public policy expenditures. Curiously, he also found that the MPO ratio possessed the opposite relationship to centralization as Hawley had claimed; instead of being smaller in the more centralized communities, the MPO ratio was smaller in the more decentralized ones. Thus, Aiken's research confirmed Hawley's claim about the link between the MPO ratio and the success of public policy, but apparently for reasons just the opposite of those advanced by Hawley.

How, then, can the curious correspondence between the decentralization of power, or its low concentration, and differential success of policies on behalf of communities be explained? Assuming that the broad hypothesis laid out by Hawley and others is in some sense true, then the problem lies with the empirical indices of "success of community policies" or "attempts to advance community welfare." All the empirical indices actually employed to measure this dimension, ranging from urban renewal expenditures to public housing expenditures, were based upon resources generated from outside the communities rather than strictly from within. The Hawley hypothesis implicitly suggests that power affects the development of communities by its use and expansion of resources somehow *internal* to the community; in other words, it suggests an image of a multitude of self-sufficient and independent communities, some of which will advance because of their more effective use of power on resources internal to them and others of which will decline because of an ineffective use of power. However, communities in modern America are by no means the self-sufficient entities they were in the eighteenth and nineteenth centuries. Thus, it is quite likely that Hawley's original notions were correct in the abstract but simply incapable of being put to the test in contemporary America.[46]

[45] Michael Aiken, "The Distribution of Community Power: Structural Bases and Social Consequences," in *The Structure of Community Power*, ed. Michael Aiken and Paul E. Mott (New York: Random House, 1970).

[46] See Aiken, "The Distribution of Community Power," for a somewhat similar explanation. Also, for further information on community power structures and production of policies, see Terry N. Clark, *Community Power and Policy Outputs* (Beverly Hills, Calif.: Sage Publications, 1973).

THE OTHER SIDE OF THE TRACKS:
THE COMMUNITY POWER OF NONELITES

So far our attention has been given exclusively to the nature and strength of elite groups in different communities. Most observers of the politics of communities seem to be especially interested in the "people at the top," reasoning that such groups probably exist, in one form or another, and act to control the public life of communities. However, the nonelites, the body of citizens, are not completely without the capacity for power or influence in the political arenas of communities. Indeed, there appear to be four essential resources upon which the nonelites can rely in attempts to exercise power and influence—the vote, through which they can collectively determine who will control the reigns of public office; legal strategies in the form of referenda and recalls that can be, but rarely are, employed by dissatisfied sectors of the masses; individual or joint efforts to intervene in the community decision-making process through such specific actions as contacting local political officials on community issues under discussion; and, most important, general forms of political organization that, if created as bodies independent of the reigning political parties and other political groups, can act to mobilize the citizens behind concerted political action. Later chapters of this book explore in some detail how citizens attempt to use these resources to exercise power in the political process; here, a few of the more salient features of the citizens' attempts to use power and influence in the local polity are touched on briefly (see chapter 12 on social and political movements and chapter 9 on political participation for other relevant discussions of these issues).

Extent of Citizen Participation
in Local Politics

Although nonelites in any community collectively hold several rich resources that can be transformed into power, the real issue is whether they take advantage of these resources. Do they actively employ the means at their disposal—the vote and community organizations—to influence the actions of public officials? In fact, they generally do not, at least not to any appreciable extent. Voting is the most minimal form in which the public can engage in the political process, but only somewhat more than four out of every ten people who are of voting age actually go to the polls for local elections.[47] This proportion dips below 40 percent in communities in which local elections are held at different times from those of the state and national elections; under these conditions, only three of every ten eligible voters go to the polls.[48]

If this picture of the involvement of the citizenry in local politics appears bleak, then that of the ways in which they attempt to directly intervene in the

[47] Robert R. Alford and Eugene C. Lee, "Voting Turnout in American Cities," *American Political Science Review*, 62 (September 1968), 796-813.
[48] Ibid.

decision making of local politics is extremely dismal. Reports from various studies indicate that perhaps no more than 30 percent of the citizens actively engage in attempts to exercise influence over specific local decisions. Gabriel Almond and Sidney Verba, for example, found in their national survey of the American public that only 28 percent of the people had attempted to exercise some form of influence over local decision making.[49] Presthus's excellent study of the communities of Edgewood and Riverview in upper New York State revealed equally small proportions of people engaging in attempts to influence specific decisions—in the former, 26 percent; in the latter, 10 percent.[50]

It appears that no matter what probe or device is used to inquire into the ways in which citizens use their local political resources, the proportion of people who actively and regularly attempt to exercise influence rarely goes above 30 percent. In one of the best quantitative studies ever undertaken of participation in politics, Sidney Verba and Norman Nie isolated several different dimensions of participation.[51] One was that of local political involvement and interest; people who engaged in these forms of activity, which ranged from working with others in solving local problems to attempting to contact a local official about local problems, were referred to by Verba and Nie as "community specialists." In their nationwide sample of American respondents interviewed in 1967, they found that only 20 percent of the people could be classified into such a category.

These and other somewhat parallel patterns of findings on the local political participation of the nonelites of communities dramatically reveal that only a small percentage of people actively attempt to use the resources available to them to exercise power and influence over the local political arena. This absence of political engagement in the local arena by citizens is perhaps especially surprising in the United States where history—the frontier—and myth—equality, individualism—have combined to create an image of the typical citizen as one who is constantly engaged in efforts to help fashion a community of some pride and joy to self and others. This portrait of the citizen actively engaged in the public arenas of his or her local residence evidently is considerably more myth nowadays than reality.

Does Citizen Participation
Influence the Decisions of Leaders?

Even though only a minority of the citizens in a community play an active role in local politics, it remains possible that these citizens strongly influence the ideas and policies of local political officials. If this is the case, then the image of elite control of community politics, which is pervasive in much of the literature on communities, is perhaps overdrawn, if not a total distortion of the actual state of political affairs in communities.

[49]Gabriel Almond and Sidney Verba, *The Civic Culture: Political Attitudes and Democracy in Five Nations* (Princeton, N.J.: Princeton University Press, 1963).

[50]Presthus, *Men at the Top.*

[51]Sidney Verba and Norman Nie, *Participation in America: Political Democracy and Social Equality* (New York: Harper & Row, Publishers, 1972).

In attempting to answer this question, the first thing that the reader must bear in mind is that those people who are highly active in community politics in particular and in politics in general are not a representative group of the population. Instead they possess qualities of mind and background that are in many ways more similar to those of the leaders than they are to those of other segments of the community. Specifically, those highly active in politics tend to be drawn disproportionately from the upper socioeconomic status (SES) groups and from among whites; they tend to be conservative in their political beliefs, opposing widespread welfare measures and supporting fiscal conservatism; and they tend to draw their strength much more heavily from among conservative Republicans than from among liberal Democrats.[52] In short, to paraphrase Schattschneider, the voice of the political activists in America is not the voice of the people but the voice of the upper crust.[53] Hence, if the political leaders of communities heed the interests and ideas proclaimed by political activists, then they will take actions that represent only a select portion of the community.

There are many observers who claim that this activist political stratum in communities, and possibly even the less active strata as well, exercise influence over the attitudes and actions of local officials. The most articulate of these among contemporary spokesmen is Robert Dahl, whose argument has already been discussed.[54] Dahl claims that citizens exercise indirect influence over their public leaders, partly through the simple exercise of their right to choose among competing candidates for office, and partly through the fact that leaders anticipate their actions and wishes and attempt to carve out policies that they—the leaders—believe will satisfy the citizenry. Dahl, like most other analysts, possesses no concrete evidence to support his argument, but his analysis does carry with it a certain intuitive appeal.

Not content simply to let this perspective rest on intuition or good faith, Verba and Nie attempted to find out whether heavy participation by citizens in politics does influence the opinions of leaders. Their analysis, which dealt with the responses of people in a large number of American communities, focused on the degree of concurrence between the opinions of citizens and leaders concerning the nature of and priorities assigned to specific community problems. Describing this procedure, Verba and Nie reported:

> Specifically, the measures were developed by pooling all leaders answers about community problems, recording the number of times the problem each citizen mentioned was also mentioned by the leaders in his community, and converting this into a ratio based on the number of "matches" that would have been possible—i.e., on the number of leaders in the community. Citizens and leaders could mention any set of problems. If the most impor-

[52] Ibid., chapter 16.

[53] E. E. Schattschneider, *The Semi-Sovereign People* (New York: Holt, Rinehart and Winston, 1960).

[54] Dahl, *Who Governs?*, pp. 163-65.

tant community problems listed by a citizen are mentioned by *all* leaders in the community, the concurrence score would be 100, indicating that 100 percent of the leaders in the community agree with the citizen's community priority schedule. If none of the problems listed by the citizen is mentioned by a leader in his community, his concurrence score is zero.[55]

They then examined the extent of concurrence between citizens and leaders in communities that vary by the level of citizen participation. Verba and Nie propose that if leaders are indeed responsive to citizen opinion, then in those communities where citizen participation is the highest one should also find that the degree of concurrence between leaders and citizens is also the highest; in fact their results tend to support the hypothesis.[56] Realizing that the similar social characteristics of both active citizens and leaders and leader manipulation of citizen opinion could also account for high levels of agreement in opinion between citizens and leaders, Verba and Nie assembled additional information to test these competing explanations of their results. An examination of the necessary data reveal that the political opinions of community leaders still appear to be significantly responsive to those of the active citizens. In short, the Verba and Nie data lend support to the argument of Dahl and others that community leaders are indeed influenced in their opinions by the concerns of those whom they lead.

As heirs to the illuminating writings of Niccolo Machiavelli, however, we would be foolish to assume that community leaders only respond to citizen participation in politics and refrain from attempting to shape or mold it. Unfortunately, evidence of leaders' manipulation of citizen participation is not as precise as that assembled by Verba and Nie, for example, but in its breadth and color it seems equally persuasive, if not more so. In Dahl's New Haven, designated by many observers as exemplary for its pluralist form of democratic politics, Mayor Lee often employed devices, such as citizens' boards, ostensibly designed to solicit and encourage citizen participation in decision making but in reality possessing little authority and no power to determine policies.[57] In communities less well-known as models of democratic politics, leaders seem even more clever at manipulating citizen participation for their own purposes. Thus in Mayor Daley's Chicago, there may well have been heavy citizen input on a variety of issues and problems, as the analysis of Banfield suggests, but it is equally clear that the mayor often allowed citizen participation to act as a safety valve of discontent and that he formulated policies that were only minimally responsive to the demands of the activists.[58]

---

[55]Verba and Nie, *Participation in America*, pp. 302-3.

[56]In fact, Verba and Nie suggest that the relationship between participation and concurrence will be curvilinear, with the lowest level of concurrence in those communities moderate in the level of citizen participation. Their explanation of curvilinearity, which proves correct on test, is less than intuitively compelling.

[57]Dahl, *Who Governs?*

[58]Banfield, *Political Influence.* On Daley's style, also see the enormously entertaining and insightful book by Mike Royko, *Boss: Richard J. Daley of Chicago* (New York: New American Library, 1971).

Even if the policies of the mayor did reveal the influence of others, it was not so much that of the activists as it was that of his key aides in city hall and the local Democratic Party. Hunter's Atlanta perhaps represents the height of leaders' apparent immunity to the concerns and interests of citizens in general and the activists in particular. As Hunter laid out in careful detail, the policies of the leaders were usually developed far in advance of expressed citizen concern.[59] Only after the leaders had carefully worked out and agreed upon their own position did they bring the issue and decision before the public, allowing citizens to participate in an act that, without their knowledge, was a *fait accompli.*

To pin down exactly the strength and direction of influence between leaders and followers in communities is a nearly impossible task. Citizens can and do influence leaders; that much is clear. However, leaders possess such a great arsenal of strategems and devices, many of which simply accompany their public office, that their capacity to shape the minds and hearts of the citizenry must be accorded the far greater weight.

Activating the Inactives in Community Politics

Relatively few citizens take an active part in the political life of their local surroundings, and among those who do there is a disproportionate number who are both financially well-off and politically conservative. Moreover, when citizens actively participate in local politics, they are apt to influence the opinions of local public officials even though the balance of power, in general, is clearly tipped in favor of the officials. Suppose we choose to intervene in this fabric of social and political circumstance, believing that through some form of intervention we could enhance the capacity of local groups—most of whom represent the poor and under-privileged—to be heard by both public and private leaders in communities and encourage them to take an active role in the local arenas of power. This issue became both the question of and quest for many distinctive political efforts of the 1960s and 1970s.

The best known and most controversial of the programs was that of Saul Alinsky, the peripatetic organizer of the poor, who established self-help political programs in a number of communities throughout the United States, including Chicago's Woodlawn area, its back-of-the-yard district, Buffalo, and Syracuse. Employing the time-tested methods of union organizers, Alinsky entered areas of poverty at the request of residents and assisted the local groups in achieving a substantial degree of internal political organization. His effort was invariably directed toward the cultivation of leadership from within the poor neighborhoods; his own role was that of alerting residents to the ways in which their lives may have been controlled by the regular political establishment (for example, government) and of helping them to implement strategies useful to the creation of a viable organization.[60] Perhaps the most successful of his ventures took place in 1961 in

---

[59] Hunter, *Community Power Structure.*

[60] For the nature of Alinsky's strategies, see Saul Alinsky, *Reveille for Radicals* (New York: Random House, 1969) and *Rules for Radicals* (New York: Random House, 1971).

the Woodlawn area of Chicago where the Woodlawn Organization (TWO) was formed. TWO eventually became the principal voice for thousands of black ghetto residents in Woodlawn as well as for the many clubs and other groups within the area. In its early days, TWO was successful in a number of ways—it mobilized a previously inert and passive citizenry for various activities; it scored a great victory in preventing the University of Chicago from embarking on an urban renewal venture that would have leveled many of the indigenous residences and stores in Woodlawn; and it achieved a number of improvements in Woodlawn. Like many such organizations, TWO has changed over the years, becoming somewhat more conventional in its tactics and conservative in its political philosophy; it has also lost a number of crucial battles both with the Daley political machine and the federal government, and has failed to achieve the measure of community progress originally envisioned by its founders. Yet, it remains today as one of the very few indigenous community organizations that can still claim to exercise considerable influence among its constituents and can still act as a spokesman in their behalf.[61]

There was also a large-scale effort in the 1960s under the sponsorship of the federal government. Included as part of the Economic Opportunity Act of 1964 and its amendments of 1966, this effort took the form of community action programs that were to be "developed, conducted, and administered with the maximum feasible participation of residents of the areas and members of the groups to be served."[62] The poor, Congress proclaimed, were to play a large part in the direction and implementation of the War on Poverty programs, serving on the boards of directors and in other ways becoming involved in the administration and guidance of the counseling, job training, child welfare, and other services of the War on Poverty agencies. As it was a nationwide effort, such a program obviously offered great hope for somehow changing the lives and conditions of the poor and, among other things, enabling them to actively influence the leaders and the sub-leaders in their communities.

The extent of success of the community action programs (CAP), however identified and measured, does not give heart to those who believe in the viability of active programs of intervention. First, those individuals who participated in the community action programs were not drawn from among the most underprivileged sectors of the poor that were rarely, if ever, heard in community affairs but rather represented the best of the poor. Thus as local participation in general draws upon the more privileged segments of the community, so the community action programs involved the most privileged sectors of the poor. (For a time, a similar problem afflicted TWO in Chicago until TWO organizers became aware of the difficulty and made a deliberate and successful effort to involve both the poorer and younger

---

[61] This analysis of TWO relies on rich description and interpretation contained in John Hall Fish, *Black Power/White Control: The Struggle of the Woodlawn Organization in Chicago* (Princeton, N.J.: Princeton University Press, 1973). For the description of another effort to organize local citizens into a community organization in Chicago, see Todd Gitlin and Nanci Hollander, *Uptown: Poor Whites in Chicago* (New York: Harper & Row, Publishers, 1970).

[62] Russell L. Curtis, Jr., and Louis A. Zurcher, Jr., "Voluntary Association and the Social Integration of the Poor," *Social Problems*, 18 (Winter 1971), 339-57.

Woodlawn residents.) Second, once the programs were underway, the successful participation by the select sectors of the poor, who still represented a voice unique to community life, acted to reduce their chances for effectively communicating their interests and changing the opinions of local leaders; as the poor became more expert in the running of the CAP programs, federal guidelines were enacted to reassert control over these programs by urban officials. As Curtis and Zurcher aptly noted, "there was the . . . irony . . . that political reaction to organizational power of the poor would serve to decrease their effective participation."[63] In one respect, however, the programs developed as part of the War on Poverty had certain benefits, particularly insofar as their political dividends were concerned; among those individuals who participated extensively in the programs, there was a marked change in certain social-psychological dimensions prerequisite for political activism —a lowered sense of individual estrangement and an enhanced sense of personal efficacy. Whether those personal changes remained and were later translated into effective forms of political expression in the local community remains in doubt, however.

What, then, can be said in general about efforts designed to intervene in the web of circumstance of the poor? Can the politically inactive be activated and given greater influence over local leaders and their own destinies? A comparison of Alinsky's intensive efforts with those taken under the auspices of the CAP program reveals that if a concerted attempt is made to involve the poor and the inactive in community organizations, as in Woodlawn, then many of those people who normally do not care for politics can be made to care and to express their special concerns. However, the Woodlawn experience as well as the CAP programs also indicate that once the fires of political crisis die away, then much of the enthusiasm and motivation necessary to sustain an extended and effective effort on the part of the poor and inactive also disappears. The web of circumstance that entraps the poor in a life of political apathy is a strong and comprehensive one, and it is one whose fibers must constantly be broken if the inactive are ever to become regular participants in the political arena. (For further details on the requirements of successful efforts at intervention on behalf of the powerless, see chapter 12 on political movements.)

COMMUNITY POWER
IN COMPARATIVE PERSPECTIVE

Although studies of communities in the United States may reveal a great deal about local power and politics, they still only present a story whose details are confined to a single nation. Other research, undertaken in different national settings, is required to round out the picture and to show whether there might not be important national variations both in the distribution of power as well as in the nature

[63] Ibid., p. 350.

of those individuals who are powerful. Moreover, such variations, if they exist, would provide important clues to the ways in which institutional structures and systems of beliefs in a broad national setting might constrain the sort of power arrangements that emerge in its local political arenas.

Such a study, or rather series of studies, was undertaken by Delbert C. Miller.[64] Using a wide variety of information assembled on the character of politics in four urban areas—Seattle, Washington; Bristol, England; Cordoba, Argentina; and Lima, Peru—Miller sought to discover whether substantial differences existed among the communities. He discovered that the relative influence of major institutional sectors, for instance, the business as compared to the governmental, did vary; in Cordoba, the religious institution, long held to be dominant in many Latin American countries, did indeed possess a reputation for great influence, while in Seattle the business and finance sectors were claimed to exercise the greatest influence. However, it is not the variation so much as the pattern of similarities that is so striking about Miller's results; the similarities stand in vivid contrast to differences in the value patterns of the different countries. In all four communities, Miller found that there existed no single elite that wielded power alone, but rather there were a cluster of influential groups and individuals that exercised some measure of power over local decisions. The pattern he uncovered was somewhat similar to the structures portrayed in figure 7-1, falling somewhere between types C and D, as there appeared to be both important points of common agreement as well as of conflict among the various institutions. In addition, Miller found that in all four settings the individuals who were reputed to exercise the greatest amount of influence over community decisions frequently came from the business and financial sectors; although Seattle and Bristol seemed to have slightly higher proportions, Cordoba and Lima showed fairly high percentages—25 percent or more of all top influential figures.

Though the comparative study of the politics of communities remains in its infancy stage, at least when contrasted with the great sophistication of method and theory achieved for studies done within the United States, Miller's study is still suggestive on two counts. First, it points to the prominence of influence by business leaders, regardless of national setting, thereby contributing to the view of those scholars who insist on the growing dominance of a worldwide capitalist economy (see chapter 11 on nation building for further details on this perspective). Second, it provides extensive support for those who claimed that the political arena of communities is open to influence from a number of different groups and individuals— a pluralist stage, in short—rather than under the reign of a single group. Indeed, such evidence is all the more important, since it originates from two Latin American countries often thought to be ruled by various oligarchies. Miller's study does leave some important questions unanswered—for example, Cordoba at the time of his investigation was governed by a military dictatorship, yet Miller claimed to have

---

[64] Delbert C. Miller, *International Community Power Structures: Comparative Studies of Four World Cities* (Bloomington, Ind.: Indiana University Press, 1970).

found a pattern of local pluralism. However, Miller's study also points to important ways in which investigators of these matters might more fully pursue the question, Who runs this town?

CONCLUSION

In concluding, let us try to bring together and highlight the major observations to be drawn from the analyses of community politics. First, students of community politics focus most of their attention on power—the resources underlying its use, and how people may or may not use these resources in exercising their will over public decisions. Second, although there are differences of opinion, as between the elitists and the pluralists, most scholars appear to agree that only a small handful of people actually control most of the political resources and exercise most of the political power in communities. The number and nature of resources may vary from community to community, but the overall pattern of elite control does not. Third, the public, the citizens, do possess some political resources that, if employed collectively, could act to counter the resources and exercise of power by the elites. Yet members of the public do not employ these means—the vote, the capacity to organize, the capacity to speak out on public decisions—to any appreciable degree. Instead, only a minority of the community use them—a minority that more closely resembles the social and economic characteristics of the leaders than of any other group. Fourth—and this represents a major irony—for all the attention they have devoted to examining community politics, analysts have failed to realize that much of the power connected with public resources, for example, the tax revenues collected by the government, has shifted over the past several decades from local to state and, especially, federal government. In particular, the federal government has become the largest holder of public revenues and the final authority on how these funds are to be disbursed. The shift has meant that local communities simply no longer possess the autonomy they once had. Nowhere in recent memory are these limitations upon the power of communities more sharply evident than in the efforts by officials of New York City to get the federal government to bail them out of their financial troubles. Thus, no matter who holds the reins of public power in New York City, the officials in Washington (and Albany) can in large measure determine who occupies the saddle.

These several points have implications both for students of community politics and for those who wish to act upon the political process in communities. It is important that students of community politics realize that a continuation in the shift of public resources from local to state and federal governments could produce communities with a lot of politics and little power. If that were the case, such observers would probably be well-advised to shift the focus of their attention to national centers of power—the federal government or national corporations— or to creative efforts by people in some communities to break out of their doldrums of community disinterest and apathy. The first of these alternative sites of academic interest would take observers much closer to the truth about power in America; the second, closer to newly emergent patterns among the public. Either alternative, however, would be far preferable to much of the scholarship currently parading under the name of community politics.

It is important for political activists to realize that citizens underuse their political resources, particularly that of the vote and political organization, and that much of the control over the public resources has shifted out of the hands of local officials and into those of state and federal officials. Citizens could be encouraged to acquire considerably more power over the decisions in their own communities by using resources there much more regularly and much more effectively. However, a reversal of the tendency for power to become concentrated in the hands of nonlocal officials seems highly unlikely. Only in certain limited respects might this occur, for example, limited revenue-sharing programs; beyond this, it is unlikely that communities in America will ever regain their former autonomy.

CHAPTER EIGHT
Political Parties
and Political Partisanship

Among the numerous advantages promised by a well-constructed Union, none deserves to be more accurately developed than its tendency to break and control the violence of faction. . . . By faction, I understand a number of citizens, whether amounting to a majority or a minority of the whole, who are united and actuated by some common impulse of passion, or of interest, adverse to the rights of other citizens, or to the permanent and aggregate interests of the community. . . . The inference to which we are brought is that the causes *of faction cannot be removed, and that relief is only to be sought in the means of controlling its* effects. . . . *A republic, by which I mean a government in which the scheme of representation takes place, . . . promises a cure for which we are seeking. . . . As each representative will be chosen by a greater number of citizens in the larger than in the smaller republic, it will be more difficult for unworthy candidates to practice with success in the vicious arts by which elections are too often carried; and the suffrages of the people, being more free, will be more likely to center in men who possess the most attractive merit and the most diffuse and established characters.*

JAMES MADISON, *The Federalist*

Like many of his fellow revolutionaries, James Madison wished to secure against various encroachments the liberty and freedom of citizens in the newly founded United States of America. One of the most serious dangers, he believed, lay in factionalism; he had in mind the factionalism based upon such interests as those of mercantilism and those of agriculture. Such groups, he felt, could attract disproportionate amounts of political power and eventually become the inevitable centers of political controversy, thus robbing politics in a free society of the fluid and responsive fashion in which it should work. To guard against such threats, Madison and the other founding fathers designed a federal republic. In *The Federalist* Number 10, he provided a stirring and elegant defense of the architecture of this constitution that would prevent the formation of factions. However, less than ten years after the ratification of the Constitution and Madison's brilliant discourse, political parties, a form of faction among the most despised by Madison, had arisen in the United States.

Had James Madison, a founding father of the United States and one of its most respected thinkers, merely been a poor judge on a minor aspect of the new republic, or had it been, perhaps, merely a strange twist of historical fate that political parties arose then? Madison was only one of the many political observers who failed to foresee and to forestall the appearance of political parties. As discussed in chapter 5 on the varieties of political rule, many of the classical writers on government and politics did not imagine that a day might come when powerful bodies would intervene between the political wishes of the mass public and its elected representatives in government. Nevertheless, in the last quarter of the twentieth century, political parties are everywhere. In industrialized nations there are parties, sometimes numbering from two to as many as fifteen, and in the developing nations as well, there are parties that often prove essential to the national aspirations and development of these countries.

How have political parties come to be established? Do they serve special functions that other forms of organization do not provide? How have parties escaped the efforts of politicians who wished to prevent their rise to power? These and other issues serve as the agenda for this chapter, which focuses on democratic (or competitive) political systems, the United States especially. The political party became a unique organization, a virtual machine in some places, that met certain vital needs of societies with a flair and efficiency lacking in other organizations. However, like all machines, the political party has begun to show signs of rust and wear, indicating that in its present form it may no longer be a viable social and political institution.

THE NATURE OF MODERN POLITICAL PARTIES

Modern political parties first came into existence in the nineteenth century. In the United States, the birthplace of modern parties, parties arose just prior to the presidential election of 1800, but the complete trappings of the modern party— the strength of organization and the involvement of the public—did not fully take place until the 1820s and 1830s. In Great Britain, political clubs and cliques existed long before the advent of nineteenth century politics, but only after the passage of

electoral reforms of 1832 and especially of 1867 did the party develop into something akin to contemporary institutions in the United States. Elsewhere in Europe,
modern parties were somewhat slower in arising; in the Scandinavian countries,
for instance, they did not emerge until the turn of the twentieth century.[1]

As the parties in the United States and Britain evolved, they began to shed
the cocoon of their former lives and to take on the special features now associated
with the modern political party. William Nisbet Chambers, in his analysis of the
early American parties—the Federalists of Hamilton and Washington, the Republicans of Jefferson—identifies the several unique qualities of the modern parties
through a comparison with their predecessors, the cliques and factions.[2] Chambers
observes, first of all, that the modern political party involves an active leadership
group committed to goals that advance the party rather than individual personalities.
The club or clique, in contrast, is typically a temporary alliance of individuals;
it is not identified by specific party labels, and members are more concerned with
their own personal advancement than that of the group to which they belong. In
addition, Chambers notes, the modern party has developed specific practices
designed to further its own expansion and to allow it to work within the
government; these include the practices of electioneering for campaigns, the
techniques of nominating candidates for office, and the special arts of compromise
required to maintain a hold over high political office. To clubs and cliques of
politicians, such practices appear quite foreign. The party, moreover, also
encompasses a wide variety of interests and supporters, each of which attempts to
shape the opinions of party leaders; in contrast, the club is only based on a narrow
range of concerns. Coherent programs, or ideologies, flow from the structure and
activities developed by the modern parties, partly as a means of further securing
its continuity both in and out of government; while clubs or factions rarely, if ever,
advance programs or statements of principle. Last, Chambers notes, modern political
parties rely heavily upon the support of the public to remain in office and thus
seek to solicit and mold opinion among the public, whereas factions or cliques,
which are highly self-contained groups, manifest little concern, or need, for broad
public support.

These are the principal features of modern political parties. These features
must in their totality be seen as an ideal-type, as an abstraction created from a
number of similar features of modern parties everywhere. There is, however, considerable diversity among modern parties; this diversity is discussed shortly. First,
some of the circumstances that gave birth to the modern parties are considered.

---

[1] A number of good general treatments of the history of parties in different countries
can be found in Sigmund Neumann, *Modern Political Parties: Approaches to Comparative
Politics* (Chicago: University of Chicago Press, 1956).

[2] William Nisbet Chambers, *Political Parties in a New Nation: The American Experience,
1776-1809* (New York: Oxford University Press, 1963), chapters 1 and 2, especially pp. 45-49.

THE BIRTH OF MODERN POLITICAL PARTIES

There are any number of reasonably good theories and accounts of the origins of modern political parties.[3] Some take a specifically historical tack, attempting to locate the origins of parties in the special circumstances and setting of a nation.[4] Others take a broad, comparative stance, identifying the origins of modern parties in features common to many nations.[5] Among these many accounts, perhaps the best is found in the work of Joseph LaPalombara and Myron Weiner; their account is notable for its emphasis on the broad preconditions and unique historical forces associated with the rise of parties.[6]

Several broad social and economic circumstances, LaPalombara and Weiner observe, probably promote the emergence of modern political parties. There are three of these that seem particularly crucial for the development of parties: secularization, voluntary associations, and communications together with transportation. First, LaPalombara and Weiner assert, it is likely that a fairly high level of secularization must take place in a society prior to the rise of modern parties; modern parties are founded on the fact that "individuals come to believe that through their actions they are capable of affecting the world in ways which are favorable to their interests and sentiments."[7] Second, they note, the emergence of modern political parties is also likely to be preceded by an extensive network and variety of voluntary groups. Modern political parties reveal an intricate organizational machinery, and it would seem that the development of this machinery is especially likely to have occurred where people have been accustomed to organizational participation and activity. Third, they suggest, the emergence of modern political parties also appears to have been encouraged by an extensive network of communications and transportation. Some of the key features of the modern party, such as electioneering and extensive contacts between the parliamentary party and the hinterlands, simply could not have come about in the absence of a system of communications and transportation.

[3] See, for instance, Hans Daalder, "Parties, Elites, and Political Development in Western Europe," in *Mass Politics in Industrial Societies: A Reader in Comparative Politics,* ed. Giuseppe Di Palma (Chicago: Markham Publishing Company, 1972), pp. 4-36; and Maurice Duverger, *Political Parties: Their Organization and Activity in the Modern State*, rev. ed., trans. Barbara and Robert North (New York: John Wiley & Sons, Inc., 1959).

[4] Along these lines, for example, see Neumann, *Modern Political Parties.*

[5] One of the most common explanations of this form is that which traces the rise of parties in both the United States and Western Europe to the extension of suffrage in the nineteenth century. See, for instance, Leon D. Epstein, *Political Parties in Western Democracies* (New York: Frederick A. Praeger, 1967), pp. 19-26.

[6] Joseph LaPalombara and Myron Weiner, eds., *Political Parties and Political Development* (Princeton, N.J.: Princeton University Press, 1966), chapter 1.

[7] Ibid., p. 21.

LaPalombara and Weiner fully realize that these three conditions only promote the emergence of modern political parties. Thus, they suggest several additional features that seem to represent the special historical precipitants for the formation of modern parties.[8] These other features they represent as three "historical crises" that occur as societies attempt to achieve nationhood—a crisis in the legitimacy of the new social-political order, a crisis in the integration of the new order, and a crisis in participation by the masses in the new order. Each of these crises seems to provide the last shove toward the formation of the modern parties; or, from another perspective, modern parties seem to be the unique devices for resolving these crises.[9]

The first crisis, that of legitimacy, concerns the broad sense of viability that a new order's institutions and symbols have for its citizens and residents. The modern political parties help, so LaPalombara and Weiner suggest, to furnish this sense of viability. The second crisis, that of integration, involves the extent to which the territories and groups of a new order are divided by seemingly irreconcilable conflicts. Often, modern political parties seem to arise to provide a means for resolving these differences, for integrating the residents of a developing nation. The third crisis, that of participation, is the most crucial; most modern political parties seem to have emerged to cope especially with this particular crisis.

The account of LaPalombara and Weiner, at first glance, seems to fit many historical circumstances. In the United States, for instance, both the general preconditions and the historical crises were present about the time of the formation of the Federalist and Republican parties at the end of the eighteenth century. For one thing, there had been a widespread network of associations in existence in the colonies long before the emergence of the two parties. The network of correspondence committees and patriotic organizations had proved instrumental to the development of the Revolution. For another thing, a system of communications and transportation also existed prior to the development of the political parties, and this, too, later proved invaluable to the development of these organizations, especially that of the Republican Party. In particular, a crisis of legitimacy of the new order and another of participation by the people were also evident at the time of the formation of the first parties. These were resolved in part through the successful efforts of the Federalists and Republicans. In addition, a second crisis of participation that occurred in the 1820s shortly after the passage of laws to extend suffrage and the disbanding of the Congressional caucus as a means of

[8] Actually, LaPalombara and Weiner consider these two sets of conditions as alternative explanations for the origins of parties; I have taken license and combined them here into a somewhat more comprehensive scheme.

[9] The logical ordering of conditions prior to the emergence of the modern parties is a sticky issue that LaPalombara and Weiner never identify. It is evident that the three general sets of preconditions act as necessary circumstances for the rise of parties, but the logical status of the crises is not so clear. For our purposes, they are assigned the status of sufficient but not necessary conditions.

political nomination was also almost immediately followed by the birth of the Democratic Party.[10]

Explaining the origins of modern political parties remains a difficult task despite the advances made by LaPalombara and Weiner. Careful examination of the LaPalombara-Weiner formulation, in fact, reveals an imprecision and vagueness in several of their concepts and in the logical formulation of their theory, as well as a notable absence of systematic empirical verification. Because the birth of parties is such an important matter for understanding ourselves and the societies in which we live, it should receive more thoughtful attention in the future.

VARIATIONS IN MODERN POLITICAL PARTIES: HIGHLIGHTS OF CURRENT AND FORMER PATTERNS

The notion of modern political parties introduced at the outset of this chapter is intended to be an abstraction or a guide that will help us to sort out and to understand better the real world. Like all such abstractions, however, it represents a composite of many common, yet subtly different, forms; it advances our understanding by showing us what apparently disparate groups hold in common, and yet retards an even deeper appreciation by downplaying important differences. This section considers some of these differences by looking at contemporary and former variations. This cannot possibly provide an exhaustive treatment, so differences are highlighted.

Current Patterns

Possibly the most illuminating and comprehensive discussion of differences among current parties is found in the analyses of Maurice Duverger in *Political Parties: Their Organization and Activity in the Modern State*. Duverger provides a most exhaustive taxonomy of party structures; two criteria he uses to distinguish among parties—their constituent units and their form of membership—are of special interest.[11]

Constituent Units. According to Duverger, there are three principal forms of the constituent units of modern parties: the caucus, the cell, and the branch. By closely examining the structure and activities of these units, Duverger suggests, one is better able to understand the nature and the relative effectiveness of the political parties that employ them.

---

[10] These events can be found in any standard treatment of American party history as, for example, Herbert Agar's *The Price of Union* (Boston: Houghton Mifflin Company, 1950). The illuminating analysis of Chambers, *Political Parties in a New Nation*, is particularly helpful in understanding this period.

[11] Duverger, *Political Parties*, rev. ed.

The caucus, which, for example, is characteristic of the Democratic and Republican parties in parts of the United States, is fairly limited as an organization. The number of its full-time members is small, and it seeks only the most minimal expansion of its membership in the public. It rarely engages in efforts to generate much enthusiasm and support in the broader society because it wishes to remain a closed and, to a large extent, select organization. Moreover, it incorporates a wide expanse of geographical territory; American caucuses cover such large units as counties and municipalities. Consonant with its limited aims for expansion, the caucus operates only on an intermittent basis, becoming active just at election times.

At the lower levels of organization, caucus leaders are typically precinct captains and other agents whose responsibility is to see that the voters turn out for the party's candidates at election time. The precinct captains also have the responsibility of disseminating information and generating enthusiasm among party members for the nominating conventions, those few occasions when party adherents gather together for the purpose of electing people to run for office. The membership, however, rarely plays a part in the selection of candidates; the primary tasks of choosing candidates are left up to the major party figures.[12]

Duverger regards the caucus with no little disdain, especially as compared with the cell and the branch forms. He notes, for instance, that in European countries the caucus is on the decline and is generally being replaced by the cell or the branch. Duverger observes that the caucus remains a viable organization only in the United States, largely because it appears to be more compatible with special features of the United States' historical setting, particularly the strength of individualism and the absence of a sense of class consciousness.[13] Among other things, he notes, "caucuses are an archaic type of political party structure [*sic*] .... In their composition as well as in their structure [weak collective organization, predominance of individual considerations] they represent the influence of the upper and lower middle class. . . . The greater efficiency of recruiting techniques directly adapted to the masses [for example, the system of branches] has usually brought about the decline of the caucus."[14]

The branch, which is characteristic of most Socialist parties in Europe, is in most respects fundamentally different from the caucus as a form of party organization. In general, the branch represents a highly centralized form of organization in which the membership is tightly locked through an intricate division of labor and in which there is a clear emphasis on control from above. It incorporates a fairly large number of members, is ever after new ones, and attempts to establish for itself a broad base among the public. It generally seeks an open stance with regard to the broader society, hoping thereby to establish itself as a permanent and broad point of reference and to be able to mobilize people for a variety of purposes.

[12] Epstein, *Political Parties in Western Democracies*, chapter 8.

[13] Duverger, *Political Parties*, pp. 22-23. Duverger, of course, is not the only observer of United States' history to point to the salience of these features for its institutions.

[14] Duverger, *Political Parties*, pp. 20-21.

One of the striking features of the branch is that it exists for more than simply the election of candidates to high political office. This explains, for example, why the branch takes an expansionist approach among the public. This also accounts for the regularity and intensity of the branch's activities; the leaders of the branch attempt to keep in constant communication with their membership and to encourage informal ties among the members. The branches of the Socialist parties, for example, generally hold meetings twice a month at which they provide a broad form of political education in addition to the more routine forms of information pertaining to elections.

Comparing the branch and the caucus, it is evident that Duverger far prefers the former type of organization, partly because he believes that it enables all people to play a much more prominent role in the internal affairs of the party and, hence, that it is fundamentally more democratic: "There is no doubt the caucus is undemocratic . . . ; this small closed group, composed of semi co-opted, well-known figures, is obviously oligarchic in character. The branch, on the other hand, which is open to all, and in which the leaders are elected by the members (at least in theory), corresponds to the requirements of political democracy."[15]

The third, and last, principal form of constituent unit of modern parties is that of the cell, a form similar in most respects to the branch. Like the branch, for example, the cell is always seeking to expand its membership base among the public and actively searches for new members through regular meetings and extensive propaganda. The cell, an invention of the Communist parties of Europe, also possesses two features that make it an even more tightly knit and cohesive unit than the branch. First, the cell is based on the occupational locus of individuals rather than the residential one—it is found not in the commune or district as the branch is but instead in the factory or the office. Naturally this provides the cell with an unusually firm and vivid presence among its membership and thereby secures its psychological hold upon the loyalties of members. Second, the size of the cell is smaller than that of the branch; whereas the branch typically has more than one hundred members, the cell rarely achieves this size. Its comparatively smaller membership provides the cell with an additional basis for creating an intense solidarity and loyalty on the part of its members.

The cell, Duverger further suggests, represents a profound change in the conception of a political party. Whereas the caucus is organized principally for electoral victory and the branch for establishing a broad base of adherents among the public in addition to electoral victory, the cell is organized as a means of overthrowing the established governmental order. He observes, moreover, that "instead of a body intended for the winning of votes, for grouping the representatives, and for maintaining contact between them and their electors, the political party [under the cell] becomes an instrument of agitation, of propaganda, of discipline, and, if necessary, of clandestine action, for which elections and parliamentary debates are only one of several means of action, and a secondary means at that. The

[15] Ibid., p. 26.

importance of this change cannot be overemphasized. It marks a breach between the political regime and the organizations it has produced to ensure its working."[16]

Form of Membership.

Form of Membership.   A second means to illuminate the differences among modern parties and thus to cast light on their relative advantages and disadvantages, Duverger claims, is through classification on the basis of form of membership. There are two broad types of parties based upon this criterion, the *cadre* party and the *mass* party. The cadre party, which most closely resembles the American political parties, is a limited enterprise that restricts membership to a very few people and attempts to attract important and familiar faces that provide the party with a blue-ribbon image. It is a party that is loosely knit in its organization and that rarely maintains a high level of control over its organizational bases in society. The cadre party, moreover, seeks only to prepare itself for the electoral battles. Therefore its leaders are principally interested in maintaining their contacts with candidates; in stirring up the public, members and nonmembers, just for electoral campaigns; and in winning the allegiance of voters, not of citizens per se. Duverger further asserts that the cadre party is generally on the decline—at least in Western countries—having been replaced in most areas at the end of the nineteenth century and beginning of the twentieth centuries by the *mass* party.

The mass party, a creation essentially of the broad modern extension of suffrage and most characteristic of the branch- or cell-based European Socialist and Communist parties, is interested in gaining converts to its cause as well as in generating voters at the polls; thus it attempts to create widespread as well as intense support among members of the public. As it is primarily interested in attracting adherents, it creates a sophisticated machinery for the recruitment and enrollment of large numbers of dues-paying members. Moreover, it is necessary to differentiate clearly between degrees or levels of membership in the mass party. There are such categories as the supporters, who simply pay dues and infrequently attend the meetings of the party; the militants, who are the active members and the ones upon whom the success of the party chiefly depends; and the inner circle, or core group, that exercises complete control over every facet of the party's structure.

Although these, and other, taxonomic devices employed by Duverger have been broadly criticized—partly because of their absence of logical and systematic rigor and partly because they make it seem that the political party, not social and economic groups, are the principal actors in modern history—they still remain highly illuminating and useful.[17] Duverger, for instance, draws attention to the fact that the cadre—caucus-based political parties, most akin to the parties in the United States—tended to develop historically from within legislatures; in his view,

[16] Ibid., pp. 35-36.

[17] For criticism, see, for example, Aaron Wildavsky, "A Methodological Critique of Duverger's *Political Parties,*" *Journal of Politics*, 21 (May 1959), 303-18; and Epstein, *Political Parties in Western Democracies*, chapters 2 and 4.

this may explain why they have also retained an emphasis on limited membership of the public and on an elitist quality. In contrast, the branch- or cell-based mass parties, like the Communist and Socialist parties in Europe, developed outside the legislature; this perhaps accounts for their greater responsiveness to the participation of the public and for their more frequent attempts to promote rank-and-file members to posts of leadership. More important, Duverger's analysis suggests possible structural grounds for the inability of political parties to develop strong working-class contingents in the United States.[18] Members of the working and lower classes are typically found to be disinterested and disinclined towards politics for a wide variety of reasons.[19] This suggests that in order to arouse the members of these classes, the party must go directly to them rather than await their voluntary arrival. The European Socialist and Communist parties, mass parties employing cells or branches, have been eager to undertake this effort and have been remarkably successful in creating a strong working-class base. By comparison, the United States' parties, cadre parties using the caucus as a form of organization, have rarely been willing to engage in such determined programs. If they had been, the working classes in the United States might be considerably better organized, if not more ideologically sensitive and cohesive, than they are at present. (Of course, this matter is extraordinarily complex, and one could equally well explain the absence of mass parties in the United States by citing the lack of a cohesive and strong working class—as many scholars have, in fact, done. Duverger's analysis as well as the general tone of his discourse reawaken us to the obvious fact that parties are not the mere reflections of the social and economic sentiments of a country; they have the capacity to cultivate and perhaps to shape those interests as well.[20])

Political parties in the United States, however, have not always been as loosely organized and as distant from the public as Duverger's analysis implies. Indeed, even though they never attained the features of mass parties, the parties

[18] The absence of a working-class political party in the United States has long been a matter of interest and fascination for historians and other scholars. For various treatments of this and related issues, see the recent anthology of writings assembled by Seymour Martin Lipset and John Laslett, eds., *Failure of a Dream? Essays in the History of American Socialism* (Garden City, N.Y.: Doubleday & Co., 1974). Also, see the excellent analysis of it by Epstein, *Political Parties in Western Democracies*, chapter 6. For a nice discussion, see Robert R. Alford, *Party and Society: The Anglo-American Democracies* (Chicago: Rand McNally, 1963).

[19] Seymour Martin Lipset, *Political Man: The Social Bases of Politics* (Garden City, N.Y.: Doubleday & Co., 1963) chapter 4; and Robert E. Lane, *Political Life* (Glencoe, Ill.: The Free Press, 1959). Lipset's treatment is better for the facts that it provides than for the personality syndrome it attempts to interpret them with.

[20] The most illuminating general treatment of this complex issue—whether parties simply mirror their social and economic environment or whether they actively shape it—is found in Giovanni Sartori, "The Sociology of Parties: A Critical Review," in *Party Systems, Party Organizations, and the Politics of New Masses*, ed. Seymour Martin Lipset and Stein Rokkan (Committee on Political Sociology of the International Sociological Association, Herausgegeben von Otto Stammer, Institut für politische Wissenschaft an der Freien Universität Berlin, Berlin, 1968), pp. 1-25.

that arose in the urban areas of the United States in the nineteenth century and remained there long into the twentieth were in many ways as sophisticated and tightly structured as their European counterparts.

Former Patterns:
The Machine of Urban America

The   political life of many large American cities was dominated by the machines of parties for a long time.[21] The rise of the machine roughly corresponded to the waves of immigration to American cities; in New York City, large numbers of immigrants arrived in the 1840s and 1850s, and the political machine showed a parallel rise in strength. In most cities, the machine was run by the Democrats, but in a few, like Philadelphia, it found its moorings among the Republicans. Control of the machine was typically in the hands of members of distinct ethnic groups. In Boston, for example, it was the Irish—most notably Boss Curley—who found their way into the positions of control over the machine; while in New York City, it was the Irish and later the Italians who controlled the party machine. As the case of New York City illustrated, moreover, it was not merely that the members of distinct ethnic groups held the machine's reins of power but also that these reins were transferred over time from one ethnic group to another—a transfer that corresponded to the length of residence of an ethnic group in the United States.[22]

What did the party machine look like? How did it wield power? The machine seemed to have both the structure and the internal discipline of an army and often worked as effectively. Typically at its top was a single leader, a boss, who exercised principal control over the operations and inner structure of the machine.[23] Slightly lower in the hierarchy were his associates, or lieutenants whom he relied upon for information and for the successful implementation of his commands. The social ties between the boss and his lieutenants often began in childhood, as Mike Royko's insightful analysis of Richard Daley's Democratic machine in Chicago reveals; these were hardened through the years by common political battles and enemies.[24] Beneath this top echelon, there were further niches in the machine's structure, including those of various party functionaries.

The principal goals of the machine were electoral victories and, through such victories, the control of the privileges and rewards of public office in the city. Insofar as the winning of political office was concerned, the strength of the machine lay far down in the recesses of the organization—in the vast networks that punctuated the many wards and precincts of cities. In each precinct, there was a

---

[21] The seminal work on the party machines in the United States during their early rise to power remains M. Ostrogorski, *Democracy and the Organization of Political Parties*, vol. II, trans. Frederick Clarke (New York: Macmillan & Co., Ltd., 1902).

[22] For an interesting analysis of this phenomenon, see Robert Dahl, *Who Governs?* (New Haven: Yale University Press, 1961), chapter 4.

[23] The following analysis is based principally on Mike Royko, *Boss: Richard J. Daley of Chicago* (New York: New American Library, 1971).

[24] Ibid., chapter 2 especially.

captain, beneath him were lieutenants, and further beneath them were other functionaries; it was these officials who helped to keep the wheels of the machine greased and upon whose shoulders rested the fate of the machine's candidates at the polls. The men of the machine knew the members of their districts, and when the time came to get them to the polls, these men had carefully laid the foundations for a large, and sometimes overwhelming, victory for the machine. The classic revelations of how the local members of the machine performed their tasks are found in the discourse on practical politics offered by George Washington Plunkitt, a member of the Tammany Machine in New York City at the height of its power in the late nineteenth and early twentieth centuries. Consider just a few of Plunkitt's pearls of practical political wisdom:

> What tells in holdin' your grip on your district is to go right down among the poor families and help them in the different ways they need help. I've got a regular system for this. If there's a fire in Ninth, Tenth, or Eleventh Avenue, for example, any hour of the day or night, I'm usually there with some of my election district captains as soon as the fire engines. If a family is burned out I don't ask whether they are Republicans or Democrats, and I don't refer them to the Charity Organization Society, which would investigate their case in a month or two and decide they were worthy of help about the time they are dead from starvation. I just get quarters for them, buy clothes for them if their clothes were burned up, and fix them up till they get things runnin' again. It's philanthropy, but it's politics, too—mighty good politics. Who can tell how many votes one of these fires bring me? The poor are the most grateful people in the world, and, let me tell you, they have more friends in their neighborhoods than the rich have in theirs.
>
> If there's a family in my district in want I know it before the charitable societies do, and me and my men are first on the ground. I have a special corps to look up such cases. The consequence is that the poor look up to George W. Plunkitt as a father, come to him in trouble—and don't forget him on election day.
>
> Another thing, I can always get a job for a deservin' man. I make it a point to keep on the track of jobs, and it seldom happens that I don't have a few up my sleeve ready for use. I know every big employer in the district and in the whole city, for that matter, and they ain't in the habit of sayin' no to me when I ask them for a job.
>
> And the children—the little roses of the district. Do I forget them? Oh, no! They know me, every one of them, and they know that a sight of Uncle George and candy means the same thing. Some of them are the best kind of vote-getters. I'll tell you a case. Last year a little Eleventh Avenue rosebud, whose father is a Republican, caught hold of his whiskers on election day and said she wouldn't let go till he'd promise to vote for me. And she didn't.[25]

For a long time, the machines of political parties exercised a tight control over municipal governments and the political arena generally in many urban settings.

---

[25] William L. Riordon, *Plunkitt of Tammany Hall: A Series of Plain Talks on Very Practical Politics* (New York: E. P. Dutton and Co., Inc., 1963), pp. 27-28.

They did so because they were able to provide the needy and dependent immigrants with material inducements not available elsewhere.[26] The machines provided jobs to recently arrived immigrants who could not otherwise secure positions. The machine provided general forms of welfare, including money and clothing, again to those people who could not otherwise secure the basic necessities of life. These, plus other benefits, served as inducements and enabled the machine to secure the compliance of voters on election day—a rather minor request after all was said and done.

POWER AND POLITICS
WITHIN MODERN POLITICAL PARTIES

Though the modern political party is recognized for a number of distinctive and innovative features, the scope and vitality of its organization—the neatly defined hierarchies, the vast network of communications, and the overriding commitments of leaders to organizational goals and growth—rank as the characteristics of singular historic significance. Many a writer has drawn special attention to them.[27] One of the most persuasive was Moise Ostrogorski, the first and possibly still the most brilliant analyst of modern parties.[28] Writing at the close of the nineteenth century, Ostrogorski took special note of the political organizations formed by the Jacksonian Democrats in the United States, especially the machinery developed under the guiding hand of Martin Van Buren, and of the Liberal Party's Birmingham Caucus in England, developed through the leadership of Joseph Chamberlain shortly after passage of the Reform Act of 1867. Painting his analysis with a good deal of cynicism and moral condemnation, Ostrogorski emphasized the ways in which the organizational strength of the Democrats in the United States and the Liberals in England enabled their leaders to manipulate the sentiments of the electorate, to induce blue-ribbon candidates to stand for office and act as front men, and occasionally, to secure public funds illegally for themselves. Ostrogorski feared, moreover, that the strength of these party organizations might grow so considerable that citizens could be deprived of their right to choose political representatives

----

[26] For the analysis in this paragraph, see Fred I. Greenstein, "The Changing Pattern of Urban Politics," *Annals of the American Academy of Political and Social Science*, 353 (May 1964), 1-13. Also see Fred I. Greenstein, *The American Party System and the American People*, 2nd ed. (Englewood Cliffs, N.J.: Prentice-Hall, Inc., 1970), chapter 4. For the relationship between power and inducements, see the discussion of the notion of power at the beginning of chapter 6 in this book. A recent insightful analysis and updating of the nature of political machines is to be found in Thomas M. Guterbock, *Machine Politics in Transition: Party and Community in Chicago* (Chicago: University of Chicago Press, 1980).

[27] See, for example, Duverger, *Political Parties*; and Philip Selznick, *The Organizational Weapon: The Study of Bolshevik Strategies and Tactics* (Glencoe, Ill.: The Free Press, 1960).

[28] M. Ostrogorski, *Democracy and the Organization of Political Parties*, I and II.

free from party interference, and that party leadership could dominate the public's representatives in the legislature.[29]

The seminal analysis of the organizational features and internal processes of modern parties, however, remains that of Robert Michels, a German-born sociologist.[30] Michels's analysis principally concerns the German Social Democratic Party at the turn of the twentieth century but deals as well with trade unions and other parties both in Europe and in the United States. He considers why seemingly fluid democratic organizations like parties become transformed into highly ossified structures with members robbed of rights to participate in decisions and leaders granted inordinate power. His examination, known chiefly by its identification of an "iron law of oligarchy," is so important that it is worth dwelling on at some length.

To begin with, Michels asserts that the members of the working classes, and by implication those of the mass public, can only achieve privileges for themselves by combining their numbers into organizations. Adopting a position roughly equivalent to that of V. I. Lenin—though apparently unaware of Lenin's own analysis—Michels maintains that the "principle of organization is an absolutely essential condition for the political struggle of the masses."[31] Nevertheless, he claims, once a party organization has been formed by the masses, the reigns of power inevitably fall into the hands of an oligarchy. Psychological factors contribute to the inability of the masses to retain control of the organization. These include their suggestibility to orators and propaganda in general and their willingness to submit to the commands of leaders.[32] Besides these there are also technical factors that produce organizational incompetence on the part of the masses. For instance, once the representatives of the membership of the organization have been elected, Michels avers, they achieve a level of expertise and a degree of control over the means of communication that individual members of the rank and file could not even hope to attain.

There are also qualities of the positions of leadership, however, that enhance the tendencies for oligarchies to emerge in party organizations. The attainment of expertise by the leaders falsely encourages them to believe that they are indispensable to the life of the party. The financial benefits that accompany office in the

---

[29] On the first point, Ostrogorski's fears may have been well-founded, even though he exaggerated them; on the second point, his fear turns out to have been less sound, as recent scholarship on British parties reveals. See R. T. McKenzie, *British Political Parties: The Distribution of Power Within the Conservative and Labour Parties*, 2nd ed. (New York: Frederick A. Praeger, Publishers, 1964), pp. 642-49.

[30] Robert Michels, *Political Parties: A Sociological Study of the Oligarchical Tendencies of Modern Democracy* (New York: Collier Books, 1962).

[31] Ibid., p. 61.

[32] Somewhat prophetically, given the rise of Hitler and the Nazi regime only decades later, Michels believed that the need for submission to a leader's will was possibly peculiar to the German people and the residue of a long tradition and of the recent leadership of Bismarck.

organization provide an incentive for leaders to retain their positions, particularly if their prior positions in the organization were as impoverished as those of other members of the rank and file. Michels writes:

> When the leaders are not persons of means and when they have no other source of income, they hold firmly to their positions for economic reasons, coming to regard the functions they exercise as theirs by inalienable right. Especially is this true of manual workers, who, since becoming leaders, have lost their aptitude for their former occupation. For them, the loss of their positions would be a financial disaster, and in most cases it would be altogether impossible for them to return to their old way of life.[33]

Ultimately those who serve as leaders become so enamored of the power and privileges of their positions that they seek to retain the positions indefinitely. Among other things, they try to co-opt future leaders from among the rank-and-file members and thus, to prevent members' free choice in the selection of their future leaders. They also create further positions within the leadership ranks, multiplying the benefits that can be obtained from holding office and simultaneously further insulating themselves from contact with and influence by the rank and file.

Michels is fully aware that leaders cannot dominate the membership of party organizations indefinitely, even by using such ploys as co-optation. To explain the eventual change that occurs in the leadership of party organization, he adopts a form of explanation similar to that which Vilfredo Pareto used to explain the changes in the composition of the governing class in society.[34] Michels argues that there never is a clear break between the composition of the old leadership group and that of the new one in an organization; instead of a *circulation des elites*, there is a *reunion des elites*, that is, an amalgam of elements from the old leadership group with elements drawn from the new one. Change in leadership through amalgamation is coupled with change through decentralization, Michels further observes, with smaller and smaller oligarchies emerging from the original large one. Nonetheless the acts of amalgamation and decentralization do not detract from the one essential fact of every party organization—oligarchy—or, the concentration of power at the top of the party organization and the resulting loss of power incurred by members of the rank and file.

Michels's thesis about the accumulation and concentration of power at the top of party organizations might as easily be cited at the "ironic law of oligarchy"— it is nothing short of major irony that socialist parties, such as the German Social Democratic Party, that preached the end of class rule and the equal dispersion of power and privilege among all people in society display vast internal inequities in the distribution of power and wealth. The irony in the discovery further convinces

[33] Michels, *Political Parties*, p. 207.

[34] Vilfredo Pareto, *The Mind and Society* (London: Jonathan Cape, 1935), III, 1427-31.

Michels that he has uncovered an eternal verity about party organizations in particular and perhaps even about mass organizations in general.

Most contemporary scholars of parties and political organizations seem about as dogmatic and unreflective in their conviction of the truth of the iron law of oligarchy as Michels is steadfast yet thoughtful in his. Some have chosen to inquire further into the nature of the iron law, seeking either to discover whether it accurately describes current party organizations or to find out the conditions under which it might fail to come true. Maurice Duverger, for example, still finds evidence of oligarchical structures in many different political parties, especially the Communist parties in Europe that have introduced systematic methods for recruiting and training new leaders.[35] He observes that even in presumably democratically administered parties, oligarchical leadership seems to surface: "In theory, the principle of election should prevent the formation of an oligarchy; in fact, it seems rather to favour it. The masses are naturally conservative; they become attached to their old leaders, they are suspicious of new faces."[36]

Renate Mayntz and Samuel Eldersveld find reasons for making revisions on Michels's iron law. Mayntz, in a 1957 study of a district unit of the Christian Democratic Union in West Berlin, uncovered some signs of oligarchy; in particular, new leaders received their positions often through the influence of older members of the leadership group, and the rank and file hardly exercised much power at all in the selection of new leaders.[37] Yet the leadership was not oligarchic in the sense portrayed by Michels; the leaders did not deliberately attempt to maintain themselves in office through the devices to which Michels pointed, for example, control of communications and monopoly of organizational skills. Instead, certain features of the party organization contributed to a high degree of autonomy on the part of the leadership that was secured independently of any conscious and self-serving interference by the leaders themselves; these included an election process that prevented the rank and file from exercising much choice over the selection of leaders, a strict hierarchy in the organization that prevented the rank and file from easily evaluating the performance of the leadership, and an absence of regular channels that would permit the rank-and-file members to participate in the formulation of party policies. Mayntz leaves readers with the conclusion that while this party organization, at least, may not strictly conform to the pattern and sources of oligarchy noted by Michels, it also is a far cry from the achievement of a democratic process in which leaders and followers freely interact and influence one another. Eldersveld, basing his ideas on his observations of local party organizations in Michigan, argues that the current political party is best conceived

[35] Duverger, *Political Parties*, pp. 116-68.

[36] Ibid., p. 135.

[37] Renate Mayntz, "Oligarchic Problems in A German Party District," in *Political Decision Makers,* ed. Dwaine Marvick (Glencoe, Ill.: The Free Press, 1961), pp. 138-92.

of as a special kind of organization in which command does not clearly flow down from the top but rather is diffusely partitioned among several layers of the organization, resulting in a very loosely coordinated structure.[38] Furthermore, he claims, the cohesiveness of the elite groups at the top of political party organizations is less real than apparent; instead of a single oligarchy, Eldersveld believes that there are several different suboligarchies that are only loosely coordinated and only infrequently in contact with one another.

Among the several recent efforts to reexamine Michels's thesis, none ranks as more imaginative and thorough than that of Seymour Martin Lipset, Martin Trow, and James Coleman.[39] Recognizing considerable truth in Michels's iron law, Lipset and his colleagues set out to discover the conditions under which oligarchies fail to arise in large organizations. The site of their study was a trade union, not a political party, but the choice was propitious nonetheless since trade unions, like parties, are often as vulnerable (if not more so) to the growth of oligarchic leadership. Moreover, the particular union they examined, the International Typographers Union (ITU), represented the single trade union in the United States that had a long history of democratic politics—there were two political parties that regularly competed for union offices and that just as consistently alternated in the control of the offices. Inasmuch as all other unions were run by oligarchies, the specific question for Lipset, Trow, and Coleman became, Why does the ITU have democratic (competitive) rule instead of oligarchic control?

There were, as Lipset and his colleagues found, both historic and structural reasons for the presence of democracy, or absence of oligarchy, in the ITU. First, at the founding of the ITU, the printers revealed a strong identification and commitment to their craft; this loyalty became transformed into an interest and concern about their union. As a result, they were less apt to fall into the trap of membership passivity that Michels thought assisted the rise of oligarchies. Second, the ITU was somewhat notable among unions for the autonomy of the local branches; instead of having been created from the top down, it had been created as a federation of autonomous units. This fact played an important part in the subsequent politics of the union, facilitating as well as sustaining dissent against established practices and policies in the union. Third, among blue-collar workers, printing carries high prestige and also considerable financial rewards. These attributes perhaps serve to reinforce the printers' commitment to their craft, and they also create less of a disparity between the job of union leader and that of rank-and-file worker. Hence, the incentive for a leader to retain his office for its special perquisites was notably absent in the ITU. Fourth, as a result of their general concern and participation in the union and as a result of their involvement with members of their own craft in social clubs and other activities not strictly

[38] Samuel J. Eldersveld, *Political Parties: A Behavioral Analysis* (Chicago: Rand McNally & Company, 1964), pp. 1-13.

[39] Seymour Martin Lipset, Martin Trow, and James Coleman, *Union Democracy: The Internal Politics of the International Typographers Union* (Garden City, N.Y.: Anchor Books, 1962).

related to the job, the printers as a group seemed to be especially skilled in the informal and formal ways of politics. Such skills on the part of the rank and file further encouraged engagement in union politics, even enabling some rank-and-file members to achieve high office in the union. These, too, are qualities that Michels did not find in the membership of the oligarchic parties and unions he observed.

In short, the study of the ITU is instructive for the lessons it may provide to political parties—and other organizations—wishing to avoid oligarchy. The following qualities are especially important to achieve democracy within parties: encourage commitment to the party, foster participation by the rank and file, create a climate receptive to dissent and innovation, and breed social and political skills in the rank and file.

The nature of the internal structure of political parties will remain an interesting matter of study as long as parties remain viable institutions in the larger society. Michels's analysis provides an important insight into the basic character of these organizations; its essential truth seems hard to disprove even now, almost three-quarters of a century after its initial declaration. Moreover, his insight raises intriguing and difficult questions about the relative advantages and disadvantages of parties that exhibit oligarchic tendencies over those that exhibit democratic ones. A true democrat may believe that any form of oligarchy is reprehensible and to be avoided at all costs. However, organizations that permit competition and dissent to arise among factions are often so debilitated by the internal conflicts that they are incapable of attaining their goals in the larger society, whereas those that insist on unity within the ranks and manifest cohesive leadership, perhaps even oligarchy, frequently are the more successful in attaining the broader goals.[40] Which is to be preferred, democracy within the ranks or victory outside the ranks? That is a question best left to the reader to ponder.

POLITICAL PARTISANSHIP: CONTEMPORARY PATTERNS AND TRENDS IN THE UNITED STATES

To what degree does some form of partisanship actually pervade the consciousness of citizens? In particular, to what extent has the public come to accept political parties as guides for their electoral behavior? To what degree do people remain loyal to political parties? To what extent does loyalty to parties interfere, if at all, with rational decision making about candidates (a process that, according to many theories of the democratic society, is supposed to occur)? These are the sorts of questions that are addressed in this section; the answers provide an assessment of the pervasiveness of partisanship in the electorate. The analysis, for the sake of

---

[40]For relevant evidence on this matter, see William A. Gamson, *The Strategy of Social Protest* (Homewood, Ill.: The Dorsey Press, 1975). Also see the discussion of Gamson in chapter 12, "Social and Political Movements."

brevity, is limited primarily to the national level of politics, to presidential or congressional elections, as well as to related phenomena at this level.

The Breadth and Depth
of Political Partisanship

There are two ways for ascertaining the degree of partisanship in the electorate. One is identification with a political party, whether a major or minor one, or nonidentification in the sense of choosing to refer to oneself as an Independent in partisan politics. Students of party identification have found generally that this dimension of partisanship is acquired very early in people's lives and, to all appearances, seems to be retained over a long period of time.[41] Still, we must ask, how pervasive is this form of identification across the voting public, and what are the specific choices of parties with which people identify? In the period prior to 1960, the patterns of partisanship broke down as shown in table 8-1, which reproduces data from *The American Voter*, a deservedly classic work in the study of voting behavior by Angus Campbell and his colleagues.[42] From October 1952 through October 1958, the proportions of people identifying with different categories of party choice remained roughly the same—about 30 percent identified themselves clearly as strong or weak Republicans; another 50 percent identified themselves as strong or weak Democrats; about 20 percent identified themselves as some form of Independents; and the remaining small proportions were identified as apolitical or had no response. Somewhat similar proportions of party identification appear in reports of other research done during roughly the same period.[43] Thus, eight of every ten American citizens identified with one or the other of the two major political parties—by any yardstick a sizable proportion of the citizenry.

Still, party identification is only a surface measure of partisanship. People may claim an identification, but this may be nothing more than a reflexive response —something pulled out on election day every four years and then put to rest during the interval between elections. Thus, it must be ascertained whether people in the United States public appreciate the ideological differences between the parties— that, since the days of Roosevelt, the Democratic Party has encouraged the growth of the federal government, the expansion of welfare programs, and government intervention in the economy, whereas the Republicans have adopted a more limited role for the federal government, believing business leadership should have more of a free reign in the growth of the economy. (Parenthetically, we must remember that ideology has a specific meaning here, not the same one as intended by Karl Marx,

---

[41] See, for example, Fred I. Greenstein, *Children and Politics* (New Haven: Yale University Press, 1965).

[42] Angus Campbell et al., *The American Voter* (New York: John Wiley & Sons, Inc., 1960). For additional results from the Michigan studies, see Angus Campbell et al., *Elections and the Political Order* (New York: John Wiley & Sons, Inc., 1966).

[43] Norval D. Glenn, "Sources of the Shift to Political Independence: Some Evidence from a Cohort Analysis," *Social Science Quarterly*, 53 (December 1972), 494-519.

Table 8-1 The distribution of party identification

	October 1952	September 1953	October 1954	April 1956	October 1956	November 1957	October 1958
Strong Republicans	13%	15%	13%	14%	15%	10%	13%
Weak Republicans	14	15	14	18	14	16	16
Independent Republicans	7	6	6	6	8	6	4
Independents	5	4	7	3	9	8	8
Independent Democrats	10	8	9	6	7	7	7
Weak Democrats	25	23	25	24	23	26	24
Strong Democrats	22	22	22	19	21	21	23
Apolitical, don't know	4	7	4	10	3	6	5
Total	100%	100%	100%	100%	100%	100%	100%
Number of cases	1614	1023	1139	1731	1772	1488	1269

Source: Adapted from Angus Campbell et al., *The American Voter* (New York: John Wiley and Sons, Inc., 1960), p. 124.

or by his followers. In this context, and that following as well, ideology refers to the specific set of principles, or program, that characterizes a party, and that makes it distinctive from other political parties. This is the sense in which William Nisbet Chambers, for example, used the notion of ideology in his analysis of parties to which we have just referred.)

Students of voting attitudes and behavior look at this matter of the depth of partisanship, or ideology, in two respects. First, they seek out possible systematic differences in the political persuasions of Democratic and Republican followers, ones consistent with the policy espoused by the party cadres and the leaders in office. The authors of *The American Voter*, Angus Campbell and his colleagues, report few significant or systematic differences in the political attitudes of Democratic and Republican followers.[44] Likewise, Herbert McClosky, Paul J. Hoffman, and Rosemary O'Hara find that followers of the Democratic and Republican parties rarely differ in their positions on such issues as public ownership of natural resources, government regulation of the economy, and tax policy.[45] To critics who might counter that American political parties lack substantial differences on matters of policy, even in the period of the 1950s when both the Campbell and the McClosky studies were conducted, McClosky and his colleagues find that a sample of leaders differ quite sharply and consistently on the very same issues on which the followers show no differences. The mass electorate, thus, does not seem

[44] Campbell et al., *The American Voter*, chapter 9.

[45] Herbert J. McClosky, Paul J. Hoffman, and Rosemary O'Hara, "Issue Conflict and Consensus Among Party Leaders and Followers," in *Political Parties and Political Behavior*, ed. William J. Crotty, Donald M. Freeman, and Douglas S. Gatlin (Boston: Allyn & Bacon, Inc., 1971), pp. 208-38.

to grasp the meaning of the issues and ideologies that divide the political parties and are evident to the parties' leaders.

Suppose, however, that one approaches the matter of the depth of partisanship from another direction and asks whether there are any signs whatsoever in the mass electorate of ideological thinking about partisan issues—that is, whether people seem to adhere consistently to a system of definite and coherent political principles. It may be, for example, that many members of the electorate think in deep and profound ways about politics but that these fail to be captured by simply examining followers of the two major political parties. Essentially, this is the tack taken both by Campbell and somewhat later by Philip Converse, one of the co-authors of *The American Voter*. Campbell and his colleagues sought to determine whether members of the mass electorate think in abstract fashion about partisan issues—about tax policy, foreign policy, and so on. Their findings revealed that only about 10 percent of the public could be classified as thinking in ideological terms; 65 percent of the public thought in terms of certain political issues but could not be classified as ideological thinkers; and about 20 percent of the public simply possessed no particular ideological slant in their thinking about politics.[46]

To illustrate the differences in the level of ideological or, better yet, the conceptual thinking that Campbell and his colleagues discovered, two reports from their study are excerpted. The first is from a respondent classified as ideological, the second from one classified as having no issue content whatsoever in his or her thoughts about politics:

(1)
(Like about Democrats?) No. (Is there anything at all you like about the Democratic Party?) No, nothing at all.
(Dislike about Democrats?) From being raised in a notoriously Republican section—a small town downstate—there were things I didn't like. . . . (What in particular was there you didn't like about the Democratic Party?) Well, the Democratic Party tends to favor socialized medicine—and I'm being influenced in that I came from a doctor's family.
(Like about Republicans?) Well, I think they're more middle-of-the-road—more conservative. (How do you mean, "conservative"?) They are not so subject to radical change. (Is there anything else in particular that you like about the Republican Party?) Oh, I like their foreign policy—and the segregation business, that's a middle-of-the-road policy. You can't push it too fast. . . .

(2)
(Like about Democrats?) No—I don't know as there is.
(Dislike about Democrats?) No.
(Like about Republicans?) No, it's the same way I am about the other party.
(Dislike about Republicans?) No. Parties are all about the same to me.[47]

[46] Campbell et al., *The American Voter*, chapter 10.
[47] Ibid., pp. 228, 248, 249.

Converse went beyond the general findings reported in *The American Voter* to investigate the depth of partisanship, or ideological thinking about politics, in other respects.[48] For example, he examined the correlations of peoples' attitudes on one domain of policy, such as employment, with other domains, such as military aid. Like McClosky and his colleagues, he also compared public views with those of congressional candidates. In the case of the general electorate, he finds little evidence of consistency of positions across attitude domains, whereas there is such evidence of consistency in the case of the congressional candidates. Drawing upon the results of this analysis, and several others, he concludes:

> For the truly involved citizen, the development of political sophistication means the absorption of contextual information that makes clear to him the connections of the policy area of his initial interest with policy differences in other areas; and that these broader configurations of policy positions are describable quite economically in the basic abstractions of ideology. Most members of the mass public, however, failed to proceed so far. Certain rather concrete issues may capture their respective individual attentions and lead to some politically relevant opinion formation. This engagement of attention remains narrow however: other issue concerns that any sophisticated observer would see as "ideologically" related to the initial concern tend not to be thus associated in any breadth or number. The common citizen fails to develop more global points of view about politics. A realistic picture of political belief systems in the mass public, then, is not one that omits issues and policy demands completely nor one that presumes widespread ideological coherence: it is rather one that captures with some fidelity the fragmentation, narrowness, and diversity of these demands.[49]

The answer to the question concerning the breadth and depth of partisanship in the mass electorate is that partisanship is pervasive but not profound. People identify in large numbers with political parties, but their identification with those parties does not seem to be the result of an appreciation of policy differences between the parties, and they do not, in other ways, show much of an ideological inclination in their consideration of political matters.

However, the research on which these conclusions are based all took place in the 1950s. The 1960s, by contrast, was a period of major political upheavals— the resurgence of demands by some groups for civil rights, the shift in the balance of power throughout the world, the appearance of violence in many nations—and the 1970s and early 1980s also have witnessed important changes in the nature of American society. Partisanship, if it has any meaning whatsoever, should have shown some response to these and other political events in the past two decades. In fact, there have been changes in the two dimensions of partisanship.

---

[48] Philip E. Converse, "The Nature of Belief Systems in Mass Politics," in *Ideology and Discontent*, ed. David Apter (New York: The Free Press, 1964), chapter 6.

[49] Ibid., pp. 246-47.

Recent studies show that there is a growing proportion of Independents in the public—a movement away from identification with either of the two major parties. Norval Glenn, for example, found that a shift to partisan independence began among young adults and people moving into adulthood in the late 1950s and early 1960s; the shift continued into the early 1970s and accounted for an overall rise in the proportion of Independents in the mass electorate.[50] Paul R. Abramson reported similar findings. In particular, 13 percent of the electorate in 1972 could be classified as "pure" Independents, roughly twice as many as there were in 1952. At the same time, there was a decline in the proportion of people who identified with the major parties, from 75 percent in 1952 to 62 percent in 1972. Abramson found that the increase in Independents and the decline in party identifiers were a result of generational change—those people who entered the electorate after World War II were more likely to show no preference for either of the major political parties.[51] Nevertheless, in both the Glenn and Abramson studies, most Americans continue to identify with the major political parties; Abramson, however, believes that this proportion will continue to decline in ensuing years. Finally, one of the most recent and reliable sources of data on partisanship, the University of Michigan election studies, reveals that the number of Independents continues to be high. In 1976, approximately 35 percent of the electorate identified themselves as Independents, and in 1980 the figure was only slightly lower, about 32 percent.[52]

Insofar as the depth of partisanship, or ideological thought, is concerned, Norman Nie, with the assistance of Kristi Andersen, recently undertook a replication of Converse's analysis.[53] Employing a variety of different forms of data, Nie

[50] Glenn, "Sources of the Shift to Political Independence."

[51] Paul R. Abramson, "Generational Change and the Decline of Party Identification in America," *American Political Science Review*, 70 (June 1976), 469-78.

[52] Martin P. Wattenberg and Arthur H. Miller, "Decay in Regional Party Coalitions: 1952-1980," in *Party Coalitions in the 1980s*, ed. Seymour Martin Lipset (San Francisco: Institute for Contemporary Studies, 1981), pp. 341-67.

[53] Norman H. Nie with Kristi Andersen, "Mass Belief Systems Revisited: Political Change and Attitude Structure," *Journal of Politics*, 36 (August 1974), 540-91. See also Norman H. Nie, Sidney Verba, and John Petrocik, *The Changing American Voter* (Cambridge, Mass.: Harvard University Press, 1976). This matter has stirred considerable controversy, and intelligent observers still are not certain about the actual extent of the reassertion of issue-oriented electoral behavior. What is self-evident, as we further argue in the text that follows, is that the parties themselves are changing quite dramatically, and that the voters are both the sources and the recipients of these shifts. For further discussion of the changes in issue-oriented voting, see the following: George F. Bishop, Alfred J. Tuchfarber, and Robert W. Oldendick, "Change in the Structure of American Political Attitudes: The Nagging Question of Question Wording," *American Journal of Political Science*, 22 (May 1978), 250-69; Philip E. Converse and Gregory B. Markus, "Plus ça change. . .: The New CPS (Center for Political Studies) Election Study Panel," *American Political Science Review*, 73 (March 1979), 32-49; James E. Piereson, "Issue Alignment and the American Party System, 1956-1976," *American Politics Quarterly*, 6 (July 1978), 275-307; and John L. Sullivan, James E. Piereson, and George E. Marcus, "Ideological Constraint in the Mass Public: A Methodological Critique and Some New Findings," *American Journal of Political Science*, 22 (May 1978), 233-49.

discovered a marked tendency for ideological consistency to increase in recent years. Figure 8-1 reproduces some of the data Nie examined. The consistency of attitudes in the mass electorate jumped dramatically between 1960 and 1964. By 1972, each of the measures of consistency on the three different dimensions—overall consistency, domestic attitude consistency, and consistency between domestic and foreign attitudes—was considerably higher than in 1956. Although Nie is unable to determine with precision the reasons for the rise in the consistency of the mass public's attitudes, some evidence points to the increased salience of politics during the 1960s as one possible source for the rise.

Comparisons of the findings on partisanship based on data collected in the 1960s with that collected later reveals two important trends—a shift away from identification with the two major parties and toward independence, and a marked increase in the consistency of attitudes among members of the mass electorate that is symptomatic of more pronounced ideological thinking among the public. It is likely that both trends reflect a broader trend toward increasing rationality in the sphere of electoral decisions on the part of the public; responses to parties are

FIGURE 8-1   Changes in attitude consistency, 1956-72 (adapted from Norman H. Nie with Kristi Andersen, "Mass Belief Systems Revisited: Political Change and Attitude Structure," *Journal of Politics,* vol. 36, no. 3 [August 1974]).

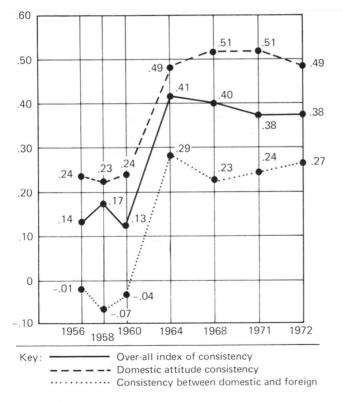

Key: ———————— Over-all index of consistency
      — — — — — — Domestic attitude consistency
      ·············· Consistency between domestic and foreign

becoming less automatic and more calculating. Evidence presented in the following section on partisanship and rationality in the electoral process tends to support this conclusion.

The Social Bases of Partisanship

Stratification. In the United States, as throughout much of the Western world, two main dimensions of stratification have been of interest to observers of the social bases of partisanship—that of social class, or socioeconomic status as it is usually measured, and that of ethnic-religious membership. Since the early sample surveys of voting behavior conducted by Paul Lazarsfeld, Bernard Berelson, and their colleagues during the 1940s, social scientists have found that socioeconomic status is positively associated with voting for the Republican Party—the higher the status, the more likely one is to vote for the Republican presidential candidate.[54] This general pattern holds true regardless of whether one measures status in objective terms—using measures of occupation, income, education, or a combination of the three—or employs a measure of subjective class identification, that is, asking people to locate themselves in the class hierarchy by giving them a choice among several classes such as the upper, middle, or working class. Moreover, parallel findings have been uncovered for party identification—the higher one's socioeconomic status, the more likely one is to identify with the Republican Party.[55]

Nevertheless the influence of social class, or socioeconomic status, on partisanship is fairly small.[56] David Knoke, for example, finds that an individual's socioeconomic status and his or her subjective social class account for a mere 4 percent of the variation in his or her party preference. Other results are roughly on the same order.[57]

Another perspective on the relatively minor impact of social class on Americans' partisanship is provided by Robert Alford, who compares the impact of social class, measured in occupational terms, on voting for left- or right-oriented parties in each of four countries, Australia, Canada, Great Britain, and the United States.[58] Alford discovers that class voting—by which he means the relative degree of support provided by manual and nonmanual workers for each party—is considerably lower in the United States than it is in either Great Britain or Australia. Even

[54] Paul F. Lazarsfeld, Bernard Berelson, and Hazel Gaudet, *The People's Choice* (New York: Duell, Sloan and Pearce, 1944); and Bernard Berelson, Paul F. Lazarsfeld, and William N. McPhee, *Voting* (Chicago: The University of Chicago Press, 1954). Also see Angus Campbell, Gerald Gurin, and Warren Miller, *The Voter Decides* (Evanston, Ill.: Row, Peterson and Co., 1954); and Campbell et al., *The American Voter.*

[55] Campbell et al., *The American Voter.*

[56] I am grateful to Norval Glenn for bringing this point to my attention.

[57] David Knoke, "A Causal Model for Political Party Preference," *American Sociological Review*, 37 (December 1972), 679-89.

[58] Alford, *Party and Society*, and Alford, "Class Voting in the Anglo-American Democracies," in *Mass Politics in Industrial Societies*, Di Palma, pp. 166-99.

in Great Britain, which Alford believes should show the most pronounced level of class voting, its degree is far from what a perfect correspondence between social class and left-wing voting might require. This pattern remains consistent during the period from 1940 to 1965.

These patterns are not unexpected. As was briefly noted earlier in this chapter, a party clearly organized on behalf of the interests of the working class never has gathered substantial support in the United States because of several peculiar features of its social and economic situation. Yet the fact that there is some degree of relationship between social class, or socioeconomic status, and partisanship is cause for speculation as to how it has been produced. The most obvious explanation is simply to rely on the differing strategies of the two major parties. The Democrats, since Roosevelt, have developed campaign appeals and occasionally policies in office that would be destined to generate support among the working classes—the Democrats' welfare program is only one such measure. Likewise, the Republicans have developed campaign appeals or strategies in office that would arouse the enthusiasm of those in the higher levels of the class hierarchy. Alford tends to adopt this form of explanation for the differences that he finds in several countries; he argues that the association between social class and party voting is a product of the extent to which parties represent, appeal to, or in other ways fashion their political base among special social classes. The relative absence of that association in the United States is a sign that American parties have not been so successful or so committed to the representation of social class interests in the mass electorate. In contrast, Philip Converse, basing his argument on the general lack of ideological thinking about politics in the mass electorate, suggests that the relationship between social class and partisanship probably develops for a variety of reasons and that only some spring from concerns about economic issues or other ideological elements.[59]

Whatever particular reasons are summoned forth to explain the kind and magnitude of class voting in the United States—and some of these are so elusive as to defy exact estimation—the fact remains that there is some variation in partisanship by social class. However, things are changing. In recent years, several studies show that the magnitude of class voting has begun to diminish in the United States. Norval Glenn, for instance, finds that in non-Southern areas of the United States there has been decline in the degree to which members of the different classes vote for the Republican presidential candidates; in 1936 there was a difference of almost 23 percent in the rate of support provided by blue-collar and white-collar workers for the candidacy of Alf Landon, whereas in 1968 there was a difference of only 11 percent between the two classes in their support for the candidacy of Richard Nixon.[60] Paul Abramson finds somewhat similar results in an analysis of patterns

[59] Converse, "The Nature of Belief Systems in Mass Publics," in *Ideology and Discontent,* Apter.

[60] Norval Glenn, "Class and Party Support in the United States: Recent and Emerging Trends," *Public Opinion Quarterly*, 37 (Spring 1973), 1-20.

of party voting during recent presidential contests. He observes, moreover, that the decline in the level of class voting can be attributed to a greater proportion of Democratic partisans among members of the post-World War II middle class as compared with the pre-World War II middle class.[61] And in an even later study, Abramson found that there was a slight increase in class voting in the 1976 presidential election, in which Jimmy Carter defeated Gerald Ford; yet the overall tendency since the end of World War II has been for a decline in such voting, and the election of Ronald Reagan in 1980, in which Reagan managed to cut into the traditional Democratic stronghold of the working class, no doubt helped to keep that tendency alive.[62]

Partisanship in the United States has also tended to differ consistently among members of separate ethnic and religious strata. The first sample surveys of voting behavior revealed some of these differences quite clearly; thus, Catholics were more likely to support the Democratic Party than Protestants, even when other influences as socioeconomic status were held constant. Since then, Democratic voting and identification tends to be disproportionately concentrated among the Jews and blacks as well. In a recent study of ethnic-religious voting in the United States, *The Ethnic Factor: How America's Minorities Decide Elections*, Mark R. Levy and Michael S. Kramer reveal the decided edge possessed by the Democratic Party among these very same groups; only among members of Slavic nationalities and Italians is there a perceptible decline in the attraction of voters for the Democrats in recent presidential elections.[63]

The reasons for the differential attraction of certain ethnic and religious groups to the Democratic Party remain about as difficult to pin down as the reasons for differential class voting in the United States. These patterns first emerged in national elections with the candidacy of Al Smith in 1928 and his appeal to a number of the urban immigrant groups in America. Moreover, they were probably reinforced in certain large urban areas by the strength of the political machine in office. Thus, in New York, the members of different ethnic or religious groups naturally would be prompted to support the Democratic presidential candidate inasmuch as the local machine, Tammany Hall, which exerted profound influence on the lives of immigrants, was controlled by Democrats. The same, of course,

[61] Paul R. Abramson, "Generational Change in American Electoral Behavior," *American Political Science Review*, 68 (March 1974), 93-105.

[62] Paul R. Abramson, "Class Voting in the 1976 Presidential Election," *The Journal of Politics,* 40 (November 1978), 1066-1072. Also see the articles by David S. Broder, Seymour Martin Lipset, and Everett Carll Ladd in *Party Coalitions in the 1980s,* ed. Seymour Martin Lipset. These articles analyze class voting in the context of changing alignments of social groups and voters over the past several presidential elections. Other articles in this collection also are worth examining in an effort to pin down the nature of changes in alignments currently taking place in American political parties.

[63] Mark R. Levy and Michael S. Kramer, *The Ethnic Factor: How America's Minorities Decide Elections* (New York: Simon and Schuster, 1972). For more recent information on the behavior of Catholics and Jews in the 1980 presidential election, see the excellent analyses by E.J. Dionne, Jr., and Alan M. Fisher in *Party Coalitions in the 1980s,* ed. Seymour Martin Lipset, pp. 307-40.

would be true in other urban areas, such as Boston and Chicago. These are only assumptions as there is no concrete data on the ethnic or religious influences on voting at those times.

Turning to the *persistence* of these patterns over the past fifty years or so, the problem is quite different and generates explanations of a different order. Finding the persistence of the ethnic effect on party identification carrying through 1968, David Knoke and Richard Felson suggest that the continuation of these patterns is due to the strength of political socialization among different ethnic groups.[64] Other observers have developed somewhat more intriguing explanations for the persistence of the influence of ethnicity and religion on partisanship. Observing that Italians in New Haven provided marked support for the local Republican Party over a long period of time, Raymond Wolfinger suggests that ethnic voting depends upon the strength of identification with a particular ethnic group and the relevance of ethnic issues during particular elections. He further observes:

> The most powerful and visible sign of ethnic political relevance is a fellow-ethnic's name at the head of the ticket, evident to everyone who enters the voting booth. Middle-class status is a virtual prerequisite for candidacy for major office; an ethnic group's development of sufficient political skill and influence to secure such a nomination also requires the development of a middle class. Therefore ethnic voting will be greatest when the ethnic group has produced a middle class, i.e. in the second and third generations, not in the first. Furthermore, the shifts in party identification resulting from this first major candidacy will persist beyond the election in which they occurred.[65]

Support for Wolfinger's thesis about the relevance of ethnicity as a means for generating support among ethnic groups comes from analyses of John F. Kennedy's victory in the presidential contest of 1960 in which some Catholics abandoned their commitment to the Republican Party to vote for Kennedy while some Protestants abandoned their loyalty to the Democrats to vote for Kennedy's opponent, Richard Nixon. Yet these shifts did not appear to remain in effect after the 1960 election, as Wolfinger's theory would have had us expect.[66]

Primary Group Influences.   Some of the earliest studies of partisanship in the mass electorate, notably those by Berelson, Lazarsfeld, and their colleagues, reflect a central concern for the impact of primary group influences. Because of the early development of party preferences, it becomes somewhat difficult to assess the manner in which primary groups influence the voting behavior of adults; that is, it is uncertain whether primary groups mold opinions or whether they are self-

---

[64] David Knoke and Richard Felson, "Ethnic Stratification and Political Cleavage in the United States, 1952-68," *American Journal of Sociology,* 80 (November 1974), 630-42.

[65] Raymond Wolfinger, "The Development and Persistence of Ethnic Voting," *American Political Science Review*, 59 (December 1965), 905.

[66] Philip E. Converse, "Religion and Politics: the 1960 Election," in *Elections and the Political Order,* Campbell et al., pp. 96-124.

selected by the individual. Nevertheless, two findings from this early research stand out as particularly interesting. First, Berelson, Lazarsfeld, and McPhee report that the greater the homogeneity in the opinions of the members of one's primary groups—family and friends—the greater the conviction of the individual for a particular political candidate. Specifically, if one's friends and family all intended to vote for or prefer the Republican candidate for president, then one would have a stronger conviction for that Republican candidate than he or she would if such persons were divided in their opinions. The second major finding of this early research emerges as a corollary to the first; people who are subject to conflicting opinions from the members of their primary groups are apt to behave reluctantly and uncertainly. For example, either they tend to put off making their decision about whom to support until the end of the campaign, or they fail to vote at all. Such a pattern became characterized as one of "cross-pressures" and, in various forms, became the basis for a considerable amount of later theoretical and empirical work.[67]

Unfortunately, as Carl Scheingold pointed out, there has been a failure to follow up on this line of research in current studies of partisanship in general and voting behavior in particular. This particular strategy, broadened to include a concern with social networks of influence, patterns of communication and information transfer prior to elections, and similar ideas, is clearly in need of further study. If some of these ideas were to be pursued, much of the present vacuity in studies of voting and partisanship could easily be overcome.[68]

Partisanship and Rationality in the Electoral Process. It is often claimed that in order for a democratic society to survive in a healthy and suitable fashion, citizens must take an active interest in public affairs. They must be willing to guard against offenses by their elected officials, to hold those officials accountable for their policies, to make sure that the ship of state is being properly guided through both the calm and rough waters of world events. Many citizens, however, have neither the time nor the interest to remain constantly vigilant. Therefore, elections are looked on by theorists of democratic politics as the one special occasion when the public can take an active interest and decide, individually and collectively, who will serve their interests and concerns best in public office. It is further assumed, by these accounts, that the public acts in a rational fashion to select their officials— that people establish priorities for themselves, weigh what candidates say, and then, through the magical device of electoral procedures, come up with candidates who will serve their interests, or those of the majority, best.

---

[67] Careful examination of the results in *Voting* reveals that the authors believed cross-pressures characterized situations of conflicting social statuses, among many others; hence, their research in a way can be directly connected to the large amount of work on the effects of status inconsistency. Moreover, their research also figured quite prominently in the development of cognitive dissonance theory by psychologist Leon Festinger.

[68] Carl Scheingold, "Social Networks and Voting: The Resurrection of a Research Agenda, *"American Sociological Review,* 38 (December 1973), 713-20.

Political parties, which are everywhere dominant in democratic societies, introduce a complicating but not an insurmountable obstacle in this reckoning about the rational method whereby the public chooses to express its will. All that is required to introduce the factor of parties into the decision-making procedure is the additional assumption that parties become the specific organizational devices whereby the public is offered a choice; parties, by this logic, have a responsibility to offer distinct choices to the electorate for their decision. At the same time, however, the electorate is expected to make its choice, now constrained by party labels, among the candidates of the parties. The policies of the parties, the special stands of the candidates, and the voter's own special priorities are expected to come together in a measured fashion and to result in a rational choice of elected officials.

This is only theory about rationality in the electoral process. How does experience work out? We have seen that prior to the 1960s in the United States, a large proportion of the electorate seemed unable to discern any of the apparent ideological differences between the major political parties and incapable of thinking about political choices and issues in any consistent conceptual fashion. That is, they seemed unaware of the issues or choices that confronted them and were in no sense prepared for exercising rationality in the electoral process. Given the sizable proportion of people who were loyal to one or the other major political party, it appeared that their motivations in elections stemmed from a *faith*, or a *loyalty*, to the party rather than from a decision based upon the issues and their own priorities.

Researchers at the University of Michigan have developed a model of the decision-making process by individual voters that highlights forces of party loyalty and concern with issues most forcefully. Campbell and his colleagues believe that choices among candidates at election time spring essentially from one of three forces: party loyalty or party identification, the attractiveness of a particular candidate, and issues of the campaign. If the rational model presupposed by democratic theories were an accurate one, issues should turn out to be the most powerful force, and candidate appeal and party loyalty should be considerably less powerful. What happens? Table 8-2 reproduces estimates of the magnitude of these effects as judged from one of the Eisenhower-Stevenson presidential contests in the 1950s.[69] Party identification refers to party loyalty; orientation to Eisenhower and Stevenson refers to the appeal of the candidates; and domestic and foreign issue partisanship refers to the impact of issues. Looking at the first row, that of the simple correlations, it is evident that party identification exerts the most powerful impact on the voter's choice but that each of the issue components also has a very powerful effect. However, examining the coefficients in the second and third rows, which represent the effects of each variable—controlling for the influence of the other variables—the pattern of coefficients is markedly different. In fact, party loyalty exerts the most powerful influence on the individual voter's choice; it is

[69] Angus Campbell and Donald Stokes, "Partisan Attitudes and the Presidential Vote," in *American Voting Behavior*, ed. Eugene Burdick and Arthur J. Brodbeck (Glencoe, Ill.: The Free Press of Glencoe, 1959), pp. 353-71.

Table 8-2 Relation of partisan attitudes to preference among all respondents expressing a preference for a major party candidate (N = 1522)

	Party Identification	Orientation to Eisenhower	Orientation to Stevenson	Domestic Issue Partisanship	Foreign Issue Partisanship
Simple correlation with preference	0.59	0.35	0.23	0.48	0.38
Partial correlation with preference (all other attitudes held fixed)	.42	.16	.12	.23	.20
Standard regression coefficients	.40	.13	.09	.20	.16

Multiple correlation of five partisan attitudes with preference 0.68

Source: Adapted from Angus Campbell and Donald Stokes, "Partisan Attitudes and the Presidential Vote," in *American Voting Behavior*, ed. Eugene Burdick and Arthur J. Brodbeck (Glencoe, Ill.: The Free Press of Glencoe, 1959), p. 356.

far greater than that of issues or candidate appeals. Thus, loyalty rather than rational calculation underlies the voter's choice.

These estimates of the effects of each of these forces on the individual voter's choice, of course, come from the pre-1960 period, which is different from the post-1960 era in several ways. In particular, in the post-1960 period there has been a decline in loyalty to each of the two major parties and, simultaneously, a marked jump in the mass electorate's consistency of conceptual thought about politics. Are these changes further reflected in the changing weights assigned to each of the three major forces that figure into the voter's choice? Unfortunately, there are no data comparable to Campbell's for the post-1960 period; thus, precise estimates are impossible. However, there are some scattered clues that there has been an increase in the extent to which issues have figured into voters' choices. Some of the increase was due to apparent short-term forces that figured into voters' decisions in particular elections. Thus, in the 1964 election that pitted Barry Goldwater against Lyndon Johnson, two researchers found that ideological, or issue forces, springing mainly from Goldwater's conservative perspective, figured more prominently in voters' decisions than had such forces in the elections of the 1950s.[70] Similarly, Converse and his colleagues found that the 1968 campaign of George Wallace generated an unusual interest, and division, among the voters on such issues as civil rights, law and order, and Vietnam.[71]

[70] John Osgood Field and Ronald E. Anderson, "Ideology in the Public's Conceptualization of the 1964 Election," in *Political Parties and Political Behavior*, Crotty et al., pp. 400-19.

[71] Philip E. Converse et al., "Continuity and Change in American Politics: Parties and Issues in the 1968 Election," in *Political Parties and Political Behavior*, Crotty et al., pp. 356-99.

However, some of the increase can be attributed to the secular rise in the salience of issues for the American public. Several articles point to the marked rise in the influence of issues on voting.[72] Nie and Andersen, for instance, find several indications of the increasing importance of issues for presidential voting and of the simultaneous decline of party loyalty. In 1956, the gamma association between attitudes toward various issues and the presidential vote was +.16; this association rose dramatically to +.58 in the 1964 election and remained at about the same level in the 1972 election. While the influence of issues was rising, that of party loyalty dropped from a high of +.89 in the 1956 election to +.70 in the 1972 election. From another perspective, the influence of party loyalty in the 1972 elections was only somewhat higher than that of issues, +.70 as compared to +.54.[73]

In sum, party loyalty exerts a more significant influence on the voter's choice in presidential elections than his or her concern with particular issues. However, this pattern of influence has been changing in recent years as issues assume a more prominent and significant role. Coupled with the increasing number of Independents and the growing ideological thinking in the electorate is a more general trend of increasing rationality and deliberation on the part of the electorate—or, its mirror image in terms of political parties, a trend of loosening of attachments and loyalty of the electorate to political parties. What has produced this trend?[74]

At best, answers to this question must be tentative; much of the hard and secure evidence is now lacking, but three possible explanations suggest themselves. First, the general increase over the past several decades in the level of education among the public has produced voters who are simply more sophisticated about the nature of parties and politics. Voters are becoming educated to be more deliberative and rational in their choices of candidates to support. Although increases in the average level of education over the past two decades are fairly slight, they could be sufficient to account in part for the growing rationality of voters. The fact that the movement toward partisan independence occurs especially among the young who are receiving the greater educational training underscores the plausibility of this explanation.[75] Second, the magnitude of domestic and

---

[72] Gerald M. Pomper, "From Confusion to Clarity: Issues and American Voters, 1956-1968," *American Political Science Review*, 66 (June 1972), 415-28; and Richard W. Boyd., "Popular Control of Public Policy: A Normal Vote Analysis of the 1968 Election," *American Political Science Review*, 66 (June 1972), 429-49.

[73] Nie with Andersen, "Mass Belief Systems Revisited."

[74] For interesting recent analyses of the matter of declining voter turnout, see Richard W. Boyd, "Decline of the U.S. Voter Turnout: Structural Explanations," *American Politics Quarterly*, 9 (April 1981), 133-59; and Stephen D. Shaffer, "A Multivariate Explanation of Decreasing Turnout in Presidential Elections, 1960-1976," *American Journal of Political Science*, 25 (February 1981), 68-95. Shaffer finds that the two key factors that appear to explain the declining turnout since the end of World War II are the changing age composition of the electorate—there are now a greater proportion of very young and very old voters—and the growing feeling on the part of the public that they, themselves, can do little to affect the course of politics—that is, the public's growing sense of political inefficacy (see our discussion of the exact nature of political efficacy in the text that follows).

[75] See Walter Dean Burnham, *Critical Elections and the Mainsprings of American Politics* (New York: W. W. Norton and Company, Inc., 1970), chapter 6.

foreign conflicts in the 1960s—the civil rights issues, the student issues, and the Vietnam War, among many others—left people with the impression that political parties are simply no longer capable of handling political conflicts, a task almost exclusively their domain. This argument is also partly supported by evidence that shows a growing cynicism on the part of the public toward the effectiveness of the federal government; the increasing cynicism toward government and the diminishing loyalty of voters to parties are an unquestionable part of a broader pattern of voter disenchantment with many political institutions.[76] The third explanation assumes that political parties are an important part of social life and that the ties of people to parties are the result of the parties' deliberate efforts to cultivate their loyalties. Thus, the declining loyalties of people to the parties is the result of diminishing strength in the party organizations and their failure to exact the commitments of people for more than electoral contests. Parties in the United States, as Duverger remarked historically, have been noted for their limited interest in the loyalties of citizens; moreover, their strength has been on the decline since the close of the nineteenth century (see the following section). Both circumstances may finally have caught up with parties and produced a reduction in the overall proportion of loyal partisans.

Any or possibly all of these explanations may help to account for the empirical patterns in this section. One that is especially important is the diminishing strength of party organizations in the United States. The next section considers this phenomenon and attempts an assessment of the future of parties in the United States.

THE PAST AND FUTURE OF MODERN POLITICAL PARTIES: THE CASE OF THE UNITED STATES

The halcyon days of the political parties in the United States were those in the last quarter of the nineteenth century. The party organizations performed with an efficiency, a discipline, and an intensity since unmatched; as Richard Jensen notes, political campaigns at this time were carried out with the vigor and precision of military campaigns.[77] The feelings engendered among the voters were also more intense than in recent years; Ostrogorski provides a most vivid description of the party feelings at the time:

> The name of the party is its own justification, in the eyes of millions of electors. They say, with a well-known politician, an ex-Senator of New York, "I am a Democrat" (or "I am a Republican," as the case may be), just as a believer says, to explain and justify his faith, "I am a Christian!" The reader

[76] For evidence on this trend, see Arthur H. Miller, "Political Issues and Trust in Government: 1964-1970," *American Political Science Review*, 68 (September 1974), 951-72.

[77] Richard Jensen, "American Election Campaigns: A Theoretical and Historical Typology," in *Critical Elections*, Burnham, p. 72.

knows how, and through what political sentiment all the world over, has been intensified in the United States and raised to the level of a dogma—the dogma of "regularity," which makes the party creed consist in voting the "straight party ticket," whatever it may be. The sins against the religion of the party are sins against the ticket.[78]

Turnout among voters for presidential, state, and local elections was considerably higher than it has been recently; it reached an average near 80 percent, while in the past several presidential elections it has declined steadily, from a figure of 63 percent in 1960 to one of 54 percent in the 1980 presidential election.[79] The competition between political parties for elective office was also usually considerably keener than at present.[80] In short, the party organizations were unusually vigorous at the end of the nineteenth century in the United States and were considerably stronger than at present. Inasmuch as the change appears to represent a more or less continuous decline that has been interrupted only occasionally, it is appropriate to inquire into the conditions that have led to the gradual atrophy of parties in the United States. There appear to be a number of sources. Perhaps the most significant is the Progressive movement that developed in the 1890s and was largely organized and advanced by white middle-class Protestant Americans who saw party organizations and their adherents as threats to their own values and lifestyles. The tensions between the Progressives and their opponents grew out of a clash of many different interests and beliefs—the genteel and impersonal outlook of the indigenous Americans against the rough and personal orientations of the ethnics; the Protestantism of the indigenous Americans against the Catholicism of the ethnics; the wealth of the middle-class Americans against the poverty of the ethnics; and so on.[81] The specific results of the Progressive movement, though designed ostensibly to promote greater participation in politics by the public, were really intended to deprive the ethnic groups of control of the party organizations that were their one hold on and source of satisfaction in American life. As the reformers intended, the ethnics ultimately lost control of the party organizations, but this loss resulted in serious and permanently crippling blows to the vitality of the party organizations.

Several products of the Progressive movement undercut the party organizations; the most prominent one was the establishment of direct primary elections. Direct primary elections took the nomination of candidates away from parties and their leaders and gave it to the public. Having lost their right to nominate candidates, parties lost their ability to establish and to enforce a firm party line among their candidates. Fights eventually came to prevail more between the personal

[78] Ostrogorski, *Democracy and the Organization of Political Parties*, II, pp. 353-54.

[79] William Nisbet Chambers, "Party Development and the American Mainstream," in *The American Party Systems*, ed. William Nisbet Chambers and Walter Dean Burnham (New York: Oxford University Press, 1967), p. 14.

[80] E. E. Schattschneider, "United States: The Functional Approach to Party Government," in *Modern Political Parties*, Neumann, pp. 194-215.

[81] See also Richard Hofstadter, *The Age of Reform* (New York: Vintage Books, 1960), chapter 6 especially; and chapter 12 in this book.

factions within political parties than between the parties themselves. The actual candidacy of people for office came to rest less on their loyalty to the party beliefs and hierarchy than on their capacity to generate funds for the political contests. In short, the direct primary stripped the political parties of an important function of identifying and nominating candidates for office; thus, it assisted in the decline of the party organizations in the United States. (One could justify the party's loss as the public's gain, but apparently the public does not see it that way for it turns out for primary elections in even smaller numbers than for regular elections.)[82]

Two other circumstances that made their first appearance at the end of the nineteenth century also contributed to a decline in the vitality of party organizations. One was the loss of patronage that was one of the mainstays of the political party. The Pendelton Act passed in 1883 opened civil service positions to competition on the basis of merit; initially, it covered only 10 percent of the civil service positions in government, but it now covers 90 percent of them. The loss of patronage meant that the parties could no longer provide the attractive inducements that secured a large and loyal staff of workers; the absence of other attractive substitutes was another crippling blow to party organizations. The other circumstance was the introduction in the early twentieth century of a new style of campaigning—advertising. Partly a consequence of the diminishing strength of the party organization and partly a cause for diminishing it even further, advertising as a mode of campaigning was adopted by candidates as an easy and efficient way to communicate with the voters.[83] The earlier style of campaigning, the militarist in the words of Richard Jensen, relied heavily on precinct workers and various other party staff members to draw out the vote for candidates. Advertising relies upon the media to appeal to voters. In recent years, advertising has become even more heavily relied upon at the expense of party workers; television now makes the house-to-house rounds among voters. The effect of this new mode of campaigning, of course, is to rob the party of yet another of its principal functions and to further contribute to the demise of the organization.

One last important historic fact working against party organizations has been a trend noted previously about the United States—that is, the gradual concentration of financial resources in the federal government and the use of these resources to provide welfare monies to the impoverished and disabled (that is, until the Presidential administration of Ronald Reagan). The party organizations in urban areas relied upon their provision of funds as a means of securing services in precincts of poor immigrants—for a little cash, one could easily drum up a few more voters in a ward. During the Roosevelt administrations, the federal government began to provide these funds in the form of unemployment compensation and countless other programs, and party organizations lost their exclusive appeal. The

[82] Frank J. Sorauf, *Party Politics in America,* 2nd ed. (Boston: Little, Brown & Company, 1972), pp. 224-29.
[83] Jensen, "American Election Campaigns," in *Critical Elections,* Burnham, p. 72.

poor could now turn to the federal government for money, and the parties had nowhere else to turn for staff replacements

In the last quarter of the twentieth century, the two most salient facts about parties in the United States are the diminished (perhaps continually diminishing) vitality of party organizations and an electorate that is slowly and steadily coming unstuck from parties. The time appears ripe for change. Should the present trends in the strength of parties continue their downward spiral, parties and partisanship might well disappear from the United States, leaving a void to be filled by some institution prepared to serve as the means whereby the public selects its leaders. A change on the part of the parties in response to the decline in their own strength and to the ebbing interest of the electorate is more likely to happen. Walter Dean Burnham and Gerald Pomper, among others, suggest that the present period might well be one of critical realignment in which the parties as well as the social groups comprising them change.[84] In particular, the Democratic coalition of ethnics and blue-collar workers created by Franklin Roosevelt, already coming apart by the late 1960s, would disappear and be replaced by another sort of combination; likewise, the composition of the Republican party would undergo transformation. Indeed, it was a deliberate part of the strategy on behalf of Ronald Reagan in the 1980 presidential campaign that the Republicans would seek to capture a number of the groups, among them low income voters and union members, who gradually over the course of the past several elections had come unglued from the Democratic banner; it was assumed that the capture of these voters would help to pave the way for the sort of critical realignment of voters envisioned by Burnham and Pomper.[85] Yet all indications are that while Reagan did indeed gain strength among some of these groups, he did not succeed in fashioning the firm new coalition he had hoped for. Everett Carll Ladd thus has come to refer to the electoral scene in America in the early 1980s as one, not of realignment, but of dealignment—a period in which more voters in more social and economic groups are regularly up for grabs in presidential elections than at any other time in the last fifty years.[86]

It also is possible, though perhaps less likely, that something more fundamental could occur to parties in the United States—that is, they might change from the cadre to the mass party structure. John Anderson, the Independent candidate in the 1980 presidential election, had hoped to create just such a mass party during his campaign. The change to this sort of party structure, in fact, seems to have been foreshadowed by the efforts of the McGovern commission to make the composition of the Democratic Party in 1972 more representative of the population by being more open to discontented groups. Even though the McGovern commission changes

[84] Burnham, *Critical Elections*, chapter 6.

[85] See Richard B. Wirthlin, "The Republican Strategy and Its Electoral Consequences," in *Party Coalitions in the 1980s*, Lipset, 235-66.

[86] Everett Carll Ladd, "The Shifting Party Coalitions—From the 1930s to the 1970s," in *Party Coalitions in the 1980s*, Lipset, 127-49.

have since been rescinded by the Democratic Party, the election reform law that limits the size of financial contributions to candidates and allows all candidates to draw upon public funds for campaign expenditures could ultimately make American parties much more similar to the European mass party structures. Such an outcome, however, would also require the parties to formulate more distinct and viable policies from among which the voters could choose.

In any event, parties and the public appear to be in the midst of a transition from a vivid past to an uncertain future. Normally an observer would caution the public to take heart and to prepare itself. In this case, however, all signs indicate that the public is fully prepared to meet the future and is becoming better equipped as the future becomes the present.

CHAPTER NINE
Citizen Participation in Politics

> *The keynote of democracy as a way of life may be expressed . . . as the necessity for the participation of every mature human being in formation of the values that regulate the living of men together. . . . no man or limited set of men is wise enough or good enough to rule others without their consent . . . all those who are affected by social institutions must have a share in producing and managing them.*

JOHN DEWEY

One of the foremost concerns of contemporary political sociologists is the manner and the degree of citizen participation in politics.[1] Taking political participation in its broadest sense—as the variety of ways in which people try to exercise influence over the political process—they have sought to identify the channels through which citizens attempt to influence leaders as well as to isolate the kinds of citizens apt to use these channels on a regular basis.[2] Besides this effort to understand political

[1] In their treatment of the concerns of contemporary political sociology, Seymour Martin Lipset and his colleagues focus heavily on political participation. See Seymour Martin Lipset et al., "The Psychology of Voting: An Analysis of Political Behavior," in *Handbook of Social Psychology,* ed. Gardner Lindzey (Cambridge, Mass.: Addison-Wesley, 1954), II, 1124-76.

[2] For alternative definitions of political participation, compare Robert Alford and Roger Friedland, "Political Participation," in *Annual Review of Sociology,* ed. Alex Inkeles, James Coleman, and Neil Smelser (Palo Alto, Calif.: Annual Reviews, Inc., 1975), I, 429-79; and Sidney Verba and Norman Nie, *Participation in America: Political Democracy and Social Equality* (New York: Harper & Row, Publishers, 1972), pp. 2-3.

participation as a general strategy employed by citizens, many observers have tried to discover the variations that exist in the degree and the meaning of participation from one society to another and have given special attention to the ways in which participation might vary between democratic and nondemocratic polities.[3] Preceding chapters of this book dealt with political participation from distinct vantage points; for instance, chapter 7 on communities considered how citizens attempt to use various political resources within their communities to exercise influence over members of the community elite. This chapter considers citizen participation in several other and equally important respects, particularly the conventional or somewhat more routine and common methods of citizen participation. The more unusual devices are reserved until chapter 12 on social and political movements.[4]

At the moment the interest in political participation is intense and fairly widespread among scholars, but this concern has a long history. One of the first modern observers to consider seriously both the practical and the theoretical significance of citizen participation in politics was Alexis de Tocqueville.[5] Tocqueville's thesis was that the United States represented the most democratic nation in the world in the nineteenth century.[6] It was democratic in the sense that its citizens—by which he meant only white adult males—had achieved a measure of social, economic, and political equality unmatched in world history; differences in general social station in life, in amount of land, in various other forms of wealth, in civil and political rights, and in other things were, if not absent, at least considerably less pronounced than in the nations of Europe. Partly a consequence of the equality of conditions but partly a force for sustaining them as well was the widespread practice of participation.[7] It seemed to Tocqueville that Americans assembled for common pursuits with far greater frequency and diversity of purpose than the citizens of any other nation. Such a tendency, he further believed, originated precisely because of the relative equality of wealth and other conditions in America; all men possessed roughly the same amount of things, no one person could exercise much influence on his own, and thus, all had to join together in forms of collective social and political enterprise. What at first was a necessity, however, soon became an educational lesson as their engagement in associations

---

[3]Seymour Martin Lipset, *Political Man* (Garden City, N.Y.: Doubleday and Company, 1960).

[4]No invidious comparisons are intended here between conventional and unconventional, or common and uncommon, methods of participation. Moreover, social and political movements tend to be fairly common occurrences, even if they are less common than some other forms such as voting. The essential difference between conventional and unconventional forms of participation is that the former are essentially intended to be supportive of the status quo, particularly the ruling political groups, whereas the latter are intended to resist the status quo. Chapter 12 elaborates upon some of these differences in detail.

[5]Of course Tocqueville was not the only nor even the very first modern observer to reflect on the role of citizen participation in politics; that honor is probably reserved for Jean Jacques Rousseau. Tocqueville, however, helped to pioneer the historical and empirical approach to citizen participation and thus contributed to the beginnings of political sociology.

[6]Alexis de Tocqueville, *Democracy in America,* vols. I and II, trans. Henry Reeve (New York: Vintage Books, 1945). For John Stuart Mill's views of this work, see volume II, 411-13.

[7]Ibid., II, chapters 5-7, especially chapter 7.

provided Americans with a wealth of practical and useful experiences: "[Men] learn to surrender their own will to that of all the rest and to make their own exertions subordinate to the common impulse. . . . Political associations may therefore be considered as large free schools, where all the members of the community go to learn the general theory of association."[8]

Tocqueville's stress on the importance of associations with his emphasis on participation in them regularly by citizens has since been echoed in the writings of other social observers as well. The eminent French sociologist Emile Durkheim suggested that the various social ills and maladies that accompany the growth of the division of labor in societies might be counteracted by the formation of associations developed on the basis of common occupational interests of individuals.[9] Durkheim maintained that such groups could serve a dual function—first, they would reduce the levels of anxiety and discomfort that affected individuals; and second, they would help to resist the tendencies toward the disintegration of the social fabric as a whole by providing channels through which the most salient interests and concerns of citizens, those based on their occupations, could be articulated to the leaders of the state. Political sociologist William Kornhauser, drawing upon the insights and analyses of Tocqueville and Durkheim, claims that the presence of widespread numbers of social and political associations, coupled with their continual employment by citizens, tends to be especially characteristic of democratic (pluralist) polities in industrialized societies and can prevent such nations from assuming forms of political rule severely detrimental to the interests of the large majority of citizens.[10] Kornhauser's assertions are based on a somewhat similar set of assumptions about the functions of associations and associating as those of Durkheim.

The list of scholars who place great emphasis upon citizen participation in politics, particularly in terms of the effect that such participation is expected to have for the foundations of democratic polities, could be multiplied here endlessly, but Tocqueville, Durkheim, and Kornhauser provide some of the most general and important points concerning it.[11]

[handwritten margin notes: Torque too stressed value of secondary assocs. for checking growth/use of central state power]

THE FORMS AND EXTENT
OF CITIZEN PARTICIPATION

Theorists who bring to the study of citizen participation a special preoccupation with the requirements of democratic politics are often most concerned with its basic attributes—the forms it takes, and the extent to which it prevails. For some,

---

[8] Ibid., pp. 124-25.

[9] Emile Durkheim, *Suicide* (Glencoe, Ill.: The Free Press, 1951), pp. 378-84.

[10] William Kornhauser, *The Politics of Mass Society* (Glencoe, Ill.: The Free Press, 1959).

[11] For an excellent treatment of other theorists who consider citizen participation in politics, particularly its role in a democratic polity, see Dennis Thompson, *The Democratic Citizen: Social Science and Democratic Theory in the Twentieth Century* (Cambridge: Cambridge University Press, 1970).

knowledge simply of the numbers of people who show up to vote for candidates at the most prominent of national elections serves as the best single index of citizen participation. With this measure, participation varies widely both within nations as well as between them. For instance, presidential elections in the United States have brought out as many as 80 percent of the eligible voters on occasion, while local elections tend to bring out only about 40 percent of the eligible voters.[12] Moreover, citizen participation in presidential elections in the United States has diminished from the peaks of almost 70 percent during the 1950s to only about 50 percent in 1972.[13] Between countries, there is also considerable variation; in many Western European nations, as many as 80 or 90 percent of those eligible to vote are likely to turn out for national elections.[14] Such differences are somewhat deceptive because voting in European nations is often compulsory, while in the United States it is voluntary.[15]

Voting turnout alone, however, is not a sufficient measure of the capacity of a body of citizens to mobilize themselves either to support or to resist those who govern. There are often much more important outlets for political participation, including the numerous civic and political associations to which Tocqueville alluded. Political scientist Lester Milbrath has attempted to isolate both the wide variety of forms of citizen participation and the varying numbers of citizens likely to perform them.[16] Milbrath identifies fourteen different forms of citizen participation in politics, ranging from the holding of public or party office to simply exposing oneself to political information. Moreover, he assembles the different forms in a hierarchy of involvement in which the greatest citizen involvement occurs in the holding of office and the least citizen involvement occurs in terms of simple exposure to political information (see figure 9-1). Several of the attributes are also clustered together to form different general political postures; thus, spectator activities include the relatively minimal acts of wearing a button, attempting to persuade someone to vote a particular way, becoming involved in a political discussion, voting, and exposure to political information. Milbrath's identification of different dimensions appears to make sense, and the conception of the hierarchy of involvement—the claim that higher levels involve considerably greater effort, even represent qualitatively different forms—seems confirmed by Milbrath's discovery that less than 1 percent of the American public engage in the top two or

[12] See, for example, Robert R. Alford and Eugene C. Lee, "Voting Turnout in American Cities," *American Political Science Review,* 62 (December 1968), 796-813; and Angus Campbell, et al., *The American Voter* (New York: John Wiley & Sons, Inc., 1960).

[13] See chapter 9.

[14] Lipset, *Political Man,* p. 181.

[15] For some of the differences between voting restrictions in the United States and Europe, see the excellent article by Stein Rokkan, "Mass Suffrage, Secret Voting and Political Participation," in *Political Sociology,* ed. Lewis A. Coser (New York: Harper & Row Publishers, 1966), pp. 101-31.

[16] Lester Milbrath, *Political Participation* (Chicago: Rand McNally, 1965). Also, see Robert Lane, *Political Life: Why People Get Involved in Politics,* (Glencoe, Ill.: The Free Press, 1959).

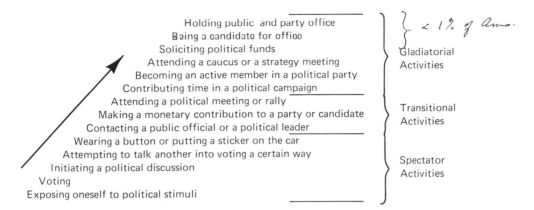

Holding public and party office

Being a candidate for office

Soliciting political funds

Attending a caucus or a strategy meeting

Becoming an active member in a political party

Contributing time in a political campaign

$\left.\begin{array}{c} \end{array}\right\} < 1\% \text{ of Ams.}$

Gladiatorial Activities

Attending a political meeting or rally

Making a monetary contribution to a party or candidate

Contacting a public official or a political leader

Transitional Activities

Wearing a button or putting a sticker on the car

Attempting to talk another into voting a certain way

Initiating a political discussion

Voting

Exposing oneself to political stimuli

Spectator Activities

FIGURE 9-1   Hierarchy of political involvement (adapted from Lester Milbrath, *Political Participation* [Chicago: Rand McNally, 1965])

three forms of gladiatorial activity, while at the other extreme anywhere from 40 through 70 percent vote in elections.

The most technically as well as theoretically sophisticated attempt to isolate the different facets of citizen participation is found in an empirical study by Sidney Verba and Norman Nie of participation among American citizens.[17] Their study, based upon interviews with a very large sample of American citizens in 1967, attempted to isolate empirically the different modes in which citizen participation occurs. First, they asked respondents about their engagement in each of several different kinds of political activities; table 9-1 presents the twelve different forms of participation they asked about and the percentages of respondents who claimed to have engaged in each of the different forms. The different forms appear to represent a hierarchy of involvement comparable to Milbrath's conception and seem to engage roughly the same proportion of citizens that Milbrath found. Thus, 72 percent of the respondents report regular voting in presidential elections (Milbrath claimed 70 percent) and only 8 percent claim membership in a political club or organization (Milbrath suggested about 5 percent). Next, Verba and Nie developed a simple theoretical model of the clusters of activities they expected to find; the model was based on the amount of initiative required for the act as well as on the scope of the act's outcome and the extent of conflict involved in the act. Thus, they expected to find that voting, an act of little initiative, would emerge as a mode of participation independent of broader campaign activity.[18] Last, they performed a statistical operation referred to as factor analysis, which in simple terms means looking for the various types of acts that tend to be performed by the same people, and came up with six different modes of participation. The six forms, as well as the percentage of people performing them, are as follows: the totally

[17]Verba and Nie, *Participation in America. (1972)*

[18]Ibid., p. 54.

Table 9-1   Percentage engaging in twelve different acts of political participation

Type of political participation	Percentage
1. Report regularly voting in Presidential elections[a]	72
2. Report always voting in local elections	47
3. Active in at least one organization involved in community problems[b]	32
4. Have worked with others in trying to solve some community problems	30
5. Have attempted to persuade others to vote as they were	28
6. Have ever actively worked for a party or candidates during an election	26
7. Have ever contacted a local government official about some issue or problem	20
8. Have attended at least one political meeting or rally in last three years	19
9. Have ever contacted a state or national government official about some issue or problem	18
10. Have ever formed a group or organization to attempt to solve some local community problem	14
11. Have ever given money to a party or candidate during an election campaign	13
12. Presently a member of a political club or organization	8

Number of Cases: weighted   3,095
unweighted 2,549

Source: Adapted from Sidney Verba and Norman Nie, *Participation in America: Political Democracy and Social Equality* (New York: Harper and Row, 1972), p. 131.

[a]Composite variable created from reports of voting in 1960 and 1964 Presidential elections. Percentage is equal to those who report they have voted in both elections.

[b]This variable is a composite index in which the proportion presented above is equal to the proportion of those in the sample who are active in at least one voluntary association that, they report, takes an active role in attempting to solve community problems. The procedure utilized was as follows: Each respondent was asked whether he was a member of fifteen types of voluntary associations. For each affirmative answer he was then asked whether he regularly attended meetings or otherwise took a leadership role in the organization. If yes, he was considered an active member. If he was an active member and if he reported that the organization regularly attempted to solve community problems, he was considered to have performed this type of political act. Membership in expressly *political* clubs or organizations was excluded from this index.

inactive, those who perform no acts whatsoever, 22 percent; the voting specialists, those who just engage in voting, 21 percent; the parochial participants, those who report contacts with state or local leaders on personal problems only, 4 percent; the communalists, those who engage in action on local problems (they report "working with others on local problems" or "forming a group to work on local problems," for instance) but in no other forms of political activity, 20 percent; the campaigners, those who report engagement only in campaign activities, such as working for a candidate, 15 percent; and, finally, the complete activists, those who engage in all forms of political activity, 11 percent.[19] The Verba and Nie results shed new

[19] Ibid., pp. 79-80.

So not really a hierarchy.

light on the patterns of participation found among citizens by revealing, among other things, that engagement in partisan politics through voting or campaigns is a substantially different form of political activity than engagement in local forms of community action.

In brief, there are various outlets for political activity that are evident among citizens at present. Voting, of course, is the most popular but also the activity that involves the least effort on the part of citizens. At the other extreme is the act of holding public or party office that attracts relatively small numbers of people but involves the greatest amount of energy and time.

SOCIAL STRATIFICATION
AND CITIZEN PARTICIPATION

Many social theorists' chief concern with citizen participation in politics centers around the correspondence between social inequalities and political inequalities. Do differences in social and economic advantages readily transform into differences in the motivation of groups to attempt the exercise of influence through their active involvement in politics? There really are two schools of thought on this matter. For one school, political participation is apt to reflect the substantial social and economic inequalities found elsewhere in societies, particularly capitalist societies. In particular, differences in the levels of citizen participation are expected. Such variations directly parallel the amounts of social and economic advantages groups possess; the greater the advantages, the more intense and extensive the level of citizen political involvement.[20] For the other school, participation in politics provides groups with the opportunity to offset their social and economic disadvantages, at least to a degree, by giving them the means to reduce such disadvantages through the active exercise of political power.[21] The granting of universal suffrage, for instance, allows individuals the freedom to participate in politics and to exercise influence regardless of differences among them in wealth or education. In this view, variations in the degree of citizen participation among different classes or status groups are also anticipated, but they might prove to be fairly minimal.[22] By and large, empirical information on the actual rates of citizen participation in politics in different classes or status groups provides greater confirmation for the view of the first school.

not exactly opposites

[20] For one example of this approach, see Alford and Friedland, "Political Participation," in *Annual Review of Sociology,* Inkeles et al.

[21] See, for example, T. H. Marshall, *Citizenship and Social Class* (London: Cambridge University Press, 1950).

[22] Thompson insists that for this school it is the sheer opportunity of participation, provided by such things as suffrage laws, rather than its actual level that is crucial to the conclusion that citizen participation prevails among all social groups. Dennis Thompson, *The Democratic Citizen,* chapter 6.

Socioeconomic Status

There is virtually no empirical study now available that does not show a reasonably strong positive correlation between socioeconomic status (SES) and political participation.[23] That is, the higher one's standing in the stratification hierarchy of a society in terms of SES, the higher the rate of one's political participation. This observation holds true for whatever measures are employed to reflect the underlying dimension of SES—occupational rank, level of educational attainment, amount of family income, or the three combined—as well as for a wide variety of indices of political participation—ranging from voting turnout to the more extensive forms.[24] So powerful is the relationship between SES and political participation relative to other structural correlates that Verba and Nie developed a basic model of participation specifically organized about differences in SES.[25] Figure 9-2 provides one set of data from their study that reveal the pattern of SES differences in Verba and Nie's general scale of political participation.[26] There is a considerable increase in the rates of participation between the lower ends of the socioeconomic scale and the higher ends of it; the group at the very lowest point on the scale shows an average rate of 46 points below the mean for the entire sample, while the group at the very highest end of the scale shows an average rate of 66 points above the mean for the entire sample.

FIGURE 9-2 Socioeconomic status and the overall participation scale (adapted from Sidney Verba and Norman Nie, *Participation in America* [New York: Harper and Row, 1972])

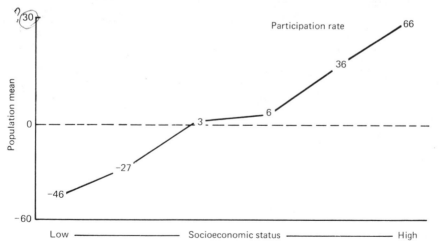

[23] See any of the following: Alford and Friedland, "Political Participation"; Lane, *Political Life;* Lipset, *Political Man;* and Milbrath, *Political Participation.*

[24] Milbrath, *Political Participation,* pp. 114-28.

[25] Verba and Nie, *Participation in America,* chapter 8.

[26] Ibid., for other relevant findings.

One point of special interest in empirical studies of the association between class, or status, rank and the level of citizen participation in politics is the amount of variation among countries. In particular, a host of writers claim that the correspondence between social and political inequalities is apt to be least pronounced in the United States; the reason is that the absence of class-linked ideologies somehow tempers the tendency for disadvantages of wealth and education to become transformed into political disadvantages.[27] Verba and Nie report to the contrary. Comparisons among the United States and several other countries, including Germany, the United Kingdom, and India, reveal that SES and political participation are more strongly correlated in America than elsewhere.[28] Verba and Nie interpret the strong correlation in the United States by turning the conventional argument on its head and claiming that the very absence of a class-based ideology for the working classes has reduced their motivation to participate in politics.

Ethnicity

Like SES, or more broadly social class, ethnicity is a dimension of stratification that is the subject of considerable empirical and theoretical interest to students of citizen participation in politics, particularly American politics. The basic theoretical vantage points with regard to the connections between ethnicity and participation roughly parallel the more general claims about social inequalities and their links to political inequalities; either participation serves as a mere reflection of other more basic forms of social inequalities, or it serves as a means of adjusting them to make them less harsh. Studies of the differences between blacks and whites in their levels of participation in politics provide a recent and perhaps the most important illustration of inquiries into the links between ethnicity and participation.

In one inquiry into the comparative levels of political participation of blacks and whites, Anthony Orum questioned whether the high degree of political mobilization of the civil rights movement on behalf of blacks in the 1960s might not be a possible outcome of a relatively high degree of political participation among blacks in general.[29] An examination of the rates of participation among blacks and whites as a whole revealed little evidence of greater rates of participation among blacks; indeed, whites were considerably more likely to belong to organizations than blacks. When blacks and whites of similar levels of socioeconomic status were compared, Orum found that the differences were not so prominent and that, in fact, middle-class blacks were as likely to participate in organizations as middle-class whites, while upper-class blacks manifested higher rates of membership. The greater propensity for political participation among blacks when differences in socioeco-

---

[27]For a number of such writings, see John H. M. Laslett and Seymour Martin Lipset, *Failure of a Dream: Essays in the History of American Socialism* (Garden City, N.Y.: Anchor Press/Doubleday, 1974).

[28]Verba and Nie, *Participation in America,* p. 340.

[29]Anthony M. Orum, "A Reappraisal of the Social and Political Participation of Negroes," *American Journal of Sociology,* 72 (July 1966), 32-46.

nomic status were removed through statistical control was confirmed by other results of his analysis as well, including higher rates of actual activity among blacks when compared with whites, a greater propensity for blacks to be active in political and civic groups in particular, and historical tendencies for the voting turnout of blacks to increase relative to that of whites.[30] Since Orum's analysis, other studies have confirmed his results as well as extended them to other dimensions of political participation besides organizational involvement and voting behavior.[31]

The more problematic aspects of the black-white differences in the levels and kinds of political participation, however, lie with the effort to explain them. While the usual pattern of SES differences can be interpreted both in broad theoretical terms as well as in more narrow ones, the differences between blacks and whites run contrary to conventional wisdom; that is, given their lower rank in the ethnic hierarchy in the United States, one expects them to participate less in politics than their white counterparts. Why do they participate at a greater rate? Alternative explanations for the differences have been proposed. Orum suggests that political participation serves different functions for blacks and whites—for whites, participation, particularly in organizations, serves the function of providing added prestige, whereas for blacks such participation provides an important collective function for the group as a whole by providing a means for creating a sense of solidarity and unity in a societal setting antagonistic to the ethnic community.[32]

Efforts to test these explanations, particularly the collective function that political participation might provide for blacks, were undertaken in two empirical inquiries. One by Marvin Olsen claims that the higher rates of political participation by blacks as compared with whites of comparable socioeconomic standing are the result of an effort by blacks to create a strong and distinct sense of ethnic community.[33] Thus, those blacks who exhibit the higher identification with the black community should tend to show a higher rate of political participation than other members of their ethnic groups who possess a lower degree of identification. His results prove his assessment correct.[34] Similar evidence on the links between ethnic consciousness among blacks and rates of political participation are revealed in the study by Verba and Nie.[35] Figure 9-3 provides some of the data for their assessment of the impact of ethnic consciousness on levels of participation of blacks. In each of the several modes of participation, those who mention race once—and hence are more ethnic conscious than those who do not mention it at all—exhibit a considerable boost in the rate of participation, while two mentions of race—the most ethnic conscious of all—affects only those who engage in voting. Orum's claims about the

30 Ibid., pp. 35-44.

31 Marvin E. Olsen, "The Social and Political Participation of Blacks," *American Sociological Review,* 35 (August 1970), 682-97.

32 Orum, "A Reappraisal of the Social and Political Participaton of Negroes," p. 45.

33 Olsen, "The Social and Political Participation of Blacks," p. 692.

34 Ibid.

35 Verba and Nie, *Participation in America,* pp. 157-60.

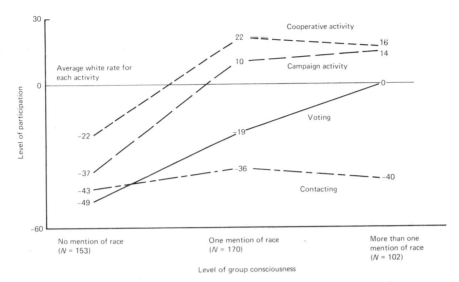

FIGURE 9-3 **Black level of activity for several activities by level of group consciousness** (adapted from Sidney Verba and Norman Nie, *Participation in America* [New York: Harper and Row, 1972])

possible functions of political participation for blacks seem confirmed by the reasonably strong correlations between ethnic consciousness among blacks and their levels of political involvement.

Summary

Social stratification and political participation are linked but in ways that may require somewhat more specialized and focused interpretations of these connections than the most general perspectives provide. Socioeconomic status is connected to variations in citizen participation in politics if the opportunities for participation reflect, in small measure at least, social inequalities of wealth and education; people of higher socioeconomic status do participate in politics in greater proportions than those of lower socioeconomic status. Such differences, indeed, may reflect some cumulative disadvantages, such as lower levels of information and less leisure time, that face those individuals who are members of the lower SES groups in society.[36] The difference between blacks and whites, however, does not follow this pattern. Thus, this difference must be explained in other terms. Specifically, for American blacks it appears that the effort to develop a sense of solidarity based on ethnic identification helps to promote among them more active and varied forms of participation in the political arena.

[36]On such disadvantages, see for example, Genevieve Knupfer, "Portrait of the Underdog," *Public Opinion Quarterly*, 11 (Spring 1947), 103-14; and Lipset, *Political Man*, chapter 4.

SOCIAL AND PSYCHOLOGICAL CONCOMITANTS
OF CITIZEN PARTICIPATION

Almost from the beginning of social scientists' interest in providing precise measurements of the various facets of citizen participation in politics there has been a special concern with the social and psychological factors associated with both low and high involvement.[37] There are both purely scientific and essentially ethical grounds for this concern. Some social scientists are chiefly interested in how and why certain personality predispositions of individuals become transformed into beliefs about or actions in the political arena; hence they seek to find out how such psychological attributes as an individual's self-esteem are linked to tendencies for political involvement.[38] Motivated by more practical and often pressing moral concerns, for example, an interest in seeking to involve citizens more actively in the political process, other social scientists seek to discover those particular psychological attributes that might be cultivated in citizens in order to assist them in participating more actively.

One characteristic of people that has been found to be associated with their participation is their sense of being able to affect politicians and the political order—sometimes referred to as their sense of political efficacy.[39] Frequently scientists measure it by questions such as, How much influence do you think people like you can have over local government activity—a lot, a moderate amount, or none at all? Those citizens who tend to score high on this kind of question, the efficacious, are also the more likely to be high on levels of citizen participation in general.[40] Verba and Nie find as well that the sense of efficacy is especially pronounced among three distinct types of participants in politics: those who engage

[37] This concern is evident in one of the first modern sample surveys of voting. See Angus Campbell, Gerald Gurin, and Warren E. Miller, *The Voter Decides* (Evanston, Ill.: Row, Peterson & Co., 1954).

[38] Although not touching on this theme directly, the emphasis on the examination of traits as a means of casting new light on politics is evident, for instance, in Fred I. Greenstein, "Personality and Politics," in *Handbook of Political Science*, ed. Fred I. Greenstein and Nelson W. Polsby (Reading, Mass.: Addison-Wesley, 1975), II, 1-92. Greenstein's other writings on the subject, cited in this article, are also most illuminating.

[39] Campbell et al., *The Voter Decides.*

[40] See any of the following: Joel D. Aberbach, "Alienation and Political Behavior," *American Political Science Review,* 63 (January 1969), 86-99; Campbell et al., *The Voter Decides;* Campbell et al., *The American Voter;* Dwight Dean, *"Alienation and Political Apathy,"* Social Forces, 38 (March 1960), 185-89; Herbert H. Hyman, "Dimensions of Social-Psychological Change in the Negro Population," in *The Human Meaning of Social Change,* ed. Angus Campbell and Philip E. Converse (New York: The Russell Sage Foundation, 1972), pp. 339-90; Edward L. McDill and Jeanne Clare Ridley, "Status Anomia, Political Alienation, and Political Participation," *American Journal of Sociology,* 68 (September 1962), 205-17; Edgar Litt, "Political Cynicism and Political Futility," *The Journal of Politics,* 25 (May 1963), 312-23; Melvin Seeman, "Alienation and Engagement," in *The Human Meaning of Social Change,* Campbell and Converse, pp. 467-527; and Wayne E. Thompson and John E. Horton, "Political Alienation as a Force in Political Action," *Social Forces,* 38 (March 1960), 190-95.

in local activity, those who campaign actively, and those who represent the complete political activists.[41] Moreover, this sense of political efficacy also appears to be related to a broader psychological attribute, a sense of personal efficacy— what loosely could be referred to as self-esteem, or what Freudian analysts might call ego-strength. Thus, those citizens who rank high on the broad attribute of personal efficacy tend to rank high as well on the more specific form of political efficacy.[42]

Another attribute of citizens related to their participation in politics is their sense of trust in the political order generally and political leaders in particular. Though somewhat related to the sense of efficacy—those high on the one dimension also are apt to be high on the other—the sense of trust attempts to measure the extent to which the citizen feels that the government acts in his or her best interests. Thus, sometimes it will be measured among samples of people through their responses to statements such as, The government in Washington does not really care about how people like me and my family feel.[43] As anticipated, those citizens who rank highest on the sense of trust in the political order also tend to rank highest on the degree of their participation in politics.[44] Two sociologists, William Gamson and Jeffery Paige, moreover, offer the intriguing idea that citizens who possess high degrees of political efficacy but low levels of trust in their government are also more easily mobilized for resistance efforts aimed at challenging the established political system and its leaders. Such citizens are likely to become heavily involved in politics but in resistance efforts such as political movements rather than in supportive efforts such as voting.[45] Evidence on this most imaginative hypothesis turns out to be mixed, however.[46]

A third and final important psychological concomitant of citizen participation in politics is the extent to which citizens feel involved in the political process.[47] Measured empirically by such standards as whether an individual attends regularly to news about politics or regularly discusses politics with friends and family members, studies invariably disclose that those citizens who manifest higher levels of involvement in politics also exhibit higher levels of participation in political activities. The particular lesson of these studies seems to be that the actual practice of participation in politics requires a regular attentiveness to the issues and currents in the political arena and, conversely, that involvement in the various activities

[41] Verba and Nie, *Participation in America,* chapter 6.

[42] See, for example, Litt, "Political Cynicism and Political Futility."

[43] See, for example, Aberbach, "Alienation and Political Behavior."

[44] Ibid.

[45] William Gamson, *Power and Discontent* (Homewood, Ill.: Dorsey Press, 1968); and Jeffery M. Paige, "Political Orientation and Riot Participation," *American Sociological Review,* 36 (October 1971), 810-20.

[46] John Fraser, "The Mistrustful-Efficacious Hypothesis and Political Participation," *The Journal of Politics,* 32 (May 1970), 444-49.

[47] Verba and Nie, *Participation in America,* chapter 6 and appendix D; and Lipset, *Political Man,* chapter 6.

that go on in the political arena leads to a regular attentiveness to political happenings.

The results on the social-psychological concomitants of political participation have stimulated alternative general interpretations that all seem to have some measure of truth. One, an informational interpretation, suggests that political participation requires the receipt of information about the general and specific nature of politics. Those people who receive such information—the more efficacious, the more psychologically involved—are more likely to participate, whereas those who do not—the less efficacious, the less psychologically involved—are less likely to participate.[48] A second interpretation, a structural one, seeks to combine both the findings on stratification correlates and those on social-psychological concomitants. It maintains that the SES differences, in particular, may be the result of the impact of economic development on the polity and political participation; those groups that have benefited from the prosperity of economic and industrial growth, the middle and upper SES groups, also receive the added advantages of greater opportunities and incentives to participate in politics.[49] By this line of reasoning, the social-psychological concomitants are a product of economic growth and serve, in particular, as intervening links to promote greater participation on the part of higher SES groups. For example, the middle SES groups participate in greater proportions than their lower SES counterparts partly because they possess the greater confidence about their ability to affect political leaders and partly because they are the more psychologically attuned to the political process.[50] A third interpretation is that the social-psychological concomitants should be viewed as the product of actual participation in politics rather than only as the causes for it. Taking this perspective, Carole Pateman, who maintains that such foremost theorists of democracy as Jean Jacques Rousseau and John Stuart Mill held basically this view of the educative functions of participation, argues for efforts to actually involve citizens in politics as a means for enhancing their competence about political matters.[51] Pateman's claims, however, receive little empirical support from the recent programs in the United States to enhance the confidence of the poor by involving them in forms of political activities; the Community Action Programs of the 1960s as well as other programs had little measurable and enduring impact on the lives of the poor (see chapter 7, "Patterns of Power and Politics in Communities").

---

[48] Ibid.

[49] Giuseppe Di Palma, *Apathy and Participation: Mass Politics in Western Societies* (New York: The Free Press, 1970), pp. 1-28; and Norman H. Nie, G. Bingham Powell, Jr., and Kenneth Prewitt, "Social Structure and Political Participation: Developmental Relationships, Parts I and II," *American Political Science Review,* 63 (June 1969, September 1969), 361-78, 808-32.

[50] Nie et al., "Social Structure and Political Participation," pp. 811-14.

[51] Carole Pateman, *Participation and Democratic Theory* (Cambridge: Cambridge University Press, 1970). Also see Thompson, *The Democratic Citizen,* chapter 3.

RECENT REASSESSMENTS OF THE MEANING
OF CITIZEN PARTICIPATION

The principal perspective that scholars have brought to the study of political parti-cipation, until very recently at least, has very much a Tocquevillian cast to it.[52] There has been the assumption that participation produces greater benefits than costs for different sectors of a society. It has been assumed, for instance, that participation tends to assist those groups and individuals who participate by provid-ing them with certain skills that come about as a result of participation and by enabling them to voice their grievances to the leading interests in society.[53] It also has been assumed that society is somehow better for the citizens' groups and participation in them by large numbers of people largely because discontent is allowed to be aired freely before all segments of the citizenry. Such a Tocquevillian image, particularly as applied to the United States, was very much called into ques-tion by the widespread and intense political protests of the 1960s. If things were going so well in the political system, many people reasoned, then why the ghetto revolts by blacks, the student protests, or the American Independent Party? Clearly, the Tocquevillian image of participation and its benefits could not easily handle the discontent and grievance that had bubbled to the surface of American politics. Scholars and concerned citizens were forced to turn elsewhere for schemes that would provide an appropriate interpretation of American politics, particularly as it was participatory politics.

There are now two interpretations of citizen participation in politics that represent important alternatives to the Tocquevillian view; one is the product of a direct reaction to the weaknesses of this or similar views, and the other is an independent creation but with stunning implications for the view. The first, repre-sented in the work of Robert Alford and Roger Friedland, insists that a distinc-tion be drawn between political participation and political power.[54] The two phenomena, Alford and Friedland observe, have been inextricably bound together by the Tocquevillian model of participation. Essentially, those who adopt the ideas of Tocqueville believe that participation automatically brings power to participants; if greater numbers of people participate collectively in politics they inevitably acquire greater power. Nothing could be further from the truth, Alford and Fried-land argue. Working largely from a theoretical frame of reference grounded in principles of political economy—that political and economic interests are subtly and complexly intertwined—they maintain that the political participation of the lower and working classes (or lower SES groups) in the United States brings them no

[52] Such scholars as David Truman, Arthur Bentley, and others who are often classified as part of the pluralist school of American political science are included here.

[53] Arnold M. Rose, *The Power Structure: Political Process in American Society* (New York: Oxford University Press, 1967), pp. 248-49.

[54] Alford and Friedland, "Political Participation," in *Annual Review of Sociology*, Inkeles et al.

But isn't the issue one of between diff. aggregate levels of partic. (in diff. hist. periods, e.g.) rather than within (individual variance)?

250 *Citizen Participation in Politics*

power, while the power of the middle and upper class (or middle and upper SES groups) is often maintained without participation.[55] To document this central assertion, they show that regardless of the levels of interest and participation in politics by the lower SES groups, these groups achieve no greater benefits, particularly in material terms, from the American political and economic systems; they receive no more substantial advantages in tax breaks, welfare assistance, and so on. Likewise, the individuals clustered in the upper SES levels of the society tend to receive considerable benefits in the forms of wealth and other such things irrespective of the extent of their involvement in politics. Thus, Alford and Friedland maintain that political participation is simply no guarantee that the material benefits of society will be more equitably distributed. (For a related discussion of benefits, power, and the distribution of both in the United States, see chapter 6, "Patterns of Power and Influence under Contemporary Capitalism: The Case of the United States.")

The other major alternative to the Tocquevillian interpretation is somewhat older than that of Alford and Friedland and has stimulated a considerable amount of empirical research and scholarly debate. This perspective originated with the work of Mancur Olson who, in a book entitled *The Logic of Collective Action*, unveiled a fundamental logical paradox concerning the realization of self-interests by individuals.[56] Until Olson's analysis, scholars, often indebted to the Tocquevillian imagery, had presumed that individuals joined groups such as political associations and organizations as a means of fulfilling their self-interests and that Americans found these devices particularly useful in the broad civic and political arena. Not only faith but also results about the social-psychological concomitants of participation—the higher efficacy and involvement of participants, for example— seemed to suggest that those individuals who embraced organizations were the more rational and were performing in ways distinctively helpful to achieving their particular goals and ends. Olson claims that this is not so, however, insisting that from the individual's point of view *the rational pursuit of self-interest dictates that the individual refrain altogether from engaging in collective pursuits with large numbers of other people.* *Yes, but not because groups aren't helpful.*

Olson's full argument goes as follows. Many groups, particularly economic but sometimes political, seek to attain benefits for their members that are indivisible. Such benefits, which are sometimes called public or collective goods, are such that members of the group are entitled to receive them regardless of whether they have paid for them or not; or, phrasing it somewhat differently, those who have not paid for the collective goods cannot be excluded from the enjoyment of them.[57] For instance, tax rebates or fringe benefits may be construed as collective

---

[55] Alford's general perspective on the links between politics and economics is further revealed in *Health Care Politics: Ideological and Interest Group Barriers to Reform* (Chicago: University of Chicago Press, 1975).

[56] Mancur Olson, *The Logic of Collective Action: Public Goods and the Theory of Groups* (Cambridge, Mass.: Harvard University Press, 1971).

[57] Ibid., pp. 14-16.

goods insofar as they represent the benefits achieved by particular groups; each and every member of the group is entitled to share in the enjoyment of the rebates or fringe benefits, regardless of whether he or she has contributed to their purchase. Noncollective, or private goods, such as merit raises or bonuses are such that those individuals who do not contribute to their achievement—through the investment of hard work, long hours, and so on—are not permitted to enjoy them. Olson further argues that as the size of a group of individuals increases, the costs of membership to the individual—in terms of effort, finances, and so on—similarly increases; beyond a certain size, the cost of membership outweighs the possible rewards it can bring to the individual in the form of public goods. In very small groups, Olson maintains, it is rational for the individual to commit himself or herself to membership through an investment of personal resources because the ultimate rewards in the form of public goods outweigh the costs—even to the extent that a single individual might wish to incur the entire set of costs for organizing the group.[58] This conclusion, however, does not hold true for large groups; from the standpoint of the rational implementation of an individual's self-interests—that is, in terms of the most economical and spare method of attaining the advantages of public goods—the individual finds it more advantageous to refrain from investing any of his or her recources in membership in the group.

The dilemma that emerges from the results of Olson's analysis is quite obvious. To attain benefits in the form of public goods, groups must enlist as many members as possible so that they actually represent a distinct and exclusive sector of the public that can exercise much power through the employment of various sanctions, such as boycotts. To the degree that the group becomes sufficiently large so that it can represent a distinct and exclusive sector of the public, it discourages the individual from membership by making the costs of membership so great as to outweigh the potential benefits to the individual member. However deceptively simple this dilemma seems, its implications are profound. Large groups that seek collective goods arise only under special conditions, and those large groups that already exist are faced with the constant agony of somehow persuading individuals to join despite the fact that membership does not serve their best interests.

If one accepts Olson's argument as valid and as applicable to the political arena, then it suggests that individuals rarely, if ever, find it in their own best interests to engage in the special forms of political activity designed to confer upon them public goods. It means, in particular, that individuals do not find it advantageous to participate in local civic and community groups. Yet, if individuals do not find it advantageous to participate in these activities, why do so many of them participate? Why does the United States, as well as the rest of the world, not consist entirely of people who are apathetic and indifferent to politics?

Olson's answer, or more precisely answers, seems to be of the following sort. Since it will not prove in the individual's own best interests to engage in the

---

[58] Ibid., pp. 32-33.

activities of large groups, then those who manage these groups or those who desire to undertake such efforts afresh must induce individuals to participate through the provision of special incentives or the exercise of powerful constraints. In the case of political organizations, specifically, this means that leaders provide people with special incentives, such as money—a noncollective good on occasion—or an atmosphere in which and people with whom to enjoy social activities; or leaders apply forms of coercive punishment, such as exclusion from the right to work, if individuals choose not to engage in their groups. The use of bribes and patronage by the old political machines in urban areas and the practice of closed shops by unions furnish historical examples of how some large groups induce individuals to join them.

The full implications of Olson's argument have not yet been felt in the study of political participation. Still, it is evident that by raising questions about the premise that political and civic associations act to further the best interests of their members, Olson confronts the conventional analysis of political participation with a serious criticism. Moreover, he helps to lay the basis for the development of an entirely new and different theoretical basis for the origins and maintenance of citizen participation in groups. This perspective views such participation more in terms of the manipulations and strategems of leaders than of the good will and intentions of the participants.[59]

Go over coercion (legal + illegal) and selective inducements (public radio)

CONCLUSIONS

Certain results appear time and again in the empirical studies of political participation both in the United States and abroad. There are several different modes of participation ranging from heavy to light involvement and from campaign- to non-campaign-related activities. Most people become only minimally involved in politics, but there seem to be differences between those who become minimally involved in campaign activities only, including voting, and those who become involved in noncampaign activities in their local communities. The conditions of social stratification are associated with the variations in the rates of participation; thus, individuals who rank in the higher levels of socioeconomic status also participate in greater proportions in political events in general. Whites in the United States also tend to participate in greater proportions than blacks. However, when differences in the proportions of these groups located in different SES groups are held constant—when blacks and whites of the same SES levels are compared with one another—the black-white disparity in participation no longer appears so pronounced, and blacks at certain SES ranks, particularly the higher ones, participate more actively than their white counterparts. Moreover, blacks who possess a greater sense of identification with the black community participate in greater proportions

[59] For an analysis of the general shift away from the good intentions approach—the hearts-and-minds analysis—and toward other perspectives in the study of citizen participation in politics, see John D. McCarthy and Mayer N. Zald, *Social Movements in Modern America: A Speculative Interpretation* (New York: General Learning Press, 1973).

than those who do not so firmly identify with other blacks. Last, there are several social-psychological attributes of people associated with inclinations for political participation; thus, active participants, as compared with inactives, are more apt to feel a sense of confidence in their ability to affect politics, to exhibit a sense of trust in the political system, and to feel psychologically involved in politics. Alone or in combination with the stratification correlates, these several social-psychological concomitants of participation have led to different broad interpretations of the causes and the consequences of political participation.

In the future we may expect to see continued interest on the part of political sociologists in the varieties and the extent of citizen participation in politics. Moreover, we can expect to find greater effort devoted to two particular sorts of matters—one, the kinds of structural conditions that both limit and enhance the possibilities of citizen participation; and two, the sorts of consequences that citizen participation can have on the polity, particularly on the political elites.[60] Clearly the latter of these two issues is the more important. If the involvement of citizens has virtually no impact over the activities and desires of their rulers, then there is some question as to why citizens choose to participate in politics. Ritual, if that is the only function of participation, can as easily be performed in the synagogue or the church as in the voting booth!

Discuss Power's theory
non-voting .

___

[60]On a pioneering effort to examine the structural variations in participation, see Seymour Martin Lipset, Martin Trow, and James Coleman, *Union Democracy* (Garden City, N.Y.: Doubleday & Co., 1956).

CHAPTER TEN
The Forms and Origins of Political Thought

War is Peace
Freedom is Slavery
Ignorance is Strength . . .
Doublethink *means the power of holding two contradictory beliefs in one's mind simultaneously, and accepting both of them. . . . To tell deliberate lies while genuinely believing them, to forget any fact that has become inconvenient, and then, when it becomes necessary again, to draw it back from oblivion for just so long as it is needed, to deny the existence of objective reality and all the while to take account of the reality which one denies—all this is indispensably necessary. . . . Ultimately it is by means of* doublethink *that the Party has been able—and may, for all we know, continue to be able for thousands of years—to arrest the course of history.*

GEORGE ORWELL, *1984*

One of the most important topics for students of politics is that of political beliefs, or thought. How people think about the world of politics, what ideals they hold to be important, which leaders and institutions they claim to be the most significant—these and other beliefs greatly influence the manner in which the political arena works. Moreover, when, and if, the salient beliefs of a polity should weaken, say if the faith of Americans in liberal democracy should flag, it is clear that the whole structure of the polity could undergo profound transformations. It is precisely because beliefs are so central to the maintenance of the polity that Antonio Gramsci, for example, invented his conception of the *hegemony* of beliefs under modern capitalism, and that Max Weber, similarly, wrote of the *legitimacy* of beliefs in political institutions (see our discussion of these ideas in chapters 2 and 3, respectively). And it is for this reason, too, that here we shall devote an entire chapter to the discussion and analysis of the nature of political beliefs.

How we talk about political beliefs, however, is a very complicated issue. For instance, if we were to use the concept of ideology, we would find ourselves beset with a multiplicity of connotations, hence problems. Karl Marx, as we discuss briefly in the following section and as we have discussed at considerably greater length in chapter 2, thought of ideology as a false-consciousness, a set of illusions that covered the grim realities of the social world; other thinkers claim that ideology simply is a set of systematic beliefs about politics; still others think of it as a set of cultural symbols that provide some meaning to the world for people.[1] To avoid these sorts of problems, and yet to get at the sorts of ideas for which the concept of ideology first was used, we shall engage in a more speculative discussion in this chapter than we have previously. We want, in particular, to grasp the several dimensions of political beliefs, for example, the existence of positive ideals but also the myths that serve to defend those ideals. In order to do so, we are compelled to invent a way for thinking about beliefs, a way that will be distinctive yet also will help to clarify the muddy waters of thinking about political beliefs. The inventions that we shall present in the text that follows are designed to help you to better grasp the complexity of beliefs that exists in the political arena, as well as the ways in which beliefs themselves can serve to structure, at least in part, how this world of politics actually looks to us.

In engaging in this discussion of beliefs it is important to remind ourselves continuously that beliefs both shape and are shaped by the actions and institutions of politics. For instance, if we believe in certain tenets of liberal democracy, that, in particular, citizens have an obligation to vote regularly, then we will show up at the polls often to vote for candidates and/or for specific issues of deep concern to us. Likewise, however, the institutions of liberal democracy in America help to implant those beliefs in our minds. Thus, when we actually vote, particularly in elections whose outcomes are claimed possibly to be close, we often come to believe—so, we tell ourselves, and are reminded by the media and friends—that our vote truly counts, that it helps to make democracy work. In other words, beliefs affect our participation, and our participation can serve to reimpress upon us the beliefs themselves. Because the actual nature of political beliefs is so complex, however, in this chapter our tendency will be to emphasize their special character, even occasionally the independent role they may play in the course of political activities. Although we shall do so here, we must never forget that beliefs do not exist in a vacuum, that they are part of the grand complexity of the political

---

[1] For discussions of ideology from different points of view see, for instance, Clifford Geertz, *The Interpretation of Cultures* (New York: Basic Books, Inc., Publishers, 1973), chapter 8; and Janet L. Dolgin, David S. Kemnitzer, and David M. Schneider, eds., *Symbolic Anthropology: A Reader in the Study of Symbols and Meanings* (New York: Columbia University Press, 1977), Part Six.

world we confront in our everyday lives. Let us turn, then, to consider the different points of view about the nature of political beliefs, and then the way we shall talk about them in this chapter.

TWO MODELS OF THOUGHT

There are essentially two different ways of thinking about the nature of political thought. On the one hand, there are those writers and thinkers who approach the nature of political thought from the point of view of society itself—those whom, for the mere convenience of our discussion here, we shall call the *structuralists.*[2] Basically, the structuralists presuppose the existence of a society, composed of its various institutions and groups, and seek to understand how it is that such a society may be reproduced from one generation of people to another. They inquire about the forces and the mediums through which the continuities, even the great changes, come about in the nature of society. Among those whom we may include in this camp are the great social thinkers, especially Marx who, with his notion of ideology, sought to explain why people think a certain way about the world. We also may include among the structuralists a scholar like Talcott Parsons. Parsons, equally interested as Marx in how society's institutions are reproduced, at one point in his own career came to adopt certain ideas from the writings of Sigmund Freud. In particular, he came to believe that through the operations of various social agencies, particularly the family, the fundamental norms and values of society are internalized by people, thus influencing their motivation and thought.[3]

Besides Marx and Parsons, in recent years there have been other scholars who also have examined thought from the point of view of society, seeking to understand how its institutions recur historically. Among them are the political scientists David Easton and Jack Dennis, who have engaged in detailed empirical study of the political ideas and beliefs of children of different ages.[4] Easton, who like Parsons construes the social world in terms of a system, believes that the policies of political leaders are sustained both in a specific fashion, as through electoral support, and in a more general way, through a broad and diffuse base of loyalty or allegiance. What Easton and Dennis have tried to discover is the precise components of this diffuse base of support, along with how it emerges over the course of peoples' lifetimes, and how it might vary among people from different backgrounds. They find that a broad base of positive support, or loyalty, occurs among virtually all people early in their lives, as youngsters; but, rather surprisingly, they also discover

---

[2]The meaning we give to the concept *structuralism* here is much different than the meaning currently associated with the movement in contemporary French intellectual thought, and with the writings of figures like Claude Lévi-Strauss. Structuralism, as we use it, simply connotes a concern with social structure rather than individual personality.

[3]See Talcott Parsons and Robert F. Bales, *Family, Socialization and Interaction Process* (Glencoe, Ill.: The Free Press, 1955).

[4]David Easton and Jack Dennis, *Children in the Political System* (New York: McGraw-Hill Book Company, 1969).

that over time such loyalty diminishes, so that by high school many people no longer exhibit strong positive beliefs toward either political institutions or their officials.[5]

To his great credit, Easton is one of the very few students of political thought and belief to have undertaken ambitious empirical examinations of the nature of such belief. Yet, his view is one with its own particular slant. Like Parsons, he thinks of the political world largely in terms of a basic consensus on values and norms rather than, as Marx and Weber do, in terms of fundamental differences and conflict. There are, in fact, scholars from within the structuralist school who advance assumptions about various and deep divisions within the nature of societies, and how, in particular, they affect the transmission of political thought by social agencies. Among them are scholars like Antonio Gramsci, whose writings are discussed earlier, in chapter 2.

The other general model of the nature of political thought is much more concerned with how the individual comes to develop his or her own ideas and beliefs rather than how society manages to reproduce its institutions. This school, which we may call merely for the sake of convenience the school of *individualists,* tries to explain the patterns of beliefs about politics found among different people. Among those scientists who have done pioneering research in this area is the Swiss psychologist Jean Piaget, who over a period of more than sixty years conducted ingenious studies of how people think and reason about the world. Piaget's early studies have had considerable influence on those scientists who presently study the nature of the individual's thought about politics. In one famous study, Piaget undertook to explain how people develop a sense of the "rules of the game," that is, a sense of morality, of what is permitted and what is prohibited, in the course of social affairs.[6] By closely observing a number of groups of children engaged in games of marbles, and by discovering how individual children responded to the games, Piaget developed the claim that there exist two different stages of the learning and application of moral rules. During the first stage, that of moral absolutism, the child tends to see rules as foreign to himself or herself and to other human beings. Rules appear to be the product of some nonhuman source, with origins in the long and distant past. In contrast, during the second stage, characteristic of children after the age of ten, the child begins to recognize that rules are the product of human effort, that they can be altered, and that application of them often depends on specific circumstances. As Piaget's own ideas matured, his attention turned from morality to the nature of basic intellectual reasoning, or cognition. Even in the case of such reasoning, however, Piaget claimed to have discovered that the way people think occurs in stages, and that there is a progressive movement over a person's lifetime from more primitive levels, of concrete reasoning, to more sophisticated ones, of abstract manipulation.[7]

[5] Easton and Dennis, *Children in the Political System.*

[6] Jean Piaget, *The Moral Judgment of the Child*, trans. M. Gabain (London: Routledge & Kegan Paul, Ltd., 1926).

[7] See, for instance, Herbert Ginsburg and Sylvia Opper, *Piaget's Theory of Intellectual Development: An Introduction* (Englewood Cliffs, N.J.: Prentice-Hall, Inc., 1969).

There are still other scholars whose work, though itself not directly devoted to examining the nature of political thought, has had a major impact upon subsequent investigations of such thought. There is the case of Sigmund Freud, for example. Freud was concerned with accounting for the origins of hysteria, and during the course of his work he developed an array of brilliant concepts about the mind as well as a new technique for uncovering hidden, or unconscious, thinking.[8] Among the notions he invented were those of three principles at work in the unconscious. They were as follows: the principle of the *id*, or the pleasure principle based upon the sex drives of people; the principle of the *superego*, or the principle founded upon the application of social morality to oneself; and the principle of the *ego*, or the reality principle, which like a gyroscope keeps the individual on life's course, transcending the strong desires prompted by the *id*, and the heavy demands originating in the *superego*. Freud also insisted that parents play the most significant role in the development of the *superego* of the individual. Many years later, this claim was extended and examined by social scientists particularly interested in the nature of political thought. Two colleagues of Easton and Dennis, Judith Torney and Robert Hess, sought to find out whether a child's early impressions of parental authority were somehow projected onto other political figures—whether, for instance, a child's conception of his or her father may have shaped his or her conception of a policeman, or even the president.[9] Their evidence turned out to be mixed. Some of it revealed that a child's positive perception of his father seems to favorably dispose him toward political figures. But other evidence suggested that the child usually perceives distinct differences between the authority of his father and that of all public figures.[10]

Between the students of society, the *structuralists*, and those of the individual, the *individualists*, there have been other thinkers with important interests and insights into the nature of political thought—but thinkers who, themselves, have not sided particularly with one camp or the other. We find prominent among this group the contemporary psychoanalyst Erik Erikson. What Erikson has done is to blend together the psychoanalyst's traditional emphases with those of the sociologist. He, like Piaget and Freud, speaks of the stages through which each and every individual passes in the course of life. But to Erikson these stages involve the intersection between the internal drives that characterize the life of the individual, and the special requirements that society has in mind for the individual.[11] Of special significance in America is the period of *identity crisis*. This occurs just on the brink of adulthood, when a person may confront social demands so pressing and urgent that he or she may be overcome by a period of deep internal conflict

[8] See, for example, Sigmund Freud, *A General Introduction to Psychoanalysis* (New York: Pocket Books, Inc., 1958).

[9] Robert Hess and Judith Torney, *The Development of Political Attitudes in Children* (Chicago: Aldine Publishing Company, 1967).

[10] Hess and Torney, *The Development of Political Attitudes in Children*, pp. 99-101, *et passim.*

[11] See, for example, Erik Erikson, *Childhood and Society* (New York: W. W. Norton, 1951); and Erik Erikson, *Identity, Youth and Crisis* (New York: W. W. Norton, 1968).

and depression. While Erikson's rich and insightful analyses have not focused so much on the development of political beliefs among individuals, other writers much influenced by him, like Kenneth Keniston, have discovered that some of the young radical students in the 1960s, in fact, did experience the sorts of crises Erikson claims do exist.[12]

We see here, then, two basic ways to think about political thought. One grows out of the great traditions in sociology and political science and attempts to discover how societies and their institutions are reproduced from one generation to another. The other grows out of the great traditions in psychology and seeks to explain how an individual comes to think about authority, about the rules of the game, about morality and, in general, about many institutions we regard to be political. So confronted with this division in the schools of interest, we could proceed by discussing a series of topics rather eclectically and then showing how the research and scholarship of members of each of the two schools bear upon these matters. That procedure, however, would likely be too difficult for the reader to follow, leading at times to considerable confusion. Thus, we have made a choice here in this chapter to emphasize the structuralist view over the individualist, to discuss the institutions and dynamics of societies insofar as they bear upon the nature of political belief and thought.

In part, our decision arises because this is a book intended to introduce you to political *sociology*, not political *psychology*. But, in part, our decision springs from our own observation that students who read this book are largely Americans and that in America we possess a cultural slant toward the individual, and psychological forms of analysis, more so than in the direction of the social. Thus, it is in keeping with good pedagogical practices that we choose to stress that which is different, if not entirely foreign, to readers, acting on the assumption that by doing so we may lay the seeds for some deeper reflection on issues of political thought and its origins.

THE STRUCTURE OF POLITICAL THOUGHT

If we are to talk about the nature of political thought among people, we must possess some sense of what political thought is. Those thinkers who have written from a structuralist point of view, like Parsons and Marx, have had certain concerns in mind when they have written of political thought, concerns often at odds with one another. Parsons, for instance, wrote of norms and values, principles that served to ground and to regulate the actions of individuals. Marx, in contrast, wrote of the ideology of the dominant, or capitalist, class, which acted contrary to the goals and purposes of the working classes. While these ideas are very important, and have inspired much writing and activity among political revolutionaries in the case of the Marxists, they fail to identify thought precisely, and political

[12]Kenneth Keniston, *Young Radicals* (New York: Harcourt Brace Jovanovich, Inc., 1968).

thought, in particular. Hence, we must turn elsewhere for useful concepts, even inventing some of our own, to seek to approximate ever more closely what it is we do when we speak and write and think about politics.

To do so, it is helpful to turn to a group of thinkers who in the twentieth century have made great headway in the course of trying to understand the substance and mechanics of thought. These are the philosophers as well as linguists who have taken up the issue of the nature of language and who have tried to discover what it is that we mean when we speak of language. What they have done, for the most part, is to assume that much of what we do when we think is in the form of language. Within the Anglo-American tradition of philosophy, John Stuart Mill was among the first to try to pin down the nature of language in a systematic fashion, though even before him John Locke had written about our ideas and impressions.[13] Mill drew an important distinction. He claimed a difference to exist between the denotative features of language, which have to do with what objects outside itself a language refers to, and the connotative aspects, which have to do with the meanings of the words rather than the objects to which they refer. Although this distinction has since been refined, as Suzanne Langer among others shows, Mill's distinction here stands us in good stead.[14] For what he drew attention to was the existence of a distinction between the language we use to speak and think about the world, and the world as it exists, apparently a far different matter than the language itself. The meaning of terms, of names, of concepts, need not, as we may think, simply be a connection between a word, or name, or concept, and an object to which it refers, but rather may involve a more subtle process in which certain meanings—logical ones—emerge out of sentences, and in which other meanings—sociological ones—emerge out of the linguistic context of language, out of the historic creation of it.

Thus, after Mill, British philosophers and even some on the Continent became much preoccupied with the nature of language and its meanings, and came, in fact, seemingly to equate language with thought. It is not farfetched to do so. Marx, for instance, in *The German Ideology* wrote very meaningfully of the role of language in human societies, insisting that

> Language is as old as consciousness, language *is* practical consciousness that exists also for other men, and for that reason alone it really exists for me personally as well; language, like consciousness, only arises from the need, the necessity of intercourse with other men.[15]

Bertrand Russell and his colleagues, following on the heels of the German mathematician Gottlob Frege, sought to develop a special theory of language that rooted

[13] John Locke, *An Essay Concerning Human Understanding*, ed. A. D. Woozley (New York: New American Library, 1964).

[14] Suzanne Langer, *Philosophy in a New Key*, 3rd ed. (Cambridge, Mass.: Harvard University Press, 1976).

[15] Karl Marx, "The German Ideology: Part I," in *The Marx-Engels Reader*, 2nd ed., ed. Robert C. Tucker (New York: W. W. Norton & Co., 1978), p. 158.

it in some fundamental realities in the world. But possibly the most famous of all the linguistic philosophers is the Austrian emigrant to England, Ludwig Wittgenstein. Wittgenstein, a student of Russell at Cambridge University in the early twentieth century, seems to have developed two very different bodies of philosophy about the nature of language. In the first, the *Tractatus Logico-Philosophicus*, he argues that the structure of language displays the structure of the world, and that somehow the way facts stand in the structure of the proposition is roughly parallel to the manner in which they stand in the world.[16] Thus, language—in particular, sentences and propositions—and the world bear an intimate connection to one another, language serving as a "picture of the world."[17] Later scholars, such as the great logician Rudolph Carnap, were much taken with Wittgenstein's claims and sought to demonstrate that scientific propositions themselves share an intimate relationship to the world, such that the proof of a scientific hypothesis lies in its verification through scientific method. In effect, these philosophers seemed to accept, with Wittgenstein, that the propositions of a language, in this case a scientific language, could be said to claim a relationship of parallelism to the world of objects so believed to exist by science. The proposition displayed, in its contents, that which was assumed to exist by the discipline of science.[18]

But Wittgenstein's genius gave birth to another body of philosophy on language as well, one wherein the role of society and the public could be seen to loom much larger. In his work, *Philosophical Investigations*, Wittgenstein wrote of what came to be known as "language games."[19] A language game, he believed, was that exercise of language in which an individual seemingly was implicated at birth. The way we use a language, the very subtlety of its use and application, Wittgenstein argued, is so complicated that we could not possibly learn it by ourselves. Indeed, he even went so far as to deny the existence of that which he called private languages, or the languages by which we name our sensations to ourselves.[20] Such languages may exist, Wittgenstein went on to claim, but if they do it is impossible for us to communicate their existence to others; and if we can communicate them, then that necessarily means they cannot be private, hence they cannot refer to some private, or internal, state of us, in particular, our sensations, feelings, desires, and the like. To social scientists, of course, Wittgenstein's second version of philosophy holds the greatest possibility for development, largely because it implies that the names, concepts, even relations we develop in the course of our language are by nature public, or social, activities, with meanings generated through public discourse. Ironically, to this point in time it is the earlier brand of Wittgenstein's

[16] Ludwig Wittgenstein, *Tractatus Logico-Philosophicus* (London: Routledge & Kegan Paul, 1961).

[17] Wittgenstein, *Tractatus Logico-Philosophicus*, p. 15 *et passim*.

[18] For an excellent discussion of the nature of logical positivism and its proponents, see Anthony Giddens, "Positivism and Its Critics," in *A History of Sociological Analysis*, ed. Tom Bottomore and Robert Nisbet (New York: Basic Books, Inc., Publishers, 1978), pp. 237-86.

[19] Ludwig Wittgenstein, *Philosophical Investigations*, 3rd ed., trans. G. E. M. Anscombe (New York: Macmillan Publishing Co., Inc., 1953).

[20] Ludwig Wittgenstein, *Philosophical Investigations*, paragraphs 246 ff.

philosophy, under the name of logical positivism, which has had the very greatest impact in the social sciences.[21]

Here, in this chapter, we shall depart from the later Wittgenstein and write of political thought as if it were a language. In this manner, we shall be able to think about thinking in more insightful fashion than if we were to work with intransigent concepts like Marx's notion of ideology, Parsons's conception of norms and values, or other such concepts. We also shall adapt the notion of language to our own purposes here, trying to show how a language of politics not only is a public medium, but how it develops against a background of historically fashioned social and economic inequalities.[22]

IDEALS, REALITIES, AND ILLUSIONS OF POLITICS

Basic Concepts

In order to write, think, or talk about political thought, we require a language ourselves, a sort of language about language, or what logicians would call a metalanguage. The chief requirement for our language about politics is that it be based upon the assumptions that politics is a public activity, carried on among people, furnishing a basis both for cooperation and conflict among them. To capture these features, in the form of thought, we shall speak of three forms of political thought, of the world of politics itself. Each of these forms is not a description of the polity, per se—for instance, of the number of voters in the polity, of how Congress works—but rather represents a set of claims that evaluates the workings of the polity, in a positive or negative fashion. These languages represent, in effect, a set of ideals, a set of bench marks, that are used to praise, or to excoriate, those who operate in the world of politics.

The Language of Ideals: Idealthink. There, first of all, is the language of ideals in any polity, that which we shall call *idealthink*.[23] Idealthink contains the basic vocabulary and terms which define the substance of that which is political.

[21] See Giddens, "Positivism and Its Critics."

[22] There are scholars and thinkers closer to the sociological tradition who also tend to emphasize the importance of language, and of forms of thought, generally, in the creation of our pictures of the world. Among the most interesting and influential of them presently are Peter Berger and Thomas Luckmann. See their *The Social Construction of Reality* (Garden City, N.Y.: Doubleday Anchor Books, 1967). Also see the excellent article on phenomenology by Kurt Wolff in *A History of Sociological Analysis*, ed. Bottomore and Nisbet, pp. 499-556.

[23] *Idealthink* is comparable in some sense to Talcott Parsons's conception of values and norms, although our conception is intended to serve somewhat different purposes than his. Moreover, our analogy between thought and language is also intended to suggest the beginnings of a logic to *idealthink*, as the other *thinks* as well, which is missing from the Parsonian conceptions. See the discussion on Parson's notions of values and norms, pp. 78ff.

It also includes a logic of relations among terms, something on the order of a syntax, or grammar, of politics. Idealthink may be viewed, moreover, as a historic product, the fruit of many previous generations of people who have created it, yet also as an entity capable of modification and reinterpretation. Idealthink functions in two important respects—first, it serves to shape our expectations of what politics is, through its basic definition of terms and the grammar of relations it posits; second, it furnishes the central definitions that are intended to guide the actual construction of political institutions. It is, in brief, something like an architectural design for the polity, though one whose guidelines, as we shall see, are far from perfectly followed.

Because a concept such as idealthink may seem very abstract, let us consider a concrete case. We might say that the idealthink of a liberal democracy emphasizes the central principles of equality and of freedom, as in the case of the United States. *Equality* is taken to refer to the positions of people, with the provision that such positions, even possibly the opportunities people possess to avail themselves of those positions, are roughly equivalent for all people who wish to occupy them. *Freedom* refers to the absence of constraints, of whatever sort, on the activities and beliefs of people in such a polity; it is, in this sense, as others have written, a negative rather than positive conception of freedom because it suggests the absence rather than the presence of something substantial. Further, the logical relations entailed by the idealthink of a liberal democracy refer to the ways that its essential elements are to be more clearly defined, the various rules to be constructed based upon them, and the manner in which they are to be realized in the actual construction of the polity. There may be certain rules, for instance, about what equality means in the case of voting for political office, or in the case of requirements for holding office. The semantics of equality and freedom—how they are implemented in the world—and the syntax of the rules of equality and freedom—the hammering out of the internal logic they entail—represent, of course, merely the minimum essential elements of an idealthink for liberal democracy. In actual fact, idealthink is likely to be far more elaborate.

Where will one find idealthink spelled out? In some, if not all, instances, there will be a document, in the way of a constitution of one form or another, that actually furnishes the language of idealthink. The Constitution of the United States, for instance, provides a detailed set of instructions about the composition of the political arena to be established in the geopolitical territory known as the United States. It describes the right of citizens to engage in free speech, as well as their right to bear arms; it also refers to their right to engage in the act of voting, regardless of race, color, or prior condition of servitude. At the same time, it furnishes a set of provisions that stipulate how it can be modified and amended. The idealthink then for a particular political arena is the articulation of cherished aspirations, of prized goals, of the deeply desired ambitions which somehow are to be achieved. It becomes a model *for*, if not *of*, the polity, and under the keen eye and guiding hand of many successive generations of interpreters, often in the form of jurists and lawyers, it helps to provide the basis for the material realization of the institutions of the polity itself.[24]

The Language of Realities: Realthink. However perfect idealthink may seem on paper, even simply as articulated by politicians or leading citizens, it rarely, if ever, seems to furnish a perfect fit for what actually takes place. As the old saying has it, "There's many a slip 'twixt cup and lip." One need not travel far or wide to recognize the correctness of such a claim. In many liberal democracies, it is proclaimed that all people shall possess the right of dissent, or of free speech; yet some people are occasionally denied such a right, and many people are denied it altogether. The Constitution of the United States intends the executive, congressional, and judicial branches of the government to serve as coequal partners; yet at certain points in history, one or the other of these branches has been far more important and powerful by comparison. The Soviet Union claims to have achieved the full fruits of a workers' state; yet there are Communist Party officials whose privileges and benefits rank considerably higher than those of the workers.[25] What actually takes place in the specific political arena, whether democratic or totalitarian, large or small, often appears very, very different from that which is claimed to happen in statements of idealthink.

We, thus, must introduce a second dimension to political thought, that of the realities of politics, for which we shall coin the term *realthink*. Realthink is a language about politics—in this case, about the realities of the political world rather than the ideals. It might first seem strange to talk about a language of realities when it always seems that what is most real is precisely *not* in the form of a language. But if we reflect a moment, we will realize that our knowledge of politics also takes the form of thought. To recognize that politics does not work the way it is intended to work is to acknowledge, in language to ourselves and to others, that there is something else happening "out there" in politics; we simply articulate this to ourselves in the form of thought, or language. Realthink, then, is a set of statements about the ways in which idealthink is incorrect, or wrong. It, too, depicts a world, as does idealthink; but this is a world almost the opposite of idealthink. It almost seems to grow up, in fact, as a criticism of idealthink so as to better correspond to the world we seem to inhabit. It, too, entails a set of relations among terms, a vocabulary which is intended to more genuinely reflect the meaning of conceptions like equality and freedom. Often, but not always, it seems to be the very antithesis of idealthink, insofar as it claims that instead of equality we have inequality, instead of freedom we have constraint, instead of democracy we have authority. There is a sense, then, in which we can say realthink seems to arise out of the very failure of idealthink to "tell it like it is."

[24] On this notion of a model *for*, but not *of*, a social world, see Clifford Geertz, *The Interpretation of Cultures*, pp. 93-95.

[25] See, for example, Milovan Djilas, *The New Class: An Analysis of the Communist System* (New York: Praeger Publishers, Inc., 1957).

Again, inasmuch as realthink is an abstract notion, let us try to put some flesh on it. Consider the case of realthink in the United States. People learn in America to think about politics as an arena in which there live power-hungry men and women out for their own gain, intent on grabbing fortune and fame, and at the end of their careers, happily ensconced in some pleasant palace in Florida or California. Those in the limelight of politics, according to realthink, are hungry for publicity, and rarely represent a consistent point of view. They only respond to the interests of those whom they represent at election time, and then for just the briefest period of time. They kiss babies in public, and lobbyists in private, and when they get the chance they take the money and run. Now if all this sounds familiar, it is because just as idealthink in the United States constitutes a logical set of interrelated ideas, so too does realthink, and it is equally as familiar to us. Moreover, as it is easy to tell, realthink here is the very opposite of idealthink—politicians are not upstanding people of integrity, but low and callous people; they speak on television and write in the newspapers not because they wish to articulate a point of view, but because they want to grab the limelight. Realthink, like idealthink, in other words, presents a composite picture of the political world, including some portrait of the motivations of those who are political actors.

The Language of Illusion and Defense: Idolthink. With virtually the same inexorable logic that brings realthink to the surface, so there arises the third and last form of political thought, that which we shall name *idolthink*.[26] Any society which confronts two competing sets of claims about its politics, idealthink and realthink, either must succumb and change the nature of its political institutions—as many do, though in a gradual manner—or it must seek to reconcile the one set of claims with the other. Such a reconciliation, given our line of emphasis here on thought as language, will again assume a form of thinking, that of idolthink. Like the two other forms of thought, idolthink, too, consists of a set of terms and logical relations among terms that constitute it as a self-contained whole. Moreover, whereas the function of idealthink is to lay out the prescribed course for politics, in terms of its basic ideals and a logic to them, and that of realthink is to act as the realistic critic of the failure of such ideals, idolthink functions to resolve the discrepancy between the two sorts of language. It provides a defense and justification of the disparity between the ideals and the realities by claiming the two to be compatible on some grounds—any grounds, in fact. From the point of view of

---

[26] The notion of *idolthink* is similar to that of Marx's notion of *ideology* in the function that it serves in society, but different in terms of its logical structure. The analogy drawn here with language as thought is, as in the case of Parsons's values and norms, intended to suggest a different logical structure to idolthink than that conveyed by Marx's notion of ideology. Moreover, as readers familiar with dialectical analysis will realize, the three conceptions introduced here—idealthink, realthink, and idolthink—are together a dialectical solution to the nature of thought. In Hegelian terms, idealthink represents the first moment, realthink the second moment, and idolthink the third moment, or the "negation of the negation." See G. W. F. Hegel, *The Phenomenology of Mind* (New York: Harper & Row, Publishers, 1967). Also see our discussion of dialectics in chapter 2, on Marx, pp. 25ff.

the observer, however, idolthink acts as an illusion, for it seeks to bridge what must otherwise be viewed as an unbridgeable hiatus. In this sense, it is a language of idols, for to think in it means to think of false gods as the true representation of the ideals of the polity. Idolthink, moreover, can become *idlethink*, for in its contents and consequences it intends to quiet an otherwise troubled polity, demanding not reflection or clamour but passive acceptance.

Again, we will find some help in grasping the nature of idolthink if we refer to some examples. Consider, once again, the case of the United States. Here is a polity with two fundamentally competing forms of thought—idealthink, which conceives politics in terms of such ideals as equality, freedom, and other associated terms; and realthink, which conceives politics in terms of such realities as the baseness of politicians and the evident inequalities and unfreedom in politics for some groups, like blacks. Given the wide disparities, idolthink takes the form of justifying the full implementation of the ideals in terms that also take cognizance of the realities. Hence, idolthink may suggest that whites are free to enjoy the benefits of equality rather than blacks because of their biological superiority—a form of thought, of course, with deep roots in Western culture; or it may claim that the rich are better able to take advantage of freedom and authority in politics because they have the necessary skills, or even because they have won out in the great Darwinian struggle for survival; or it may argue that men occupy the center stage of politics because they possess the greater skills and/or display superior physical strength. Idolthink, in other words, provides the ground—the "reasons"—why the dominant groups are dominant in this polity at this time, and it intends to shut off debate on those grounds. Idolthink, in brief, acts as the language of dominance, of the status quo. The ideals of the polity are retained but in a dispirited form, as idols rather than as the genuine articles.

THE REPRODUCTION OF SOCIETY

Any society in order that it may survive, so the argument goes, must succeed in implanting in its members' minds the manner of thought most closely geared to keeping its institutions intact.[27] It must generate respect for its ideals, yet do so in such a way that the realities a person encounters in the everyday world do not differ too sharply from proclaimed ideals. Most students of the reproduction of society, of socialization as it is sometimes called, claim that what people are taught as the basic form of indoctrination is idealthink; they claim that realthink develops on its own, and that idolthink probably is not taught at all. Yet, if we adhere to the logic of our argument here, then the basic medium of intellectual indoctrination is not idealthink at all, but rather idolthink. Why? Because idolthink is the language of reconciliation, of the marriage of the disparity between the ideals and the

[27]This is an argument made essentially by Parsons and by Marx, though with entirely different implications.

realities of the political world in a form that is palatable, at least on some ground, or for some reasons. In the following discussion, we will discover, in fact, that the agencies of indoctrination, those which are charged with the actual reproduction of society, rely in some part on the communication of idolthink—especially the school. But idolthink is not the only thought taught; in some instances, as we shall learn, the agents of society teach forms of idealthink and realthink, too.

Schools

In all modern societies, regardless of the particular complexion of their ideals, the school is expected to take a major role in the instruction of people in political thought. Its task is to sustain the institutions of society, to ensure somehow that future generations come to think of the world of politics in the same way as past ones. What this means, in practice, is that the school is expected to train the good citizen for society—someone who will prove to be responsible, to respect the on-going social and political institutions, and thereby to assist in the preservation and continuation of the body politic. So much for general expectations. What actually seems to happen is far different.

In the United States, as in all liberal democracies, the school faces a doubly difficult task, one that makes it virtually inevitable that idolthink rather than idealthink will be the language of instruction. For if the school were to teach the full course of idealthink, comprised of the principles of equality and freedom and their application to dissent, the vote, holding office, and other similar areas, this would invite self-contradictions in the ongoing character of liberal democratic institutions. It would mean, in particular, that children would learn it was appropriate to question authority, to exercise the right of free speech, and to engage in other acts that could ultimately undermine the stability of the government. Hence, schools in these settings are compelled, in part at least, to rely upon a form of idolthink. Teachers, so we learn from such researchers as Robert Hess and Judith Torney, place heavy emphasis on respect and veneration of political institutions and figures, particularly in the early grades when, it is believed, children are most vulnerable and most in need of strict guidelines.[28] Children are taught not so much the meaning and logical implications of liberal democratic ideals as they are led to believe in the awesome and venerable qualities of liberal democracies. And their own views give evidence of the idolthink they learn. For schoolchildren appear to come away with a distinctive sense that individuals, not institutions, constitute government; and that people who occupy offices, such as that of the presidency, or even policemen, are basically kind, benevolent, and trustworthy. Hess and Torney, for instance, report that 75 percent of second grade schoolchildren believe the president would "care a lot" if they wrote to him; and even 92 percent of the eighth graders believed the president either would "care a lot," or "care some."[29]

---

[28] Hess and Torney, *The Development of Political Attitudes in Children*, pp. 101-115.
[29] Hess and Torney, *The Development of Political Attitudes in Children*, p. 40, table 8.

And yet, schoolchildren in American schools are not taught merely idolthink. Judging from age trends that appear in the beliefs of children, from elementary grades through late high school, they also appear to be receiving liberal doses of realthink as well. Again, Hess and Torney find that there is a steadily diminishing reverence for political institutions in the United States between the third and eighth grades in school.[30] And this is no anomalous result—virtually every other study of schoolchildren in the United States uncovers the same diminishing degree of awe and reverence for political authority.[31] How do we explain the pattern? Have children, themselves, developed into more critical observers of the world—are they more worldly-wise? Some would prefer this explanation. Yet, if we adhere to a structuralist argument, it is equally likely that what has happened is that teachers have altered their messages from strict idolthink to realthink, and that children themselves are beginning to be influenced by the typical counter-adult authority thinking of their peers, a contributor ultimately, of course, to realthink. There is evidence, in fact, to suggest that at least the first part of this argument is correct. Teachers in the higher grades do expose their pupils to much greater criticism of the government and its officials than do those in the lower grades.[32]

American schoolchildren, thus, appear to learn both idolthink and realthink from schools and peers, with idolthink diminishing in importance among the older children. The obviously missing form of political thought in all this instruction is that of idealthink, the very heart of political instruction by most accounts. And strangely enough, it is in the instruction of ideals that the Soviet Union appears to excell over the United States. In the 1960s Urie Bronfenbrenner studied the nature of Soviet education.[33] He observed how instruction was carried out in the schools and had the opportunity to examine leading manuals on Soviet education as well. The major ideals the Soviet system intends to teach children, he found, are those of respect for others, obedience to both adult and peer authority, and the importance of collectivism as a basis of responsibility, even of achievement. These lessons, he further learned, are taught chiefly through the school, which displays all manner of collective efforts, and are reinforced by peer groups within the school as well as by parents. At an early age the responsibility of training children is taken over by the State. The child becomes a part of a small collective in the school classroom, which becomes the base from which he or she competes with other children as well as the means through which he or she is aided in learning the importance of responsibility and obedience. At each level of Soviet society—the small collectives within the classroom, the classroom itself, the school, the community—the principles

[30] Hess and Torney, *The Development of Political Attitudes in Children*, chapter 3.

[31] Fred I. Greenstein, "The Benevolent Leader: Children's Images of Political Authority," *American Political Science Review*, 54 (December 1960), 934-43; Fred I. Greenstein, *Children and Politics* (New Haven, Conn.: Yale University Press, 1965), pp. 35-42; Robert D. Hess and David Easton, "The Child's Changing Image of the President," *Public Opinion Quarterly*, 24 (Winter 1960), 632-44.

[32] Hess and Torney, *The Development of Political Attitudes in Children*, pp. 101-115.

[33] Urie Bronfenbrenner, with the assistance of John C. Condry, Jr., *Two Worlds of Childhood: U.S. and U.S.S.R.* (New York: Russell Sage Foundation, 1970).

of collective responsibility, collective achievement, and collective cooperation are continuously emphasized. And these ideals, which are ever on display, seem to produce their intended effects. As compared to their American counterparts, children in the Soviet Union, Bronfenbrenner concluded, seemed to be more conformist and dependent on the group for direction as well as less disrespectful to the State itself.

Schools are expected to train the good citizen in modern society, but the Soviet Union appears to do a far better job in this regard than the United States. It could well be one of the many ironies of democracy that the type of educational system so necessary to raising people to appreciate and to fulfill democratic ideals is inherently incapable of doing so.

Parents

In more traditional societies, ones that are relatively small and not yet in the grips of industrialization, the kinship group plays an active role in basic instruction. But in the more highly advanced societies, especially in ones like the Soviet Union, such a role is played little anymore. Parents, in effect, have had their role usurped, at least so far as politics is concerned, by the school as well as by the other sorts of transmission belts of political thought. All the evidence we now have on hand, particularly from the very large number of studies accomplished of early political learning, clearly underscore the very limited influence of parents over children's political thought. By and large, parents and their children are hardly at all alike in terms of their fundamental political beliefs. In a lengthy reanalysis of a number of studies conducted of familial resemblances between parents and children, R. W. Connell, for example, found few topics on which the two groups were similar.[34] And an important study by M. Kent Jennings and Richard J. Niemi of the political beliefs of American high school seniors discovered few areas of politics on which parents and their children resembled one another.[35]

Yet there exist some important exceptions in the materials on parental influence, ones that show the way in which parents might shape the thinking of their children. For example, Jennings and Niemi also discovered that among parents who expressed a high degree of interest in politics, the correspondences with their children's beliefs was higher than in those families in which parents expressed minimal interest.[36] And a discovery of Kenneth Keniston's study of young anti-War in Vietnam volunteers in the 1960s displays the important influence parents may have on some children.[37] Keniston found that virtually without exception all children claimed to be carrying on the ideals taught them by their parents. Some students clearly had been instructed deeply and thoroughly by their parents

---

[34] R. W. Connell, "Political Socialization of the American Family: The Evidence Reexamined," *Public Opinion Quarterly*, 36 (Fall 1972), 323-33.

[35] M. Kent Jennings and Richard G. Niemi, *The Political Character of Adolescence* (Princeton, N.J.: Princeton University Press, 1974).

[36] Jennings and Niemi, *The Political Character of Adolescence*, p. 48, table 2.3.

[37] Keniston, *Young Radicals*.

in elements of liberal democratic idealthink, such as one young girl who vividly recalled the approval her father voiced over the 1954 Supreme Court decision which outlawed school segregation.

Parents, in short, rarely have much influence over the development of how their children think about the political world. Yet, when they do, as in the case of the 1960s radical students, it is in the form of a deep and lasting influence.

Mass Media

Without question the mass media play a major role in today's instruction in political thought. Their role, of course, will vary from nation to nation, and regime to regime. In countries in which the government controls the media, the media is apt to articulate a point of view fully in keeping with the principles of the regime itself—as in the Soviet Union, where the media present a view supportive of the Communist party, and in an earlier era, in Nazi Germany. In the United States, however, the media have come to operate in a vastly different fashion. In fact, we can go so far as to say that they are, in large part, the instrument both of realthink and idolthink in modern America.

The mass media typically act in the United States as a critic. In their own words, the media make, or construct, the news. That which is news is that which reveals that the institutions of government do not operate in the manner claimed by the ideals of American politics—that is to say, it is pure and essential realthink. In the 1950s and 1960s in particular, the media by and large took the side of the civil rights activists, informing in print and showing in pictures that equality, in fact, was far from prevalent in the United States. They went to considerable lengths to report the evident inequities as well as to excoriate political leaders for actions seemingly at odds with the ideals of the American polity, and of its venerable institutions. The media also acted to display the evident hypocrisy with regard to the issue of freedom in America. No better or more tragic reminder of this exists than in the media's coverage of the activities of the police force in Chicago in 1968, when the force, so it was later charged, engaged in a riot against dissidents outside the Democratic convention.

The media's critical—or, realistic—stance continued well into the 1970s. It was two newspaper reporters on the staff of the *Washington Post*, Robert Woodward and Carl Bernstein, who were responsible for bringing down the Nixon administration, in effect, through the revelations about the Watergate break in. It was the *New York Times*, moreover, which was responsible for publishing the first excerpts from *The Pentagon Papers*, materials that illuminated the secret operations of the Pentagon officials as well as Nixon administration officials like Henry Kissinger during the War in Vietnam. Whatever the intentions on the part of the media during the course of these and many other exposés during the 1960s and 1970s, the effect was to heighten the incongruity between what politics was intended to be in America—in the language of democratic idealthink first forged by the founding fathers—and what it actually had become—realthink. Moreover, by giving special attention to those groups who acted on behalf of black Americans, as well as those who acted against the War in Vietnam, the media effectively reinforced the claims of these disparities between the language of American ideals and that of its realities.

Yet, if the media lift the veils of illusion from politics with the one hand, they serve to restore it with the other. The entertainment programs on television, in particular, speak in the language of idolthink; they portray a world in which there are the free and the unfree, the equal and the unequal, and in which the privileges of power and authority are to be had by those who are dominant—that is, the wealthy, men, and Anglo citizens. The success of such recent television shows as "Dallas" and "The Incredible Hulk" clearly displays how television entertainment fulfills the fantasies of people, taking them into a world where dominance justifies all acts—and where it is the liberating force, easily propelling people into a world where only the powerful are equal and free. On "Dallas," the freedom to use, and to abuse, power and authority by J. R. Ewing is justified in the name of profit and wealth. But J. R., while occasionally hoisted with his own petard, also makes a virtue out of his manhood—which gives him freedom not allowed his wife, freedom to engage in various dalliances that either produce bouts with the bottle or visits to the psychiatrist by his wife Sue Ellen. "The Incredible Hulk," a program specifically designed for and frequently watched by youngsters, mixes realthink and idealthink into a medium of idolthink exquisitely, revealing that might makes right, so long as it is used for just causes.

Even the friend of television, *TV Guide*, recently has underscored the ways in which the medium is highly critical of liberal democratic institutions and ideals as well as the ways in which it portrays, and sustains, the power of dominant groups in American society. Reporting on the results of a recent study of programs watched by children, *TV Guide* notes that the researchers "found that the entertainment programs children are most likely to watch show them little about the nuts and bolts of the institutions that run our society: federal, state and local government; the legal system; the business community. And what is shown is not heartening. Overall, negative portrayals of these institutions appear two and a half times more often than those that present institutions (and their representatives) sympathetically."[38] And *TV Guide* goes on to state that the investigation "also looked at the messages about power that children absorbed from television. Predictably, most characters representing powerful institutions were white males; and on Saturday-morning programs, no women or black males held positions of authority. . . . The characters whose power, competence and skill were proved by deeds—and results—tended to be loners outside all institutions, sometimes even outside the human race: Fonzie, Rockford, the Hulk, or Scooby-Doo."[39]

It is easy of course to claim, along with Marshall McLuhan, that the media are the message.[40] They are, and have been, much more. Newspapers dish out

---

[38] *TV Guide,* vol. 29, no. 26, June 27, 1981. "As We See It," p. A-2.

[39] *TV Guide,* "As We See It," p. A-2.

[40] Marshall McLuhan, *The Medium Is the Message* (New York: Random House, 1967).

criticism and display inconsistencies in the American polity, while television's entertainment programs mask such disparities once more. Yet, perhaps the very great success of some of these programs, notably "Dallas," underlines the fact that many, if not most, people would prefer to retain dreams and illusions about politics, worshiping false idols, than to face the hidden incongruities in the world of the *thinks.*

THE REPRODUCTION OF DOMINANCE IN SOCIETY

Just as society, as a whole, requires the reproduction of itself, so especially do the dominant segments of society. The logic that has permitted the smooth operation of the social machine—whether economic, sexual, or ethnic—can only continue so long as the groups that are dominant retain their favored station and those that are subordinate continue to "know their place." Nowhere do the three types of political language clarify patterns of results so well as in our efforts to understand why it is that dominant groups come to display one form of thought about politics, and subordinate groups quite another. Consider, first, the case of social class and political thought.

Social Class

If the middle and upper classes are to remain dominant in society, then the patterns of thought to be learned by children must work to their advantage. That is, we must suppose that those from the higher classes will eventually come to think about the world of politics in such a way as to sustain their dominance—not merely in the world of economics, but in the world of politics, too. The lesson we learn, in fact, from studies of the way young schoolchildren think about politics entirely supports this general line of reasoning. Edgar Litt undertook one of the more interesting studies of this matter.[41] In three communities which varied in their general social class composition—or more precisely, their socioeconomic composition—Litt examined the contents of the civics textbooks used in the secondary schools. He found that in each community the textbooks included some reference to the "basic democratic creed," that is, the right of citizens to seek to influence the actions of government. But in the upper-middle class community, Alpha, the textbooks implemented the basic lesson of the democratic creed with an emphasis on the mechanics of government and the importance of citizen participation in politics, whereas in the working-class community, Gamma, the textbooks wrote of politics as an arena of harmony and downplayed the importance of citizen involvement.

[41] Edgar Litt, "Civic Education, Community Norms and Political Indoctrination," *American Sociological Review*, 28 (February 1963), 69-75.

> . . . students in the three communities are being trained to play different political roles, and to respond to political phenomena in different ways. In the working-class community, where political involvement is low, the arena of civic education offers training in the basic democratic procedures without stressing political participation or the citizen's view of conflict and disagreement as indigenous to the political system. Politics is conducted by formal governmental institutions working in harmony for the benefit of citizens. . . . Only in the affluent and politically vibrant community . . . are insights into political processes and functions of politics passed on to those who, judging from their socioeconomic and political environment, will likely man those positions that involve them in influencing or making political decisions.[42]

To put these results into the forms of political thought we have advanced here, upper-middle class children were taught the language of idealthink, the ideals of the American polity in a full and complete fashion, whereas the working-class children were taught idolthink, the language of dispirited ideals that serves the long-term interests of the dominant classes.

Litt's study is not the only one to reveal how the forms of political thought differ among schoolchildren from different class backgrounds. Fred Greenstein, in a pioneering study conducted in the late 1950s, examined the political beliefs of youngsters from different socioeconomic backgrounds.[43] Like Litt, he found that children from the upper and lower socioeconomic backgrounds appeared to have received different lessons about the nature of the political world. The children from the lower-class backgrounds, in a way similar to young schoolchildren generally, thought of political figures and institutions as typically more benevolent and awesome than their counterparts from more privileged backgrounds. In effect, the children from the poorer homes were more likely to idolize institutions, to give them unquestioned respect and obedience—an attitude so necessary to the continuing dominance of the upper and middle classes. Greenstein observes the results of the variable patterns of thought among these groups clearly, and, in his own terms, how idolthink may become idlethink among the lower classes. "It is especially notable," he writes, "that lower socioeconomic status children do not share the explicit unwillingness to participate in politics found among adults of the same background. But they *do* show a greater deference toward political leadership; unlike upper-status children they do not begin to display in sixth, seventh, and eighth grades a sense that political choices are theirs to make—that *their* judgments are worth acting upon. And this seems part of a much larger pattern in the socialization practices of American status groups."[44]

The nature of political thought to which schoolchildren from different classes are exposed, in brief, serves to explain how the more privileged sectors of society maintain their position. They learn a language fully in keeping with the

---

[42] Litt, "Civic Education, Community Norms and Political Indoctrination," 74.

[43] Greenstein, *Children and Politics.*

[44] Greenstein, *Children and Politics,* p. 106.

fundamental meaning of the basic ideals of liberal democracy in America, including an emphasis on the active participation in politics. Their counterparts, on the lower rungs of the social hierarchy, however, are instructed in a language tailored to compliance with a set of empty ideals, a language of illusions. One, in effect, learns the spirit of liberal ideals, the other the mere letter of them.

Sex Roles

The story of dominance and subordination, of freedom for some and un-freedom for others, is the same among children of the different sexes as it is among children of different class backgrounds. But it does have a somewhat different ending—one that alerts us to how people might modify the impact of political thought by making themselves conscious of what it entails. Many studies which have examined the nature of political beliefs among boys and girls clearly reveal that boys think about politics much differently than girls.[45] They seem to learn political thought, in general, more quickly than girls do. They seem to identify with figures in the midst of active battle in politics much more than girls do. And they also are less apt than girls to idolize the institutions and figures of the government. As Robert Hess and Judith Torney report, for instance, girls even in eighth grade are distinctly more likely than boys to think of the president as a kind of caring figure.[46] Girls, like lower- and working-class children, seem to learn the language of idolatry.

Yet, the most recent evidence shows that differences between the boys and girls no longer are so sharp. In a study undertaken by myself and colleagues, we found that among young schoolchildren the girls were generally no more likely than the boys to display reverence for the president, to idolize him in other words.[47] Table 10-1 presents some of the results from our study, showing the generally insignificant differences between boys' and girls' average scores in terms of their perception of the helpfulness of the president. What could the few differences here possibly portend as compared to the large differences noted in the past between the thinking of boys and girls? Adhering to our structuralist argument here, we may conjecture that the women's liberation movement of the past fifteen years or so could well have begun to modify the thought learned by young girls, inducing them to display a less compliant and reverent attitude toward political institutions.

[45] Richard E. Dawson, Kenneth Prewitt, and Karen Dawson, *Political Socialization*, 2nd ed. (Boston: Little, Brown & Company, 1979); Robert E. Dowse and John A. Hughes, "Girls, Boys and Politics," *British Journal of Sociology*, 22 (March 1971), 53-67; Joseph Ellis, "The Effects of Same-Sex Class Organization on Junior High School Students' Academic Achievement, Self-Discipline, Self-Concept, Sex-Role Identification and Attitude Toward School," (Educational Resources Information Center, United States Office of Education: Project Number 7-E115, 1968); Joseph Forbes and Dale Dykstra, "Children's Attribution of Negative Traits to Authority Figures as a Function of Family Size and Sex," *Psychological Reports*, 28 (April 1971), 363-66.

[46] Hess and Torney, *The Development of Political Attitudes in Children*, chapter 8.

[47] Anthony M. Orum, Roberta S. Cohen, Sherri Grasmuck, and Amy W. Orum, "Sex, Socialization and Politics," *American Sociological Review*, 38 (April 1974), 197-209.

Table 10-1 Sex, Race, Grade in School, and Occupation of the Chief Wage Earner by Image of the President (mean scores on image of President)

Grade	Sex	Race			
		Black		White	
		CWE Occupation		CWE Occupation	
		White-Collar	Blue-Collar	White-Collar	Blue-Collar
4-6	Female	2.74 (39)	3.23 (49)	3.34 (128)	3.81 (40)
	Male	3.07 (24)	3.13 (46)	3.00 (101)	3.44 (32)
		Partial Correlation: −.029		Partial Correlation: +.166*	
7-8	Female	2.54 (42)	2.57 (74)	2.99 (69)	3.17 (17)
	Male	2.40 (33)	2.61 (93)	2.91 (65)	3.00 (17)
		Partial Correlation: −.018		Partial Correlation: +.063	
9-10	Female	2.45 (28)	2.41 (86)	2.48 (25)	2.91 (46)
	Male	2.43 (33)	2.63 (80)	2.74 (27)	2.99 (57)
		Partial Correlation: −.124		Partial Correlation: −.051	
11-12	Female	2.47 (25)	2.48 (100)	2.88 (55)	2.88 (70)
	Male	2.55 (27)	2.56 (107)	2.70 (39)	2.68 (65)
		Partial Correlation: −.034		Partial Correlation: +.110	

actually, the gender dif. remains considerably larger here than the "class" one.

*p ≤ .05

Source: Anthony M. Orum *et al.*, "Sex, Socialization and Politics," *American Sociological Review*, 39 (April 1974), p. 201.

The scores reported above are mean scores, based upon answers to the following items:

1. Would the president always want to help you if you needed help?
2. Does the president protect you more than anyone else?
3. When you write to the president, do you think he cares about what you think?

The higher average score means the more favorable the image of the president.

It is especially notable here that the women's movement has confronted directly the issue of consciousness, and done so by drawing attention to the elements of thought that display the dominance of men over women, for example, that the generic expression for human beings often is "man," or "mankind." This is a matter about which we shall say more shortly, however.

In brief, the dominance of men over women seems to have revealed itself, until very recently, in the same differences and manners of political thought as produced the dominance of the more financially privileged over the less privileged. Yet, it is a phenomenon that seems to have yielded, however slightly, to the assaults by the protest movements of the recent past. Such assaults, we now shall learn, have only minimally altered the picture of dominance among girls and boys compared to that among blacks and whites.

Race

Dominant groups, we have argued, seek to reproduce themselves in society. In part, we have also insisted, they do so through the forms of political thought that exist. The more privileged remain so because they are instructed in a language that will foster their active participation in the political arena; and men have remained dominant because they, too, have learned a manner of thought about politics that will produce a greater involvement on their part. But what happens when the dominance of a group comes into open and obvious conflict with the ideals of the polity; in particular, what alterations are brought about in the thought of the subordinate groups when idolthink is shown to be a language of false gods and illusions? What happens is visibly evident when we look at the character of political thought among young black and white schoolchildren.

Since the late 1960s, much of the research into the nature of political thought and how it is indoctrinated in young children has been done among young black and white Americans. Further, no matter where the research has been done, or who has conducted it, the same result appears time and again. Black children, whether they are in the third grade or in the twelfth grade, consistently are less apt than white children to revere political institutions and figures in the United States.[48] When asked, for instance, about whether the president is a kind and helpful figure, black children routinely have claimed that he is not. Consider the data displayed in table 10-2, again taken from our study of schoolchildren in Illinois.[49] Without exception, black children think in less positive terms than white children. Likewise, when asked similar questions about such officials as the policeman, black children give evidence of a decidedly more negative view. In short, black children display all the signs of a greater realthink, the language of criticism and realities, than white children.

Multiple explanations have been offered of the differences, ranging from the obvious, that black children think more "realistically" than white children, to the claim that black children learn a different set of cultural beliefs.[50] But the realism argument is deceptive in its simplicity. It does not say where the messages children are exposed to come from, nor does it even say what the contents of these messages are in a *theoretical* sense—it is a naive realism rather than a sophisticated one. And the subcultural argument, while based upon the plausible notion of a plurality of worlds in politics, fails to recognize that some groups *may be* more dominant than others. It seems much more parsimonious, and fruitful, to claim that black

---

[48] For a thoughtful review of all these studies, see Paul Abramson, "Political Efficacy and Political Trust among Black Schoolchildren: Two Explanations," *Journal of Politics*, 34 (November 1972), 1243-75.

[49] Anthony M. Orum and Roberta S. Cohen, "The Development of Political Orientations among Black and White Children," *American Sociological Review*, 38 (February 1973), 62-74.

[50] Abramson, "Political Efficacy and Political Trust among Black Schoolchildren: Two Explanations"; Milton D. Morris, *The Politics of Black America* (New York: Harper & Row, Publishers, 1975); and Orum and Cohen, "The Development of Political Orientations among Black and White Children."

Table 10-2 Race, Grade in School, and Occupation of
the Chief Wage Earner by Image of the President
(mean scores)

		Image of the President		
Grade in School	Chief Wage Earner Occupation	Black $\overline{X}$	White $\overline{X}$	Partial r (Occupation controlled)
4-7	White Collar	2.87	3.19	−.151*
	Blue Collar	3.18	3.65	
7-8	White Collar	2.47	2.95	−.248**
	Blue Collar	2.59	3.08	
9-10	White Collar	2.44	2.62	−.183**
	Blue Collar	2.52	2.96	
11-12	White Collar	2.51	2.81	−.150**
	Blue Collar	2.52	2.79	

Source: Adapted from Anthony M. Orum and Roberta S. Cohen, "The Development of Political Orientations among Black and White Children," *American Sociological Review*, 38 (February 1973), p. 67.

*Significant at .05 level.
**Significant at .01 level.

See table 10-1 for explanation of the Image of the President scale.

children have acquired the language of realthink, from multiple sources in recent American history. They have learned that there is a great disparity between the ideals and realities in American politics, that in particular there is equality for whites but not for blacks, and thus whatever elements of idolthink may have captured their minds have been removed. From parents, from friends, but probably especially from television, they have learned to criticize American political institutions for their failure to achieve the goals established in the Constitution. This is the language to which they have been intensively exposed because they are black, and it would seem they have learned the language quite well indeed.

CHANGING THOUGHTS, CHANGING TIMES

To think of the political world in terms of political thought as we have proposed here is intended to be more than simply a clever ploy. It should assist us as well in making better sense out of the "known facts" about politics. One topic on which this scheme may shed some light is that of change—specifically, change in the political world. There are several inferences which follow from our scheme, and our earlier discussion, that bear upon the nature of political change. Firstly, to bring about change in the political world is enormously difficult, as we have discovered in the recent past, particularly in America. Now we understand why this is so. The world "out there," as it were, is not something constituted independently of us but rather is constituted by the way we think about it. To modify that world, therefore, means to alter the way we think; to transform politics is to transform the character of our political thought. Perhaps it is in recognition of this insight into the nature of politics that the women's liberation movement has devoted itself so intensively to the effort to transform the way people think about sex, power, and freedom. With modifications in the nature of our language of politics, with the substitution of "person" for "man" after occupational positions, with the replacement of "man" as the reference to human beings generically by "people," if not by "woman," advocates of the women's movement hope to free people by liberating their thought. Many people now dismiss such efforts as mere symbolic gestures; but they have missed the point completely. It is precisely in the form of these symbolic transformations that supporters of the women's movement seek to change the structure of the political world.

Secondly, to conceive the possibility of change in the terms we have suggested—that is, as thought—is to gain a certain insight into what must take place if change is to occur. What must happen, in brief, is that people become sensitive to the way they think about the political world. More than that, they must have some version of idealthink to replace the idolthink. Karl Marx and V. I. Lenin, among others, recognized these facts, and so addressed themselves not merely to the inevitable tendencies in the world but to the consciousness of people who would become the bearers of change. Marx spoke of this, we recall, as class consciousness, a form of awareness that, he believed, was necessary to mobilization of the revolutionary class.[51] Lenin too devoted some thought to the matter, believing, among other things, that the revolution had to be battled in terms of ideas as well as in terms of property and power.[52] The revolutionary forces, he believed, had to be brought to an awareness of their destiny, first through a criticism of the current regime—realthink as applied to idolthink—and second through the introduction of a set of ideals to furnish the basis of a new regime—which, to Lenin and the Bolsheviks, represented a form of idealthink. Any group, then, that desires change would seem, like the Bolsheviks or the women's movement, to be compelled to confront the dominant form of thought, idolthink, and to do battle for the minds of revolutionaries with the weapon of criticism and the promise of a new set of ideals.

Thirdly, once the "winds of change are blowing," that is, once idolthink is, in the eyes of some persons at least, revealed to be a language of false prophets, various possibilities exist for the direction of change. These we may derive directly from the forms of political thought, for they represent the "political worlds" that people will seek to establish, or reestablish. Naturally, there will be the dominant groups, whether men, feudal lords, or Anglos, who will seek to maintain the world

---

[51] See chapter 2, pp. 32-33.
[52] Again, see our discussion of Lenin in chapter 2, pp. 40-41.

as it is—we may call them *idolatrists*—and they will seek fundamentally to preserve the world by, of course, preserving their own form of thought. Then there are those who emerge virtually on a realistic course of action, whom we may call the *realists*. The aim of the realists is to draw attention to the failure of the ideals, yet to do so almost in a critical fashion with little left to replace them. Indeed, when the language of realism is carried to an extreme it can become nihilism, an orgy of destruction let loose sheerly for its own sake. In some sense the movement to mobilize blacks during the 1960s and 1970s may have produced nihilism as the dominant point of view—at least, that is what the evidence from the political beliefs of black youths might suggest.

A third group, and form of political world, can emerge from the winds of change, this being those whom we may call *idealists.* The idealists stand for a form of thought that exclusively attends to the ideals of the polity—whether they be cast as democratic or authoritarian—and wishes to implement those ideals. Idealism, when itself carried to an extreme, can become a form of romanticism. In fact, it is important to observe in this connection that some of the students who were involved in the antiwar efforts of the 1960s and who were interviewed at the time displayed precisely a blend of democratic ideals, in the form of participatory democracy, and an emphasis upon romanticism.[53] Lastly, there is a group that recognizes the imbalance between the ideals and the realities of the political world— that is, precisely, the discrepancy between idealthink and realthink—and would hope to narrow the difference. These people, whom we may call *tempered idealists,* in some sense suffer the greatest agony, for they are fully cognizant of the disparities in the world and wish somehow to redress them. Again in the 1960s a number of such youths were observed, by Kenneth Keniston, Richard Flacks, Jacob Fishman, and Frederick Solomon, among others.[54] Numbers of students professed a view based on liberal democratic ideals, adhered closely to such ideals, and wished to reconstruct the polity based on the distance the ideals stood from reality. Some youths even went so far as to claim that it was the disparity they observed in their own parents—between their parents' professed attachment to liberal democratic ideals and the real ways their parents thought—that prompted them to become involved in radical activities.[55]

To change the political world, in sum, is a formidable task—in part because it entails a rethinking of the world itself, and in part because it can unleash alternative systems of thought whose proponents do battle over what the new world should look like.

[53]See, for instance, Richard Flacks, "The Liberated Generation: An Exploration of the Roots of Student Protest," *The Journal of Social Issues*, 23 (July 1967), 52-63.

[54]Jacob R. Fishman and Frederic Solomon, "Youth and Social Action: I. Perspectives on the Student Sit-In Movement," *American Journal of Orthopsychiatry*, 33 (October 1963), 872-82; Frederic Solomon and Jacob R. Fishman, "Youth and Social Action: II. Action and Identity Formation in the First Student Sit-In Demonstration," *Journal of Social Issues*, 20 (April 1964), 36-45; Flacks, "The Liberated Generation"; and Keniston, *Young Radicals.*

[55]Keniston, *Young Radicals.*

CONCLUSIONS

Social scientists who represent the structuralist view have spoken in two different ways about the nature of peoples' beliefs—what we have called thought—and how they operate in the realm of politics. Many structuralists, like Talcott Parsons, have spoken about a system of ideals that more or less act to guide the nature of the polity. Taking this cue, then, David Easton looked to the nature of such ideals in the form of a widespread diffuse loyalty that could serve as the foundations of any ongoing political system. But we recognize, because all of us have become well versed in realthink, that the system often does not work that way at all. In societies which proclaim themselves to be democratic, there is considerable undemocracy; those which proclaim themselves to be the bastions of liberty often house large numbers of citizens in prison. In light of this, other structuralists have had to invent certain ways of dealing with the discrepancies between ideals and the real world. Marx, thus, spoke of ideology to capture the illusions, the "false consciousness," that gripped the members of societies which, while proclaiming justice for all, were in fact settling it upon the very few. Many thinkers, following in the footsteps of Marx, have taken other tacks—drawing attention to the illusion committed in politics by the principle of equality, while in fact there is much inequality in the marketplace.

Yet, equality and inequality do not seem to occur merely under capitalist systems, as a simple reading of history will show. Even communist nations that attempt to remedy private ownership with some form of public ownership have their own brand—that based upon the Party. The problem, then, for any reflective student of these matters is to construct a picture of the world of thought which attends both to the ideals and to the realities, and which also seeks to recognize the device, the illusions, whereby bodies of thought are invented and used by dominant groups to secure their position. We have sought to perform that task here, in this chapter, by distinguishing three forms of thought, or language, in societies, and showing how they are transmitted as well as how change might grow out of them. All of the evidence on this perspective, of course, is not yet in; but we hope at least to have pointed the way to the issues that any sound structuralist view must cope with.

CHAPTER ELEVEN
Nation Building
in the Modern World

We hold these truths to be self-evident, that all men are created equal, that they are endowed by their Creator with certain unalienable rights, that among these are life, liberty, and the pursuit of happiness. That to secure these rights, governments are instituted among men, deriving their just powers from the consent of the governed, that whenever any form of government becomes destructive of these ends, it is the right of the people to alter or to abolish it, and to institute new government, laying its foundation on such principles, and organizing its powers in such form, as to them shall seem most likely to effect their safety and happiness.

DECLARATION OF INDEPENDENCE

For every scientist the quest after truth inevitably comes down to the simple query, How did things become the way they are today? In political sociology, political scientists and sociologists invest considerable time, passion, and energy into the quest for the fundamental roots of modern social and political forms. How did the contemporary nation-state come into being? Why did there develop such different political structures as parliamentary democracy and totalitarian rule? What common elements might the very different and special political and social orders of the modern world hold in common?

These issues were ones that inspired the imagination and intelligence of the great intellectual forebears of political sociology. Karl Marx devoted a considerable amount of thought to the roots of the modern capitalist order. In particular, he wondered how capitalists first acquired the material wealth that became the basis of capitalism, and he discovered that this wealth originated from plunder and piracy. With the origins of this accumulated wealth, Marx believed, came the great developments of capitalism that later produced the political domination of worker by owner.[1] Max Weber entertained somewhat similar questions and produced a number of treatises on the economic, religious, and legal origins of the modern world. Among other things, he discovered that bureaucracy appeared to represent the heart of the modern world; its origins lay in the centralization of authority and the extension of the state enterprise that occurred prior to the nineteenth century. Talcott Parsons also sought to discover the origins of modern social and political forms and found many of them in the seminal innovations of ancient Greece and Israel.

Since the close of World War II, students have had ample opportunity to enrich their understanding and to sharpen their perceptions of these issues. Estimates indicate that since that time at least sixty-six different countries have attained de jure independence and been freed from their bonds of subordination to such colonial empires as those of the English and the French.[2] During this period of rapid nation building, many scholars examined how rulers go about the process of fashioning a modern nation-state anew and how the masses of citizens are likely to respond to these efforts. The riddles that remain despite the discoveries and insights of Marx and Weber, for instance, are explored in nation building in the present as scholars seek to learn what the invariant and variable features of this process are.

This chapter reviews some of the answers that social scientists provide about the origins of the modern world. The focus is specifically on the origins of the modern nation-states—on the various roots of those vast political structures that are singularly characteristic of the twentieth century.[3] There are now many controversies that beset the study of nation building, as there are in several other areas of political sociology. These controversies stem largely from the different visions with which scholars embark on their scientific studies; some scholars begin from Marxist (or neo-Marxist) premises, others from Weberian (or neo-Weberian) principles, still others from Parsonian ideas. Naturally the different starting points yield alternative interpretations of nation building and lead, for example, to differential emphases on the significance of economic and political forces. The following discussions tend to gloss over such differences to provide a reasonably smooth and simple introduction. Those who wish to pursue the inquiries into nation building in greater detail

---

[1] Karl Marx, *Capital,* Volume 1 (Moscow: Foreign Languages Publishing House, 1961), chapter 26.

[2] Clifford Geertz, *The Interpretation of Cultures* (New York: Basic Books, Inc., Publishers, 1973), p. 234.

[3] The focus here is deliberately restricted to fairly recent nation building efforts. For excellent analyses of the creaton of great states and empires in earlier times, see S. N. Eisenstadt, *The Political Systems of Empires* (New York: The Free Press, 1963); and S. N. Eisenstadt, ed., *Political Sociology* (New York: Basic Books, Inc., Publishers, 1971), especially chapters 2-8.

and to study the controversies at length might wish to examine articles by Joseph Gusfield, Mark Kesselman, Alejandro Portes, and Lucian Pye.[4]

MAJOR FEATURES OF THE MODERN NATION-STATE AND OF NATION BUILDING

In the face of considerable diversity among modern political forms—some old, some new, some democratic, some totalitarian—the reader might well wonder whether there are any common features to the structure of the modern nation-state and to the process that produced it. Observers agree on at least a few shared qualities. By far the single most comprehensive rendition of them comes from the pen of a scholar accustomed to telling a good story, the historian C. E. Black.[5] Providing a lucid synthesis of many writings on the form and origins of contemporary nation-states, Black suggests that the major feature of the modern nation-state is the consolidation of policy making—or, in other words, the centralization of political authority. Noting that this consolidation has been encouraged by the introduction of sophisticated forms of communication and transportation, Black nevertheless declares that it is "due more . . . to the desire on the part of modernizing leaders in both government and private enterprise to mobilize and rationalize the resources of society with a view to achieving greater control, efficiency and production."[6] The history of European nation-states since the Middle Ages discloses this feature to us most clearly, whereas that of the United States, since the end of the eighteenth century at least, reveals a less marked trend in this direction.[7] Another quality of the modern nation-state, Black points out, lies in the expansion of its functions over previous political forms. Special functions involving, among other things, the provision of services to the poor and destitute as well as the establishment and maintenance of national defense have gradually been taken over by the modern nation-state and have given this body a degree of power unforeseen by its creators. As Black observes, "modern states today collect revenues in an amount equivalent to between one-quarter and one-half of the gross national product to reimburse the costs of general administration, public enterprises, and social

---

[4] Joseph Gusfield, "Tradition and Modernity: Misplaced Polarities in the Study of Social Change," in *Political Development and Social Change*, 2nd ed., ed. Jason L. Finkle and Richard W. Gable (New York: John Wiley and Sons, 1971), pp. 15-26; Mark Kesselman, "Order or Movement? The Literature of Political Development as Ideology," *World Politics, 26* (October 1973), 139-54; Alejandro Portes, "On the Sociology of National Development: Theories and Issues," *American Journal of Sociology, 82* (July 1976), 55-85; and Lucian Pye, "The Concept of Political Development," in *Political Development and Social Change*, Finkle and Gable, pp. 83-91.

[5] C. E. Black, *The Dynamics of Modernization* (New York: Harper & Row, Publishers, Inc., 1966), pp. 13-18.

[6] Ibid., p. 13.

[7] James MacGregor Burns, *The Deadlock of Democracy* (Englewood Cliffs, N.J.: Prentice-Hall, Inc., 1967); and Samuel P. Huntington, *Political Order in Changing Societies* (New Haven, Conn.: Yale University Press, 1968), chapter 2.

security, whereas in traditional societies such revenues may be as low as 5 percent or less of the wealth produced."[8]

The modern nation-state is also characterized by the proliferation of legal standards. This, in turn, has led to the growth of equally distinctive and formidable bureaucracies to which attention was first drawn by Weber. Almost everywhere in the world, political officials undertake efforts to create and expand bureaucracies; new nations often turn first to the establishment of a large civil service, while nations long underway inevitably—and to some partisans regrettably—seem bound to keep the bureaucracy alive and well. A related and final feature of modern nation-states, according to Black, is the expansion of the citizen's part in public affairs. On this quality, or course, the differences between equally modern democratic and totalitarian nation-states stand out sharply. Nevertheless, as Black correctly observes, twentieth-century leaders of democratic and of totalitarian regimes seem to find it necessary to clothe the legitimacy of their rule in the guise of widespread popular support.

Some social scientists are interested in identifying more than these few rather elementary features. They inquire as well into the timing and the sequence of events that are characteristic of the development of modern nation-states and hope thereby to specify ever more precisely the process of nation building—the general ways in which nation-states arise, continue to survive, even may die.[9] At least part of the reason behind their concern with this process lies in the obvious differences between the creation of old and new nations. While countries like England took two or three centuries to assume the outlines of their present political form, others, like Nigeria and Ghana, are compelled to accomplish nationhood in only two or three decades, if only as a means of keeping pace with the older nations. What effects might the greater speed of nation building have on the newer countries? Would an alternative chain of events—the establishment of large and complex political institutions before rather than after economic growth—alter the likelihood of achieving a viable form of nationhood? These rank among the most important questions for current students of nation building. Hans Daalder provides intriguing thoughts on these matters.[10] He claims, for instance, that countries like England whose leaders gradually accepted the demands for full participation in politics from the new social classes (for example, the working class) were better able to develop a more viable and widespread form of democracy than countries like France whose

[8] Black, *The Dynamics of Modernization,* p. 14.

[9] For example, see the following: Black, *The Dynamics of Modernization;* T. H. Marshall, *Citizenship and Social Class and Other Essays* (Cambridge: Cambridge University Press, 1950), chapter 1; Eric A. Nordlinger, "Political Development: Time Sequences and Rate of Change," in *Politics and Society: Studies in Comparative Political Sociology,* ed. Eric A. Nordlinger (Englewood Cliffs, N.J.: Prentice-Hall, Inc., 1970), pp. 329-47; and Sidney Verba, "Sequences and Development," in *Crises and Sequences in Political Development,* ed. Leonard Binder et al. (Princeton, N.J.: Princeton University Press, 1971), pp. 283-316.

[10] Hans Daalder, "Parties, Elites, and Political Development in Western Europe," in *Mass Politics in Industrial Societies: A Reader in Comparative Politics,* ed. Giuseppe Di Palma (Chicago: Markham Publishing Company, 1972), pp. 4-36.

rulers continued to discourage and to resist such participation. A similar circumstance that accounts for the greater stability of British politics over French, he argues, is the earlier development of industrialization in England that permitted "many new links [to be] forged between the state and its citizens through the expansion of administration and the establishment of a great number of new political groups."[11] Many more facts remain to be discovered about the timing and the chain of events that lead to the successful accomplishment of nationhood, but certainly Daalder is on the right path.

CONCOMITANTS OF NATION BUILDING

The creation of the nation-state often, if not invariably, occurs as the result of other developments in a society; these changes are sometimes dubbed in academic shorthand as "modernizaton." Nation building represents the political aspects of these changes, while the social and economic ones go under such names as urban migration and economic growth.[12] So much do these various events appear to go hand in hand that it becomes difficult to disentangle them from one another.[13] Moreover, it is impossible to say in general which of these several strands of development take primacy over the others. In fact, among the older nation-states, such as England, economic growth and leadership seemed to be more important to subsequent development, while among the newer ones, as for example those of Africa, political leadership provided the principal impetus for economic growth.[14] The most judicious empirical view of these several strands of change is to view them as concomitants of one another. Three are singled out for special consideration: economic development, growth and spread of nationalism, and political instability.

Economic Development

European nations, like England, most vividly illustrate the close links between economic development and nation building. In Britain, the gradual growth and expansion of the economy into a full-blown capitalist enterprise was paralleled by an equally gradual enlargement of the political arena. As the means and setting of production changed from simple utensils of the artisan and the comfortable location of the home or guild, so, too, the aristocracy of England ever so slowly and smoothly accommodated themselves to new circumstances in politics; for instance,

---

[11] Ibid., p. 12.

[12] Actually many scholars of development, or modernization, use nation building to cover all manner of changes from social to economic. Here it is used strictly to describe the political aspects of development, in effect shortening the term *nation-state* to *nation* when it is used with the term *building*.

[13] Karl W. Deutsch, "Social Mobilization and Political Development," *American Political Science Review*, 55 (September 1961), 493-514.

[14] The difference here sometimes is described as that between unplanned and planned forms of social change.

in the nineteenth century the franchise was extended first to the manufacturing classes and then to the working classes.[15] Though peaceful compared with nation building in countries such as France, the process of development in England was nevertheless punctuated by moments of violence and upheaval.

No doubt the British case has suggested to many observers that economic development inevitably accompanies the emergence of the modern nation-state. W. W. Rostow, in a pioneering thesis, gives special significance to the importance of economic development in nation building and suggests a multistage sequence whereby countries ultimately achieve an economic "take-off" that propels them into extensive and sustained economic growth.[16] Many economic factors appear to Rostow as part of this sequence of events, and chief among them is change in the form of agriculture techniques and market organization in a country, emergence of an economic elite that shifts its attention from traditional practices of enterprise to new forms of production, and a marked increase in the investment of a country in the technical means of production. Other observers draw upon the Rostow thesis, or one very similar to it, to claim that governmental structures are compelled to undergo corresponding changes by, among other things, enlarging the part they play in the development of the economy and increasing the number of political personnel. Observers claim that sometimes the political leaders act to initiate the economic growth, and other times such leaders, and the state machinery in general, act in response to such growth.[17]

While economic development assisted the early nation builders gradually to achieve the accouterments of a modern nation-state, economic development often appears to be more of an obstacle than an aid to more recent nation builders in Asia, Africa, and Latin America. This is particularly true in the case of nations that are required to develop rapidly in the effort to accomplish economic parity with other nations. Mancur Olson, Jr., presents some of the reasons why rapid economic growth may disturb a country's effort to become a modern nation-state.[18] He observes that rapid economic growth produces new social groups of both economic gainers and losers; these are people whose routines and life outlooks may be so radically upset by their newly won fortunes or lost wealth that they become the easy targets of organized efforts to displace the current political regime. A brief scan of history reveals, he notes, a variety of specific instances in which both gainers and losers from rapid economic growth contributed to widespread political violence; thus, he cites some well-known cases of economic gainers:

[15] For a description of these events in the form of an ideal-typical analysis, see Neil J. Smelser, "Mechanisms of Change and Adjustment to Change," *Political Development and Social Change,* Finkle and Gable, pp. 27-42; and Neil J. Smelser, *The Sociology of Economic Life,* 2nd ed. (Englewood Cliffs, N.J.: Prentice-Hall, Inc., 1975), chapter 5.

[16] W. W. Rostow, "The Take-Off Into Self-Sustained Growth," in *Political Development and Social Change,* Finkle and Gable, pp. 141-61.

[17] For an example of the first type of argument, see Black, *Dynamics of Modernization;* and for an illustration of the second, see J. J. Spengler, "Economic Development: Political Preconditions and Political Consequences," in *Political Development and Social Change,* Finkle and Gable, pp. 161-76.

[18] Mancur Olson, Jr., "Rapid Growth as a Destabilizing Force," in *Political Development and Social Change,* Finkle and Gable, pp. 557-68.

The growth of commerce and industry in early modern Europe created a larger and wealthier middle class; and as this middle class gained in numbers and in wealth, especially in relation to the landed aristocracy, it demanded, and it got, extra political power to match that wealth. These demands were obviously behind the middle class participation in the French Revolution, and were also fundamental to many other instances of political instability in the history of modern Europe. . . . In Sweden, and still more in Norway, industrialization and the absorption of rural migrants was later and faster, and the labor movements in turn revealed, especially in Norway, more disaffection and political extremism. . . . The radical elements in Jacksonian democracy, in Populism, in the unusually strong Socialist parties of some of the frontier states of the Great Plains, in the violent western mining unions, and in the Non-Partisan League [developed in] western areas near the frontier [that] were growing rapidly when these destabilizing movements began, and [that] were often filled with people who had gained from this expansion.[19]

However imaginative the thesis of Olson, the relationship between rapid economic growth and political instability in nation building is not nearly so clear and simple as he portrays. An examination of this same argument by Samuel P. Huntington, for instance, reveals that political instability results from rapid economic growth only among some of the newly emerging nations in which economic development begins at a very low level.[20] Other research suggests that in both new and old nations the tendencies for economic development to somehow impede the gradual process of building a comprehensive and effective nation-state may be slight.[21] The discussion in the next chapter on social and political movements covers this issue in greater detail.[22]

[19] Ibid., pp. 560-61.

[20] Huntington, *Political Order in Changing Societies*, pp. 52-53.

[21] See, for instance, Douglas A. Hibbs, Jr., *Mass Political Violence* (New York: John Wiley & Sons, 1973); and David Snyder and Charles Tilly, "Hardship and Collective Violence in France, 1830 to 1960," *American Sociological Review*, 37 (October 1972), 520-32.

[22] There is a special version of the economic development thesis that claims that economic affluence encourages the growth of democratic regimes. The argument has been fraught with controversy for several years, however, because of the special difficulties involved in constructing a suitable measure of democracy. To examine the evidence both for and against the assertion that economic affluence accompanies democratic developments in a nation, see the following: Phillips Cutright, "National Political Development: Measurement and Analysis," *American Sociological Review*, 28 (April 1963), 253-64; Robert A. Dahl, *Polyarchy: Participation and Opposition* (New Haven: Yale University Press, 1971), chapter 5; Robert W. Jackman, "On the Relation of Economic Development to Democratic Performance," *American Journal of Political Science*, 17 (August 1973), 611-21; Robert W. Jackman, *Politics and Social Equality: A Comparative Analysis* (New York: John Wiley & Sons, 1975), pp. 66-73; Seymour Martin Lipset, "Some Social Requisites of Democracy," *American Political Science Review*, 53 (March 1959), 69-105; Seymour Martin Lipset, *Political Man: The Social Bases of Politics* (Garden City, N.Y.: Doubleday Anchor, 1969), chapter 2; Deanne E. Neubauer, *"Some Conditions of Democracy,"* *American Political Science Review*, 61 (December 1967), 1002-1009; and David M. Potter, *People of Plenty: Economic Abundance and the American Character* (Chicago: University of Chicago Press, 1958), chapter 5 especially. The discussion of David Potter is the most stimulating and imaginative, while the various analyses of Robert Jackman provide the most sophisticated and sensitive empirical measurements of the different concepts. Jackman, whose work represents the most recent and, thus, has had the benefit of instruction from the errors of previous analysts, concludes that "while economic development may lead to increased political democracy at earlier stages of industrialization, a threshold is reached at later stages of this process beyond which the effects of economic development on political democracy become progressively weaker" (Jackman, *Political and Social Equality*, p. 84).

Growth and Spread of Nationalism

Nowhere is the significance of ideas more vividly illustrated in political sociology than in the process of nation building. The forming of a nation seems to depend on the capacity of leaders and of led to find a common set of symbols on which they can agree and that furnish some of the most important foundations for the edifice of the nation-state. To some observers, in fact, the long and often circuitous struggle to locate and to sustain a common set of symbols is the very heart of nation building. Writing of the ideology that is characteristic of nation building, the anthropologist Clifford Geertz, certainly one of the most brilliant students of nation building, puts the matter best: "Nationalism is not a mere byproduct but the very stuff of social change in so many new states; not its reflection, its cause, its expression, or its engine, but the thing itself."[23]

All modern nation-states seem to go through a process of attempting to forge a set of beliefs that serve as their cornerstone. In the United States, for example, Louis Hartz has found this set of beliefs in a "liberal ethos," a congeries of ideas whose origins lay principally in the writings of John Locke and whose clearest articulation is found in the Declaration of Independence and the Bill of Rights.[24] Running as a theme throughout American history, the liberal ethos, which proclaims the freedom and equality of all individuals, is evident at one point in the significance of the frontier and at another point in the unparalleled rate of economic expansion in the nineteenth century. In a related inquiry, Seymour Martin Lipset claims that the prevailing kind of religious institutions and beliefs in the United States—those of Protestantism—greatly contributed to the formation and the maintenance of the liberal ethos, by stressing among other things, the egalitarianism of people among themselves as well as before the law.[25]

Elsewhere, for instance the founding of nation-states in Europe, the important place of beliefs in the process of nation building is equally clear. In the events that led up to the emergence of Germany as a modern nation-state, the dogma of race and nation of Adolf Hitler certainly helped to create, at least for a time, a unique national identity for the German people. The importance of an ideology around which the disparate members of a country might unite is equally significant in the founding of Communist nations as well. Remarking on this in the case of Yugoslavia, R. V. Burks writes that "the lesson of Yugoslavia . . . is that nationalism is not a temporary impediment to the revolution; it is more nearly its motor force. . . . The [Communist] Partisans won out over their better equipped and better fed local enemies in large part because they stood for Yugoslav nationalism. . . . They were able to do this probably because they represented a new [if secular] religion, which pushed aside and replaced the characteristic Catholicism,

[23] Geertz, *The Interpretation of Cultures,* pp. 251-52.

[24] Louis Hartz, *The Liberal Tradition in America: An Interpretation of American Political Thought Since the Revolution* (New York: Harcourt Brace Jovanovich, Inc., 1955).

[25] Seymour Martin Lipset, *The First New Nation* (Garden City, N.Y.: Doubleday Anchor, 1967), pp. 177-80.

288

Orthodoxy, and Islam of such discrete national groups as the Croats, the Serbs, and the Bosniaks."[26]

Though obviously of crucial significance to the process of nation building in the modern world, beliefs also remain the most elusive element to study, perhaps because they also are the most difficult aspect of nation building to secure. Geertz underscores this problematic character of beliefs noting, for instance, that newer nations are caught up in a constant search for the appropriate and delicate balance between beliefs that arise out of the traditions of a society, and beliefs that are part of the currents of the times, the *Zeitgeist*.[27] The search for underlying identities, for shared commitments to the same set of symbols, no doubt will continue to be the most challenging feature of nation building and one to arouse ancient rivalries within new and old nations. The recent religious upheavals in Lebanon and in Northern Ireland and the longstanding racial and ethnic conflicts in the United States provide some vivid testimony to the difficulty of this achievement.

Political Instability

Becoming a modern nation-state is by no means a smooth and easy task. For each success attained there may be one or more failures. Often these interruptions are most evident in the political challenges and tensions encountered by leaders of the regime. Nation building among the older nation-states, for example, provides evidence of political conflicts. In England some major conflicts occurred in the seventeenth century and ultimately produced a fundamental change in the distribution of political power; Parliament replaced the king as the sovereign body. In France the battles were even more intense and widespread; they reached their peak in 1789 but continued long into the nineteenth century. German history, too, is marked by periods of political tension, though the German leaders succeeded in suppressing most extreme forms of opposition until 1848 and later in 1918, 1923, and 1932. The United States as well is a country whose steps in the direction of nationhood were marked in the late eighteenth century by a successful challenge to a colonial power and whose later efforts to achieve a more or less pacific nationhood were interrupted by a great Civil War. In the newly emerging nation-states of today there are equally intense and violent conflicts among the inhabitants—in Asia, in Africa, and in Latin America.[28]

What is it, besides growing pains, that seems to account for the sporadic punctuation of nation building with political conflicts and challenges to the reigning leaders? Samuel P. Huntington, a political scientist and close student of nation building, presents one of the more provocative explanations.[29] He argues that

---

[26] R. V. Burks, "Eastern Europe," in *Communist Systems in Comparative Perspective,* ed. Lenard Cohen and Jane P. Shapiro (Garden City, N.Y.: Doubleday, 1974), pp. 72-73.

[27] Geertz, *The Interpretation of Cultures,* pp. 243-54 especially.

[28] No claims are made here for the source of the conflicts, only for their presence. One could make a handsome argument for the significance of outside agents in the political tensions of nation-states, particularly among the newer nation-states.

[29] Huntington, *Political Order in Changing Societies.*

nation building involves the unparalleled growth of political participation that is partly brought about by economic development.[30] Participation, by itself, is not a sufficient stimulus for political instability, however; it must be further joined with an inadequate number and growth of political institutions. Thus, instability is produced because there exist an insufficient number of channels and of sponsors available to embrace the newly enlarged and aroused citizenry. By channels and sponsors, Huntington has in mind such groups as political parties, trade unions, and voluntary organizations that commonly dot the twentieth century landscape of such older nations as the United States.

To prove his case Huntington provides a variety of pieces of evidence and documentation. Asserting, for example, that political instability is characteristic of the transition between a relatively peaceful traditional social order and a relatively peaceful modern one—that is, of the process of modernizing—he displays evidence that shows that political violence reaches its peak among those nations midway in the level of literacy. Other research, by Ivo and Rosalind Feierabend, tends to support his view (see table 11-1).[31] However, other analysts who examined evidence for the argument have not found overwhelming support for it. For instance, P. R. Brass sought to examine the thesis among the different states of India.[32] Instead of finding that political instability came about when the level of political institutionalization was low, as Huntington's thesis claims, Brass found that instability resulted from high levels of institutionalization. Indeed, Brass's analysis, rather than Huntington's, tends to support the most advanced thinking on the matters of instability and violence in nation building; but these are issues that are considered in the following chapter.

Table 11–1   Literacy and stability

Level of Literacy	Number of Countries	Number of Unstable Countries	Percent Unstable
Below 10%	6	3	50.0
10%–25%	12	10	83.3
25%–60%	23	22	95.6
60%–90%	15	12	80.0
Over 90%	23	5	21.7

Source: Adapted from Ivo K. Feierabend, Rosalind L. Feierabend, and Betty A. Nesvold, "Correlates of Political Stability" (paper presented at Annual Meeting, American Political Science Association, September 1963).

[30] Ibid., pp. 39-59.

[31] Ivo K. Feierabend, Rosalind L. Feierabend, and Betty A. Nesvold, "Social Change and Political Violence: Cross-National Patterns," in *Political Development and Social Change,* Finkle and Gable, pp. 569-604.

[32] Paul R. Brass, "Political Participation, Institutionalization and Stability in India," *Government and Opposition,* 4 (Winter 1969), 23-53.

Regardless of the current balance of evidence on Huntington's argument, its implication is that political stability exists only where political institutions are durable and strong, at least sufficiently strong to withstand the sudden numbers of newly enfranchised political participants. Huntington explores this implication and embellishes it with an exploration into the many ways in which political parties, as institutions, succeed in the control of political participation.[33] Particular cases come to mind that clearly illustrate this angle of Huntington's vision. In the United States, for instance, both of the major contemporary political parties, and that which some analysts refer to as the party system, developed at a pace so that they were able to withstand what otherwise might have been severe shocks to the incipient nation-state.[34] The same degree of institutional durability was evident in the case of England in which first the political clubs and later the full-fledged parties readily accommodated the ever growing numbers of enfranchised citizens, thus, the process of nation building, at least since the late eighteenth century, has been a reasonably uninterrupted one.[35] The great challenge facing the newer nations of today, of course, is that they must seek simultaneously to cope with an expanded body of citizenry and a fragile system of parties; this heightens the chances of political instability. (For further details on parties as institutions, see chapter 8, "Political Parties and Political Partisanship. ")

THE PLACE OF SOCIAL GROUPS
IN NATION BUILDING

Several of the concomitants that are part of contemporary development have been explored. Besides these, there are special segments of the population of incipient nation-states that play a prominent part in their development by taking the lead in its direction or acting as the principal supporter for the effort to change. Three of the social groups that have played a major role in the nation-building efforts of modern nation-states, particularly in those many countries caught up with great intensity in nation building in the twentieth century, are the intellectuals, the military, and the peasants. The intellectuals and the military have mainly acted as leaders of organized attempts to change; the peasants have been major suppliers of personnel for the ultimate victories of national liberation.

Intellectuals

Some figures prominently associated with the heights of nation building among countries of the modern world are Jefferson, Madison, and Hamilton in the United States; Lenin and Trotsky in the Soviet Union; Mao in China; and Nehru

---

[33] Huntington, *Political Order in Changing Societies,* chapter 7 especially.

[34] William Nisbet Chambers, *Political Parties in a New Nation: The American Experience, 1776-1809* (New York: Oxford University Press, 1963); and Lipset, *The First New Nation,* chapter 9 especially.

[35] M. Ostrogorski, *Democracy and the Organization of Political Parties,* vol. I, trans. Frederick Clarke (New York: Macmillan and Co., Ltd., 1902).

in India. What did all of these figures have in common? Attentive students of the nation-building experience suggest that these and other individuals who led the effort to construct new nations were people of ideas that were receptive to new knowledge and anxious to challenge the status quo in an effort to create for themselves and for their followers a new social and political order. Whatever their special motivations and talents for revolution and reform—and often, to all outward appearances, such motivation consisted principally of an overwhelming ambition to secure positions of great power—the minds of these individuals were of a different cut from those of their fellow conspirators and were equally tuned to the world of ideas and to that of action. They were the individuals responsible for both creating and for articulating the symbolic threads that, as we have already seen, play so crucial a part in the creation of the nation-state in the modern world; in short, they were intellectuals.[36] (The reader is urged to reconsider our distinction among the three different forms of thought examined in chapter 10. In particular, intellectuals appear to engage in a process of seeking to create a new nation-state through articulating a form of idealthink; yet, for many of them, even Lenin and Jefferson among them, the idealthink of regimes quickly seems to turn to idolthink. Why does this happen? And, is it inevitable?)

One of the foremost students of nation building in the twentieth century and of the prominent part assumed by intellectuals is Edward Shils. Writing with great insight and wisdom, Shils maintains that intellectuals, whom he defines as possessed of "an advanced modern education," occupy a special role in nation-building efforts in Asia and Africa.[37] In part this occurs because no other groups are available for the task. The merchants who achieve great success in the world of business, for instance, obviously have no special reason or desire to embark on an effort to sever ties with colonial nations; and other social groups that in earlier times had undertaken the effort to challenge the old orders, such as trade unions, are insufficiently organized to assume this part in the colonies. However, it is not just the absence of others that prompted the intellectuals to become revolutionaries or reformers. Often those who receive advanced educational training in their home countries, or more typically in England and France, are unable to find sufficiently rewarding and satisfying professions in which to employ their skills and talents; hence they are open to the opportunity to engage in political activities. Their willingness to participate in political protests receives added encouragement from circumstances peculiar to their role as educated individuals—their uncomfortable position vis-à-vis colonial authority. "For an intellectual in an underdeveloped

---

[36]On various analyses of these sorts of leaders, see for instance, Black, *Dynamics of Modernization,* pp. 9-13, 62-89; and Lipset, *The First New Nation,* pp. 75-85. For slightly different perspectives on these leaders, see Reinhard Bendix, "Charismatic Leadership," in *State and Society: A Reader in Comparative Political Sociology,* ed. Reinhard Bendix et al. (Boston: Little, Brown and Co., 1969), pp. 616-29; and Reinhard Bendix, "A Case Study in Cultural and Educational Mobility: Japan and the Protestant Ethic," in *Social Structure and Mobility in Economic Development,* ed. Neil J. Smelser and Seymour Martin Lipset (Chicago: Aldine Publishing Co., 1966), pp. 626-79.

[37]Edward A. Shils, "The Intellectuals in the Political Development of the New States," in *Political Development and Social Change,* Finkle and Gable, pp. 249-76.

country," Shils writes, "authority is usually something into which he must be absorbed or against which he must be in opposition. It is seldom something about which he can be neutral while he goes about his business. . . . The distance of authority renders revolt against it psychologically practicable."[38]

Twentieth-century intellectuals were led to voice ideas that tend to echo those found in earlier nation-building efforts as well. Overriding all other ideas were those of national independence and unity; these were themes that had a special attraction for the intellectuals because they seemed to reconcile the tension between the appeal of the urbane life in the older nation-states, like England and the United States, and the parochial tug of ties to family and friends in the colonial country. The theme of nationalism frequently was couched in two other sets of ideas—populism and socialism. Populism possessed a particularly strong and almost natural appeal to the intellectuals because it provided a means of articulating the feeling of loyalty to home as well as a device destined to arouse the mass of newly awakened peoples to the tactical efforts required by nation building. These were themes, incidentally, equally as characteristic of the nation-building experience of older nation-states in Europe and the United States as of the newer ones.[39] Socialism, on the other hand, came to be attractive to the intellectuals for many reasons—the hatred that the intellectuals felt toward nations they perceived as engaged in imperialist expansion and rape of lesser countries; the practical political successes that communism had to its credit in the twentieth century in nations like the Soviet Union and China; and, of course, the demonstrated ease with which socialist doctrines could accommodate the themes of nationalism and populism.[40]

The future role of intellectuals in nation building, Shils maintains, is somewhat ambiguous. Undermining whatever incentive they might have to involve themselves in political challenges to established regimes, particularly in the newer nations, are the expansion of employment opportunities that come with economic development—once positions commensurate with their skills become available to them, then one major source of dissatisfaction will be gone. Yet, if the experience of the older nation-states is any guide, intellectuals may continue to be a thorn in the side of established political regimes, by challenging the right of those who hold high office to continue in their positions of power. Although there are many counterexamples from the recent past that severely test the validity of this conclusion, as in the case of intellectuals who participated in the administrations of presidents John F. Kennedy and Lyndon Johnson in the United States, there are still at least some intellectuals who are born skeptics; and skepticism, now as throughout all history, stands as the principal germ of revolution.[41]

[38] Ibid., p. 257.

[39] Hannah Arendt, *The Origins of Totalitarianism* (Cleveland, Ohio: The World Publishing Co., 1958), chapter 8 especially.

[40] For an interesting discussion of the way in which communism has become the political model for state building in the twentieth century, see Huntington, *Political Order in Changing Societies,* chapter 7.

[41] For an important account of how intellectuals can become defenders rather than challengers of the established ways, see David Halberstam, *The Best and the Brightest* (Greenwich, Conn.: Fawcett, 1972).

The Military

Students of the military have been struck by the degree to which military personnel become involved in nation-building efforts.[42] Perhaps the prototype of recent cases is that of Gamal Abdel Nasser and other members of the Egyptian army who deposed King Farouk in 1952 and assisted Egypt and later the United Arab Republic in political and economic success. There are many other examples as well, including Ahmed Ben Bella of Algeria and Mustafa Kemal in Turkey. There are a number of qualities associated with the military profession and with military training that are compatible with an active and vigorous role in politics, such as aspirations for positions of power and skills useful for coping with the special nuances of politics.[43] Moreover, military officers, like intellectuals, have often found themselves propelled to the forefront of organized efforts to change simply because there are no other groups that might assume the part.[44]

Some of the most recent inquiries into the part that the military plays in nation building tend to divide over whether the military occupies a position of encouraging greater economic and political self-sufficiency or one of halting, if not reversing, such development.[45] Huntington, in a provocative analysis, resolves the seeming contradiction between equally sound investigations by suggesting that the role of the military depends not so much on features of the profession but rather on the stage of nation building in the larger society.[46] In the first place, Huntington draws a distinction among six types of political regimes and relies on the circumstances mentioned in an earlier discussion of his analysis—namely, political participation and political institutions (see table 11-2). Societies may be equally advanced in their development, at least in terms of the extent of political participation within them, but differ in the degree to which participation is bound within existing political organizations. Thus, the Soviet Union is an example of a society displaying high levels of participation as well as high levels of institutionalization, whereas Argentina represents a society exhibiting high levels of participation but low levels of institutionalization. The praetorian political orders are those societies in which political institutions are insufficiently developed or strong to cope with the extent of citizen participation; Huntington focuses his analysis of the origins and development of military intervention in nation building on these societies.

Huntington finds that the military plays its most vigorous role as a champion of nation building in the shift from traditional to transitional political orders. In

---

[42] Morris Janowitz, *The Military in the Political Development of New Nations* (Chicago: University of Chicago Press, 1964).

[43] Ibid.

[44] On these and many other features associated with military intervention see the review of materials in Robert D. Putnam, "Toward Explaining Military Intervention in Latin American Politics," in *Political Development and Social Change,* Finkle and Gable, pp. 284-304.

[45] See George A. Kourvetaris and Betty A. Dobratz, "The Present State and Development of Sociology of the Military," *Journal of Political and Military Sociology,* 4 (Spring 1976), 91-92, as well as the many references cited therein.

[46] Huntington, *Political Order in Changing Societies,* chapter 4.

Table 11-2 Types of political systems

Political Participation	Ratio of Institutionalization to Participation	
	High: Civic	*Low: Praetorian*
Low: traditional	Organic (Ethiopia)	Oligarchical (Paraguay)
Medium: transitional	Whig (Chile)	Radical (Egypt)
High: modern	Participant (Soviet Union)	Mass (Argentina)

Source: Adapted from Samuel P. Huntington, *Political Order in Changing Societies* (New Haven, Conn.: Yale University Press, 1968).

these cases, the military represents virtually the only group in the society willing and able to undertake the challenge of the existing political regime. Upon the success of its overthrow of the established political rulers—its coup d'etat—it initiates a large-scale effort to upgrade the economy and to replace existing political institutions with somewhat more popular and representative ones. Huntington writes:

> In these early stages of political modernization the military officers play a highly modernizing and progressive role. They challenge the oligarchy, and they promote social and economic reform, national integration, and, in some measure, the extension of political participation. They assail waste, backwardness, and corruption, and they introduce into the society highly middle-class ideas of efficiency, honesty, and national loyalty. Like the Protestant entrepreneurs of western Europe, the soldier reformers in non-Western societies embody and promote a puritanism which, while not perhaps as extreme as that of the radical revolutionaries, is nonetheless a distinctive innovation in their societies.[47]

Huntington finds that change in which the military assumes a highly innovative role in nation building was characteristic of nations such as Iraq until 1958, Egypt until 1952, and many Latin American nations in the nineteenth century.

With the transformation of a nation-state from oligarchical to radical praetorianism, and thence to mass praetorianism, the role of the military changes accordingly. In particular, as "society changes, so does the role of the military. In the world of oligarchy, the solider is a radical; in the middle-class world he is a participant and arbiter; as the mass society looms on the horizon he becomes the conservative guardian of the existing order."[48] Citing a number of cases in Latin America in the 1950s—Argentina, Venezuela, Colombia, and Brazil—as well as Turkey, Huntington suggests that the military at this stage tends to assume the role of a guardian of the established regime and constitution by suppressing forces aimed at the overthrow of the government and securing the reign of representatives

[47]Ibid., p. 205.
[48]Ibid., p. 221.

of the middle classes. Further, instead of aggressively seeking economic and other reforms, it merely serves as the agent for those middle-class groups currently the most popular and powerful; it assists them in deposing recalcitrant leaders but then withdraws from an active part in governing the new nation-state.

Whether the military will continue to play the part of a force for innovation or for conservatism in nation building remains to be seen. At a minimum, the implication of Huntington's analysis is that the role of the military will depend on the main features of the larger society. If the more technically advanced societies and older nation-states, like the United States, England, or even the Soviet Union, serve as any sort of guide, then it appears that the role of the military in the developing nation-states will ultimately become subordinate to that of civilian leaders. (See chapter 6 for a discussion of the military leadership as well as the importance of the defense sector of federal expenditures in the United States.)

Peasants

While the effort to build a new nation-state must often rely (and in the past has relied) on the leadership and guidance of intellectuals and military officers, in the end it will fail unless it manages to incorporate a large and willing band of foot soldiers. Marx, of course, anticipated that the foot soldiers would come principally from the urban proletariat—individuals so stripped of their humanity that they would become willing accomplices in the effort to create a new society. To a degree Marx proved correct in his prognosis, for instance in Russia. However, there have been far more instances, particularly in the twentieth century, in which the foot soldiers for radical change in nation building came not from the urban proletariat but from the peasant laborers—not from the city, but from the country.[49]

The story of the role of the peasants in the nation-building efforts of the twentieth century has been particularly well told by anthropologist Eric Wolf.[50] He examines in close detail the distant as well as immediate histories of twentieth-century peasant wars and revolutions in six different countries—Mexico, Russia, China, Vietnam, Algeria, and Cuba—searching for both the common and the unique factors of peasant rebellion. He claims that the peasant wars and revolts had their distant origins in the growth and spread of capitalism in Northern Europe; it was capitalism that succeeded in upsetting the settled and customary routine of life among peasants, as among every other social group.[51] The meaning of land and of labor became transformed from objects of long-standing pride and respect to objects that, in the capitalist scheme of things, merely represented commodities. The spread of capitalism, moreover, had the effect of at least unleashing a chain of

---

[49] Ibid., pp. 279-300.

[50] Eric R. Wolf, *Peasant Wars of the Twentieth Century* (New York: Harper & Row, Publishers, 1969).

[51] For a similar frame of reference, see, for instance, Susanne Bodenheimer, "Dependency and Imperialism: The Roots of Latin American Underdevelopment," in *Politics and Society,* 1 (May, 1971), 327-57. Some of these issues are discussed at greater length later.

events that comprise the general sorts of processes that were previously referred to, economic development among them:

> The spread of the market has torn men up by their roots, and shaken them loose from the social relationships into which they were born. Industrialization and expanded communication have given rise to new social clusters, as yet unsure of their own social positions and interests, but forced by the imbalance of their lives to seek a new adjustment.[52]

Thus aroused, people of all groups, principally peasants, became available to engage in the organized political efforts to free societies from their traditional, often debilitating forms of rule.

In all six countries studied by Wolf there ultimately resulted a political victory of more or less sustained duration that was accomplished on behalf of peasants, if not mainly by peasant forces. However, this victory neither came easily nor transpired quickly. Invariably it was preceded by an effort to establish a dictatorship on behalf of other social forces and groups. In China the victory of the Communists on behalf and with the aid of the peasants was preceded by the dictatorship of Chiang Kai-shek; in Vietnam the victory of Ho Chi Minh and the Communists was preceded by the efforts of the French to impose an unpopular rule. Where peasant forces did not succeed in establishing a central political authority on their own behalf, as in Germany and Japan, the failure was due to the strength of the feudal barons who controlled the land.

Peasants are not everywhere free or eager to engage in nation-building efforts, regardless of the ruin visited upon them by capitalism. Indeed, Wolf suggests, peasants are naturally disinclined to engage in rebellions or revolutions because of circumstances inherent in their mode of life. As all peasants tend to work alone, they come to prize the strength of their individual efforts—to view themselves, as capitalism advances, as competitors for scarce bounty rather than as collaborators. Equally true of the life of peasants is the lack of skill, not to say interest, in matters of power; life to peasants consists entirely of the workaday routine of farming the land, of harvesting the crops, and of occasionally praying for the protection of food and family.

Hence, it is in special circumstances that rebellious forces are comprised of peasants. Wolf claims, in the first place, that peasants become active in widespread rebellions only when they are led by outside agents such as military officers, political parties, and independent intellectuals:[53]

> Poor peasants and landless laborers, therefore, are unlikely to pursue the course of rebellion, *unless* they are able to rely on some external power to challenge the power which constrains them. Such external power is repre-

[52] Wolf, *Peasant Wars*, p. 295.

[53] On a similar theme, but in terms of the urban poor in the United States, see Michael Lipsky, "Protest as a Political Resource," *American Political Science Review,* 62 (December 1968), 1144-58.

sented in the Mexican case by the Constitutionalist army in Yucatan . . . by the collapse of the Russian Army in 1917 and the reflux of the peasant soldiery, weapons in hand, into the villages; by the creation of the Chinese Red Army as an instrument designed to break up the landlord power in the villages.[54]

In the second place, Wolf argues that only the middle and the land-free peasants are the likeliest candidates for rebellions because the former are most thoroughly caught up in the tensions of transition from a rural agrarian economy to an urban capitalist one and the latter are least subject to the power of the landlords and to the continuing attachment to the land.

Will peasants continue to play a vital part in the efforts to build nation-states in the future—either as the dominant troops or as the principal beneficiaries? Wolf suggests that the political efforts conducted in their name may prove to be limited. As societies become more complex, he observes, the consequences of peasant rebellions tend to become more narrow in scope and more reduced in intensity, owing perhaps to the more minor role of peasants in the economy and society. "[A] peasant rebellion which takes place in a complex society already caught up in commercialization and industrialization," he writes, "tends to be self-limiting, and, hence, anachronistic."[55]

THE ALTERNATIVE OUTCOMES
OF NATION BUILDING AND THEIR ORIGINS

There are important differences between the political forms of modern nation-states that range from parliamentary democracies to totalitarian regimes. If the general question asked by analysts concerns the origins and form of the typical modern nation-state, then the specific question is obviously, How is it that parliamentary democracy and totalitarian rule, as principal types of modern nation-states, have developed?

The analyst of these matters must be equipped with the knowledge and the skill to probe not only the common features of modern nation-states but also to examine with intelligence the detailed histories of individual nation-states. There are few scholars capable of this sort of task, and perhaps for this reason, there are few detailed and thoughtful comparative treatments of nation building. Despite this, it is instructive to present some of the available conclusions about the origins of different modern nation-states, however tentative they now are. At the very least they provide the directions that analysts take on these issues.

Possibly the most significant of current analyses into comparative nation building is that of Barrington Moore, Jr., a sociologist and historian. In a work widely regarded as a classic, *Social Origins of Dictatorship and Democracy: Lord and Peasant in the Making of the Modern World*, Moore arrives at a number of

[54] Wolf, *Peasant Wars,* pp. 290-91.
[55] Ibid., p. 294.

important conclusions about the wellsprings of different forms of nation-states in the modern world, particularly parliamentary democracy and fascist and communist varieties of totalitarian rule.[56] Detailed studies of England, France, the United States, India, Japan, Germany, Russia, and China that in some cases trace their social history as far back as the fourteenth century provide the empirical materials for Moore's analysis.

What are the special conditions that provided the groundwork for democracy in the twentieth century—for the political regimes in England, in France, in the United States, and in more preliminary fashion, in India? The first of these, Moore claims, is the emergence of a balance of power between the principal social groups in a society that reduces the possibilities of too powerful a royal authority or too strong a landed upper class.[57] The classic illustration for this conclusion comes from English history; the ascending social groups in the seventeenth century managed to make the king subordinate to parliament, and by the close of the nineteenth century, the manufacturing classes had overtaken the landed ones in both economic and political resources. French history illustrates a considerably different chain of events; the royal authority remained dominant far longer but was overthrown far more abruptly, leaving the balance among groups to be worked out through a long and difficult struggle in the nineteenth century.

A second major condition producing democracy in the twentieth century is the development of commercial agriculture by some social groups within a society.[58] This provides a way for promoting the growth of a class of capitalists whose power can eventually counteract that of urban manufacturing groups; it also gradually displaces the peasants from the land, which is an indispensable event in undercutting the seeds of peasant revolution as China and the Soviet Union show.

The third condition, the absence of a coalition between an equally powerful landed aristocracy and capitalist class, clearly suggests why democracy first arose in France but failed to do so in Germany until much later. In France, the Revolution of 1789 and its immediate aftermath dramatically reduced the power of the landed aristocracy and left the expanding bourgeois groups, both the financial and the manufacturing capitalists, to develop unhindered by a declining aristocracy's claims to a social and economic glory long past.[59] In Germany, the landed aristocracy, the Junkers, remained dominant well through the nineteenth century and succeeded in manipulating the destinies of both manufacturing classes and peasants alike.[60]

---

[56] Barrington Moore, Jr., *Social Origins of Dictatorship and Democracy: Lord and Peasant in the Making of the Modern World* (Boston: Beacon Press, 1966).

[57] Ibid., p. 430.

[58] Ibid.

[59] Alexis de Tocqueville's analysis of this matter still remains the most penetrating. See Alexis de Tocqueville, *The Old Regime and the French Revolution,* trans. Gilbert Stuart (Garden City, N.Y.: Doubleday Anchor, 1955).

[60] For other details on the political significance of Junkers, see, for instance, Reinhard Bendix, *Max Weber: An Intellectual Portrait* (Garden City, N.Y.: Doubleday Anchor, 1960), pp. 42-45 especially; and W. N. Medlicott, *Bismarck and Modern Germany* (New York: Harper & Row, Publishers, 1965).

The fourth stimulus for the development of a democratic regime in the modern world is the occurrence of a radical and abrupt break with the past. This condition, while insufficient for the emergence of a democracy, is necessary for it; that is, while such breaks do not invariably lead to democratic regimes, as the case of Russia indicates, a break with the past produces democracy when combined with all the previously noted conditions. In this light, incidentally, Moore is able to claim that the failure of a strong and viable democracy to materialize in India is due to the failure there of a radical break with the past.[61]

Within those nation-states that have experienced episodes of fascism in the twentieth century—Germany, Italy, and Japan—Moore finds a number of conditions that distinctly differ from those that lead to the enduring parliamentary democracies. Some of them represent just the opposite set of circumstances, in fact. In Germany and Japan, the landed upper classes remained a strong and vital force well through the nineteenth century and were never eclipsed by the industrial capitalists. Indeed, the landed elites in these societies were sufficiently adept to have manipulated the growth of industrialism; they delayed its rise at first and later exercised considerable political control over its beneficiaries, the industrial capitalists. In so doing, they prevented a balance of power, a condition that was so crucial to the flowering of demoracy in England and France. Also, in contrast to the experiences of both England and France, there remained in nineteenth-century Germany and Japan large clusters of peasants. The peasants were continuously subject to the demands of the landed upper classes whose authority could be traced to the introduction of feudalism.[62] Hence the peasants were to become a source, not of rebellion, but of support for the upper classes. When revolutionary forces later emerged in the twenieth century, they failed to build a large, dissident peasant base, as in China, but turned to transforming the society by reconstructing its higher echelons.

Still, these circumstances were not sufficient to encourage the rise of fascism, at least not in Moore's view. Though he indicates a large number of highly specific additional events—so many in fact to obscure the general conditions—both the early failure of parliamentary democracy and a strong state bureaucracy played equally prominent parts in the emergence of fascism. The failure of parliamentary democracy—in Germany, for example, the demise of the brief and fragile Weimar Republic—left a void that other social and political forces inevitably had to fill. Naturally, those that came to occupy the void represented the durable forces of the past, those of an upper class accustomed to rule without accommodating itself to ascending social groups, and a mass of peasants and laborers accustomed to an almost passive compliance with the commands from the higher ranks of society. In other words, the relations and the forces that became evident in the demise of parliamentary democracy quickly assumed the basic outlines of fascism. Equally crucial to the growth of fascism was the presence of a large and vigorous state bureaucracy. Taking Germany again as an illustration, this bureaucracy had origi-

---

[61] Moore, *Social Origins of Dictatorship and Democracy,* p. 431.
[62] Ibid., 228-29.

nally been formed during the reign of Frederick the Great of Prussia in the eighteenth century; under the iron hand of Bismarck it gained added strength while the German Parliament, the *Reichstag*, declined.[63] The collapse of the Weimar Republic left this bureaucracy intact and allowed Hitler and the National Socialist Party to use it, to duplicate it, and perhaps most importantly, to rely upon the Germans' customary obedience to its commands.

Last, what conditions promoted the growth of communism in the modern world? Like societies in which fascism appeared, but unlike those in which parliamentary democracy arose, the nation-states that would turn to communism entered the twentieth century still comprised of a large and significant force of peasants. Thus, such societies were compelled to deal with the peasants either through outright repression or through enlisting their aid in fundamental political change; the former route proved characteristic of fascism, the latter of communism. The reasons that lay behind the support of the peasants for the overthrow of the existing political order are informative of the preconditions of peasant revolutions and, subsequently, of the rise of communism.

In Russia and China, the landed upper classes failed to become involved in commercial agriculture. This meant, among other things, that they were only able to secure their own livelihood through an increasingly harsh oppression of the peasants and that, partly in consequence, they came to appear both to those below and to those above them as a parasitic and retrogressive class. While landlords in Germany continued into the twentieth century to secure the respect of the peasants and thus contributed to the growth of fascism, those in China and Russia succeeded only in attracting their anger and thus promoting a peasant revolution. At the same time, the peasant revolutions in China and Russia were aided by the retention from an earlier period of an active solidarity and cooperation among the peasants. Moore indicates some difficulty in ascertaining the singular importance of this condition, but despite the problems, he observes that in "a rebellious and revolutionary form of solidarity, institutional arrangements are such as to spread grievances through the peasant community and turn it into a solidarity group hostile to the overlord."[64]

Besides the failure of the landed aristocracy to embark successfully upon commercial agriculture and the success of the peasants in retaining their customary cooperative alliances, the survival of the great agrarian bureaucracy under royal authority also favored the emergence of peasant revolution and later of a communist form of totalitarianism. The power of the crown and of the bureaucracy enabled it to stifle the growth of industrialism and capitalism and thus prevented the emergence of rival centers of power. In addition, the royal authority acted to prevent the emergence of a bourgeois revolution, such as one that levelled the crown in France, and prevented whatever impetus might have been given both to capitalism and to parliamentary democracy. Finally, the presence of a vigorous royal authority, which through its favors and rewards was able to sustain the

---

[63] For further details, see Medlicott, *Bismarck and Modern Germany*.
[64] Moore, *Social Origins of Dictatorship and Democracy*, p. 475.

livelihood of all other principal classes, could intervene in the relationship between the lords and the peasants. Since the royal authority acted to tax the peasants and to secure surplus goods from them directly, no opportunity arose for any sort of strong bonds of affection and respect to grow between the landlords and the peasants.

The intellectual achievement of Moore is something close to remarkable. Not only did he manage to cover the social history of a single nation in close detail, but he also succeeded in making extensive comparisons among several nations, producing in the end a series of general statements about the conditions fostering one sort of government or another.[65] Still there are some serious drawbacks to his analysis; these are discussed as a means of showing the immense task that still lies ahead for analysts of nation building, not as a way of casting any doubt on Moore's notable accomplishment. First, Moore seems to freeze arbitrarily the political forms of different nation-states. He seeks to examine the emergence of fascism in Germany and Japan, yet those particular regimes remained in office only a short time. This comment thus raises a more general question that all such analysis poses, How can the political form of a nation-state be accurately characterized without making the analysis appear unduly arbitrary and the society unduly frozen? The fact is that any such analysis encounters this sort of problem and has to solve it. Moore's solution seems less satisfactory than one that attempts to capture the most enduring political form of a modern nation-state.

Second, Moore's analysis is cut entirely out of historical cloth. For instance, certain arrangements between peasants and lords may produce a peasant revolution that, in turn, can quickly turn into a communist reigme. What political forms might we expect in the future when lords and peasants no longer represent the principal social groups? Again, Moore's problem raises the more general problem that faces analysts of all social phenomena—the extent to which generalizations and predictions may be made to other settings and to the future. Moore, in contrast to other analysts, seems to remain so close to the actual historical forms and figures in which he works that any effort to go beyond his materials has little chance of success. For the same reason, his historical analysis fails to suggest more than a few interesting hypotheses that other observers might wish to explore in other places and times.

Third, Moore does not give much credence to the existence and the power of international ties and exchanges that exist among incipient nation-states. Essentially developments that produce parliamentary democracy in one country and fascism in another are entirely the creations of the internal circumstances of each; the network of trade relations and other such matters have only the smallest effect on the roots of political rule. India is the only exception to which Moore draws close attention. Of course, to take into account such networks of relations *in addition* to all the other issues to which one must attend represents close to an impossible task. Yet that is the task; as recent research and theory show, the hierarchy and

---

[65] An excellent compendium of reviews of Moore's analysis can be found in David C. Potter, *Lords, Peasants and Politics* (Sussex, England: The Open University Press), block 2, units 5-8, at unit 8.

substance of the relations among nations, even as far back as the sixteenth century, play a major part in determining the subsequent developments of all nation-states.[66]

Finally, Moore's analysis makes it appear as though political forms represent only the outcome of nation building, not actors in their own right. That is, fascism in Nazi Germany played a considerable part in the development of capitalism there during the period from 1933 to 1945; yet Moore's analysis makes it seem as though fascism was merely the product of a long chain of events, economic and otherwise, prior to 1933. This criticism also brings to light the fact that the analyst must somehow choose whether the form of the modern nation-state is to be represented as cause or consequence, if only to make his or her task more manageable. Generally speaking, it seems to make sense to regard it as either, depending on the nature of the question addressed by the analyst. Even more generally, it makes sense, as noted earlier in this chapter, to see the political form of the modern nation-state as being part of a broader set of developments whose character might be determined by a great master tendency set off early in history.[67]

SUCCESS AND FAILURE IN NATION BUILDING

One of the major current issues in the study of nation building is why some societies achieve great success in creating a modern nation-state whereas others accomplish next to nothing. The concern really comes down to two distinct and related matters: one, how to define the features of success, and two, how to assess the origins of success. The definition of successful nation building presents some very difficult problems. Some observers, for instance, prefer the notion of political order, or stability, as the criterion of success and, thus, describe the successful nation-state as one in which there is no instability or violence.[68] Other observers prefer the notion of change and upheaval as the criterion of success, particularly where current governments appear to be extremely oppressive of citizens' civil and political freedoms.[69] Looking at nation building from a slightly different angle, still other observers prefer to think of success as anything that resembles the demo-

[66]Bodenheimer, "Dependency and Imperialism." Also see the following discussion of Immanuel Wallerstein and André Gunder Frank.

[67]Along these lines, a work by Immanuel Wallerstein remedies some of the problems encountered in Moore's analysis; eventually to comprise four volumes, this project promises to provide the most thorough and innovative treatment of the issues dealt with in this section. Wallerstein is discussed at length later. See Immanuel Wallerstein, *The Modern World-System: Capitalist Agriculture and the Origins of the European World Economy in the Sixteenth Century* (New York: Academic Press, 1974).

[68]Huntington, *Political Order in Changing Societies.*

[69]Mark Kesselman, "Order or Movement? The Literature of Political Development as Ideology." This is a review article of Huntington's *Political Order in Changing Societies* and of *Crises and Sequences in Political Development* by Leonard Binder, et al.

cratic regimes of Western Europe or the United States.[70] They, too, have their critics who believe that successful nation building requires the erection of a communist regime.[71] These and many other issues plague the conceptual definition and empirical identification of success in nation building.[72]

For our purposes, success in nation building is defined in terms used at the outset of this chapter—the features of the modern nation-state summarized by Black. In particular, a successful outcome of nation building is a nation-state in which policy making has become consolidated and routine, there is some regular means of replenishing political leadership, the interests of the citizens regularly receive recognition from political leaders, and there exists a complex and active machinery of the state. Failure, thus, means the absence of at least one of these conditions; more often, it seems, failure entails the absence of two or more of these conditions.

What is it that accounts for the success of some societies in achieving the qualities of the modern nation-state as compared with the failure of others? The immediate answer might have something to do with time; some societies, particularly those of Africa, simply have not had the benefit of several centuries during which they could erect a viable nation-state. However, as current theories and evidence inform us, the principal obstacle to success lies not in the realm of time but in a system of economic interdependence among advanced and developing nation-states. It is this system that accounts for the great political accomplishments of some societies and the tragic failures of others.

The conception of interdependence among societies actually comes in a variety of shapes and sizes, but all of them touch on practical and theoretical issues first dealt with by Marx and later embellished by Weber. To understand this general point of view, its basic premises are sketched here.[73] The initial premise is that a world-system exists that had its beginnings in the transformation of agriculture from that for use to that for profit in sixteenth century Europe. This world-system is one in which some countries, the core states, are dominant over others, the peripheral and semiperipheral territories; the dominant ones receive a greater share of material and symbolic tribute in the world mainly because they con-

[70] Lucian W. Pye, "The Concept of Political Development," in *Political Development and Social Change,* Finkle and Gable. Pye provides a nice analysis of the concept of political development, including the various Western democratic connotations it sometimes has. One observer among many who is clearly guilty of this sort of conception is Seymour Martin Lipset. See his *Political Man: The Social Bases of Politics* (Garden City, N.Y.: Doubleday Anchor, 1963).

[71] For instance, see James D. Cockcroft, André Gunder Frank, and Dale L. Johnson, eds., *Dependence and Underdevelopment: Latin America's Political Economy* (Garden City, N.Y.: Doubleday Anchor, 1972).

[72] For recent analyses that attempt to shed some light on these matters, see Alejandro Portes, "Modernity and Development: A Critique," *Studies in Comparative International Development,* 9 (Spring 1974), 247-79; and Alejandro Portes, "On the Sociology of National Development: Theories and Issues."

[73] The sketch here relies primarily on the interesting book by Immanuel Wallerstein, *The Modern World-System: Capitalist Agriculture and the Origins of the European World-Economy in the Sixteenth Century,* chapter 7 especially. See footnote 67.

tribute more than others to the survival and expansion of the system. It is a system whose foundations lie in a world-economy that had its origins in capitalist agriculture but that over time has changed in the forms of technology it employs as well as the products it creates. Nation-states, in this scheme, represent a narrower social expanse than the classes that develop from the economic mode of production; that is, the situations and interests of the classes spill over the boundaries of those entities conventionally regarded as nation-states, such as England, France, Belgium, and Italy. Those people who sit in positions of control of state machinery—the kings, the queens, the ministers—still represent major actors in the world-system, but over the long haul they are subordinate to the capitalist class that sits in positions of control in the world-economy.

As in any such system, there exists in the modern world-system a vast network of ties that link parts to one another and on whose continued survival the survival of the system itself depends. The network of ties is evident in specific forms of economic trade, political relations, and social exchanges that flow from one country to another. Moreover, there exists in the world-system a social division of labor in which those individuals in the labor force of a single country and those in the labor forces of other countries may perform different functions; for instance, the labor force in one country might engage principally in the production of raw materials, such as minerals, whereas labor in another might engage mainly in the manufacture of final products, such as clothing. The capitalist class resides within those countries in which the principal control of the productive enterprise is located and garners for themselves and for their nation-states the major forms and amounts of wealth.

This world-system is not a creature that remains dormant, but one that has over the past five hundred years grown ever larger. The world-economy, which represents the heart of the system, is responsible ultimately for the expansion of the world-system; as technology expands and becomes more sophisticated, for instance, the boundaries and the content of the economy incorporate more and more territories into the system as well as more and more individuals within distinct countries. Manufacture for profit represents the force that drives the economy to expand. As the system expands, its constitutent units may change in the degree of their importance to the system and hence in the position they occupy in the world-system of stratification. For example, individual countries can change in their position of dominance from one century to another, representing a core state at one time and a peripheral territory at another. (To understand the conception of world-system better, the reader might wish to review the discussions of social theorists in chapters 2 through 4. The discussion of Talcott Parsons might prove particularly helpful.)

From the sixteenth through the twentieth centuries, those countries that have represented the dominant positions (core states) in the world-system have been those of Northwest Europe, particularly England and France, where capitalist agriculture first appeared. Those countries and territories that occupied the subordinate niches lay elsewhere, specifically in the Americas, in Africa, and in Asia.

Over the five centuries, positions of dominance shifted, particularly within great regions, but the overall structure of dominance, the hierarchy of positions within the world division of labor, retained its original form, which was first established in the sixteenth century.

In light of this grand conception, it should be easy for the reader to answer the question about the origins of successful nation building in the twentieth century. Why have some societies been less successful in establishing the accouterments of modern nation-states than others? They have occupied subordinate positions in the modern world-system or, more precisely, the modern world-economy. Whereas some nation-states, mainly those in Northwestern Europe, long ago established positions of dominance as core states in this system, others—now regarded as "developing" nations—at the very same time became junior members of this system, and so they remain to this very day.

What are the network and hierarchy of relations that relegate some countries to the top position and others to mere followers? Concrete facts come to us from those scholars who have articulated this grand conception in whole or in part. At the turn of this century, for instance, J. A. Hobson published *Imperialism* in which he tried to show how the nation-states of Western Europe, particularly England, had established economic dominance over those elsewhere in the world, particularly in Asia and Africa.[74] Capitalism in Europe had worked through the auspices of the state machinery—the government—to control territories that were essential to its own success. Moreover, an important distinction existed between colonialism and imperialism:

> This recent imperial expansion stands entirely distinct from the colonization of sparsely peopled lands in temperate zones, where white colonists carry with them the modes of government, the industrial and other arts of civilization of the mother country. The "occupation" of these new territories was comprised in the presence of a small minority of white men, officials, traders, and industrial organisers, exercising political and economic sway over great hordes of population regarded as inferior and as incapable of exercising any considerable rights of self-government, in politics or industry.[75]

The imperialism of the Western European countries cast a wide net over the entire world and embraced lands of people that came to serve merely as the resources and as the labor force of the great capitalist machine. Most significant, at least from the perspective here, Hobson went into great historical detail to show that the domination of the imperialist countries wreaked havoc on the indigenous political structures of the subordinate territories and crippled them to such an extent as to make success at nation building, in the terms previously outlined, an impossibility for years to come.[76]

---

[74] J. A. Hobson, *Imperialism* (Ann Arbor, Mich.: University of Michigan Press, 1965).

[75] Ibid., p. 27.

[76] Ibid., part II, chapter 1. Incidentally, Lenin, in one of his most famous works, *Imperialism: The Highest Stage of Capitalism,* was greatly influenced by Hobson's analysis. For

Because colonialism insists on the political character of subordination and imperialism on its economic tone, the end to colonialism in the 1950s and 1960s did not free the former colonies to become independent, not at least in this scheme of things. The network of interdependence among core states and peripheries continued to exist and to undermine the capacity of former colonies to achieve actual economic and political self-sufficiency. Harry Magdoff provides recent facts and analysis to support this aspect of the conception of a world-economy and world-system; his discussion echoes many of the themes first sounded by Hobson.[77] Magdoff claims that a new form of imperialism arose with the end of World War II in which the United States came to replace England as the major figure of economic and political strength, competition among capitalists quickened in pace, and corporations expanded both their size and the territorial scope of their operations.[78] Corporations in the United States as well as financial institutions enlarged the extent of their investments abroad and ultimately changed the position of the United States and England in the world-economy (see table 11-3). Magdoff maintains, moreover, that the various programs of the United States government assist in securing the economic dominance of North America corporations abroad by establishing, among other things, a deficit in the balance of payments for foreign countries, particularly former colonies, and providing the United States with unhampered access to raw materials of the subordinate countries. Like Hobson's analysis of England, Magdoff's analysis insists that the effort of the United States

Table 11–3   Foreign investments of leading capital exporting countries

	1914	1930	1960
		—Percent of Total—	
United Kingdom	50.3	43.8	24.5
France	22.2	8.4	4.7[a]
Germany	17.3	2.6	1.1
Netherlands	3.1	5.5	4.2[a]
Sweden	0.3	1.3	0.9[a]
United States	6.3	35.3	59.1
Canada	0.5	3.1	5.5
Total	100	100	100

Source: Adapted from Harry Magdoff, *The Age of Imperialism: The Economics of U.S. Foreign Policy* (New York: Modern Reader Paperbacks, 1969).

[a] The data for 1960 are estimates made solely to simplify the presentation on the relative change of the U.S. position.

---

a discussion of these connections, together with an exhaustive exposition of a wide variety of different views of imperialism, see Michael Barrat Brown, *The Economics of Imperialism* (Middlesex, England: Penguin Books, Ltd., 1974), chapter 3. Also see our discussion of Lenin in chapter 2.

[77] Harry Magdoff, *The Age of Imperialism: The Economics of U.S. Foreign Policy* (New York: Modern Reader Paperbacks, 1969).

[78] Ibid., pp. 15-26; 34-40.

to secure economic dominance over other nations has it major political repercussions; the effort severely, if not entirely, reduces the likelihood that the subordinate nation can develop a viable state apparatus of the sort outlined earlier.

The conception of a world-economy has been used to special advantage to explain why particular countries and settings may fail in the creation of a viable nation-state. One such setting is Latin America. André Gunder Frank, for example, has used a conception much like the one previously presented to explain the current economic and political dependence of Latin American countries on the United States.[79] It is Frank's belief that a system of dependence originated in the sixteenth century and that this system has been gradually modified, largely to meet the changing economic needs and interests of the dominant countries. Those countries in Latin America that display economic underdevelopment as well as atrophied polities, Frank maintains, owe their failures to the dominant nation-states. To provide some confirmation for his point of view, Frank shows that when the economic ties between the dominant and the subordinate nation-states weaken, as during the depression of the 1930s, then the subordinate nations become considerably more successful in cultivating indigenous forms of economic production. Other support for his claims lies in evidence that reveals that even during periods when the United States proclaimed its effort to provide great financial aid to Latin America, as in the 1960s, it succeeded in extracting considerably more capital out of Latin America than it invested in it (see table 11-4).[80]

There are other perspectives on the success and failure of nation building in the modern world that grew out of careful observations of the nation-building efforts of Asian and African countries in the 1950s and 1960s.[81] None of these

Table 11–4

	(Billions of Dollars)			
	Europe	Canada	Latin America	All other Areas
Flow of direct investments from U.S.	$8.1	$6.8	$3.8	$5.2
Income on this capital transferred to U.S.	5.5	5.9	11.3	14.3
Net	+$2.6	+$ .9	-$ 7.5	-$ 9.1

Source: Adapted from Harry Magdoff, *The Age of Imperialism: The Economics of U.S. Foreign Policy* (New York: Modern Reader Paperbacks, 1969).

[79] André Gunder Frank, *Capitalism and Underdevelopment in Latin America,* rev. ed. (New York: Monthly Review Press, 1969). For a brief review of this analysis, also see André Gunder Frank, "The Development of Underdevelopment," in *Dependence and Underdevelopment,* Cockcroft et al., pp. 1-17.

[80] For a somewhat parallel treatment of the same themes, see Bodenheimer, "Dependency and Imperialism."

[81] See, for instance, Gabriel A. Almond and G. Bingham Powell, Jr., *Comparative Politics: A Developmental Approach* (Boston: Little, Brown & Company, 1966); and David E. Apter, *The Politics of Modernization* (Chicago: University of Chicago Press, 1965).

views promise as much for the explanation of successful nation building as the general conception of a world-system.[82] This conception is not without its drawbacks, however; the major one is that it now represents an idea in search of confirmation. Immanuel Wallerstein, who has outlined this conception with the greatest intellectual vigor and imagination, expects to complete an additional three volumes that may prove to be an epic history of the modern world-system. Upon the completion of his project and related ones by other scholars, our knowledge of the circumstances that have contributed to success and failure in nation building in the modern world may be far more precise.[83]

CONCLUSION: PROSPECTS FOR NATION BUILDING AND ITS ANALYSIS

Nation building represents a continuing adventure that is destined to remain unfinished. The older nation-states possess certain advantages over the newer ones, although the extent of these advantages depends on whether one accepts the idea of a great capitalist world-economy or some other notion. Irrespective of this, however, old and new nation-states face a number of uncertainties in the years immediately ahead that will put the enterprise of the nation-state through its most severe tests. Two of these are most important. One is the continuing effort of leaders of nation-states to submerge the vigor of primordial ties beneath a broad commitment among all social groups to the nation-state. Until fairly recently, observers of these matters seemed to think that primordial ties were only a problem for the newer nations, particularly those of Africa. Racial and religious conflicts in the United States, in Northern Ireland, and even in the Soviet Union in recent times have revealed that both old and new nations face a formidable foe in the strength of these loyalties among their citizens. Nation building, indeed, may prove to involve a constant interplay between national and primordial identities, and the strength and purpose of the nation-state may depend on the balance that can be achieved between the two sets of allegiances.

The second uncertainty involves the tensions and conflicts between the nation-state as an entity and the multinational, or transnational, corporations.[84]

[82] For criticisms of these views, see: Bodenheimer, "Dependency and Imperialism," pp. 328-30, 340-42; André Gunder Frank, "Sociology of Development and Underdevelopment of Sociology," in *Dependence and Underdevelopment*, Cockcroft et al., pp. 321-97; José F. Ocampo and Dale L. Johnson, "The Concept of Political Development," in *Dependence and Underdevelopment*, Cockcroft et al., pp. 399-424. For an excellent compendium of recent essays that suggest the grounds for criticizing earlier views, see Julio Cotler and Richard R. Fagen, eds., *Latin America and the United States: The Changing Political Realities* (Stanford, Calif.: Stanford University Press, 1974), particularly essays by Ianni, Kaplan, and Martins.

[83] Although very recent, Wallerstein's analysis already has begun to inspire the sort of research necessary to support and to extend it. See Richard Rubinson, "The World-Economy and the Distribution of Income Within States: A Cross-National Study," *American Sociological Review*, 41 (August 1976), 638-59.

[84] An excellent analysis of these issues is found in Brown, *The Economics of Imperialism*, chapters 9-11, and 13.

The growth of these corporations over the past two decades has been phenomenal; corporations like Exxon, Mobil, and other great oil companies seemed for a time to be on the verge of rivaling in the scope and strength of their operations the great empires of the past. Decisions by leaders of Arab nations in the mid-1970s clearly had the effect of warning the multinational corporations that some nation-states would not permit themselves to be subdued quite so easily. Still, it appears that this conflict—one that produced a world-wide recession dramatically affecting nations like England—may represent only the first in a series of skirmishes that will occur over the next couple of decades. It is likely that the survival of the nation-state, the most distinctive modern political enterprise, will depend on the outcome of this conflict.

Just as there are pitfalls ahead for the development of nation-states, there are also pitfalls for the analysis of this development. Historians will ultimately be better able to sort out these matters, but even from this proximate point in time, we can see that several of the analytical schemes that were developed in the 1950s and 1960s to examine nation building have proven inadequate to the task. The discussion in this chapter touched only briefly, if at all, on a few of these schemes—those of Almond and Powell, for instance—preferring the more vivid historical treatment of Moore as well as the more suggestive theoretical discussion of Wallerstein.[85] Briefly, these earlier schemes often proved neither sufficiently attentive to historical events nor sufficiently sensitive to the necessary requirements of scientific theories.[86]

In fact, if the reader takes the time and patience to search through many of these materials, he or she will discover that Marx, Weber, and Parsons still remain in many ways better analysts and collectors of rare facts than their successors in modern social science. At the same time, with the appearance of works like those of Moore and Wallerstein, the prospects are good that in the next few years both the construction of fruitful theories and the identification of important facts will begin to keep abreast of nation building itself.

[85] Almond and Powell, *Comparative Politics: A Developmental Approach.*

[86] A thoughtful treatment of the defects of some earlier schemes is contained in Robert T. Hold and John E. Turner, "Crises and Sequences in Collective Theory Development," *American Political Science Review,* 69 (September 1975), 979-94.

CHAPTER TWELVE
Social and
Political Movements

That which causes conditions leading to change is chiefly and generally what we have just been speaking of—inequality. For those who are bent on equality start a revolution if they believe that they, having less, are yet the equals of those who have more. And so too do those who aim at inequality and superiority, if they think that they, being unequal, are not getting more, but equal or less. The lesser rebel in order to be equal, the equal in order to be greater.

ARISTOTLE, *The Politics*

Scholars now commonly agree that social and political movements are as endemic to social life as any other group or institution; movements appear to have existed throughout history, competing in their own special arenas for their own special goals. Indeed, from one perspective, the arena of politics often looks as if it consists mainly of the established political institutions of a society—the status quo—and those small, sometimes informal groups that are attempting to wrest power from the establishment and to refashion the nature of the rules that govern the arena of politics. If one looks back over mankind's past, as Pitirim Sorokin did, time and again one finds evidence of the ubiquity of movements that sometimes produce the overthrow of particular leaders or regimes, sometimes take the form of organized series of strikes against certain work conditions, and sometimes take the form of minor attempts to change a piece of legislation or a law viewed as unjust and disagreeable by a segment of a society's population.[1]

The historical record of the twentieth century reveals the degree to which movements have virtually a natural place in the social order and body politic. The turn of the century saw the Progressive Era in the United States and a wide variety of different movements; in Great Britain, it witnessed the crystallization of the labor movement, and soon thereafter a viable Labour Party. In the second decade of this century, one of the more profound movements on record occurred, the Russian Revolution; the Bolsheviks seized power soon after the revolution of February 1917 and subsequently provided a remarkable and enduring transformation of the whole of Russia. A variety of movements erupted in the 1920s in the United States. There were the diffuse movements that emerged in response to the "Red Scare," resulting in the sacrifice of such innocent victims as Sacco and Vanzetti. There was also the resurgence of the Ku Klux Klan's efforts to eliminate the imagined threats of Negroes in the North and South. Hitler and the National Socialist Party of Germany effectively dominated the history of political movements for more than fifteen years; the Nazi Party, and its atrocities and massacres, became the theoretical model for many subsequent discussions of social and political movements, most in an effort to provide ways to avoid such events in the future.[2]

The late 1940s and early 1950s in the United States saw the development of left- and right-wing movements. The Progressive Party, which ran Henry Wallace as its candidate for president in 1948, was supported in subtle ways by members of some of the traditional leftist groups in America, such as the Communists and the Socialists; and the Dixiecrat bolt from the Democratic Party in 1948 was a response to the civil rights positions of many of their fellows and resulted in a third party with its own candidate for president, Strom Thurmond. Senator Joseph McCarthy, and the diffuse sentiments generated by him, bridged the period of the late 1940s and early 1950s; some initial impetus was given by the hearings of the House Un-American Activities Committee and such counsels as Richard Nixon. McCarthyism was more a mood than an effective social or political movement, but a mood that carried a good deal of weight and appeared to effectively silence whatever political dissent and criticism may have lurked beneath the surface of the American political fabric at that time. The civil rights effort on behalf of black Americans arose shortly after the Supreme Court decision of 1954 that banned segregation of public school facilities; events that followed included the Montgomery Bus Boycott in 1956 and the violence in Little Rock in 1957 upon the integration of schools there.

Still, it was not until the 1960s that in the United States, and even worldwide, one could observe social and political movements on a massive and rich scale

---

[1] Pitirim Sorokin, *Social and Cultural Dynamics, Volume III: Fluctuations of Social Relationships, War and Revolutions* (New York: American Book Company, 1973).

[2] See, for example, Hannah Arendt, *The Origins of Totalitarianism,* (Cleveland, Ohio: World Publishing Company, 1958); and Franz Neumann, *Behemoth: The Structure and Practice of National Socialism* (New York: Oxford University Press, 1942).

of intensity. In the United States, the black civil rights movement came together with a greater intensity and direction of effort than in the preceding decade, but it also gave rise to a greater number of branches than had previously existed—new groups emerged, such as the Student Non-Violent Coordinating Committee (SNCC), the Southern Christian Leadership Conference (SCLC), and the Black Panther Party of Mississippi and California. Old civil rights organizations were rejuvenated, and the membership of the National Association for the Advancement of Colored People (NAACP) and of the Congress of Racial Equality (CORE) increased over their numbers in the 1950s. The trend of the times was in the liberal or radical direction; this was revealed not only by the emergence of the civil rights groups, but also by the groups working to improve the conditions of students and youth here and abroad. For example, in 1962 a small group of students met in Port Huron, Michigan, and founded the Students for a Democratic Society (SDS), which later played a major part in shaping and guiding the political history of youth during the 1960s. Much of the political turmoil of the times was found not simply in the broad trends, such as civil rights, or in the specific organizational phenomena, such as the SDS, but in the eruptions of dissatisfaction evident among the people—in the riots in Watts in 1965, in the riot in Detroit in 1967, and in other riots that were less massive and bloody. Contrary to outward appearances, there is good reason to believe that many of these riots were not spontaneous but rather planned and organized in large measure by members of different political groups within the communities in which they took place. Even when the riots were not specifically planned or organized, there are analysts who believe that the riots represented deliberate attempts to gain new privileges by participants and supporters.[3]

This chapter discusses the character and consequences of movements that have occurred at various points in recent history, particularly American history. Judging from the diversity of events labeled as movements, the topic is vast and to a great extent virtually without boundaries. There are two consequences of this ambiguous nature of social and political movements that figure into the presentation in this chapter. One is to try to isolate the special characteristics of those phenomena called movements. Many analysts of movements fail to give this problem sufficient attention and thus produce discussions that must necessarily be doomed to fail since the analysts seem generally ignorant of the nature of the beast (or beauty?) they are attempting to portray. The other is to provide several different kinds of paradigms that are more or less useful to the analysis of movements. The whole topic of social and political movements is now so diffuse and so challenging that one finds competing theories being used to describe the events that have happened, or are taking place—there is, for example, a neo-Marxist paradigm on the other hand, an elitist on the other, and a wide variety of other perspectives.

One other remark about the nature of the presentation is important; the discussion is not confined to political movements, because the distinction between political and social is so hard to define. The most powerful and profound of the

---

[3] Joe Feagin and Harlan Hahn, *Ghetto Revolts* (New York: Macmillan Co., 1973).

movements during the twentieth century—the revolutions in Russia and in China, for instance—could hardly be called just political revolutions, for they involved vast transformations of the entire structure of their societies from the state institutions to those of kinship. To maintain some degree of clarity in the focus of the presentation, however, religious movements are not discussed. They are a form of movement that normally excludes contact with politics in any way; they are concerned more with changing the minds of members than the structure of society and could hardly be said to be interested in power, which is the distinguishing feature of most social and political movements. Some of these matters come into sharper focus in the following discussion.

THE NATURE OF MOVEMENTS

It is difficult to grasp clearly the nature of social and political movements. Does one mean a vast revolution, like the French Revolution of 1789? Should the discussion of movements be simply confined to events and episodes on the scale of such revolutions? Or does one mean something quite different, such as the John Birch Society in the United States or the student left throughout the world? Clearly, all of these phenomena are different, and yet they are also classified by many analysts as movements. Thus, they must hold something in common that ties them together in a way that analysis of one sheds some light on the character of the others.

In identifying the nature of social and political movements, we must begin from our earlier premise that social and political movements are omnipresent phenomena and as natural a part of most social settings as any other element or institution. The necessary and sufficient definition of social and political movements consists of three elements found in everyday social life: (1) organization, or structure; (2) beliefs or ideals; and (3) actions, or behaviors, in which people engage. It is the particular shape of each of these elements that gives social and political movements their own particular cast.

Perhaps the most essential feature of any successful social or political movement is some form of organization; in the absence of some degree of organization, movements fail to capture advantages from established groups in the social and political arenas. In general, organization means that a group exists with more or less well-defined boundaries that distinguish between members and nonmembers; with a hierarchy of positions, such that some roles are subordinate to other roles; and with means for establishing the goals for which both members and leaders work. Organization, in this sense, provides a means for effecting the coordination *as well as control of* efforts on the part of members of the movement; it is the device that enables a movement to operate smoothly and to generate, if and when it is required, a broader base of support in the public. For example, in the Russian Revolution of October 1917, the key organization was the Bolshevik Party; in the student left activities in the United States during the 1960s, the key organization was the SDS.

Sometimes movements consist of more than one organization, and those several organizations may express different political tendencies as well as compete for the same small share of benefits and audience support in a society. Again, in the case of the Russian Revolution of 1917, there were a number of different groups—the Social Democrats, the Mensheviks, and the Bolsheviks. In the student left in the United States, there initially existed the SDS, but this later split into different factions—the most radical, the Weathermen, also became the most famous.

It is the style of organization, for lack of a better term, above and beyond the fact of organization that often provides a distinctive cast to social and political movements. The style of organization must frequently be covert and secretive due to the challenges that the movement poses to established organizations. If the organization becomes less covert, it faces the danger of eradication or infiltration and subversion of its aims. If a movement organization is public, such as the NAACP, then it means that the organization does not pose recognizable threats to the existing institutions and that its aims fall within the existing fabric of the social and political orders. In addition, the style of movement organizations sometimes assumes the form of a small, militant band—the prototypes of this kind of organization are the Bolsheviks in Russia and later the Communist Party in different nations of the world. Partly because of the success of both the Russian and Chinese movements, it is believed that organizations that hope to gain substantial advantages for themselves must be small and flexible; otherwise they face the dangers of bureaucratization and paralysis in the pursuit of their aims.

Although organization does not represent a distinctive feature of many social and political movements, the second element comprising the definition of movements, the beliefs of movement adherents, does represent a unique characteristic. Such beliefs always propose some form of change in the established social and political institutions. These beliefs also generally attack the legitimacy of prevailing institutions and challenge them on any of a variety of grounds. Furthermore, such beliefs may contain some plans for redressing the grievances of the particular group on behalf of which the movement has been undertaken that range from broad utopian visions to specific legal strategies. One illustration is the Republican Party that, like nearly all political parties in the modern world, began as a movement; it originally focused exclusively on the issue of slavery and fought for the prohibition of slavery in the United States. It was largely supported by moral principles—slavery, its leaders claimed, was morally indefensible—and it advanced legal strategies designed to outlaw slavery. Another illustraton is SNCC; it began with an effort to attack the legitimacy of segregation in the United States and to encourage in its place equal rights and opportunities for blacks and whites. In the early stages of this movement organization, this specifically meant efforts to bring about equal opportunities for blacks to dine in public restaurants, to use public swimming pools, and to attend public schools. Religious principles provided the foundations upon which these beliefs were built and also led to the development of a particular strategy for action, nonviolent resistance, employed in the first few years of the students' efforts.

Sometimes analysts include as movements those groups whose beliefs call for resistance to change rather than sponsorship of it. However, such groups are not movements but are countermovements that arise in reaction to positive efforts to promote change in a society. Social scientists sometimes refer to them as counter-revolutions or counterreforms. For example, in the late 1950s and early 1960s groups that went under the name of White Citizens' Councils arose in some communities in the South. These groups were intent on preventing blacks from achieving changes such as integration in public schools. Some social scientists have identified these groups as movement organizations; however, they are countermovements because they do not call for changes in the established order but for the prevention of such changes.[4]

The third element of definition of movements is the actions that comprise them. Movements are typically characterized by actions ranging from nonviolent passive resistance to terrorism that distinguish them from other groups in a society. Moreover, the most successful of movements employ a plan of action, or a strategy, that provides the specific designs to be employed to achieve their goals. On occasion, the strategy is dictated by the abstract, guiding principles in which the members believe; this was the case for the SNCC, for the movement that supported Mahatma Ghandi in India, and at the other extreme, for the elements of the Narodniki in nineteenth-century Russia who advocated violence for the sake of violence. However, the strategy is usually developed independently of the general beliefs associated with the movement; the broad, utopian ends toward which a movement is working become disassociated from the means employed to achieve those ends. Again, the prototype for the evolution of this disassociation with emphasis on the means used to secure power occurred in the case of the Bolsheviks in Russia under the leadership of Lenin and Trotsky. Indeed, in the years immediately following the October Revolution of 1917, Trotsky engaged in massacres against the dissidents and was severely criticized for these actions by those who nonetheless agreed with him on the overall aims of the Bolsheviks.[5]

Like the occasional separate development of beliefs and actions, the actions of a movement may arise in the absence of any specific organization to guide them. For instance, a certain number of actions associated with the recent women's liberation movement in the United States arose almost spontaneously and without the benefit of an organization to guide them. Instead, through personal associations built simply upon friendships, some women and men came together and developed various plans for encouraging greater equality for women in the United States.[6] Nevertheless, the effectiveness of the organization of a movement readily manifests itself in the movement's strategy. Although generalizations are difficult on the topic of social and political movements because sound evidence is often lacking, it seems

[4] See Ralph Turner and Lewis Killian, *Collective Behavior* (Englewood Cliffs, N.J.: Prentice-Hall, Inc., 1972), pp. 317-19.

[5] Irving Howe, ed., *The Basic Writings of Trotsky* (New York: Random House, 1963).

[6] Jo Freeman, "The Origins of the Women's Liberation Movement," *American Journal of Sociology*, 78 (January 1972), 792-811.

true that movements that are better organized—or that possess sounder individual organizations—are more apt to have better plans for action. It also seems to hold true that more flexible plans for action are likely to produce surer results and to achieve greater success for movements. For instance, the Communists in China only achieved success with their efforts to secure power after fundamentally altering their plans for action but keeping their overall goals for the new society basically intact. In the first period of their efforts, between 1927 and 1934, they attempted to create entirely new institutions, such as land reforms; these efforts proved so unsuccessful that they resulted in greater strength for their opponents. In the second period of their efforts, from 1934 to 1945, however, they revamped their plans and worked through organizations that already existed as part of the Chinese social structure; in general, this strategy seems to pay dividends to movements.[7] The new strategy produced far greater success and resulted in the Communists' takeover in 1949. Commenting on this experience, David Cameron notes that "the Chinese experience suggests ... that the success or failure of [a political movement's capacity to mobilize support] depends to a large extent on the [movement's] tactics."[8]

To repeat, there are three elements that define a political or social movement: organization(s), beliefs, and actions, including the strategies designed to effect change through actions. Any particular movement is likely to emphasize one of these elements at the expense of the others; thus, the Weatherman faction of the SDS appeared to emphasize certain terrorist actions at the expense of formulating doctrines, whereas the John Birch Society appears to stress the formulation of a doctrine of beliefs over engagement in specific actions. Moreover, a glance at the successes and failures in the recent history of movements clearly recommends the view that success comes more often to those movements that have better organizations and, in consequence, better plans for action. The key to the *successful* movement is the effectiveness of its organization; beliefs play a secondary role. Successful movements such as the Nazi Party in Germany and the Communists in both China and Russia seem to bear out this observation. The recent analysis of William Gamson provides more refined and systematic evidence for it.[9]

It is important to recognize that scholars of movements have tended to pay more attention in recent years to the various elements of actions, particularly to characteristics of participants in actions, than they have either to the dimensions of organization or beliefs. Many of the empirical studies done of political and social movements during the 1960s, for instance, drew conclusions based largely on comparisons of participants and nonparticipants in the activities of movements. Obviously this is a legitimate strategy; but operating apart from examinations of both

[7]Kenneth L. Wilson and Anthony M. Orum, "The Mobilization of Individuals for Political Movements," *Journal of Political and Military Sociology,* 4 (Fall 1976), 187-202.

[8]David R. Cameron, "Toward a Theory of Political Mobilization," *Journal of Politics,* 36 (1974), 150.

[9]William A. Gamson, *The Strategy of Social Protest* (Homewood, Ill.: The Dorsey Press, 1975).

the organizational structures and the beliefs associated with movements, especially the former, it can lead to a very one-sided and distorted perspective about movements. Advances in knowledge in this area will only occur as efforts are made to probe the substance of movement organization, especially the manner in which the organization influences the strategies or actions designed to achieve specific ends.

Movements and Other Phenomena

Two other phenomena with which movements are often confused are political parties and movement organizations. Movements are not political parties, although they may give rise to parties. For instance, prior to its assumption of the reigns of power in Germany in 1933, the Nazi Party was more than just another political party contending for political office. It undertook, among other things, to indoctrinate large numbers of people, especially children, to its way of thought; it engaged in large, mass rallies that were designed to involve people in an intense cause; and in particular, it developed and disseminated a rather systematic set of beliefs that identified a core group of beneficiaries, *das Deutsche Volk*, and a core group of antagonists, *die Juden*, and outlined some fundamental ways for returning the German state to its past days of glory. Many other movements also exhibit a parallel link between the larger movement and a political party, among them the Progressive and the Populist movements in the United States. Movements and movement organizations, moreover, are also not identical; movements consist of organizations, but they can also embrace a cluster of adherents who do not belong specifically to their organizations. For example, the student left in the United States undoubtedly included many more adherents than those students registered or actively involved in such organizations as the SDS. The same holds true for the black civil rights effort in the United States during the 1950s and 1960s, and many other movements. For some purposes, such fellow-travelers of movements are most helpful, as in assembling financial contributions or mobilizing people for mass demonstrations; nonetheless, the movement organizations, their leaders and their prime supporters, prove to be the most significant element in the makeup and ultimate successes of the movement.

THE CONDITIONS FOSTERING
THE RISE OF MOVEMENTS

The matter to which most movement analysts have given their attention and thought is the origins of movements. Those figures who provide political sociology with its intellectual foundations and core issues—Marx and Weber especially—were vitally concerned with this topic. Marx provided some of the most explicit and stimulating of insights; these give rise to special concern among contemporary analysts with the economic forces likely to produce social and political movements.

Weber highlighted the character and development of status groups as well as variation in types of authority in modern societies, these lead to frames of reference that have as their special focus the dynamics of status groups in the evolution of movements. Tocqueville, that most perceptive observer of the American landscape, produced an equally profound analysis of the French Revolution; his analysis draws attention to the social-psychological elements of movements.

This section deals with several current theories about the rise of movements; most derive their perspective in one way or another from the forebears of political sociology. Each of these theories represents a current contender for the position of the most useful and valid explanation for the rise and development of movements. Although they share an interest in the origins and development of movements, these theories are vastly different. Some, for instance, look to characteristics of the stratification system of a society, while others devote exclusive attention to the worries and fears burdening individuals. To organize them in a way that provides maximum comparability and yet highlights their unique features, they are distinguished based upon their principal mode of explanation—structural theories that search for the origins of movements largely in the structural conditions of a society, such as economic trends or patterns in stratification, and regard these as the prime movers for the development of a movement; organizational theories, of which there is only one viable contender, that seek out the origins of movements in organizational terms; and finally, social-psychological theories that regard social-psychological variables, for example, feelings of distrust in the government, as the most significant in the rise of movements. One would hope that an explanation for the development of movements would emerge that satisfactorily synthesizes key forces under each of these broad sets of conditions; at present, there is no such contender, though some come close.[10]

Structural Theories

Among modern treatments to account for the origins of movements, one of the earliest and most sensitive is that of the historian Crane Brinton.[11] Brinton's special interest is in a comparison of the causes, the development, and the conclusion of four events commonly identified as revolutions: the English Revolutions of the 1640s and 1688, the American Revolution of the late eighteenth century, the French Revolution of 1789, and the Russian Revolution of 1917. Revolution for him is radical transformations in the leadership and government of a society, and consequences of these changes that filter into other institutions of society. Revolutionary movements are those organizations, beliefs, and actions that have produced the revolutions. In contrast to many scholars, he manages to examine these phe-

[10]However, for an excellent treatment of revolutions that, through an integration of different theories, provides one such perspective, see Mark N. Hagopian, *The Phenomenon of Revolution* (New York: Dodd, Mead and Company, 1974).

[11]Crane Brinton, *The Anatomy of Revolution* (New York: Random House, Vintage, 1965).

nomena in depth, probing the substance of their actions, beliefs, and organizations with intensity and insight.

Examining the events leading up to revolution in these four settings, Brinton finds considerable flux and variation. Nevertheless, there appear to be some general patterns in the conditions preceding the revolutions that he formalizes into tentative theorems about their origins. First, he observes that in all four nations economic conditions were improving rather than worsening. In America, for example, he finds no evidence of poverty and misery but rather conditions of immediate prosperity prior to the revolutionary situation. Adding further fuel to his claims about the prosperity of the populations is his analysis of those who were among the first and most active participants in the revolutionary movements; they were not the poor but people who were fairly prosperous and who, if anything, simply wished to add more to their coffers of accumulated wealth.[12]

Next, he finds serious conflicts among major social classes in each of the societies. In contrast to a conventional Marxist interpretation of revolutions, which would presume the antagonisms to occur between the bourgeoisie and the feudal nobility in precapitalist societies or between the bourgeoisie and the proletariat in capitalist ones, Brinton sees the antagonisms occurring between classes near to one another in the stratification system. Writing in his characteristically lucid and graceful fashion, he notes, " 'Untouchables' very rarely revolt against a God-given aristocracy. . . . But rich merchants whose daughters can marry aristocrats are likely to feel that God is at least as interested in merchants as in aristocrats."[13]

Third, in all four societies large numbers of intellectuals became disaffected with the reigning powers prior to the revolutions. In America, for instance, a number of the most prominent thinkers among the colonists, among them Jefferson, Madison, and Franklin, deserted the ranks of the supporters of the British government and aided in the creation of a set of arguments and an organizational apparatus for an entirely new system of government. The same was true, of course, in Tsarist Russia as well as in the other two countries prior to their revolutions.

The fourth, and one of the most visible features in all four countries in the revolutionary period, was the ineffectiveness of the established governmental machinery.[14] Reigning authorities would attempt to repress dissent, only to find it occurring later with greater vigor; leaders would vacillate in their policies, being unable to decide if compromise or outright concession with dissidents was the best

---

[12] Tocqueville much earlier had pointed to similar conditions that preceded the outbreak of the French Revolution in France in 1789. He wrote: "It is a singular fact that steadily increasing prosperity, far from tranquilizing the population, everywhere promoted a spirit of unrest. The general public became more and more hostile to every ancient institution, more and more discontented; indeed, it was increasingly obvious that the nation was heading for a revolution. Moreover, those parts of France in which the improvement in the standard of living was most pronounced were the chief centers of the revolutionary movement" (Alexis de Tocqueville, *The Old Regime and the French Revolution,* trans. Gilbert Stuart [Garden City, N.Y.: Doubleday and Company, 1955], p. 175).

[13] Brinton, *The Anatomy of Revolution,* p. 265.

[14] For similar points, see Tocqueville, *The Old Regime and the French Revolution.*

policy, the government began to lack for funds and thus turned to measures, such as further taxation, that only provoked the public more, and so it went. In all four countries, developments (particularly economic ones) began to outstrip the government's capacity to handle problems attendant upon these developments.

Finally, all four revolutions were preceded by a decay in the ruling classes of the country. Bickering took place among different sectors of the political and economic elite groups, leaving some to go over to the side of the revolutionaries. Russia exhibited this symptom to a greater degree than any of the other countries. There it became the rule for the nobility to criticize the government, the Tsar and his family. Where once loyalty and trust of the regime reigned, there came cynicism; many members of the nobility sympathized more actively with the peasants and lower classes than with the ruling class.

So perceptive is Brinton's analysis of these conditions leading to the formation of revolutionary movements that many current analyses of movements, revolutionary and otherwise, fix on quite similar conditions. In large part, of course, this occurs because both Brinton and contemporary analysts are indebted to the original inspiration of Marx in attempting to trace the forces producing the rise of movements. Brinton, however, points more forcefully to the *political* conditions producing movements than Marx, and many analysts find this particular insight more useful in explaining political movements or those that have important political consequences.[15] At this point in our knowledge of the structural underpinnings of revolutionary movements and situations, it is virtually impossible to bring together all the current evidence and draw final conclusions about the validity of the general conditions (such as economic) or the specific ones (such as prosperity) that Brinton analyzes. However, many current studies of movements, past and present, seem to agree that economic conditions are not as important in providing forecasts of the occurrence of movements and related phenomena as Brinton thought and that political ones, particularly those involving the ineptitude of the government and the reigning political elites, may be even more significant than he estimated.[16]

From the most historically specific of the contending theories, it is instructive to move to the most theoretically abstract and sophisticated of them, that of Neil Smelser.[17] Using a paradigm based largely on the theories of Parsons, Smelser

---

[15] See, for instance, David Snyder and Charles Tilly, "Hardship and Collective Violence in France, 1830 to 1960," *American Sociological Review,* 37 (October 1972), 520-32. For a general discussion of the political elements, see Anthony Oberschall, *Social Conflict and Social Movements* (Englewood Cliffs, N.J.: Prentice-Hall, Inc., 1972), pp. 43-49.

[16] On the former point, see, among other works, Douglas A. Hibbs, Jr., *Mass Political Violence* (New York: John Wiley & Sons, 1973); and on the latter one, see Snyder and Tilly, "Hardship and Collective Violence in France, 1830 to 1960," including the works cited therein. Nevertheless, the Brinton point of view, especially that which sees economic growth as conductive to revolutionary situations, continues to receive the support of additional theorizing. For an excellent example of this, see Mancur Olson, "Rapid Growth as a Destabilizing Force," *Journal of Economic History,* 23 (December 1963), 529-52.

[17] Neil Smelser, *Theory of Collective Behavior* (New York: The Free Press, 1963).

interests himself in explaining all manner and form of collective activities that take place outside the normal routinized channels of societies, that is, "uninstitutionalized" behavior (see chapter 4). In particular, he constructs a theory that tries to account for the origins of activities as diverse as panics and revolutionary movements. The two types of phenomena that fall into the category of movements are norm-oriented movements and value-oriented movements. Here, for purposes of brevity, only his explanation of the nature and origins of norm-oriented movements is reviewed.

Smelser defines a norm-oriented social movement as one that "is an attempt to restore, protect, modify, or create norms in the name of a generalized belief." [18] In conceptualizing such movements, Smelser has in mind those movements that other observers tend to label as reform movements; that is, they are collective activities such as the Know Nothing, the Progressive, and the anti-Masonry movements of nineteenth-century America that have as their aim to somehow alter the statutes, laws, or informal norms in a society. If such movements actually produce changes, a result that is not a necessary part of their definition, such changes are of a more minor sort in contrast to value-oriented movements. Instead of revolution, simple acts of reform result.

As an apt observer of history, Smelser considers that social and political norm-oriented movements are comprised of the three elements that comprise the definition of a movement—organization, beliefs, and strategies for action. Nevertheless, Smelser clearly assumes that beliefs are the most important of the three elements. Beliefs are the views of movement adherents that, in response to the appearance of a problem in society, identify for the adherents both a source of the problem and a way for solving the problem through the creation of a new set of norms. Such beliefs, however, have a flavor that distinguishes them from people's routine beliefs and standards. In particular, they are *generalized* beliefs in the sense that they explain a particular problem through a general instead of a specific source, and they are *short-circuited* beliefs in the sense that they suggest a remedy to the problem through bypassing the normal steps of solution to correct the problem. [19] To illustrate, if wheat farmers suffer a drought, their normal reaction might be to attempt to improve their irrigation systems or their farm machinery and thus to improve the amount of their product during the period of the drought. Action based on the beliefs associated with a movement, in contrast, might involve attributing to the government a failure to forewarn farmers of the imminence of the drought as well as a failure to advise farmers on how to deal with the effects of the drought. Furthermore, such beliefs would probably demand that the government establish a regulatory agency designed to aid farmers in the future. The actions recommended by a movement's beliefs, in other words, are *generalized,* since they may move the source of the problem from the level of techniques to the government, and *short-circuited* in the sense that they suggest the problem can

[18]Ibid., p. 270.
[19]Ibid., pp. 71-73.

be solved through altering the current system of government rather than the methods of farming. Because of the character of the beliefs, movements appear to Smelser as irrational responses to problems; they represent "the action of the impatient . . . [and differ from] the processes of social readjustment that do not short-circuit the journey from generalized belief to specific situations."[20]

The rise of norm-oriented movements, Smelser claims, is fostered by several different conditions. Each is a necessary circumstance leading to the appearance of a movement, and all can be regarded as a sufficient condition. Smelser goes on to emphasize that these conditions need not occur in any given temporal order; all that is important is that the conditions occur in a logical sequence, moving from the appearance of the most to the least general. The first is *structural conduciveness.* A norm-oriented movement can occur only when conditions in the social structure permit it to arise. In particular, norm-oriented movements are able to take place in societies in which major institutions are highly differentiated from one another in form but especially in terms of articulation and aggregation of interests (political parties represent the interests of the public to the government, but the government is mainly responsible for arriving at decisions on public policy); in which the channels for expressing dissatisfaction are limited but not altogether absent from an aggrieved group (a group of people can voice their concerns through their representatives in government, although such access to their representatives involves many difficulties); and in which people who are aggrieved are able to communicate with one another because of a common heritage and through such specific devices as the mass media.

Second, a norm-oriented movement may occur after a group of people have experienced a condition of *strain.* Strain can result from economic disasters and misfortunes, from sudden growth and change in a society that manifests itself in a lack of fit between people's normative expectations and the actual conditions in society, and from the advance of processes like urbanization and industrialization. Moreover, some strains may be real, such as society-wide economic depression, whereas others may be imagined, such as the deprivation people feel when their achievements fall short of their expectations. Finally, Smelser urges, strain can only give rise to a norm-oriented movement when it combines with the earlier circumstances of structural conduciveness.

Smelser next suggests that the emergence of a norm-oriented movement depends on the growth and spread of a *generalized belief.* Such beliefs, as already intimated, attribute the source of a group's discomfort to particular agents, suggest ways for improving a bad situation, and are often made public in the form of a systematic platform or document. They are especially characterized by elements of wish fulfillment that give them their irrational flavor.

In addition, the occurrence of certain *precipitating factors* always precedes the rise of a norm-oriented movement when joined with the other conditions of conduciveness, strain, and generalized belief. Any of a wide variety of circum-

[20] Ibid., pp. 72-73.

stances may precipitate a norm-oriented movement, including the arrest of leaders, attacks on movement adherents, and illegal acts.[21] Smelser is quick to point out, moreover, that some concrete circumstances that serve to represent such conditions as strain might also serve as a precipitant to a norm-oriented movement; for example, an economic recession could be both a source of strain and a precipitating factor encouraging the rise of norm-oriented movements.

There is one final condition, Smelser suggests, that accounts for the rise of norm-oriented movements. *Mobilization for action* includes many of the general characteristics discussed earlier in considering actions and strategies as an integral part of the definition of movements. Thus, Smelser notes, leadership is of crucial importance to the emergence of movements; earlier organizations may have had to exist for movement organizations to appear, but the organizations of movements, if the movements are to be a success, must use alternative plans of action.

Taking these several types of conditions together—conduciveness, strain, generalized belief, precipitating factors, and mobilization for action—then, one would expect the emergence of a norm-oriented movement. However, if the agencies of *social control,* such as the police, the CIA, or the gendarmes, behave in a certain way, the emergence of a movement can either be forestalled altogether or the probabilities of its appearance considerably strengthened. There are several things the agencies can do to encourage the rise of a norm-oriented movement. Among others, these include support of the movement so as to secure the cooperation of movement adherents for other efforts. Other actions, such as vacillation in the face of a movement's demands, Smelser claims, may produce other forms of collective action, including more extreme forms. The obvious importance of social control to Smelser's sequence of events has suggested to some interpreters that the theory would be better identified as one of conflict regulation than of collective behavior.[22]

Because of its high level of abstraction, Smelser's theory can be both faulted and praised. Those who fault it claim the theory is far too abstract to be useful in the concrete prediction of the appearance of social movements, while those who praise it believe the theory can encompass an enormous range and richness in the variety of structural conditions that it suggests prompt the rise of movements. Beyond such comments, the theory has come in for an increasing amount of criticism in recent years because of its allusion to the irrational beliefs of the adherents of movements. By having begun from a Parsonian paradigm for the analysis of societies, Smelser was virtually compelled to assert that movements were somewhat abnormal phenomena; in fact, the very large and diverse number of them on which his theory is based should have suggested to him quite the opposite.[23]

[21] Ibid., pp. 294-95.

[22] William A. Gamson, *Power and Discontent* (Homewood, Ill.: Dorsey Press: 1968).

[23] For other criticisms of Smelser's theory, see Elliott Currie and Jerome H. Skolnick, "A Critical Note on Conceptions of Collective Behavior," and Neil Smelser's rebuttal, "Two Critics in Search of a Bias: A Response to Currie and Skolnick," in *Collective Violence,* ed. James F. Short, Jr., and Marvin E. Wolfgang (Chicago and New York: Aldine Publishing Co., 1972), pp. 60-81.

A third structural theory that is designed to account for the origins of certain social and political movements is that of status politics. The phrase covers a perspective whose development is due largely to the work of three scholars, Richard Hofstadter, Seymour Martin Lipset, and Joseph Gusfield.[24] The theory of status politics is based on an extension of two of Weber's insights—first, status groups rather than social classes are the principal actors in some historical and social settings; and second, members of self-conscious status groups may act to advance their ideal or symbolic interests through collective action. Hofstadter, Lipset, and Gusfield also believe that the theory is especially useful to an explanation of American politics, since status groups appeared to play a much more prominent role in the unfolding developments of this country than they have in many European nations.[25]

There are only certain types of movements whose origins can lend themselves to an explanation in terms of status groups and of status group conflict. These are all movements whose prime social carriers are not social classes, and whose prime doctrines have little, if any, relationship to economic concerns and woes. They are movements that some scholars label as reform efforts. Moreover, the beliefs associated with these movements often appear as symbols for something else—as status resentments for Hofstadter, or as attempts to generate status deference, for Gusfield. The beliefs of such movements, in other words, appear to be devices for enhancing the psychological needs of movement supporters instead of a camouflage designed to distract an unwary opponent and pave the way for victory.

The special historical instances of movements with which Hofstadter, Lipset, and Gusfield concern themselves are the Populist movement, the Mugwumps, the Progressive movement, McCarthyism, and the Women's Christian Temperance Union. In all these cases, it is important to observe, the analysts have focused their attention almost exclusively on the beliefs of adherents and spokespersons as the means for identifying the movement itself; thus, they ignore for all intents and purposes the organization and the actions that comprise social and political movements.

According to the theory of status politics, certain movements arise during prosperous times rather than difficult ones. Analysts, trained in the rigors of Marxian thought and alerted to the significance of economic issues, confront the dilemma, Why do social and political movements occur, or gain strength, when

---

[24] See the following works: Richard Hofstadter, *The Age of Reform* (New York: Vintage Books, 1969); Richard Hofstadter, "The Pseudo-Conservative Revolt (1955)," and "Pseudo-Conservatism Revisited: A Postscript (1962)," in *The Radical Right*, ed. Daniel Bell (Garden City, N.Y.: Doubleday and Co., 1962), pp. 63-86; Seymour Martin Lipset, "The Sources of the 'Radical Right' (1955)," in *The Radical Right*, Bell, pp. 259-312; and Joseph Gusfield, *Symbolic Crusade: Status Politics and the American Temperance Movement* (Urbana, Ill.: University of Illinois Press, 1963). For one of the earliest works on this theme, see Hadley Cantril, *The Psychology of Social Movements* (New York: John Wiley & Sons, Inc., 1963).

[25] Gusfield, *Symbolic Crusade*, p. 1.

economic conditions are going so well?[26] The answer, they suggest, lies in the fact that as a result of economic growth, there emerge certain status groups that believe their style of life will be threatened by the gains of those who have become newly prosperous.[27] Through the vehicle of a social or political movement, members of such status groups hope to protect their style of life and prestige against the new claims to deference made by those groups ascending on the social ladder. To illustrate, at the end of the nineteenth and beginning of the twentieth centuries, rapid industrial growth took place in the United States. Among other things, many men became millionaires almost overnight, including J. Pierpont Morgan and John D. Rockefeller. Simultaneously several movements developed. The Mugwumps, for example, consisted of many individuals from families of tradition and wealth in America—the old Protestant middle and upper-middle classes—who undertook to turn back the new industrial growth by advancing plans to limit corporate expansion such as antitrust laws. In the early part of the twentieth century, the Progressive movement emerged, taking up the cry of the Mugwumps and adding special messages of their own, such as attacks on big city political machines. Again, as in the case of the Mugwumps, those who articulated the Progressive message and supported the Progressive movement in large numbers did not fit the conventional picture of the political radical, coming from backgrounds of high standing and prestige in American life. Like those who supported the Mugwumps, those who adhered to the Progressive banner did so for reasons of status; they "were Progressives not because of economic deprivations but primarily because they were victims of an upheaval in status . . .[and they were] men who suffered from the events of their time not through a shrinkage in their means but through the changed pattern in the distribution of deference and power."[28]

While some status groups are prompted to become part of protest movements in order to protect their styles of life and deference, there are other status groups who become involved in movements as a means of securing some rather precarious and tentative amounts of deference. They are groups, often based upon a common ethnic heritage, who stand on the lower rungs of the status hierarchy in a society but are in the process of rising. For instance, Catholics and members of other groups who supported Senator Joseph McCarthy in the early 1950s, Lipset points out, did so because they were ascending in the status hierarchy and wished to solidify their position in American society by embracing the intensely pro-America, anti-Communism beliefs of the McCarthy mood.[29] Gusfield suggests that the civil rights movement on behalf of American blacks in the 1950s and 1960s occurred in part because blacks hoped to achieve greater respect in the eyes of their fellow Americans.[30]

[26] Brinton, of course, observed a similar pattern in his analysis of revolutions, but he dealt with it somewhat differently than status politics theorists.

[27] For a similar thesis, see Mancur Olson, "Rapid Growth as a Destabilizing Force."

[28] Hofstadter, *The Age of Reform,* p. 135.

[29] Lipset, "The Sources of the 'Radical Right' (1955)."

[30] Gusfield, *Symbolic Crusade,* pp. 172-73.

Analyses of the origins of social and political movements cast in terms of status groups and status group conflicts have naturally drawn a large number of admirers in the United States because of their compatibility with salient features of American society. At a minimum, such explanations appear to provide almost a natural fit for the richness and diversity of movements in American history that are not easily captured by a framework based mainly, if not exclusively, on the dynamics of class conflict. Nevertheless, empirical efforts designed to carefully test the claims of the theory of status politics provide little firm support for them. Using empirical indices of such dimensions as social mobility—both upward and downward—as well as status inconsistency, observers have not found that those people who are mobile, or inconsistent, are any more prone to exhibit ethnic intolerance or to support reactionary political beliefs, as the theory of status politics would have one believe.[31] Status politics theory, at this point in its development, thus emerges as a somewhat weaker contender than the other theories designed to account for the origins of movements. Its major value perhaps lies more in its ability to describe dramatically and gracefully the history of popular support for movements than in identifying the intricate structural dynamics leading to their appearance.

Organizational Theory

Years ago Lenin suggested the key to the successful development of a social movement lay in the capacity of movement sympathizers to organize people for protests and related activities. He observed that "the building of a fighting organization and the conduct of political agitation are essential under any 'drab, peaceful' circumstances, in any period, no matter how marked by a 'declining revolutionary spirit'; moreover, it is precisely in such periods and under such circumstances that work of this kind is particularly necessary, since it is too late to form the organization in times of explosion and outbursts; the party must be in a state of readiness to launch activity at a moment's notice."[32] Whether for conscious or unwitting reasons, in recent years growing numbers of social scientists have come to recognize the critical importance of organizations and organization-linked conditions for the successful emergence of social and political movements. The effort to formalize this sort of perspective has thus far been most adroitly accomplished through the convergence of the efforts of three scholars, William

---

[31] For a review of some of this literature, see Anthony Orum, "On Participation in Political Protest Movements," *Journal of Applied Behavioral Science,* 10 (May-June-July 1974), 181-207. For other relevant materials see Barbara S. Stone, "The John Birch Society: A Profile," *Journal of Politics,* 36 (February 1974), 184-97; and Raymond E. Wolfinger et al., "America's Radical Right; Politics and Ideology," in *Ideology and Discontent,* ed. David Apter (Glencoe, Ill.: The Free Press, 1964), chapter 7. For materials which tend to support the claims of the theory of status politics, see Ira S. Rohter, "The Righteous Rightists," *Society,* 4 (May 1967), 1-8.

[32] V. I. Lenin, "Where to Begin" in *Collected Works* (London: Lawrence and Wishart, 1961), V, 18. The more widely known statement of this position is found in V. I. Lenin, *What Is to Be Done?* (New York: International Publishers, 1943).

Gamson, Anthony Oberschall, and Charles Tilly. Their model is variously referred to as a group conflict perspective and as a resource management model.[33]

Theorists of the resource management school regard social and political movements in as broad a fashion as Smelser, though their perspective is fundamentally different. To them, conflict and violence are endemic to social life. Social and political movements thus are common occurrences rather than unusual phenomena, and their explanation rests upon the same kinds of forces and motivations that go into everyday behavior.[34] Indeed, the absence of movements and collective violence is uncommon in social life, not their presence.[35]

There are two elements of the definition of social and political movements that seem to come in for special attention by those who employ the resource management approach. One is the organization of movements. In Gamson's recent work, for example, the characteristics of social and political movements are closely observed, including such things as the number of factions, the centralization of authority, and the bureaucratic character of movement organizations.[36] The other element of movements that comes in for special attention are the actions of movement participants as well as the strategies for actions. Tilly, for instance, concentrates his attention on a large number of episodes of collective disturbances and protest in Europe prior to the twentieth century, while Gamson has drawn attention to the types of strategies of action employed by dissenting groups through both his empirical research and theoretical analyses.[37]

Society, according to theorists of the resource management school, is viewed as consisting of groups that are constantly moving between a state of diffusion and concentration. Often groups emerge in a congealed state and attempt to challenge the legitimacy of opposing groups—most often the established governmental authorities—in an effort to increase their own resources and benefits in society. The rise of such groups that, for our purposes, may be considered as movements, occurs in response to "changes in five sets of variables: (1) articulated group interests, (2) prevailing standards of justice, (3) resources controlled by groups and their

[33] See the following works for various formulations of this theory: William A. Gamson, *Power and Discontent* (Homewood, Ill.: Dorsey Press, 1968); Gamson, *The Strategy of Social Protest;* Anthony Oberschall, *Social Conflict and Social Movements* (Englewood Cliffs, N.J.: Prentice-Hall, Inc., 1972); Charles Tilly, *The Vendeé* (Cambridge, Mass.: Harvard University Press, 1964); Charles Tilly, "Collective Violence in European Perspective," in *Violence in America,* ed. Hugh Davis Graham and Ted Robert Gurr (New York: Signet Special, 1969); and Charles Tilly, Louise Tilly, and Richard Tilly, *The Rebellious Century: 1830-1930* (Cambridge, Mass.: Harvard University Press, 1975).

[34] Oberschall, *Social Conflict and Social Movements,* pp. 27-29.

[35] Charles Tilly, "The Chaos of the Living City," in *Conceptions of Social Life,* ed. William Gamson and André Modigliani (Boston: Little, Brown, & Company, 1974), pp. 535-44.

[36] Gamson, *The Strategy of Social Protest.*

[37] See, for example, Snyder and Tilly, "Hardship and Collective Violence in France, 1830 to 1960" and references cited therein; Gamson, *Power and Discontent;* and Gamson, *The Strategy of Social Protest.*

members, (4) resources controlled by other groups (especially governments), and (5) costs of mobilization and collective action."[38]

In sharp contrast to other theories that try to account for the emergence of social and political movements, the theory of resource management regards movements, or more precisely movement organizations, as the principal actors in situations of conflict. Such organizations are viewed as having goals that they attempt to achieve; actions in the pursuit of those goals are regarded as instrumental. In any given case, the goals appear as defined by the leaders of the movement organizations or are revealed by the nature of the actions in which movement participants engage.

The actual form that the actions of movement organizations are likely to assume depends on a variety of critical factors. For one thing, there is a distinction between groups normally regarded as lying within the boundaries of the polity and groups lying outside. Those groups on the outside are forced to resort to actions of a more extreme sort than those lying inside, partly because they are not regarded as legitimate contenders for power by the polity's members and partly because they have no vested interests in the continuation of the polity as it currently exists. For another, distinctions are made concerning the amount and type of resources held by groups in conflict situations. Groups with few, if any, material or symbolic resources such as money or prestige, that is, "powerless" groups, may be encouraged to resort to mass actions because that may be the only form of resource they can muster.[39] Often such groups must turn to third parties as a means of enlisting support for their cause.[40]

A final important feature of the resource management approach is its attempt to conceptualize dissent in general and movement organizations in particular as involved in a continuing interaction with their rivals. The specific actions of movement organizations are modified according to the requirements of specific situations of conflict. At times, street protests may be chosen as the most effective way for generating success, whereas different means may be employed on other occasions. This aspect of the approach thus removes the study of movements from a static form of analysis and substitutes a dynamic one.[41]

So far the resource management approach to the origins of movements remains at a fairly immature stage, and specific hypotheses and predictions are wanting. Nevertheless there is some evidence to support certain of the principal premises underlying the perspective. Most critical in this regard is evidence that collective violence and protests emerge in settings in which organizations play key roles. After finding a host of findings disconfirming various other hypotheses to

---

[38] Charles Tilly, "Collective Action and Conflict in Large-Scale Social Change: Research Plans, 1974-78," cited in Gamson, *The Strategy of Social Protest,* p. 138.

[39] Gamson, *Power and Discontent.*

[40] Gamson, *The Strategy of Social Protest,* p. 140.

[41] Oberschall, *Social Conflict and Social Movements.*

account for the emergence of collective violence in France from 1830 through 1960, Tilly, for example, observes that "the whole array of evidence we have been examining suggests a positive connection between *organization* and conflict." A number of other studies also appear to support the contention that organizations can play a key role in the evolution of conflict and dissent by political and other groups.[42] The most recent work of Tilly and his colleagues supports the resource management theorists' claim that the actions and inactions of governmental authorities in particular go a long way toward explaining the emergence and evolution of collective protests.[43]

Social-Psychological Theories

A house may be large or small; as long as the surrounding houses are small it satisfies all social demands for a dwelling. But let a palace arise beside the little house, and it shrinks from a little house to a hut.[44]

The most popular of recent theories of the origins of movements are a handful of social-psychological theories, sometimes labeled "rising expectations" and other times simply "dissatisfactions." Of all these, that of relative deprivation has attracted more attention than its competitors. A wide variety of students have employed this paradigm to explain movements and, in the process of exploration, have extended the model to include actions far beyond the reaches of that simply captured by the concept of movement. Thus under the microscope of scholars interested in the importance of relative deprivation are broad social movements, such as the civil rights movement in the United States; specific organizational forms, such as the National Farmers' Organization; rebellious protests, such as Dorr's Rebellion of 1842 in the United States; and an assortment of other activities ranging from political strikes to mass warfare.[45] Disguised by the broad variety of

[42] For a review of such studies, see Anthony Orum, "On Participation in Political Protest Movements." For some additional theorizing along these lines, see the important work by Maurice Pinard, *The Rise of Third Parties* (Englewood Cliffs, N.J.: Prentice-Hall, Inc., 1971). It is important to note that all of this work, together with the previous writings of theorists in the resource management tradition, serves to disconfirm the theory of mass society that was once thought to be the most productive of theories concerning the origins of movements. In particular, its chief proponent, William Kornhauser, claimed that the absence of intermediate structures in societies could produce mass actions, since people in such settings lack the organizational ties necessary to provide them with a sense of security and to prevent them from being manipulated by political elites. An important derivation of Kornhauser's hypothesis was that those people who lacked organizational affiliations would be the most likely candidates for social and political movements. In view of the results of most recent research, quite the opposite conclusion prevails. See William Kornhauser, *The Politics of Mass Society* (Glencoe, Ill.: The Free Press, 1959).

[43] Tilly, et al., *The Rebellious Century: 1830-1930,* chapter 6 especially.

[44] Karl Marx, *Wage, Labour and Capital,* quoted in Everett Carll Ladd, Jr., *Negro Leadership in the South* (Ithaca, N.Y.: Cornell University Press, 1961), p. 24.

[45] See, for example, James A. Geschwender, "Social Structure and the Negro Revolt: An Examination of Some Hypotheses," *Social Forces,* 43 (December 1964), 248-56; James C. Davies, "Toward a Theory of Revolution," *American Sociological Review,* 27 (February 1962),

phenomena to which the concept of relative deprivation is applied is the simple fact that most theorists sympathetic to this view want to explain the violent actions in which people engage or, at the very most, certain of their beliefs; the element of movement organizations is really of little concern to them.[46]

What is relative deprivation, and how does it help to explain the origins of people's engagement in social and political movements? The basic theory begins with the notion that every individual has certain essential needs or wants—for example, the need for material comfort. There are different degrees to which that need can be fulfilled; one can attain a great deal of material comfort or very little. The fulfillment of the need can be divided into two categories, actual and expected; actual refers to the real extent to which the need is fulfilled, and expected to the anticipated extent to which one feels justified in fulfilling the need. Thus, we may actually fulfill our need for material comfort only a very little—we have a little hut—but our expectation is to fill the need a great deal—we want a big palace. To the degree that there is a gap between our actual fulfillment of the need and our anticipated fulfillment of the need and that the former is smaller than the latter, we feel *relatively* deprived. That is, we feel deprived in the actual fulfillment of our need for material comfort relative to our expectations for its fulfillment.

People who are relatively deprived begin to feel unhappy after awhile. Under the right circumstances, these relatively deprived people can become active recruits to movements. They just must become convinced that feelings of tension and irritability are not the result of a bad night's sleep, a fight with the wife, or high blood pressure; but instead that they are the result of some problem in society and, in particular, that their feelings of tension are *caused* by inept governmental officers or other similar political authorities. In other words, their feelings of anger must become transformed and channeled into the beliefs or actions of movements whose collective targets of change can be regarded by individuals as the source of their tension. If all goes well to this point, individuals become actively involved in a movement in order to rid themselves of tensions; wipe out the government, and presto, no more unjustified deprivation!

Now there are certain critical junctures in this theory that call for special attention. One concerns how a person comes to expect a greater amount of comfort than what he or she actually possesses. To answer this, proponents of the relative deprivation argument suggest that the individual's expectations for need fulfillment are acquired from the social groups with which he or she identifies, that is, *reference groups,* or from past experience.[47] Thus, if one happens to identify

---

5-19; Denton Morrison and A. D. Steeves, "Deprivation, Discontent, and Social Movement Participation: Evidence on a Contemporary Farmer's Movement, the NFO," *Rural Sociology* (December 1967), 414-34; and Ted Robert Gurr, *Why Men Rebel* (Princeton, N.J.: Princeton University Press, 1970). For related literature, see especially Gurr's *Why Men Rebel,* and Orum, "On Participation in Political Protest Movements."

[46] For one attempt to apply the concept to the origins of movement-linked beliefs, see James A. Geschwender, "Explorations in the Theory of Social Movements and Revolutions," *Social Forces,* 47 (December 1968), 127-35.

[47] On a discussion of reference groups, see Robert K. Merton, *Social Theory and Social Structure* (Glencoe, Ill.: The Free Press, 1957).

with a group whose material comforts are greater than one's own or one happens to have had greater comforts in the past than in the present, then one experiences relative deprivation with regard to the fulfillment of needs. The other juncture concerns the transformation of tension into anger and thence its focus on some external objects, such as political authorities. Such tension is thought to become anger because of the general principle of *frustration-aggression*; if a person is frustrated, according to this principle, then this frustration will become changed into aggressive behavior, including the violent actions often associated with political and social movements.[48] Naturally there are many qualifications to this last principle; sometimes people turn their anger inwards, becoming depressed, and other times they will shrug off the frustration. What people do with their anger depends to a large extent on their personality characteristics and forces in their larger social and political environment. It is at this juncture in the theoretical argument that the connections between relative deprivation and the violence associated with social and political movements are the weakest.[49]

Among the more elegant efforts to examine the theory of relative deprivation for its applicability to an explanation of the origins of revolutions is that of James C. Davies.[50] Though referring to his explanation in somewhat different terms than those described here, Davies's argument is based on roughly the same kind of reasoning; a gap occurs between the levels of people's fulfilled needs and their desired ones so that they come to feel discontent about their achievements relative to their own expectations. Frustration quickly follows, and from this grows revolution. Davies provides a graph that nicely illustrates his claims and to which he refers as the J-curve pattern preceding revolutions (see figure 12-1).

Although the locus of Davies's explanation for the origins of revolution lies in the state of people's minds, these feelings are preceded by fluctuations in the social and economic development of a society. In particular, Davies suggests, a period of rapid improvement in a society followed by reversals is sufficient to promote the state of mind that leads to revolution. To examine his theory, Davies looks at the economic conditions preceding three forms of rebellion—Dorr's Rebellion in America in 1842, the Russian Revolution of 1917, and the Egyptian Revolution of 1952. In all three cases, he observes, the efforts at reform or revolution followed the upswing-downswing development phenomenon; for instance, figure 12-2 illustrates how this occurred in the Russian Revolution. Ingenious as his explanation for the origins of revolution is, however, Davies, like most other students sympathetic to the relative deprivation model, lacks the actual information on people's moods prior to the revolution. In other words, all that is known after having examined Davies's materials is that a major episode of collective violence followed on the heels of fluctuations in the developmental cycle of a

[48] For a general discussion of the principle of frustration-aggression, see John Dollard et al., *Frustration and Aggression* (New Haven, Conn.: Yale University Press, 1939).

[49] For additional qualifications, see Leonard Berkowitz, *Aggression: A Social Psychological Analysis* (New York: McGraw-Hill, 1962).

[50] Davies, "Toward a Theory of Revolution."

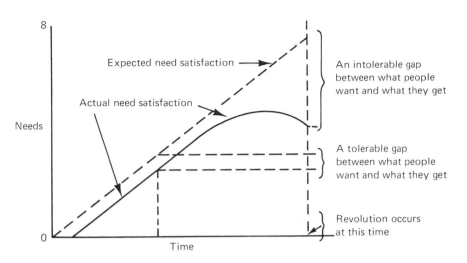

FIGURE 12-1   Need satisfaction and revolution (adapted from James C. Davies, ed., *When Men Revolt and Why: A Reader in Political Violence and Revolution* [New York: The Free Press, 1971])

society; since it is not actually known whether the people in the society at that time, especially the revolutionaries, felt deprived and frustrated, one might equally well explain the revolutions with other factors associated with fluctuations in the developmental cycle—for instance, simply the emergence of opposition political parties to the government (this happened, in fact, in Russia).

Nevertheless, although an observer can easily pass judgments such as these, the claims of this theory have received considerable empirical support beyond that produced by Davies. Thus, Ted Robert Gurr has conducted an extensive empirical study of the various societal determinants of "civil strife," including under this label such things as "relatively spontaneous, unstructured mass strife [such as] riots," "intensively organized, relatively small-scale civil strife, including political assassinations," and "large-scale organized, focused civil strife . . . including large-scale terrorism and guerilla wars."[51] Like Davies, the underpinnings of Gurr's argument and hypotheses rest on a relative deprivation-frustration theory. To test his theory, Gurr assembles data from one hundred fourteen different nations and colonial countries on such dimensions as the extent of economic and political deprivation, the number of political parties that could serve to facilitate the outbreak of civil strife, and of course, the extent of civil strife. He finds that his measures of deprivation provide the most powerful predictions of the extent of civil strife across the many nations; thus, his three measures of deprivation in the nations accounted for the largest proportion of variance in the degree of civil strife, 36 percent. Gurr, too, has no direct evidence on the actual feelings of people

[51] Ted Robert Gurr, "A Causal Mode of Civil Strife: A Comparative Analysis Using New Indices," *American Political Science Review,* 62 (December 1968), 1104-24.

FIGURE 12-2   Need satisfaction and the Russian Revolution (adapted from James C. Davies, ed., *When Men Revolt and Why: A Reader in Political Violence and Revolution* [New York: The Free Press, 1971])

prior to civil strife so his evidence is at best indirect support for his theory, but he rightly asserts that "there is only one scientifically acceptable alternative to regarding the results . . . as strong indirect evidence for the psychological propositions relating deprivation . . . to civil violence [that being] to provide reasonably parsimonious, alternative explanations [of our findings]."[52]

There are other studies, besides those of Davies and Gurr, that provide additional empirical confirmation for the relative deprivation argument or at least one sufficiently similar to it. Among these are the extensive studies by Ivo Feierabend and his colleagues on systematic frustration and the outbreak of violence in different nations.[53] The most recent research in this area, however, casts very serious doubts on the validity of the relative deprivation thesis. Douglas H. Hibbs uncovers very little empirical support for the relevance of deprivation-related measures to explanations of violence in different nations; Anthony Orum finds no relationship between the feelings of deprivation and movement participation among black students involved in the black student movement of the early 1960s in the United States; and David Snyder and Charles Tilly find no evidence to support the arguments of proponents of the relative deprivation school in their recent analysis of outbreaks of collective violence in France during parts of the nineteenth and twentieth centuries.[54] At best, final judgments on the ability of

[52] Ibid., p. 1124.

[53] See, for example, Ivo K. Feierabend and Rosalind L. Feierabend, "Aggressive Behaviors Within Polities, 1948-1962," in James C. Davies, *When Men Revolt—and Why* (New York: The Free Press, 1971), pp. 229-49, and the many references to the Feierabends' work cited therein.

[54] Douglas H. Hibbs, Jr., *Mass Political Violence;* Anthony M. Orum, *Black Students in Protest: A Study of the Origins of the Black Student Movement* (Washington, D.C.: American Sociological Association, 1972); and Snyder and Tilly, "Hardship and Collective Violence in France, 1830 to 1960."

the relative deprivation perspective to contend in the same ring with the other theories must await solid proof that what goes on in individuals' minds prior to their engagement in movements are feelings of tension or anger, not something else, and that such feelings are the product of situations of relative deprivation. These are tough matters to solve, but perhaps theorists of this school will eventually devise studies sufficiently ingenious to produce solutions.

Comparing Contenders:
Requiem for Some Lightweights?

Several of the theories point to changing economic and political circumstances as significant determinants of the rise of movements. In particular, it appears that economic improvements (Brinton, Hofstadter et al., and Smelser), economic declines (Hofstadter et al. and Smelser), and the improvement of economic conditions followed by rapid deterioration of them (Davies) can produce the seeds of revolution or reform. So varied are the economic conditions that can produce movements and movement-related phenomena that this is perhaps one reason why other observers (Gamson et al.) have turned to political circumstances as being the more viable of contending theories. In fact, several of the theories converge on the significance of political conditions as determinants of movements; vacillation in the actions of governmental authorities (Brinton, Smelser, Gamson et al., and Gurr), on the one side, and crystallization of the efforts of opposing political groups (Brinton, Smelser, and Gamson et al.), on the other, appear to rank among the most prominent of these circumstances.

Moreover, almost all of the theories, with the exception of the resource management approach, assume an intimate connection between the effects of changing social and economic conditions on the psychological makeup of individuals; such changes, it is thought, bring on various forms of tension that, in turn, can lead people to engage in collective outbursts, whether highly spontaneous or highly organized. Naturally the theory of relative deprivation is more explicit about these connections than others, but this sort of logic appears even in a theory as strongly emphatic about the importance of structural conditions as that of Smelser. Such assumptions seem to cast the participants in movements in a bad light, making them seem as something less than human and rational creatures; this is an implication that some theorists, particularly those advocating the resource management point of view, explicitly reject.

One of the chief problems of most of the theories concerns their frequent failure to carefully identify the nature of the beast they are attempting to explain. In the case of applications of the theory of relative deprivation, this is a particularly serious problem. Although most researchers confine their attention to the actions of people, some, such as Gurr, indiscriminately mix actions with beliefs and organizations. Someday the theory of relative deprivation might prove to be a most powerful device for the explanation and prediction of movements and movement-related phenomena, but it is too much to expect that the theory can explain equally well the psychological states of mind in people, the actual behavior of people, and the social creation of organizational forms among people.

This brings us to a most important point. At the outset of this chapter, the characteristics of movements were carefully delimited, in part to consider what facets of movements different observers try to explain. Many of the theories, and the research upon which they are based, do not try to account for all three facets of movements; for example, the status politics theory focuses almost exclusively on the beliefs associated with movements. Two critical implications follow from this differential attention of theorists to the composition of movements. First, the logic of scientific explanation suggests that some theories can easily account for some things but not for others. For example, the theory of relative deprivation may account for the behavior of people, but it is extremely unlikely that it will ever be able to explain the growth and persistence of movement organizations among them. Likewise, a structural theory such as that of status politics might readily account for the growth or origins of social organizations, like those of movements, but it is a far more difficult task to ask it, as theorists like Hofstadter and Lipset have done, to account for the origins of people's beliefs. One of the last intellectual occasions on which that task was successfully accomplished was Max Weber's famous thesis expounded in *The Protestant Ethic and the Spirit of Capitalism*; even on this matter some scholars have serious reservations.[55] Where Weber was careful to suggest that an "elective affinity" existed between the social conditions of men and their beliefs, the theorists who have employed the status politics approach to explain the origins of movements have been downright sloppy, assuming connections where none may even exist.

Second, as noted earlier, the pivotal element in movements, particularly successful ones, is their organization. Hence theories like that of relative deprivation are not the best kinds of explanatory devices to seek. Instead, a theory that tries to capture the reasons for the growth and evolution of movement organizations, like that of resource management, is the most powerful and intelligent sort of theory. Perhaps other theories of this kind will soon be developed.

Where do we go from here? One answer would be a synthesis of those significant points on which the theories concur, in general and in particular, and to suggest that such points are the ones to which attention should be addressed in the future. For example, most of the theorists, if they say anything at all about such forces, claim that the vacillation of political authorities appears to be a logical precondition for the origins of a movement. Thus, scholars and students simply need to attend to such conditions as a means of understanding how movements arise; but that is too easy and facile a strategy. Instead, it is crucial that one formulate some significant questions in the manner of C. Wright Mills, with an eye to such

[55] See, for example, the greatly penetrating analysis by R. H. Tawney, *Religion and the Rise of Capitalism* (New York: New American Library, 1958), pp. 261-62 especially.

matters as those we have mentioned. Those important to the task here are the following:

- What is the character of the society? Where does the economy, in particular, seem to be heading, if it is heading anywhere at all?
- What categories of people are left out from the distribution of political power in the society?
- What means are employed to keep out those groups who are left out? Who controls these means? How extensive are they? What do they comprise —for example, weapons of force or propaganda?
- Are there sufficient intellectual and material resources to create the organizations necessary for the emergence of movements?
- Is there a burgeoning discontent in the society? How easy is it for this discontent to rise to the surface? How much is likely to be drawn off into apolitical rather than political forms of opposition?

These and other similar questions must be asked if one is to assess the potential for the formation of movements in any society. They are questions that in general call for a greater sensitivity to the nuances of history and a greater breadth and depth of imagination than many past theorists and researchers on these issues have been willing or able to employ.

MOVEMENTS TRANSFORMED

Once movements actually arise, the direction of one's analytical concern shifts from their origins to the circumstances that aid their later growth or foster their decline. Much of the inspiration for the intellectual focus on this issue comes from Max Weber and Robert Michels. Weber, as we recall from chapter 3, developed a theory to account for the rise and fall of different groups based on the strength of their authority and legitimacy in the eyes of their members. As older groups declined, new groups tended to arise and to crystallize around individuals of singular skill and brilliance, that is, charismatic figures. Such was the course of life, Weber asserted, that charismatic authority inevitably gave way to new forms and to different styles of social organization. In particular, the authority of charisma became routinized, leading to the embodiment of authority in less graceful but more systematic organizational procedures. Christ gives way to Christianity and the Church; Hitler to Nazism and the Third Reich, and so on.

In compressed form, this same type of analysis has been applied time and again to describe the transformation of social and political movements. Often the sort of picture conveyed by Weber's analysis seems to provide an excellent fit to the course of growth taken by movements. However, just as frequently the picture of growth portrayed by Weber's scheme can prove an imperfect model, obscuring the subtleties of movements' changes as well as the circumstances accounting for them.

Michels's theory provides a complementary, if not different, conception.[56] In a wide variety of circumstances, ranging from Socialist parties to labor unions, he notes the tendency for movement organizations to become nothing more than sources of self-aggrandizement for their leadership. There are many reasons, both primary and secondary ones, for this tendency. The principal one is that the leaders of movements emerge from the very social groups on whose behalf the movement has originated; the overnight transformation of their standing from one of destitution to one of prosperity leads them, Michels argues, to protect their new gains at any cost. Leaders are aided in this effort by their expertise in management and social relations that is simply a consequence of their tenure of office. Moving with deft actions, they prevent challengers from replacing them in office; often they are supported in such actions by the organization's membership, who have come to admire the leaders, not suspecting for a moment that the leaders' special qualities are available to anyone who comes to hold a position of leadership. Leaders are assisted as well by their control over the vast resources of the organization, including those of communications that may be used to deceive the members and other contenders for power in a variety of ways. This model, like Weber's, often provides so close an approximation to the sequence of events in the development of movements that it seems more real, and inevitable, than it actually is.

To improve upon the imperfections in both the Weber and the Michels formulations, Mayer Zald and Roberta Ash developed a series of propositions that would describe the ebb and flow of change in movement organizations.[57] Going a step beyond the earlier analyses, they observe that the elements of potential change in movement organizations can be identified as goal transformations, shifts to organizational maintenance, and increases in the concentration of power. To account for these potential forms of change, they stress, one must look at the nature of the movement organization, in particular whether the organization demands only minimal commitment (inclusive) or intense commitment (exclusive) from its members, and at its position within the larger society.

Among a series of propositions they develop, several are worth noting. They observe that a transformation in the goals of a movement organization is likely to happen because of its competition with other organizations within the same movement. For instance, in the black civil rights movement in the 1960s, organizations like the NAACP and the Urban League were compelled to become more ideologically radical simply to retain their hold on material resources that were beginning to shift to the more radical groups like the Student Non-Violent Coordinating Committee (SNCC). They also contend that a movement that has lost its original dynamic quality and become a part of the status quo is most apt to follow

[56] Robert Michels, *Political Parties* (New York: Collier Books, 1962).
[57] Mayer Zald and Roberta Ash, "Social Movement Organizations: Growth, Decay and Change," *Social Forces,* 44 (March 1966), 327-40.

the sort of sequence outlined by Weber and Michels. This happens because the viability of the movement no longer lies in the acquisition of major new gains from the established social and political institutions but rather in the protection of old gains. For no segment is this pattern more important than for that of the leadership. In one of their more insightful assertions, Zald and Ash remark that movement organizations whose ideology strongly recommends distrust of societal and political authorities are very likely to produce factions and splits among their members. The stance of distrust of authority almost inevitably shifts from a focus on authority outside the movement to that within it, leading to opposition groups which challenge the original leadership of the movement. Both the SDS and SNCC eventually experienced the development of factions, and later decay, precisely because of the pattern Zald and Ash formulate.

On many occasions, movements become transformed as a result of their success, either disappearing altogether or assuming a position as part of the status quo—perhaps another political party or interest group. Success, in other words, breeds change, a rule that can be observed elsewhere in social life. Attention naturally shifts then to the question, What breeds success?

ASSESSING THE SUCCESS OR FAILURE OF MOVEMENTS

One of the more crucial questions involved in the study of social and political movements has escaped careful attention thus far. This is the matter of the success or failure of movements. In large part, attentive students have tended to overlook it because it is so difficult to answer. How can one determine success or failure of movements? Is a movement successful if it is perceived as such by its adherents, regardless of whether it achieves some specific goals?[58] Is it a success if it simply manages to survive and turn into a part of the established social structure? For each of these questions, there seem to have been a variety of answers, and few scholars reached solid agreement on any. To a degree, moreover, the assessment of whether a movement is a success or failure is often obscured by the conceptual haze that engulfs the study of it. For many analysts, movements are not goal-oriented actors but epiphenomena that give vent to anger and passion but whose principles and beliefs are mere words "signifying nothing." Clearly such a perspective does not lend itself to an evaluation of the effectiveness of a movement, apart from a clinical diagnosis of the therapeutic value of involvement for movement participants.

An ingenious attempt that corrects for the absence of an intelligent approach to the goal-seeking actions of movements is the work of William Gamson.[59] Gamson

---

[58]One pioneering study took just this point of view. See Leon Festinger, H. W. Riecken, Jr., and S. Schacter, *When Prophecy Fails* (Minneapolis, Minn.: University of Minnesota Press, 1956).

[59]William A. Gamson, *The Strategy of Social Protest.*

sets out to identify movements that are successful and those that are failures and then to locate the characteristics of movements and their social surroundings that are associated with success and failure. His analysis is based upon a representative sample of fifty-three social movement organizations in America, or what he refers to as "challenging groups," since the organizations represent innovative attempts to secure benefits from members of the status quo. Among groups represented in the sample are those as diverse as the American Association of University Professors, the Bull Moose Party (Progressive Party under Theodore Roosevelt, 1912-1916), and the Communist Labor Party. The time frame from which Gamson drew his sample is the period from 1800 to 1945, during which there were about five or six hundred groups that could be classified as challenging ones.

Gamson defines success and failure with two separate indices. One is an index of *acceptance;* if a challenging group is invited to negotiate or consult, granted formal recognition, or actually incorporated as part of the organization of its antagonist, then it has received acceptance by its antagonist and qualifies as successful. The other is an index of *new advantages;* if the goals of a challenging group are somehow met, then the challenging group has received new advantages. How does one determine whether the goals have been met? As illustrations, Gamson suggests that "new advantages for the American Birth Control League . . . meant a change in practice by Americans—increased usage of contraceptive techniques. New advantages for the North Carolina Manumission Society are measured by their success in persuading individual plantation owners to grant freedom to their slaves."[60] In some cases, groups are identified as having more than one goal, and so they stand to gain more than one kind of new advantage. Of the fifty-three groups in his study, approximately the same proportion—38 percent—achieved success on both indices as achieved success on neither—42 percent. Six of the groups were not accepted in any way by their antagonists but did gain new advantages, while five achieved acceptance but no new advantages.

There are two kinds of results which prove to be the most illuminating from this study. First, Gamson finds that violence and other forms of constraints such as boycotts or strikes bring success to challenging groups. Separating the challenging groups into those that use violence, those subject to it, and those that fall into neither group, for instance, he finds that the greater proportion of the groups that use violence achieve both acceptance and new advantages. Figure 12-3 reproduces these materials from Gamson. While there is a difference in the rates of acceptance, the difference is not statistically significant. "Virtue, of course, has its own, intrinsic rewards," Gamson concludes. "And a lucky thing it does too, since its instrumental value appears to be dubious."[61]

Gamson also discovers that, in general, challenging groups that are better equipped as organizations also achieve the higher rates of success, thus confirming with hard evidence the kind of intuitive understandings possessed by such successful revolutionaries as Lenin. For one thing, the challenging groups that are bureau-

[60] Ibid., p. 35.
[61] Ibid., p. 87.

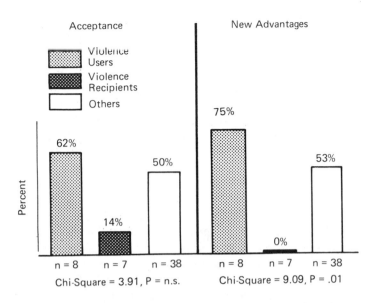

FIGURE 12-3 Violence and outcome (adapted from William A. Gamson, *The Strategy of Social Protest* [Homewood, Ill.: The Dorsey Press, 1975])

cratic, that is, possess a written charter or constitution, have a formal list of members, and have at least three levels of authority, are far more likely to achieve acceptance and new advantages than their nonbureaucratic counterparts. For another, groups in which power is centralized, that is, there is only one center of power, are also the more likely to achieve success, though the achievement is more likely to occur in the case of new advantages than in that of acceptance. Both circumstances, moreover, operate independently so, for instance, 75 percent of those groups both bureaucratic and centralized achieve new advantages compared to only 15 percent of those groups neither bureaucratic nor centralized.[62]

Gamson's research has only scratched the surface of this important matter. Nevertheless, it represents a significant beginning. With more research on this topic, we will be in a position to understand the goal-directed actions of social and political movements with the same degree of precision we currently possess with regard to other kinds of organizations.

CONCLUSIONS

That each new generation of men and women tries to give a different interpretation of the past and the future is by now accepted as commonplace. This tendency is perhaps nowhere more evident than among the students of reform and revolu-

[62] Ibid., p. 95.

tionary action. Some of them have been active in the movements of their times, and impressions gained from such experiences as these help them to modify the notions of earlier scholars. The special changes now found in the interpretations of movements and collective violence in general grow out of and are filtered through the sensibilities of people close to the turbulence of the 1960s. So many attempts at reform and revolution erupted with such force and brought about so much publicity that views radically at variance with those of the past were inevitable. The overall result has been the creation of a new set of ideas, such as those represented by the resource management school, that challenge the older claims about the abnormality of collective violence and replace them with assertions of the normal and common character of such actions. If movement participants occasionally stomp their feet, so this point of view implies, well so do other human beings.

Interpretations of movements during the 1960s, moreover, have not merely transformed our views, they have furthered them. The elements of movements can now be identified with far greater precision and explained with far deeper appreciation than in earlier times. The new interpretations also reveal themselves not as outright rejections of the ideas of the past, but as selective applications of them; instead of turning to Gustav Le Bon or Sigmund Freud for a suitable statement about the character of movements and collective violence, the newer scholars turn to the statements of Marx and modify them as seems appropriate to social settings more than one hundred years removed from 1848. Over the next few years, as violent and nonviolent attempts at change go, so will the efforts to interpret and reinterpret the meaning of these things. However, it is doubtful that such interpretations will ever retreat quite so far as to proclaim once again that movements and their bands of supporters are irrational actors on a rational stage.

Selected Bibliography

For readers who wish to pursue the issues and topics that have been discussed in this book, the following list of books and articles represent especially good places to begin your research. Although a few may be relatively old, they are nevertheless so excellent that they ought to be among the very first sources to which you turn.

INTRODUCTION

COSER, LEWIS A., ed., *Political Sociology: Selected Essays.* New York: Harper & Row, Publishers, 1966.

LIPSET, SEYMOUR MARTIN, *Political Man: The Social Bases of Politics,* rev. ed., Baltimore, Md.: The Johns Hopkins Press, 1982.

THE VISION OF KARL MARX

BERLIN, ISAIAH, *Karl Marx: His Life and Environment.* London: Oxford University Press, 1963.

BOTTOMORE, TOM, ed., *Karl Marx.* Englewood Cliffs, N.J.: Prentice-Hall, Inc., 1973.

MARX, KARL, *Capital,* vol. I. Moscow: Foreign Languages Publishing House, 1961.

TUCKER, ROBERT C., ed., *The Marx-Engels Reader.* New York: W. W. Norton & Co., Inc., 1972.

THE VISION OF MAX WEBER

BENDIX, REINHARD, *Max Weber: An Intellectual Portrait.* Garden City, N.Y.: Doubleday and Co., Inc., 1962.

BENDIX, REINHARD, AND GUENTHER ROTH, *Scholarship and Partisanship: Essays on Max Weber.* Berkeley, Calif.: University of California Press, 1971.

COLLINS, RANDALL, "A Comparative Approach to Political Sociology," in *State and Society: A Reader in Comparative Political Sociology,* ed. Reinhard Bendix et al. Boston: Little, Brown & Co., 1968.

WEBER, MAX, *Economy and Society: An Outline of Interpretive Sociology,* vols. I-III, ed. and trans. in part by Guenther Roth and Claus Wittich. New York: Bedminister Press, 1968.

THE VISION OF TALCOTT PARSONS

PARSONS, TALCOTT, "An Outline of the Social System," in *Theories of Society: Foundations of Modern Sociological Theory,* vol. I, ed. Talcott Parsons et al. New York: The Free Press, 1961.

———, *Politics and Social Structure.* New York: The Free Press, 1969.

———, *Societies: Evolutionary and Comparative Perspectives.* Englewood Cliffs, N.J.: Prentice-Hall, Inc., 1966.

———, *The Structure of Social Action,* vols. I and II. New York: The Free Press, 1968.

———, *The System of Modern Societies.* Englewood Cliffs, N.J.: Prentice-Hall, Inc., 1971.

BASIC FORMS OF POLITICAL RULE: DEMOCRACY AND OLIGARCHY IN THE MODERN WORLD

ARENDT, HANNAH, *The Origins of Totalitarianism.* Cleveland, Ohio: World Publishing Co., 1958.

ARISTOTLE, *The Politics of Aristotle,* ed. and trans. Ernest Barker. London: Oxford University Press, 1975.

FRIEDRICH, CARL J., AND ZBIGNIEW K. BRZEZINSKI, *Totalitarian Dictatorship and Autocracy,* 2nd ed., rev. Carl J. Friedrich. Cambridge, Mass.: Harvard University Press, 1965.

KARIEL, HENRY, ed., *Frontiers of Democratic Theory.* New York: Random House, Inc., 1970.

PATEMAN, CAROLE, *Participation and Democratic Theory.* Cambridge: Cambridge University Press, 1970.

SHILS, EDWARD, *Political Development in the New States.* The Hague: Mouton, 1962.

THOMPSON, DENNIS R., *The Democratic Citizen.* Cambridge: Cambridge University Press, 1970.

PATTERNS OF POWER AND INFLUENCE
UNDER CONTEMPORARY CAPITALISM:
THE CASE OF THE UNITED STATES

BARAN, PAUL A., AND PAUL M. SWEEZY, *Monopoly Capital: An Essay on the American Economic and Social Order.* New York: Monthly Review Press, 1968.

DOMHOFF, G. WILLIAM, *Who Rules America?* Englewood Cliffs, N.J.: Prentice-Hall, Inc., 1967.

GALBRAITH, JOHN KENNETH, *The New Industrial State.* Boston: Houghton Mifflin Co., 1971.

JANOWITZ, MORRIS, *The Last Half Century: Societal Change and Politics in America.* Chicago: University of Chicago Press, 1978.

KELLER, SUZANNE, *Beyond the Ruling Class: Strategic Elites in Modern Society.* New York: Random House, 1963.

MILLS, C. WRIGHT, *The Power Elite.* New York: Oxford University Press, 1959.

ROSE, ARNOLD, *The Power Structure: Political Process in American Society.* New York: Oxford University Press, 1967.

TOCQUEVILLE, ALEXIS DE, *Democracy in America,* vol. I and II, trans. Henry Reeve. New York: Vintage Books, 1945.

WOLFE, ALAN, *The Limits of Legitimacy: Political Contradictions of Contemporary Capitalism.* New York: The Free Press, 1977.

WRONG, DENNIS, *Power: Its Form, Bases and Uses.* New York: Harper & Row, Publishers, 1979.

Lukes

PATTERNS OF POWER AND POLITICS
IN COMMUNITIES

ANTON, THOMAS J., "Power, Pluralism and Local Politics," *Administrative Science Quarterly,* 7 (March 1963), 448-57.

BACHRACH, PETER, AND MORTON BARATZ, "Two Faces of Power," *American Political Science Review,* 51 (December 1962), 947-52.

BANFIELD, EDWARD, *Political Influence.* New York: The Free Press, 1961.

BONJEAN, CHARLES M. ET AL., ed., *Community Politics: A Behavioral Approach.* New York: The Free Press, 1971.

CASTELLS, MANUEL, *The Urban Question.* London: Arnold, 1977.

HAWLEY, AMOS H., "Community Power and Urban Renewal Success," *American Journal of Sociology,* 68 (January 1963), 422-31.

HUNTER, FLOYD, *Community Power Structure: A Study of Decision Makers.* New York: Doubleday and Co., 1963.

PRESTHUS, ROBERT, *Men at the Top: A Study in Community Power.* New York: Oxford University Press, 1964.

POLITICAL PARTIES
AND POLITICAL PARTISANSHIP

BURNHAM, WALTER DEAN, *Critical Elections and the Mainsprings of American Politics.* New York: W. W. Norton & Co., Inc., 1970.

CHAMBERS, WILLIAM NISBET, *Political Parties in a New Nation: The American Experience, 1776-1809.* New York: Oxford University Press, 1963.

DUVERGER, MAURICE, *Political Parties: Their Organization and Activity in the Modern State,* 2nd ed., trans. Barbara and Robert North, with a foreword by D. W. Brogan. New York: John Wiley & Sons, Inc., 1959.

EPSTEIN, LEON D., *Political Parties in Western Democracies.* New York: Frederick A. Praeger, 1967.

MICHELS, ROBERT, *Political Parties: A Sociological Study of the Oligarchical Tendencies of Modern Democracy.* New York: Collier-Macmillan Books, 1962.

NIE, NORMAN H. ET AL., *The Changing American Voter.* Cambridge, Mass.: Harvard University Press, 1976.

OSTROGORSKI, M., *Democracy and the Organization of Political Parties,* vol. II, trans. Frederick Clarke. New York: Macmillan and Co., Ltd., 1902.

POMPER, GERALD, *Voters Choice: Varieties of American Electoral Behavior.* New York: Dodd Mead, 1975.

SARTORI, GIOVANNI, "The Sociology of Parties: A Critical Review," in *Party Systems, Party Organizations and the Politics of New Masses,* ed. Seymour Martin Lipset and Stein Rokkan, pp. 1-25. Berlin: Institüt fur politische Wissenschaft an der Freien Universität Berlin, 1968.

Kornblum, Wm. Blue Collar Community

CITIZEN PARTICIPATION IN POLITICS

ABERBACH, JOEL D., "Alienation and Political Behavior," *American Political Science Review,* 63 (January 1969), 86-99.

ALFORD, ROBERT, AND ROGER FRIEDLAND, "Political Participation," in *Annual Review of Sociology,* vol. I, ed. Alex Inkeles, James Coleman, and Neil Smelser. Palo Alto, Calif.: Annual Reviews, Inc., 1975.

MILBRATH, LESTER W., AND M. L. GOEL, *Political Participation: How and Why Do People Get Involved in Politics?* 2nd ed. Chicago: Rand McNally College Publishing Co., 1977.

OLSON, MANCUR, *The Logic of Collective Action: Public Goods and the Theory of Groups.* Cambridge, Mass.: Harvard University Press, 1971.

VERBA, SIDNEY, AND NORMAN H. NIE, *Participation in America: Political Democracy and Social Equality.* New York: Harper & Row Publishers, 1972.

THE FORMS AND ORIGINS OF POLITICAL THOUGHT

BERGER, PETER, AND THOMAS LUCKMANN, *The Social Construction of Reality.* Garden City, N.Y.: Anchor Doubleday, 1967.

ELKIN, FREDERICK, AND GERALD HANDEL, *The Child and Society,* 2nd ed. New York: Random House, 1972.

GREENSTEIN, FRED, *Children and Politics.* New Haven, Conn.: Yale University Press, 1965.

JENNINGS, M. KENT, AND RICHARD G. NIEMI, *The Political Character of Adolescence.* Princeton: Princeton University Press, 1972.

KENISTON, KENNETH, *Young Radicals.* New York: Harcourt Brace Jovanovich, Inc., 1968.

ORUM, ANTHONY M., "On the Explanation of Political Socialization and Political Change," *Youth and Society,* 8 (December 1976), 147-74.

Lane, Pol. Ideology

NATION BUILDING IN THE MODERN WORLD

BLACK, C. E., *The Dynamics of Modernization.* New York: Harper & Row, Publishers, 1966.

FRANK, ANDRÉ GUNDER, *Capitalism and Underdevelopment in Latin America.* New York: Monthly Review Press, 1969.

GEERTZ, CLIFFORD, *The Interpretation of Cultures.* New York: Basic Books, Inc., Publishers, 1973.

GUSFIELD, JOSEPH, "Tradition and Modernity: Misplaced Polarities in the Study of Social Change," in *Political Development and Social Change,* 2nd ed., ed. Jason L. Finkle and Richard W. Gable, pp. 15-26. New York: John Wiley & Sons, Inc., 1971.

HUNTINGTON, SAMUEL P., *Political Order in Changing Societies.* New Haven, Conn.: Yale University Press, 1968.

LIPSET, SEYMOUR MARTIN, *The First New Nation.* Garden City, N.Y.: Doubleday and Co., 1963.

MOORE, BARRINGTON, JR., *Social Origins of Dictatorship and Democracy: Lord and Peasant in the Making of the Modern World.* Boston: Beacon Press, 1966.

PORTES, ALEJANDRO, "On the Sociology of National Development: Theories and Issues," *American Journal of Sociology,* 82 (July 1976), 55-85.

WALLERSTEIN, IMMANUEL, *The Capitalist World-Economy: Essays.* New York: Cambridge University Press, 1979.

WALLERSTEIN, IMMANUEL, *The Modern World-System: Capitalist Agriculture and the Origins of the European World-Economy in the Sixteenth Century.* New York: Academic Press, 1974.

WALLERSTEIN, IMMANUEL, AND TERENCE K. HOPKINS, eds., *Processes of the World-System.* Beverly Hills, Calif.: Sage Publications, Inc., 1980.

SOCIAL AND POLITICAL MOVEMENTS

BRINTON, CRANE, *The Anatomy of Revolution.* New York: Random House, 1965.

GAMSON, WILLIAM A. *The Strategy of Social Protest.* Homewood, Ill.: Dorsey Press, 1975.

———, *Power and Discontent.* Homewood, Ill.: Dorsey Press, 1968.

GARNER, ROBERTA ASH, *Social Movements in America,* 2nd ed. Chicago: Rand McNally College Publishing Company, 1977.

HIBBS, DOUGLAS A., JR., *Mass Political Violence.* New York: John Wiley & Sons, 1973.

LENIN, V. I., *What Is to Be Done?* New York: International Publishers, 1943.

McCARTHY, JOHN D., AND MAYER N. ZALD, *Social Movements in Modern America: A Speculative Interpretation.* New York: General Learning Press, 1973.

OBERSCHALL, ANTHONY, *Social Conflict and Social Movements.* Englewood Cliffs, N.J.: Prentice-Hall, Inc., 1972.

ORUM, ANTHONY M., "On Participation in Political Protest Movements," *Journal of Applied Behavioral Science,* 10 (April-May-June 1974), 181-207.

SKOCPOL, THEDA, *States and Social Revolutions: A Comparative Analysis of France, Russia, and China.* New York: Cambridge University Press, 1979.

SMELSER, NEIL J., *Theory of Collective Behavior.* New York: The Free Press, 1973.

TILLY, CHARLES ET AL., *The Rebellious Century: 1830-1930.* Cambridge, Mass.: Harvard University Press, 1975.

Index